SAFE
DANCE
PRACTICE

Edel Quin, MSc, FHEA
Sonia Rafferty, MSc, FHEA
Charlotte Tomlinson, MSc, PGCE

**HUMAN
KINETICS**

Library of Congress Cataloging-in-Publication Data

Quin, Edel.
  Safe dance practice / Edel Quin, Sonia Rafferty, Charlotte Tomlinson.
    pages cm
  Includes bibliographical references and index.
  1. Dance--Safety measures. 2. Dancing injuries--Prevention. 3. Dance--Physiological aspects. I. Title.
  GV1782.3.Q85 2015
  792.8028'9--dc23

                                        2014044343

ISBN: 978-1-4504-9645-2 (print)

The web addresses cited in this text were current as of February 2015, unless otherwise noted.

Acquisitions Editor: Chris Wright; **Developmental Editor:** Bethany J. Bentley; **Managing Editor:** Anne E. Mrozek; **Copyeditor:** Joy Wotherspoon; **Indexer:** Andrea J. Hepner; **Permissions Manager:** Dalene Reeder; **Graphic Designer:** Fred Starbird; **Cover Designer:** Jonathan Kay; **Photograph (cover):** © Chris Nash, dancer is Vanessa Michielon; **Photographs (interior):** © Human Kinetics, unless otherwise noted; **Photo Asset Manager:** Laura Fitch; **Visual Production Assistant:** Joyce Brumfield; **Photo Production Manager:** Jason Allen; **Art Manager:** Kelly Hendren; **Associate Art Manager:** Alan L. Wilborn; **Illustrations:** © Human Kinetics; **Printer:** Sheridan Books

Printed in the United States of America   10   9   8   7   6   5   4   3   2   1

The paper in this book is certified under a sustainable forestry program.

Human Kinetics
Website: www.HumanKinetics.com

United States: Human Kinetics
P.O. Box 5076
Champaign, IL 61825-5076
800-747-4457
e-mail: humank@hkusa.com

Canada: Human Kinetics
475 Devonshire Road Unit 100
Windsor, ON N8Y 2L5
800-465-7301 (in Canada only)
e-mail: info@hkcanada.com

Europe: Human Kinetics
107 Bradford Road
Stanningley
Leeds LS28 6AT, United Kingdom
+44 (0) 113 255 5665
e-mail: hk@hkeurope.com

Australia: Human Kinetics

57A Price Avenue
Lower Mitcham, South Australia 5062
08 8372 0999
e-mail: info@hkaustralia.com

New Zealand: Human Kinetics
P.O. Box 80
Torrens Park, South Australia 5062
0800 222 062
e-mail: info@hknewzealand.com

                                        E6308

SAFE
DANCE
PRACTICE

This book is dedicated to our friends and families,
especially Dan, Kevin, Luke, Phil and Zélie,
for their invaluable and constant support.

Contents

Foreword

The field of dance science is reaching maturity and this book provides evidence of that progress. Over the last few decades, we have seen an exponential growth in the body of scientific research concerning the physiological, biomechanical and psychological considerations of dance practice. Yet the prevalence of dance injuries is still high and some suggest that this is because the research is yet to be translated and made available for all those who work with dancers on a daily basis.

While it is often remarked that research is not complete until it is published, I would go further and say, research has little value unless it is applied, understood, and has impact. At last, research findings have been transformed into this practical and informative resource. The first book of its kind, *Safe Dance Practice* combines scientific evidence with practitioner wisdom. It will have broad appeal, connecting with all those interested in becoming better informed about both safe dance practice and performance enhancement. Presented in an accessible and user-friendly format, useful recommendations from a dance science perspective can be readily applied by a wide range of dance practitioners in their classes, rehearsals, schedules and performances. The principles advocated in this book have direct relevance for leaders working with professional or recreational dancers, teachers of all genres and levels of experience, and students and lecturers within undergraduate and postgraduate courses. The focus on the interrelated components of safe practice will help to promote health and well-being for any dancer, minimizing injury and encouraging optimal performance and engagement.

The authors are highly regarded within the world of dance and the field of dance science. They are trained dancers with professional performing and choreographing experience and continue to teach on a daily basis. While all three writers hold postgraduate degrees in dance science and have presented and published numerous academic papers in journals and at various international forums, their primary focus remains the quality of their teaching. They share a deep desire to promote dance-science-informed teaching practices and to disseminate their knowledge and expertise in safe practice. Having created several new undergraduate and postgraduate modules, as well as international certificates and qualifications in safe dance practice, the authors continue to serve as assessors and consultants with various examining bodies. They maintain a strong relationship with both the National Institute of Dance Medicine and Science (NIDMS) and the International Association for Dance Medicine and Science (IADMS) and serve on various committees advising on matters that concern teachers all over the world.

There are many anecdotal accounts of how best to teach dance and it has been commented that dance teaching relies upon tradition and personal experience rather than scientific understanding. Yet I often hear teachers say that change is long overdue. This book has the potential to significantly influence dance practice worldwide both now and in years to come. Mahatma Gandhi once said, '*be the change you want to see in the world*'. This is a book that could help you make that change.

Dr. Emma Redding

Head of Dance Science, Trinity Laban Conservatoire of Music and Dance

Past-President, International Association for Dance Medicine and Science

Safe dance practice has become a prominent issue in recent years. With more people interested in taking part in dance activities, not just as a possible career, but as a recreational or fitness activity, the requirement for greater understanding of the effects of physical activity on *every* body is being highlighted. In addition, the evolution of dance science as an area of research and study is encouraging ongoing investigation and application of effective and research-informed dance practice. Dance leaders also seem to be striving to enhance the overall health and well-being of dance participants at every level, through an examination of teaching, training, and performance practices. As a result, there is increased recognition that knowledge of how to safeguard dancers while continuing to challenge physical potential, is absolutely necessary.

A wealth of information on elements of safe practice is available across the dance sector. However, the source of this knowledge ranges from informal advice to complex scientific studies. There are advantages and disadvantages to both of these approaches. Journal articles are not always an accessible read, and would benefit from being distilled into a user-friendly format. Yet all too often the informal approach can be subjective, confusing, and potentially damaging. The solution is to translate the extensive theories and scholarly research and present it in a way that supports accessibility and encourages application.

As the title proposes, the purpose of *Safe Dance Practice* is to present an applied dance science perspective of the integrated principles that are essential to any dance experience and to provide guidelines on how to implement these in practice. The book is intended as a manual that can inform and support dance practitioners as they carry out their activities across an ever-growing pool of styles and genres and with a potentially diverse range of participants. The subject matter is explicitly relevant to dancers and dance teachers; however, the term *dance leader* is used throughout this book to encompass any position of leadership within dance. Therefore, accountability for knowledge and application of the subject matter lies also with choreographers, rehearsal or company directors, studio managers, school or university principals, directors, heads of departments or course leaders.

The integration of the following key aspects of safe practice is central to the theme of the book, distilling theory and research, combining it with informed practitioner wisdom and presenting it through easy to understand guidelines that deal with the what, where, when, how and why of working safely in dance:

- Creating a physically and psychologically safe and supportive dance environment
- Understanding relevant anatomical principles and biomechanically sound alignment
- Implementing effective physiological preparation and progression
- Minimising injury risk and understanding injury management
- Tailoring delivery to the specific needs of the participants

The content is divided into 11 comprehensive chapters, following an introduction that provides an overview of safe dance practice principles and their intended application. The chapters are purposefully organised so that the reader can progressively advance through the book in sequential order or engage with specific chapters independently, if preferred. Cross-referencing is included throughout in order to guide the reader to related information that may appear in other areas of the book. Common to all chapters are clear headings, subheadings, highlighted key points, case studies and at-a-glance summaries that provide quick access to key information and encapsulate the main messages of each chapter, allowing readers to easily relate the content to their own practice.

Chapters 1 to 8 present fundamental environmental, anatomical, physical and psychological principles of safe dance practice. Each of these chapters includes strategies and examples for putting the principles into practice in relation to different dance styles and settings. Chapter 9 acknowledges that dancers as a population are susceptible to injury due to the nature of the activity and therefore includes strategies for injury management. Chapter 10 focuses on possible adaptations of the principles to a range of specific dancing populations and stresses the importance of identifying the needs of different learners. Ongoing monitoring and self-evaluation of personal practice in order to regularly reflect on the effectiveness of safe dance application is addressed in the concluding chapter, including a useful safe practice checklist and personal evaluation template. In addition, a series of useful aides and pro formas, as well as a contact list of sources for additional information, are included as appendices.

While a research-informed grounding is integral to the whole book, certain chapters lend themselves to a more pragmatic approach, resulting in a collation of published research, standardised recommendations, practitioner wisdom and real-life experiences. Some chapters present theoretical principles that relate to safe practice application, while other chapters include discussions of the evidence-based research that is emerging. All chapters draw from the extensive experience of the authors in research and application of the principles of safe practice in dance.

The book exceeds the scope of what already exists due to a number of features, which include the following:

- A research-informed approach
- Real-life case studies
- Pragmatic recommendations that combine published fact with practitioner expertise
- Specific examples applicable to a range of dance styles and a variety of dance settings
- Tailored information for dance leaders and educators that also has relevance for dancers and dance students
- A focus on psychological aspects of safe practice

- Clear take-home messages, checklists, templates, and pro formas for personal application
- Relevant anatomical principles and biomechanically sound alignment

A primary function of *Safe Dance Practice* is to raise the profile of safe practice as a vital element of dance activity. The intention of this text is not to dwell on risk, but to illuminate fundamental principles of working safely in dance so as to support best practice. This book aims to encourage both experienced and upcoming generations of dance practitioners and leaders to develop a better understanding, communication and application of safe dance principles, while continuing to encourage creative and physical challenge. The combination of physical, psychological and environmental variables promotes an interdisciplinary approach. Benefits of increased understanding of safe practice principles will include a more knowledgeable community where dancers and dance leaders can be confident that, regardless of style, situation or ability level, individual performance potential is optimised and injury risk is minimised.

The authors of *Safe Dance Practice* collectively have almost 60 years of experience in the dance profession as creative artists, teachers and researchers. Individually they are experienced lecturers and assessors who promote a dance science perspective to the application of safe practice. In creating this resource they aim to provide a key text for dance leaders and practitioners of different levels, settings and styles. For all readers, this book empowers individuals to take responsibility for their own safe dance practice and that of others with whom they interact.

available at
HumanKinetics.com

Credits

Introduction
Overview of Safe Dance Practice

The popularity of dance is growing due to its exposure on primetime television shows and the increasing participation through schools, community centres, dance agencies, independent studios and vocational and university dance courses. A dance mapping report (Burns & Harrison, 2009) noted that the UK dance workforce is increasing and provided an estimated figure of 40,000 people employed in the sector, the majority of whom are engaged in teaching. An additional 10,000 people were said to be in training, an increase of 97 percent in the five years leading up to the report. In the United States, the National Dance Education Organisation (2014) estimated figures of 32,000 private dance studios and 665 higher education programmes in dance. Perhaps as a result of this increasing magnitude of dance participation at all levels, more and more dance genres are gaining popularity. Cultural forms, such as the many varieties of folk and ethnic dance, are enjoying something of a renaissance, while emerging popular styles, such as breaking and pole dancing, are appealing to a wider audience than ever before. Established dance forms are also being fused together to produce imaginative hybrids, such as the combination of Irish and street dance, that often move away from conventional structures and further challenge the body's capabilities beyond what might previously have been considered possible.

The increased interest, and the growing diversity of styles, is very encouraging for the development of dance as both an art form and a recreational activity. However, the importance of effective care and maintenance of the dancer's body and mind remains frequently undervalued or misunderstood. Dancers are often portrayed in both the media and in dance literature as driven, dedicated individuals who will do what it takes to make it. All too often injury is seen as a marker of what dancers are prepared to do to succeed. As a result, the adage of 'no pain, no gain' is upheld. While dedication and determination can be positive attributes, researchers in both dance psychology and injury note that excessive drive can sometimes become a negative. Personal pressure to succeed or pressure from external sources, such as parents, teachers, choreographers, directors or fellow dancers, have been reported as contributing factors to ill health, injury occurrence and dropout (Shah, Weiss, & Burchette, 2012; Aujla, 2012; Laws, 2005; Mainwaring, Krasnow, & Kerr, 2001).

Thankfully change is happening. Ever-increasing dance science knowledge is emerging on how and why to safeguard the dancing body. This knowledge can be enlightening, but at times can challenge existing practices. Because both the art and science of dance are evolving, ongoing examination of dance practice is increasingly necessary. Understanding the fundamental functioning of the dancer's body and mind, within a variety of dance contexts, is becoming a crucial aspect of working safely in dance and ensuring longevity of participation. Therefore, dance leaders and participants in all styles – from aerial dance to Zumba – should empower themselves by questioning their practice and updating their knowledge and application of the essential principles of safe dance practice.

WHAT IS SAFE DANCE PRACTICE?

Safe dance is about allowing all dancers of every age, ability and style to engage fully in the act of dancing without risk of harm to the body or mind, while also supporting them to achieve their full potential. It therefore requires an ability to identify risk, not with the intention of curtailing the activity, but rather to apply mediating strategies that allow the activity to take place in a safe and effective manner. It is necessary to understand that while adherence to basic health and safety procedures is important, experiencing safe practice goes beyond this. A multidisciplinary understanding of the workings of the human body and mind in relation to the specific context of the dance activity is also essential, allowing for appropriate choices to be made regarding the learning, teaching and practice of dance. As illustrated in figure I.1, safe dance practice calls for knowledge and application of key environmental, physical and psychological components, which results in increased dancer well-being through reducing injury risk, promoting enhanced performance potential and ultimately prolonging dance participation.

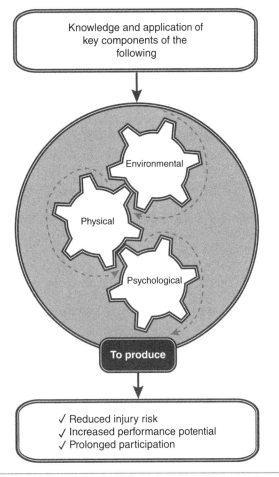

Figure I.1   The inter-related principles of safe dance practice.

Environmental components include the following:

- Knowledge of appropriate dance space, flooring, temperature, ventilation, clothing, footwear and equipment recommendations
- First aid and general health and safety considerations, including risk assessments, preparticipation questionnaires and relevant policies or codes of conduct
- Insurance and other legal considerations for protection of both the dance leader and participant

Physical components include the following:

- Basic anatomical and biomechanical principles and awareness of relevant alignment variations
- Physiological preparation for and recovery from dance activity through appropriate warm-up and cool-down processes

- Knowledge and application of physical training and fitness principles
- Knowledge and application of rest and recovery principles
- Effective session planning, progression and sequencing in relation to physical demands, expectations and capabilities
- Supportive nutrition and hydration

Psychological components include the following:

- Promotion of well-being through creating a positive psychological environment
- Understanding the effect of feedback, behaviours, and expectations on physical and mental well-being
- Effective psychological engagement and preparation through the use of psychological skills

It is important to note that alongside integrating these generic principles of safe practice, consideration needs to be given to the individual participant and to the stylistic requirements of the specific dance genre. Although dance is predominantly a group activity, within any dance class one participant might be working with a misalignment of the spine (such as scoliosis), while another might be excessively hypermobile, another might be asthmatic and yet another might be recovering from a previous injury. All of these dancers will require individual modifications in order to safely and optimally participate. In addition, some stylistic requirements can be considered counter-intuitive to safe practice principles. For example, Irish dancers are required to dance on the tip of their big toes with little cushioning or support provided by their dance shoe. This position results in increased physical stress on an area of the body that is not anatomically designed to take such forces. However, this is the requirement of the style, and therefore to state that this is unsafe and must be stopped would be to challenge an aspect that is integral to the historical development and current execution of Irish dance. Therefore it is more realistic to openly acknowledge the potential issues of this position, or any other controversial elements in any dance style, by assessing the effects on the individual dancing body and then integrating safe practice training mechanisms to mediate against potential short- and long-term negative outcomes.

The example of the conflict between inappropriate anatomical stresses and stylistic demands, offered in the previous paragraph, highlights a complex interplay between safe practice recommendations and stylistic requirements. Add to this the individual needs of each unique dancer's body and mind. Therefore the dance practitioner will need to be skilled in managing a triangulation of factors, where adherence to specific stylistic or choreographic requirements, awareness of individual physical and psychological variations and an understanding of ideal safe practice recommendations need to realistically meet (see figure I.2). Through careful consideration, the convergence of these elements should produce appropriate and informed modifications, inclusions and adaptations to participation, as necessary.

BENEFITS OF SAFE DANCE PRACTICE

One positive outcome of safe practice is reduced injury risk. Dance research reports injury rates of up to 97 percent within a 12-month period (Russell, 2013). The causes of injury are deemed multifactorial, but include elements such as insufficient warm-up, pressure to succeed, demanding or repetitive choreography and unsuitable environments (Laws, 2005). While the complex nature of injury incidence in dance is coming to light through research, this information is only of benefit if the emerging trends are heeded. Practitioner knowledge of safe practice principles should be updated and then applied in order to mediate against the known locations, causes and

implications of injuries that are being highlighted in the literature, thereby supporting safer dance experiences for all. Accidents and injuries in dance will never be wholly eliminated, due to the activity's physical nature and also the artistic and expressionistic desire to challenge and explore the physical boundaries of the art form. Therefore, understanding methods of injury management are also beneficial.

Increased performance potential is another positive outcome of safe practice. The application of effective preparation and training and recovery methods not only results in limited time away from dance participation due to injury or ill-being, but also supports performance improvements in their own right. The term *performance* here is referring to the optimum functioning of the dancer's body and mind, regardless of the context (such as class, rehearsal, competition or performance). More healthful experiences promote optimised physical functioning, which reduces unwanted wear and tear on the body's musculoskeletal system. The combination of increased performance potential and reduced injury risk result in the third outcome of safe practice: a healthy and efficient dancing body that can keep dancing for longer.

Of course, there are those who believe that overtly focusing on safety in dance participation can restrict enjoyment and development of the art form. However, awareness and implementation of safe dance practice will not take away the excitement or physical challenge of dancing. On the contrary, the recommendations from dance science and medicine research are helping to support advancement and innovation in dance by both protecting and rehabilitating dancers more

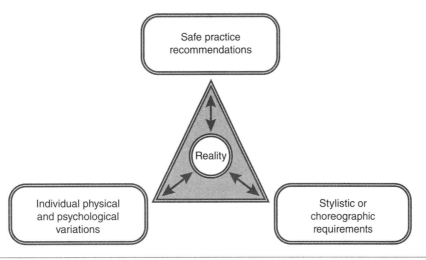

Figure I.2 Managing realistic applications of safe dance principles.

successfully. In this way, dance leaders can still pursue creative risk while minimising detrimental aspects that prevent dancers from fully participating in their dance activities or cause them to prematurely stop dance participation. Truly effective safe practitioners will be able to realistically challenge current physical boundaries and push the potential of both the individual dancer and the art form without negatively affecting the dancer's well-being or the artistic product.

IMPLEMENTING SAFE DANCE PRACTICE

Safe practice requires knowledge, understanding and application. While there are clear crossovers with pedagogical best practice, safe practice brings a particular focus and attention to principles that are not, as yet, commonplace within all dance settings. Teaching theories suggest that two broad categories of requisite knowledge exist: content knowledge (for example, familiarity with the style being taught) and pedagogical knowledge (for example, familiarity with techniques for the teaching of the style; Warburton, 2008; Mosston & Ashworth, 2002). Understanding how to create and select appropriate dance content and material and then finding the best way to communicate it to a diverse range of dancing bodies and minds can be supported by both content and pedagogical knowledge, employing teaching strategies such as devising session plans, defining class objectives and identifying learning outcomes. However, safe practice additionally encourages the dance leader to interrogate the anatomical, physiological and psychological reasoning behind the choices made. It further suggests that these choices should be based on a combination of up-to-date research in dance medicine and science and informed common-sense ideals. As an example, simply including a grand plié exercise as the second exercise at the barre because that is what has always been done is not appropriate. Instead the dance leader should question the function of this specific action, in this specific location of the session planning,

for these specific dancers. By engaging with the research-informed facts and following the practical guidelines that are offered throughout this text, dance leaders and practitioners will be able to integrate the principles of safe and effective dance practice into their session planning and delivery.

Everyone involved in dance is responsible for upholding safe practice. No dance experiences are exempt because of the manner in which they are practised, be that in a competitive, media, training, recreational or professional setting. Community and professional artists, choreographers, directors, producers and managers, teachers, as well as students of dance at every level should understand and integrate the principles into their specific role and context. Needless to say the level of responsibility differs depending on that role and context; consider the dance teacher leading a group of 6- to 8-year-olds in a creative dance session, versus the freelance hip-hop choreographer working with an adolescent youth group that have never danced before, versus the director of a professional ballet company deciding on rehearsal schedules and venues for the next tour. Fundamentals of ensuring effective working environments and safe physical and psychological functioning are a common responsibility in all of these cases, but each situation also requires specific considerations based on the dance style and the age range and level of participant. Scenarios such as these are presented throughout this text, with examples provided of how the key principles of safe practice can be adapted to specific situations.

Widespread communication of safe practice principles can positively influence future generations of dance practitioners, making such approaches to dance planning, delivery and participation commonplace. Through application of the information and guidance contained within this book, the processes for working safely and effectively in dance will be possible. Dancers in every context need to be reassured that they can work in any style, in any situation and at any level with minimised injury risk, and that their leaders are promoting optimum functioning and supporting longevity of participation.

KEY POINTS

Dancers, dance leaders and managers should be able to do the following:

- Understand the generic physical, psychological and environmental research-informed guidelines for safe dance practice.
- Apply these generic principles to their daily practice with consideration of the specific needs of their dance style and dance population.
- Work towards reducing injury risk, enhancing performance potential and prolonging involvement in dance activity across all genres and ages of dance participation.
- Appreciate that identification and mediation of risk goes beyond health and safety legislation.
- Engage with the theory and follow recommendations that are detailed within this text.

The Dance Environment

After reading this chapter you should be able to do the following:

- Select and maintain a fit-for-purpose space for dance activities.
- Choose appropriate clothing and footwear for your activity.
- Provide or locate first aid equipment in your own dance context.
- Adhere to legal policies that ensure health and safety in the dance workplace.
- Protect yourself and your participants with relevant insurance.
- Ensure that your behaviour and that of your participants comply with recommended codes of conduct and safeguarding principles.
- Conduct a risk assessment for your dance activity.
- Follow reporting procedures for accidents and injuries.

≡ *Key Terms*

accident and injury report	duty of care	liability
child protection	equal opportunities	risk assessment
codes of conduct	first aid	safeguarding
discrimination	health and safety	sprung floor
	insurance	touch

Safe dance practice begins with an awareness of the setting of the dance activity. Making sure that dance takes place in the most suitable environment possible is within the grasp of any dance leader. The intention of this chapter is to simply and clearly set out recommendations that maximise safety in the dance workplace and highlight basic practical strategies and support systems; therefore some of the advice provided is legislation based.

Health and safety regulations are a set of codified rules that, although they protect workers and the general public, can sometimes be seen as restrictive. However, safe dance practice is much more than this. Discussion on the optimal dance environment goes beyond a simple definition of site, location or facilities used for practice and performance—it also includes the contribution of psychological factors and the importance of care and **safeguarding** while leading dance activities and highlights additional moral and legal responsibilities. Policies and procedures that can

protect all involved in dance activity are becoming a necessity. Dance leaders must be familiar with **liability**, **insurance** and **risk assessment** in order to ensure that their working environment is safe and secure. The ideal is not always realistic, but understanding the positive and negative characteristics of the available environment will help leaders to prepare, adapt and monitor their sessions and take responsibility for ensuring the dance space is as free of risk as possible.

PREPARING FOR DANCE ACTIVITY

Thorough preparation can help prevent accidents and injuries. Physical preparation (warming up) is addressed in detail in chapter 3, but this section deals with the practical steps that dance leaders can take in advance of their sessions in order to help both themselves and their dancers avoid risks. Some of these are relatively straightforward, but nevertheless they can reduce the likelihood that detrimental incidents will occur.

Clothing, Footwear and Personal Effects

All dancers should be equipped with the appropriate clothing and footwear. Clothing needs to be suited to the activity. Ideally it should not be too tight so as to restrict movement or too loose as to cause an accident or obstruct or mask a teacher's appreciation of dancers' technical execution. The leader must advise dancers on suitable attire, explaining the reasons if necessary. Children and young people might need more guidance on appropriate dancewear, and parents could be provided with a uniform or suggested clothing list. Professional dancers, students in training and older adults may exercise individual choices, but dance leaders might need to remind them that dancewear should be functional as well as fashionable. Different genres have regulations or trends that make their style recognisable and distinctive, both in performance and in practice: For example, a ballet dancer's usual practice wear is pared down and designed to explicitly reveal the working of the body, while the hip-hop or street dancer's clothing is usually loose or baggy, partially obscuring the body. Dancers' own choices for their practice wear should complement their style and make them feel comfortable, but should also not pose any risk in the performance of their vocabulary. Dance leaders could also be aware of any body image issues with certain groups of dancers, especially in a community dance context when it may be neither necessary nor appropriate to insist that dancers conform to specific clothing requirements if this will affect their confidence. Some cultures require that certain garments be worn for religious reasons, for example to preserve modesty. Although it can be a sensitive issue, in this situation, participants should be informed of any implications should the items of clothing impede movement or interfere with their own safety or that of others (Whitlam, 2012).

Dancers, particularly young people, can be advised to wear layers and remove or add clothing in response to changing temperatures in dance spaces or to their own increasing or decreasing body temperature. Care should be taken, where possible, to avoid both clothing that encourages overheating or lack of clothing, which can cause unwanted cooling of the working body (more skin exposure allows sweat to evaporate, therefore reducing the body temperature).

Costumes that enhance choreography for presentation and performance are often considered at the last minute. If costumes are complicated in any way, perhaps in weight or length, or create additional restriction, dancers should have several opportunities to work in the costumes so that they can become accustomed to any challenges to the dancing and make adjustments if issues arise. In class or rehearsal, the use of protective clothing or equipment, such as knee pads or wrist guards, can be implemented to minimise any repetitive impact (e.g., in Graham technique and hip-hop or street dance vocabulary).

Long hair should be tied back for dance practice otherwise it can obscure the dancer's view of the space and their fellow dancers. It can affect balance and hinder execution in floor work, when others may step on a dancer's long hair. However, if a choreographer requires loose hair for the staging of a work, then dancers should practise the material with the performance hairstyle in advance to anticipate problems.

Footwear can be an injury risk when it is not appropriate for the activity or the environment. All dance shoes should fit the dancer well and provide proper support for the activity. Dancers should wear their shoes in gradually and discard them when worn out. In the recreational context the need for specialist footwear may not always be emphasised, so dancers might wear running or sports shoes that do not have the correct properties for safely practising specific styles. Dance leaders should advise their participants on the most suitable footwear for the activity.

Dance shoes vary in construction depending on the style. Unlike sports shoes that can be highly developed and rigorously tested for their specific activity, dance footwear is not particularly designed for shock absorption, and it often focuses on aesthetics as well as function (Wanke et al., 2012). The effects of footwear on foot motion are at present under-researched, but it is recognised that shoes have the potential to enhance or restrict movement, and can lead to consequential changes in alignment that affect the whole body (Fong Yan, Hiller, Smith, & Vanwanseele, 2011). The effect of footwear on alignment is discussed in more detail in chapter 2. Different genres either work with bare feet or use specific shoe types to accommodate the vocabulary. Examples include ballet slippers and pointe shoes, jazz sneakers or trainers, high heels for ballroom or some jazz styles, flamenco or character heels, and Irish and Highland dance slippers, jig shoes or pumps.

The interaction between the footwear and the floor surface, in terms of shock absorption, stability and friction, affects the body's biomechanics and therefore affects the potential for injury (see the section Dance Floor later in this chapter for more on floor properties). The use of socks (worn in place of shoes) is very common. Although many dancers would plead for the benefits of improved traction and the perceived comfort or performance-enhancing powers of wearing socks (smoother turns, easier gliding motions of the feet and so on), socks can affect the surface properties of a dance floor by polishing it and actually creating slippery patches (Wanke et al., 2012), as well as presenting a slip hazard due to reduced grip (Whitlam, 2012). If socks need to be worn for any reason, they should be used only by experienced dancers performing well-controlled, low-risk movements (Stein et al., 2014). Regardless of any protective benefits or negative consequences of footwear, shoes should be fitted properly to reduce the effects of prolonged exposure. Aesthetic preferences can lead dancers to choose shoes (particularly pointe shoes) that are too small, short or narrow. Poorly fitted shoes and those that lack shock-absorbing properties have been identified as a cause of injury (Fong Yan et al., 2011). Some dancers insert shock-absorbing insoles into their shoes for repeated practice.

The ballet pointe shoe is an exceptionally specialised type of footwear. Safety when working in pointe shoes is based on the dancer's physical capacity to perform effectively while wearing them. (See chapter 10 for clear recommendations on assessing a young dancer's readiness to begin pointe work.) Well-fitting pointe shoes, of the correct length and width and with the appropriate level of support, are essential. Research has also shown that soft ballet shoes and pointe shoes significantly vary in the amount of pressure they impose on the foot, and that it may be beneficial for young dancers to adapt gradually to the pressure of the stiffer full-pointe shoes by conditioning the feet using demi-pointe shoes (Pearson & Whitaker, 2012).

Tying ribbons and laces correctly on dance shoes is important for preventing tripping over loose laces and incurring injury due to pressure on the foot and ankle. On pointe shoes, the ribbons should be sewn on to match the individual shape of the feet and ankles and tied at the side of the ankle, rather than directly over the Achilles tendon (Huwyler, 1999). Similarly, Highland or Irish dancers should practise correct shoe-lacing techniques. Although a normal practice in some styles, tying laces around the arch of the foot affects foot function and might result in sore feet, while tying them too tightly at the ankle results in compression and possible reduction in blood flow, and may cause Achilles tendon problems (Coussins, 2009). Specialist dance shoe manufacturers can supply advice if necessary.

Finally, it is preferable to change into a different pair of shoes for use on the dance floor to avoid dirt being brought into the dance space; for example, when using the same pair of outdoor trainers or sneakers for indoor dance fitness or street dance sessions.

The term *personal effects* refers to any additional accessories that might constitute a hazard, minor or major, while dancing. These usually mean jewellery, watches, hair slides, belts and so on, but also can include spectacles, medical bracelets or hearing aids (BAALPE, 2004). Ideally, all personal effects should be removed before dancing. However, some dancers might need to use specific items, such as spectacles, in order to appreciate the session fully. Leaders should speak with the dancer and decide whether the hazard is more or less pronounced with or without the personal effects. Dance leaders can use their discretion. For example, elderly dancers might not need to remove all their jewellery, and they would probably prefer to wear their hearing aids or spectacles to get the maximum benefit from the session—with the type of activity level to be expected here, the associated risk may be minimal. Dancers with specific health conditions such as diabetes (see chapter 10) may need to wear their medical information on a bracelet or necklace. In these cases, alternatives to jewellery include shoe tags (if footwear is worn in the session) or identification attached to kit bags and personal belongings that are present in the dancing space. If the dancer cannot find a suitable alternative or feels more comfortable wearing medical tags, the item could be covered or taped if it might present a significant risk to the individual or to other dancers.

Face and body piercing have gained popularity, and dancers are often reluctant to remove this type of jewellery. However, it is certain that accidents involving hoops or rings could cause particular discomfort and damage for a dancer, and sharp or pointed types of jewellery would also affect other dancers in partnering material.

Older dancers will be able to wear jewellery safely during their dance sessions if their activities do not involve large ranges of movement or unpredictable contact. They are likely to enjoy and appreciate their activities more if they wear their spectacles or hearing aids.

If it is not possible to remove them completely, then all piercings should be taped over. Security arrangements for storing valuables might need to be organised, especially when the leader is in charge of younger dancers.

Health and Injury Check

Conducting an health and injury check before dance sessions provides key information for responsive dance leaders and prepares them to adapt their activities and strategies accordingly, either for individuals or for the group as a whole. The significance of this check will become increasingly apparent as this book unfolds. Understanding the health and injury status of individual participants is a vital part of safe dance practice that is frequently highlighted in these chapters. Information can be gathered in advance of a course or series of lessons by giving students a preparticipation health and injury questionnaire or, alternatively, immediately before a single session by asking the group a few simple questions. The first involves more planning for the dance

leader, but the second can be both quick and very beneficial. A health questionnaire pro forma can be found in appendix A.

The following types of questions should be included in a preparticipation questionnaire:

- Do you have any health conditions that might affect your capabilities in the dance session, for example, asthma, diabetes, epilepsy, heart or blood pressure irregularities? Have you recently experienced any other significant physical changes, for example, pregnancy or childbirth?

- Do you have any disabilities or specific learning difficulties you would like us to consider?

- Do you have any previous or ongoing injuries that could affect your participation?

- Do you need to use any specialised equipment or medication during the session, for example, inhalers or insulin pumps?

- Do you have any relevant allergies that could be affected during the dance session?

• Are there any permanent or long-term physical issues that might require movement adaptation, for example, scoliosis, leg length discrepancies or arthritis?

Prior written consent could also be considered, if the answer is yes to any of the preceding questions. Providing a handout in advance with clear expectations for the session, health and safety rules and guidelines for proper conduct gives participants an opportunity to sign in agreement and evidence their understanding and compliance. Both participants and leaders should be accountable and responsible for their actions (Hernandez & Strickland, 2005).

Leaders who tend to work with groups of people in a community or recreational setting should provide the preparticipation questionnaire, which will help them identify people with relevant conditions. Knowing if dancers in the group have any allergies or need to use insulin pens or pumps for diabetes or asthma inhalers will also support the leader's ability to react quickly should the need arise. Dancers should also be encouraged, reassured or reminded to use these aids before or during sessions if necessary. If leaders are uncertain of the suitability of their activity for dancers with specific conditions, they can refer dancers to their healthcare provider to request a medical assessment before participation. In a formal educational training environment, dance leaders need to be briefed on students with health issues so that they can create informed strategies for dealing with possible incidents and can correctly follow institutional procedures. Chapter 10 provides detailed information on a variety of factors to consider when working with dancers with some common health conditions.

If the dance session provided is an informal, drop-in type of class, it is more difficult to check on all participants over time, but teachers can do an on-the-spot health check before every session. In fact, all leaders in all teaching and practice environments should regularly conduct an injury check at the beginning of their sessions. Knowing if any dancers are either carrying or recovering from an injury prompts the leader to be aware of any possible repercussions, including lack of concentration, focus and co-ordination, which can be contributory risk factors for accidents. If dancers report that they have any transient health issues (for example, a viral infection), leaders can give relevant guidance on whether or not to participate (see chapter 9 for more details on health

and injury risk factors). Examples of questions to include in a regular check at the beginning of each session would be:

• Are there any short-term, unresolved or current injuries that will prevent the dancer from performing specific actions (for example, jumping or rolling on the floor) or that may be exacerbated by certain movements?

• Does the dancer have any viral infections (colds, sore throats)? Or is the dancer temporarily feeling unwell, lightheaded or faint?

It is also good practice to prepare participants for a dance session with a briefing on what they can expect. This will give them the opportunity to assess their own readiness for the demands of that activity and make an informed decision on their ability to meet them safely. Some advance information on the activities to be encountered during the session is helpful, and leaders should advise against full participation or identify aspects that may involve modification for specific groups when necessary (for example, providing a disclaimer for sufferers of heart conditions or guidelines for pregnant dancers). During the session, the dance leader should be also aware of dancers in recovery from injury and make appropriate adaptations for them in the material.

Clear rules and instruction on the use of props or equipment should be established prior to the activity in which they are involved. Any equipment that is used during the activity, including portable or fixed barres, props, mats, poles, or ropes or wires, should be fit for purpose, in good working order and inspected frequently. If it is in any way defective, the equipment should be either professionally repaired or replaced. Regular tests for electrical equipment are also advised. All materials must comply with industry standards in terms of safety. For example, there are recommendations regarding the optimal height for ballet barres. Commercially available barres often use a double rail system to simultaneously accommodate dancers of different heights: minimum to maximum heights are approximately 82 to 105 centimetres (32.5 to 41.5 inches). If permanently fixed, the distance from the wall is approximately 15 to 20 centimetres (6 to 8 inches). Free-standing barres should have adjustable feet to accommodate the height variations and possibly uneven floor levels (Hernandez & Strickland, 2005; Harlequin, 2013). Before each session, dance leaders are responsible for checking any equipment they personally provide and for assessing any equipment they use that is provided by the facility. If they are not satisfied with the safety level of any equipment, they should report the condition or damage and request repairs by the managers of the facility.

MAINTAINING PROPER FACILITIES

It is unlikely that the space will be perfect in every way unless it has been built specifically for dance. The expectations mentioned in this section are features of an ideal space rather than definitive prerequisites for successful dance activity. The practice and performance environment can range from specialised studios and traditional theatres to shared-use venues or unusual, site-specific spaces and events staged in the open air. Each one has different aspects that can affect safe participation.

Size and Amenities

In an ideal scenario, entrances to and exits from the dance space should be safe for all participants. Both able and disabled dancers would have access to the space. If not, arrangements should be made to assist access where necessary. Each dancer should have an adequate amount of room to move with enough personal space so as not to come into contact with an obstruction or a fellow dancer when their limbs are outstretched (Dance UK, 2011). Ideally, the space should not have any obstructions such as pillars or columns in the centre. Recommendations suggest that a standard dance space should be approximately 12 to 15 meters (40 to 50 feet) square by 4.5 metres (approximately 15 feet) high to accommodate on average 30 people: Smaller studios for 12 to 15 people are acceptable, with dimensions not smaller than 10 metres by 9 metres (approximately 33 by 30 feet) by 4.5 metres (15 feet) high (NDTA, n.d; Sport England, 2008; Youth Dance England, 2013). In addition to floor area, the room's height needs to take into account jumping and lifting movements as well as individual choreographic or genre-specific needs.

The factors to consider in assessing the suitability of space for a dance session are the number of expected participants, their age and the type of activity. For example, young children can use more space than perhaps expected since they often use free, less formal types of movement material such as running, which needs unimpeded space (NDTA, n.d.).

Different dance genres have unique spatial components—not all require as much space for travelling, for example, belly dancing or other ethnic forms. When designing dance activities, the leader should bear the size of the space in mind, manage the participants effectively in the space and encourage individual spatial awareness (Bramley, 2002). If dance leaders regularly rely on the use of mirrors, emphasising frontal orientation, they should take care to encourage dancers not to focus on themselves in the mirror all the time but to be aware of three-dimensional relationships to others in space to avoid accidents.

A dance space may not always be indoors—often events and public performances are held outside. In this case, the effects of the weather should be considered. Decisions to continue working in cold and wet conditions are detrimental for dancers' health and well-being. Prolonged sun exposure also has dangerous consequences. If dancers, especially children, are expected to work at length outside in hot weather, they should be directed to cover their skin with light clothing and to wear a hat if possible. Dance leaders should encourage the use of sunscreen (provided by parents in the case of children) and ensure that water for rehydration is available. Indoor facilities should also include access to drinking water. Water bottles taken into the dance area are best stored out of the way. If water is spilled onto the dance floor, it should be wiped and dried immediately.

The provision of changing facilities can sometimes be overlooked as an aspect of safe dance practice. However, to avoid any potential issues, an ideal space will include single-gender changing rooms that are not accessible to non-participants, with separate toilets for male and female dancers. Adult leaders should not change at the same time or in the same facility as child participants. There needs to be an awareness of security and individual safety, particularly for young people. It is not advised to allow children and young people to leave the main working space unattended, or to leave them alone once the session is over. They can be sent to the changing areas or toilets either with a friend or with a designated second responsible adult, and they must be collected by parents after their session if necessary. Even for older teenage dancers, the leader should request information as to how they will return home following events or performances so that parents and guardians are aware of the arrangements.

The responsibility for the provision of adequate facilities lies with the owner or manager of larger, built-for-purpose premises. Dance leaders who rent a space independently should construct their own strategies to combat a lack of facilities, for example, implementing set changing times for different sexes or groups or organising comfort breaks in larger groups. When dealing with younger children, a second responsible adult can assist in managing such situations. Participants can also be advised to arrive already dressed in practice wear under their street clothes. Further detail on related issues is included in the Safeguarding section later in this chapter.

All areas that are regularly used by dancers in practice venues or in their workplace need to be well maintained, clean and hygienic. This includes toilets, dressing rooms and corridors as well as the immediate dance area. General untidiness, for example, participants leaving their belongings in a haphazard arrangement around the space, can contribute to workplace accidents. Any unavoidable sharp or protruding edges should be highlighted, taped or padded if necessary, particularly at head or foot height (Equity, 2011). When the space to be used is not completely dedicated to dance activities and involves shared use, additional safety factors might need to be taken in to account. The condition of the floor area should be monitored between each type of activity. The storage of equipment in the dance space needs to be secure, and should not interfere with any dance traffic. Independent dance leaders might have to allow time in advance of their session to prepare the space if sharing it with other activities, for example, in church halls or community centres.

Dance Floor

The state of the dance floor is extremely important for safe dance practice. The balance of its prop-erties and characteristics can negatively affect the resilience of the dancer's body and can significantly contribute to injury. In research studies examining dance floor properties and injury risk factors, 20 to 28 percent of professional dancers associated an unsuitable floor surface with the progression of a previous injury (Hopper et al., 2014).

There are different types of dance floors: **sprung floor**, semisprung and cushioned. They can be permanent or temporary. For regular and frequent dance practice, the ideal is a permanent, fully sprung floor, sometimes termed an *area-elastic* floor (Foley, 1998). Even in the short term, dancing on unsuitable floors, especially those based on concrete, can potentially cause pain and lasting damage to the body. Dancers may complain of pain in the feet, legs (especially at the front of the shins) and back during or following dancing activities on such floors, but ultimately the whole body can be affected. The lower extremity is the most common site of injury attributed to the dance floor, and these type of injuries are sustained by both experienced and novice dancers, suggesting that lack of technical ability is not the only contributory factor (Wanke et al., 2012). To prevent injury, a dance floor should have a balance of friction and elasticity or resiliency, absorbing some of the impact forces inherent in dance movement (Laws, 2008; Shell, 1984). This translates into a two-component structure, a surface and a solid or suspended sub-floor, each of which has different properties (see figure 1.1). Both are equally important, and one does not compensate for the absence of the other (Wanke et al., 2012). Simply laying a vinyl floor over unyielding floors will not eradicate the risk.

The visible part is the surface: This may be wooden, including parquet, or heavy-duty, slip-resistant vinyl (such as Marley). The purpose of the surface is to provide the right amount of friction

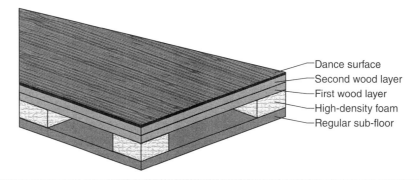

Figure 1.1   Ideal multilayered dance floor.

between the floor and the feet or the shoes. Generally, although the mechanics may depend on the genre of dance and the footwear used, dancers need to be able to turn, pivot, balance or slide comfortably. A sticky or slippery surface can either provide too much resistance for the foot, producing unnatural twisting in the joints, or not allow enough friction, encouraging excessive tension and gripping or accidental falls. Genre-specific differentiations have been suggested. For dancing with shoes (for example, in ballet) the floor should have a good degree of grip while allowing the foot to slide, while a floor for dancing in bare feet needs a finer finish to avoid friction burns, but should still provide enough grip for control of dynamic movement (Foley, 1998). As mentioned earlier, a large number of dancers regularly working in socks may alter the surface properties of the floor by polishing it unnecessarily.

Caution must be exercised when evaluating a dance floor, since some commercial vinyl floors are not dance specific, and the non-slip quality can cause friction injuries and discomfort for dancers (Ausdance, 2012). Thin floor surfaces can develop folds and ridges, and the adhesive tape used to secure individual rolls and edges works itself free as it deteriorates (Wanke et al., 2012). While a wooden floor, waxed, sanded or lacquered, may be acceptable for some ballroom styles or social dance, it has been reported to be unpredictable for many other dance styles (Dance UK, 2011). Unmaintained wooden floors may present risks due to splinters, nails and uneven boards (Ausdance, 2012).

Frequent care and regular cleaning of the floor surface are essential. Potential injuries arise as a result of unwanted dirt, liquid or chemicals: this includes water or other drinks, excess sweat and skin care products that dancers sometimes apply to their feet, either for relief from pain or hard skin or to create moisture in an attempt to alter their traction with the floor. Ideally, these scenarios should be avoided. Keeping an eye on sweat patches on the studio or stage floor as they accumulate and wiping them as soon as possible will deter accidents and make things more pleasant for everyone using the dancing space. Dancers could keep their own towels handy at the side of the studio or backstage. Similarly, the use of rosin (an antislip resin powder usually used with ballet shoes) will affect a shared dance space. If barefoot dancers come into contact with it following a previous ballet class in the same space, it affects their ability to work smoothly through their feet and

roll on the floor. It is also a skin irritant. Managers of commercial sport or dance spaces are likely to ensure regular cleaning of their floors, but in the private, multi-use spaces frequently used in community or recreational dance sessions, individual dance leaders might need to assume the responsibility for cleaning the floor before their session if necessary.

The shock-absorbing properties of the dance floor come from its substructure. A space under the top layers creates the cushioned floating effect and allows for elasticity and reactivity to the dancers' movements. Industry markers exist for the shock-absorbing qualities of a floor (for example, European DIN standards and American National Standards), but dancers have their own intuitive opinions about the feel of a good floor, and might describe one as having give and a feeling of buoyancy or rebound. Recommendations on the shock absorption of different floors suggest a minimum value of approximately 55 percent (Ausdance, 2012; Youth Dance England, 2013). The rest of the impact from high-intensity activities such as jumping is absorbed by the dancer's body on landing. For comparison, the shock-absorption value of concrete is 0 percent. The relationship between supportive footwear and the shock-absorbing properties of the floor therefore becomes more important. Dance leaders might be able to minimise some of the impact risks by the choice of footwear they direct their dancers to use; if the work is barefoot, or protection is not offered by style-specific footwear, then a fully sprung floor becomes imperative.

The dancer would usually expect to work on a flat floor surface. However, some theatres may have a raked stage, which means that the floor has a slight, or sometimes quite steep (approximately 1:12) forward incline. Sloped stages can affect dancers' perception of balance (Motta-Valencia, 2006), particularly if they are unused to performing on this type of surface. Reports show that raked stages are seen in approximately 20 percent of Broadway productions, and working on this surface might double or triple the risk of injury to professional dancers (Pappas & Hagins, 2008). This comes about because the dancer accommodates in alignment by shifting the centre of gravity backwards (Evans, Evans, & Carvajal, 1998). The steeper the rake, the less suitable it is for choreographed movement, especially in high-heeled shoes, but even standing still for long periods of time can be more difficult on raked stages than on standard ones. Performers usually receive training to help them work in this environment. Also, if the rake is steep, the quality of the finish is more important, since greater grip is needed, and footwear should be supportive with a sole surface that is compatible to the floor surface (Theatre Safety Committee, 2007). Equipment and props should also be rake-proofed, that is, stabilised to match the degree of tilt, for example, for dancers standing or moving on additional platforms or tables.

To help dancers successfully negotiate different types of floor, leaders can draw attention to changing characteristics if necessary, for example, allowing greater time to become familiar with the practice floor versus the performance floor (moving from rehearsal room to performance space) because injuries due to the floor appear to be a particular risk on stage, as opposed to in the studio (Wanke et al., 2012). It has been suggested that floor variability, rather than the hardness, may have a greater influence in injury (Hopper et al., 2014). Young dancers changing studios between classes might be reminded to change their class-specific footwear to non-slip, supportive types if they are walking through buildings and corridors that are constructed of concrete or tiles.

It could be supposed that the responsibility for the composition of the dance floor on which dancers are expected to work rests with the venue provider (including the educational institution, the private studio, the school, the performance venue or the dance company manager booking tour dates). However, independent dance leaders can choose their space carefully. The planning decisions of the dance leader who directs the activities on that floor will affect the likelihood of injury in a compromised working environment. If the use of an unsuitable floor is unavoidable, dance leaders should pay greater attention to warming dancers up thoroughly and modifying high-impact activities, for example, minimising unnecessary rehearsal time and reducing the frequency of, or even removing, jumps, lifts or floor work.

Temperature and Ventilation

A room temperature that is too cold prevents effective warm-up and maintenance of muscle heat, while one that is too hot can generate excessive sweating, resulting in dehydration and muscle fatigue. The average person works best at temperatures between 16 and 24 degrees Celsius (61 to 75 degrees Fahrenheit) but this depends on the type of work being done. Dance industry standards quote a minimum of 18.3 degrees Celsius (65 degrees

Fahrenheit), with an ideal air temperature of 21 to 24 degrees Celsius (70 to 75 degrees Fahrenheit; Dance UK, 2011; Equity, 2011; NDTA, n.d.; Youth Dance England, 2013). A rise in temperature is inevitable in hot weather, but it can be offset by the use of ventilation systems. In an ideal dance space, reactive and efficient heating or ventilation systems will maintain an even working temperature and humidity, preferably below 60 percent (Sport England, 2008). Simply opening and closing doors or windows cannot stabilise the environment in the same way, and may affect fire regulations. Too many people for the size of the space will also affect the efficiency of the ventilation systems. If heaters are used, there should be no danger of burns or from fumes. Dance leaders need to be aware of the effects of adjusting temperature by opening windows, using heaters, and switching air conditioning on and off. Dance leaders should follow guidelines provided by the venue and use common sense in the absence of guidelines.

In performance and rehearsal, heavy costumes, suits or masks will affect dancers' ability to regulate their own temperature, so the ambient temperature may need to be adjusted. Similarly, if dancers express that they are too cold in a particular environment, additional clothing should be allowed. Age and body composition can affect the regulation of body temperature during exercise. For example, small children have a larger ratio of surface area to mass than adults, which makes it more difficult for them to maintain normal body temperature in the cold, and adults with more fat mass can conserve heat more efficiently (Kenney,Wilmore & Costill, 2012). However, as a general rule, if the temperature varies too much (up or down), then safety is compromised. Overheating can result in dehydration, loss of concentration and fatigue, then dizziness, fainting or muscle cramps. More seriously, if the blood temperature rises above 39 degrees Celsius (102.2 degrees Fahrenheit), there is a risk of heat stroke and collapse (Equity, 2011). In touring situations, giving dancers an opportunity to acclimatise to unaccustomed heat will allow physiological adaptations that can increase their tolerance, including lowered heart rate, increased rate of perspiration and a delay in the onset of fatigue (Kenney, Wilmore & Costill, 2012).

Light and Noise Levels

Common sense dictates that lighting should be sufficient for seeing the teacher in a dance class, but other lighting factors can affect concentration, such as direct sunlight or glare (which can be managed through the use of adjustable curtains or blinds) and flickering fluorescent lights or disorientating strobing effects, which should be avoided by dancers who suffer from particular types of epilepsy. Dancers frequently have to work in low levels of lighting on stage. If the performance lighting is significantly low, dancers should be given adequate time to rehearse in the expected levels so that they can negotiate the space and their fellow dancers safely. If there are problems, the dancers' viewpoint should be considered by choreographers, lighting designers and technicians, since safety can be compromised for the sake of atmospheric ambience and stage effects.

Exposure to noise is not usually seen as a great problem in dance practice, but in some circumstances, the noise levels can affect dancers if the exposure is long enough or the decibel level is high enough. A limit of around 85 decibels, or a noise rating of NR40, are given as a general guideline (long-term exposure to 85 decibels is generally considered to result in hearing loss; Equity, 2011; Sport England, 2008). This noise level is approximate to one in which you must raise your voice to be heard. This situation may not be uncommon for dance leaders who regularly use amplified live or recorded music or for dancers who are involved with commercial types of work, for example, supporting the music industry in videos or as backing dancers. For dancers working in theatres, it is likely that there will be an in-house amplification system. Regulations stipulate that if the volume exposure is above the first action level (the level that steps must be taken to limit harmful effects), then a noise risk assessment must be undertaken by a competent person (Equity, 2011).

Fire and Emergency Procedures

All dance leaders need to be familiar with the fire regulations and procedures of the venue in which they practise. Ideally leaders should communicate these to their participants.

Adapting the Performance Environment to Meet Dancers' Needs

■ ■ ■

An urban youth dance group have been asked to perform in a showcase of mixed-genre dance. Their routine involves floor work and some semi-acrobatic moves. Because this is a one-day event, they have not previously seen their performance space. On arrival, their leader discovers that they have been allocated a space outside with a concrete foundation, which also has a small amount of grit and dirt on the surface. The weather is cold and there is the threat of rain.

The leader speaks to the organisers, letting them know that this space is not ideal for the type of dancing the group will perform. Unfortunately, the schedule means that all the other performance spaces are fully booked for the duration of the event, so the only alternative for the group would be to pull out.

The dance leader has several concerns about the well-being of his group. He feels that he should refuse to perform, but also feels compromised and pressured not to do so by both the organisers and his dancers, who would be disappointed. He decides to put some mediating factors into practice.

He asks that the space be swept thoroughly and covered with a waterproof tarpaulin between each act. He directs the dancers to add a long-sleeved layer to their costumes and to wear their costumes under their regular clothes with a rainproof layer on top to keep warm up to the point of performance. He tells them that they will wear their sports shoes and trainers instead of dancing barefoot. After finding a grassy area that is under cover, he warms the dancers up thoroughly before making some adaptations to the choreography. He removes any movements that involve lying on the floor and takes out the athletic aspects that would be risky on the hard surface, making sure that the dancers are all happy with the changes at short notice.

Following the event, the dance leader has a conversation with the event managers. He explains that an advance risk assessment would have been extremely helpful. Together they put plans in place for this to happen the following year, highlighting the need for increased communication between all participating groups and the organisers.

The emergency fire exits and fire extinguisher sites need to be located and access kept clear of obstructions at all times. The fire doors must be able to be opened from the inside, and it is illegal to wedge open a fire door. Leaders must understand evacuation procedures, assembly points and obligations for taking registers or roll calls to account for all participants in emergency situations. They should be aware of the presence and situation of alarms and phones, as well as know whom to contact in an emergency. It goes without saying that dance activities should not take place in a smoky environment and that smoking should be restricted to designated areas. The proper disposal of cigarettes and litter is advised. Leaders must pay attention to the use and storage of potentially flammable material in the dance space (Bramley, 2002; Equity, 2011). Information on adhering to fire regulations is usually included in contracts, either of employment or space hire, and dance leaders should read these carefully so they are prepared in the event of an incident. In the unlikely event that a venue does not have adequate procedures, dance leaders should formulate their own guidelines. It will be beneficial to frequently rehearse a fire drill.

First Aid Procedures and Supplies

For all leaders, when an accident occurs during their sessions, standard procedures and statutory policies should be followed, along with recommendations for immediate treatment of any injury (see chapter 9). **First aid** training for dance leaders is not always a legal requirement, but it is recommended, either through completing a recognised course or by maintaining a working knowledge of basic first aid procedures that are relevant in the dance workplace. An employer or venue owner must legally provide appropriate first aid equipment and have a registered first-aider on site. Dance leaders who are employed should take responsibility for finding out where the first aid kit is kept and how to contact the designated first-aider. Independent practitioners should carry their own kit.

A basic first aid kit usually contains:

- Sterile disposable gloves
- Individual alcohol wipes and saline solution
- Assorted individually wrapped sterile adhesive dressings
- Unmedicated sterile wound dressings
- Individually wrapped triangular bandages
- Sterile eye pads
- Gauze
- Scissors
- Safety pins

Additional items that might be found include an air cast, crutches and instant cold compresses

Dance leaders should ensure that a first aid kit is available in their dance environment. A fully-equipped kit enables them to offer immediate basic first aid treatment to deal with on-site injuries and minimise their effects.

if there is no ice provision. The contents of the first aid kit should be replaced as they are used. Whether or not to provide medication in a first aid kit is controversial because of possible allergies. Children (under 10) should not be given any medication that is not provided by their parents (BAALPE, 2004; Carlon, 2011). When attending to children, (ideally as a trained first-aider), permission should be sought from their parents if the situation allows, rather than from the children themselves. This is why it is essential to have a list of parent contact numbers. It is advised to always tell the child exactly what you are doing and why, and preferably to treat them in the presence of another adult (Royal Academy of Dance, n.d.).

If an accident occurs that results in bleeding, it is important to clean up any blood spill immediately. It is very common for dancers who work in bare feet to get small splits or friction burns that result in bleeding onto the dance floor, and cuts can easily occur on any site of the body through physical contact or collisions. While it might seem unlikely that any contamination could occur from small spots of blood, leaders should always follow standard blood spill procedures and prevent any other dancers from coming into contact with the blood to avoid any chance of infection. If leaders are responsible for cleaning up the blood (that is, there are no other specified individuals charged with the task), then they should follow these guidelines:

- Wear disposable gloves.
- Ensure that any cuts or lesions (on the injured dancer or themselves) are covered with a dressing.
- Wipe up the blood with paper towels soaked in a weak solution of bleach (1:10 bleach to water) or use disinfectant wipes.
- Respray the area with bleach if necessary, then wash the floor area with detergent and allow it to dry.
- Follow procedures to dispose of the gloves and towels as contaminated waste.
- Wash hands thoroughly.

ENSURING MORAL SAFETY

Apart from providing activities that are safe and knowing how to deal with accidents if they occur, dance leaders also need to ensure that they are aware of their moral responsibilities in dealing with different groups of people. Chapter 8 discusses in detail the psychological issues related to creating a positive learning environment, but this chapter concentrates on factors that affect the optimal learning and working environment from a legal perspective. The responsibility for maintaining a morally safe environment can be shared between employers and independent leaders, but each must understand their role within the legal framework. This can be easily done if all concerned are aware of the relevant **codes of conduct** that apply to safe dance practice.

Codes of Conduct

Dance is a fun, social, professional, commercial and very physical activity that necessarily involves relating to, communicating with and coming into close contact with other bodies. In an age of heightened awareness of **discrimination** and litigation in society in general, dance leaders must be vigilant that their behaviour, language and associations with participants in their capacity as a leader are appropriate. Ensuring moral safety is key to protecting all parties involved.

To begin, professional behaviour underpins the relationship between leader and participant.

In the first instance, although this could be taken for granted, it is worth emphasising that the dance leader must have the requisite skills and knowledge to be able to deliver dance activities competently. Secondly, the activities they deliver should comply with national or regional statutory legal requirements to protect the rights of all involved. Knowing how their activity is affected by legislation allows dance leaders to formulate the proper strategies and adjust their behaviour to maintain appropriate boundaries. Leaders have an obligation to their participants, termed a **duty of care**, and in turn can expect to be treated fairly themselves. This means that interactions between leader and participant should be mutually respectful regardless of age, gender or level of ability or disability.

Safeguarding

Safeguarding refers to the protection of specific groups of people in terms of health, well-being and welfare, keeping them free from harm or potential abuse. Dance leaders working with children, young people and vulnerable adults must comply with legal policies and national, federal, state or local laws that are specifically put in place to care for these individuals. Most institutions or organisations will have such policies in place and, if employed, the leader will be required to understand the practical application of these. For independent leaders, it is good practice to provide their own statement dealing with these issues that can be publicised or distributed if necessary. Many dance organisations, unions, teaching associations and network sites worldwide offer guidance and pro formas that can be used and adapted (some of these issues are included in the sample Equal Opportunities Statement in appendix B).

Child protection is one of the most important safeguarding issues to consider. It has become a legal requirement in many countries that dance practitioners working with children must have undertaken a disclosure certification, in which they are checked for any convictions or previous history of abuse in relation to young people. It is worth remembering that a child is usually considered to be 18 years old or younger. The United Nations Convention of the Rights of the Child defines a child as being below the age of 18, unless the law of a particular country sets the legal age for adulthood younger. In most countries this legal age is also 18, but there are exceptions (UNICEF, n.d.).

In addition to the international agencies that promote rights for children and vulnerable people, such as UNICEF, Unesco and the United Nations, there are a multitude of acts and treaties that originate in each continent, country, state, territory or district. Each local authority will be driven by country-specific, national or federal laws, but they will also have their own policies on safeguarding and the reporting of abuse. Specific legislation is also frequently changing and being updated. For this reason, it is extremely difficult to provide a checklist on what dance leaders must adhere to in order to comply with the law in their workplace.

However, the most common essential requirement is the criminal record check. In most countries, local police or local government agencies such as the following conduct these checks:

- Australia: National Police (Working with Children Check)
- France: Ministries of Justice
- Germany: Federal Criminal Register
- Greece: Penal Records
- Ireland: Garda Central Vetting Unit
- India: Crime Record Office
- Italy: Criminal Records Bureau

- UK: Disclosure and Barring Service (DBS)
- United States: Local police or FBI checks, Department of Justice

Dance leaders must take responsibility in addressing the issue of their compliance with local regulations when working with children and vulnerable adults in order to both protect their participants and themselves. It is up to the individual (although some institutions will organise the service for their employees) to provide a document stating that there is no history of a criminal record.

When working with children, young people and vulnerable adults in dance practice or performance, a responsible adult must be present at all times—this may be their teacher, a chaperone or parent or guardian. These groups cannot be left alone without supervision by a designated responsible adult.

Licensed chaperones also take care of individual children working in entertainment (NNCEE, 2014). Leaders should observe recommended adult-to-child ratios for supervision, which may vary internationally. For example, in supervising children who are between the ages of 2 and 3 in the UK, there should ideally be one adult for every four children; for children between the ages of 4 and 8, the ratio is 1:6; for children between the ages of 8 and 12, 1:8; and for adolescents between 13 and 18, 1:10 (Exercise, Movement and Dance Partnership, n.d). In the United States, the recommendations differ: The suggested teacher–pupil ratio is 1:12 for pre-school children, 1:15 for those of school age, then dropping to 1:20 as dancers reach the ages of 14 to 18 (Hernandez & Strickland, 2005). These figures are guidelines only—there may be further needs for particular groups or occasions, such as performance events.

Private, one-to-one dance sessions are not advised unless prior authorisation (and written consent) is provided by the parents of guardians. Ideally, such sessions would be recorded (Royal Academy of Dance, n.d.).

Any filming, photography and digital images of dance activity with children participating must be managed securely. Unfortunately, there are reasons why taking photographs of children has the potential to be unacceptable. International evidence indicates that images made available through Internet sites, in newspapers or magazines may lead to the targeting of children (including locating and conditioning them) for the purposes of abuse and exploitation (Ausport,

2014). Therefore most countries have initiated recommendations, if not legislation, for regulating the use of digital images of children. This translates down into the dance studio. Now certain rules apply to taking pictures of a group or individuals, or simply allowing the participants or their parents to record dance sessions without prior permission of everyone concerned. This is one area in which parents understandably become frustrated that they cannot capture their own child's performances and achievements on film, but it is in everyone's interests to consider the guidance given. Dance leaders organising concerts and performances can counteract this by arranging for a photographer or filmmaker to make a recording of the event that can be then accessed by participants' families though controlled means. In this way, prior permission and restricted access can be ensured.

The following guidelines can ensure compliance with safeguarding policies (Ausaid, 2013; Ausport, 2014; NSPCC, 2013; Royal Academy of Dance, n.d.; Whitlam, 2012):

- To take photographs or recordings and to reproduce them, the permission of the individual and a parent or guardian should be obtained in advance. Written consent is advised.
- Only images of a child in suitable dress, that is, adequately clothed, should be recorded and distributed.
- Unusual body positions that could be interpreted as sexually suggestive should be avoided.
- The full name of any individual should not be provided alongside the photograph.

Dance leaders must take appropriate action to prevent any safeguarding issues arising, but if issues do occur, they also have legal obligations to report them. For example, there are recommended procedures to follow if the dance leader either suspects or is directly approached about allegations of inappropriate behaviour by adults or other children or young people. If a young or vulnerable person discloses this type of information, the dance leader must take action.

Other factors come into play when considering appropriate behaviour and language for all participant groups. The use of **touch** has sometimes been considered controversial in dance practice, but it is a key communication and feedback tool with a clear rationale if used correctly, for example,

Addressing Safeguarding Concerns

1. Ensure that you listen to all concerns regarding abuse disclosed to you and refrain from making judgements as to whether any allegations made are true or unfounded.

2. Make a detailed report (in the concerned individual's own words) of any incidents that have been reported to you.

3. Ensure confidentiality but explain that you will need to pass on the information to appropriate authorities.

4. Report your concerns to a designated safeguarding or welfare officer if your place of work has one. Alternatively, seek advice from appropriate authorities, organisations or charities specialising in child protection (for example, Social and Family Services, the NSPCC in the UK or Love Our Children in the United States). Contacting the local police is another option.

5. Do not take independent action to resolve or confront any issues if you suspect abuse.

(Council for Dance Education and Training, n.d.; NSPCC, 2013; Royal Academy of Dance, n.d.; Love Our Children USA, 2014)

in correcting alignment or preparing for contact and lifting work. The rules of using touch need to be agreed and explained in advance with different groups and communicated to parents if necessary. Physical contact between leader and participant should be used openly in front of the whole group rather than following the dance session or privately.

Again, in some situations, providing a document for participants to highlight teaching strategies that include the use of touch and requesting written confirmation that these are acceptable would be beneficial. Explaining why and how touch is to be used is particularly important when working with children, young people and vulnerable adults, but also when there is a cultural range of participants, who might have contrasting previous experiences and expectations, and when the group is mixed gender. It goes without saying that physical correction or hands-on feedback would be light and indicative, not rough or aggressive.

An understanding of policies on **equal opportunities** and discrimination is also necessary. The parameters for upholding civil and human rights are the same for most countries: Everyone should be treated equally with regard to age, gender, race, ethnicity, religion, sexuality or disability. Dance leaders need to demonstrate that they are familiar with equal opportunities with respect to diversity in dance participation and ensure that their behaviour and language are inclusive and culturally appropriate (Bramley, 2002; Foundation for Community Dance, 2014). National agencies can provide advice and support on equal opportunities issues, usually called Equal Opportunity Commission, Equality and Human Rights Commission, Equal Employment Opportunity Commission or similar, depending on the individual country. Institutional policies can provide the framework and guidelines, but independent dance leaders should also prepare their own statement to highlight their awareness of these issues. Equal opportunities statement templates are freely available on the Internet, and an example can be found in appendix B.

Leaders must be aware of how their communication with participants can be perceived and interpreted. Language used needs to be positive and free from discrimination, removing any references or comments that can be interpreted as racist, sexist or humiliating in any other context. Feedback should be framed positively; that is, it should be constructive and not unnecessarily critical. Leaders should never make comments that could be misconstrued as insulting or demeaning. Language that is age and group specific but not patronising is helpful. Humour should be used carefully so as not to be interpreted as making fun of any individual or group. Dance leaders, including directors and choreographers, should be mindful if they are singling out an individual for excessive negative feedback or consistently praising one individual to the exception of others. For more on providing feedback to support a positive learning environment, see chapter 8. Participants, including children, have a right to express their views, but they can be directed to frame their language appropriately. Dance leaders may need to set appropriate boundaries for the relationship between themselves and their participants to avoid placing themselves in a vulnerable position.

Many of the recommendations provided here appear to be very rigorous, academic and overly cautious, potentially far removed from what a dancer or dance leader might encounter on day-to-day basis. However, small incidents can escalate through misunderstanding, immaturity or chance. For example, teenage girls in a youth dance company might innocently share photographs of themselves in their dance costumes on freely accessible social networking sites. Teachers of either gender in positions of authority should be acutely aware of their behaviour towards students of the either sex so that any comments, favourable or otherwise, are not taken out of context or misinterpreted. An off-the-cuff, ill-thought comment by a teacher about weight may be misconstrued as discriminatory, or perhaps could contribute to a negative body image. Young dancers may be subject to improper propositions in order to be considered for career-developing roles. These are all real-life scenarios that bring up many of the issues discussed.

Dance practitioners should follow the following guidelines and codes of conduct:

- Behave professionally and treat all participants with equal respect.
- Communicate at an appropriate level and with constructive language and feedback that is free from potential misinterpretation.
- Do not pressure any individual into an activity in which he or she is uncomfortable.
- Use touch appropriately and with advance explanation and rationale.
- Be aware of all relevant safeguarding and equal opportunities issues, policies and procedures. Independent dance leaders should have their own policies in place.

These will provide a foundation for a supportive and psychologically and emotionally sound environment in which to work and learn.

CONSIDERING LIABILITY AND INSURANCE

In recent years, there has been an increase in the effects of consumerism in society in general. Inevitably this has also affected the dance workplace. Anyone charging a fee for their services is subject to legal scrutiny, and dance leaders must ensure that they do their utmost to protect their participants and themselves from risk so as not to be held liable in claims questioning the safe delivery of their activity. Dance professionals are frequently advised to maintain up-to-date knowledge of current standards and legislation and investigate the main areas of legal vulnerability (ACSM, 2000; Bramley, 2002). This contributes to their duty of care to their participants and helps them to avoid or manage accusations of negligence if serious accidents occur.

In sport, failure to provide adequate facilities and protocols is seen as negligence, and therefore subject to litigation. The following examples could easily be transferred to the dance setting (BAALPE, 2004):

- Poor condition of training and performance area and equipment, including extraneous objects in the training area
- Lack of warning of risk or danger, failure to teach safe techniques for the activity or disclose potential injury consequences of participating and failure to intervene when participants use unsafe techniques
- Lack of injury documentation and failure to maintain injury records
- Failure to follow appropriate care protocols, refer to a healthcare professional and remove the injured athlete from participation

However, the possibility of accidents and injury cannot be fully removed. Dance leaders need to be aware that, however careful and diligent they are in conducting their sessions, there is a possibility that the dance material they deliver could have negative effects on a participant, who may seek compensation. Even day-to-day tasks can result in major or minor incidents, and the philosophy of safe dance practice is not to stifle the creativity or innovation that results from risk-taking but to enhance it. Therefore it has become the norm, and it is strongly advised, for dance leaders to invest in **insurance** policies that support them in doing their job with confidence so that they and their participants are protected.

Fears over litigation are growing worldwide. In some countries, for example, in the United States, these are particularly intense (Howard, 2009). Professionals working in dance must have a clear understanding of their legal responsibilities and accountability with regard to the safety of their participants within their own teaching environment. Practitioners should investigate which insurance policies best suit their needs and which are required to practise in their own

country or region. They first need to determine whether they are covered by their employer's or institution's insurance or whether they need their own or additional policies.

Terms for describing types of insurance are generally universal, and the following guidelines can reasonably be applied to international practice. The main types to consider are as follows:

- *Professional indemnity insurance.* This type of insurance provides cover against allegations of personal professional negligence, that is, a loss that occurs because of errors made by the dance leader. For example, as a result of following instructions given by the leader, a dancer becomes injured and blames the leader for the incident and for any financial disadvantage.

- *Public liability insurance.* This protects individual leaders against claims made against them due to accidents resulting from their failure to maintain a safe environment and causing damage to a third party or their property. For example, this might include accidents due to the floor surface or tripping over hazards that have not been secured. Most organisations or venues will have this in place, but policies may exclude personal negligence if this has contributed to the accident.

As a minimum requirement, it is wise for all dance leaders to consider both of the preceding types of insurance. The following might also be valuable or applicable in specific contexts.

- *Personal accident and personal injury.* This protects leaders against injuries to themselves that occur during the course of their practice.

- *Employer's liability.* If a leader employs any other practitioners, this is a legal requirement. It covers the employer against claims from employees for illness or accidents incurred that are a result of their employment.

- *Income protection insurance or permanent health insurance.* Professional dancers and dance leaders may benefit from this type of insurance to protect their income if they cannot work for significant periods due to illness or disability.

- *Travel insurance.* When travelling independently to work in various areas worldwide, dance practitioners should check that medical expenses include injuries or accidents due to their dance activity. While insurers may recognise particular sports or even high-risk activities, injuries incurred through professional activities may be discounted in some cases.

• *Specialist events insurance.* This may apply if dance practitioners organise special events in specific locations away from their usual venue. They might also consider additional travel insurance if personally transporting participants to events.

• *Products liability insurance.* This is relevant for practitioners who supply or sell goods to their participants.

• *Building insurance.* If dance practitioners own their own studio, they are likely to be insured against damage to their premises.

• *Defamation cover.* Some policies include clauses regarding support for defence costs arising from harassment or sexual abuse, as well as infringement of copyright, for example, choreographic plagiarism. If an insurance broker regards these as important factors in particular countries or in particular contexts, the dance practitioner would be wise to consider the additional cover.

Other important questions to consider when choosing an insurance policy include the following: Does it cover practitioners when working outside their own country? Do the policy limits adequately cover the likely costs for claims? Does it cover the specific activity in all practice situations? For example, while regular travel policies include participation in sporting or leisure pastimes, they will not automatically cover dance in a professional context. Practitioners should check if they need additional specialist cover in case they are injured or have an accident during the course of their work. Some dance activities are deemed to involve greater risk than others. For example, activities when the dancer is suspended or elevated above the floor (as in pole dance or vertical dance) are sometimes excluded from general policies.

ASSESSING RISKS

It might be supposed that an individual decision to participate in dance activity could be seen as agreement to accept any risks, but this cannot be taken for granted. Dance leaders are responsible for carefully appraising all aspects of their dance environment to avoid potential risks.

Because of the awareness of litigation mentioned earlier, employers may demand formal risk assessments and independent practitioners might carry out their own assessments to show that they understand their responsibilities. In order to try to predict potential risk and formulate strategies for dealing with them effectively, dance leaders should work independently or in conjunction with the managers of premises and venues as well as health and safety officers in schools or institutions. The responsibility for identifying the risk and putting appropriate precautions in place must be charged to specific people so the measures taken can be registered and action confirmed. In this respect, a formal risk assessment would involve a two-part process (BAALPE, 2004):

1. To identify foreseeable risks that may result in injury
2. To take reasonable practical steps to reduce the risk to an acceptable level

A risk assessment form gives details of the dance activity in terms of content and delivery, the characteristics of the participants and the environmental factors such as amount of space, specific location details, condition of the dancing area, temperature, light and noise levels, and equipment or costume requirements. Many of the factors discussed in this chapter can form the basis for risk assessment questions. For example, is there a requirement that participants wear the recommended footwear and clothing? Has a health and injury questionnaire been distributed? Is there a potential danger from equipment or other hazards likely to be encountered in the dance space?

Anyone who enters the dance space should be factored into the risk assessment, including all participants, leaders, assistants or additional and visiting personnel if necessary, such as musicians, photographers or costume designers. Remember that the dance space may extend to waiting areas or toilets and changing rooms, so these areas should also be taken into account. As well as a risk assessment for their individual sessions, dance leaders might also want to look at evaluating possible risks for specific events, for example, a one-off performance in an outdoors location, a trip to a competitive event that involves overnight travel and supervision of participants, or a workshop that uses unfamiliar equipment or props. Different people may be at risk in any one situation, so each factor needs to be put into context and recorded. Dance leaders should highlight any mediating steps that are to be taken as well as note who is assessing the risk. Once an evaluation of the risk has been completed, it can be determined whether it is significant and judgments can be made about the suitability of the activity. The risk can then be put into perspective, controlled and monitored.

Risk is a positive element in dance learning and practice. Rather than eradicating it, dance leaders can support their efforts to challenge their dancers and protect all concerned by considering appropriate insurance policies and conducting risk assessments, which can prepare for and mediate the risk where necessary.

The following steps are suggested for carrying out effective risk assessments (Bramley, 2002; Health and Safety Executive, 2011; Foundation for Community Dance, 2013; Whitlam, 2012):

1. Identify as many of the potential hazards as possible.
2. Decide who might be at risk as a result of these and why.
3. Evaluate the likelihood of the risks (high, medium or low?).
4. Implement practical strategies to address the risk, reduce it or take appropriate precautions.
5. Assign roles and specific personnel to deal with each action point (all of these might fall to the individual leader).
6. Sign off each action point when it has been completed.
7. Record all findings and action points, and sign and date the document.
8. Review the risk assessment and update when necessary.

An adaptable pro forma incorporating these points can be found in appendix C.

By identifying the possible hazards, leaders can either eliminate them or draw attention to them to forewarn all involved. It is not essential to remove risks completely, but leaders should anticipate and control them to reduce the likelihood of harm. An example to illustrate this process is included in figure 1.2.

REPORTING AND DOCUMENTING ACCIDENTS

In terms of injury reporting and logging of workplace accidents, national regulations usually require collection of data and information. Certainly larger institutions will need to comply with rules on this. Information can be found from the appropriate government departments, for example, the Health and Safety Executive (HSE) in the UK, the Occupational Safety and Health Administration (OSHA) in the United States, the European Agency for Safety and Health at Work (EU-OSHA) and the Occupational Health and Safety department (OSH) in Australia. The person in control of the dance premises is ultimately responsible for reporting relevant accidents, but individual dance leaders need to play their part by bringing incidents to the attention of building managers. As with other legal requirements, dance leaders should check the procedure within their workplace for logging incidents or writing an **accident and injury report** for their own records. This is good practice that can support insurance and liability claims.

An accident report would include the following:

- The name of the injured party.
- The time and location of the accident.
- The type of activity (with detail if possible) in which the incident occurred and whether it happened under supervision.
- Any environmental factors that could have contributed to the accident, for example, tripping hazards, faulty equipment or inappropriate temperature or lighting levels.
- The level of training or ability of the injured person.
- Details of protective measures that were already in operation (perhaps previously identified on a risk assessment).
- How the injury was addressed—for example, were PRICED procedures applied (see chapter 9)? Were paramedics called? Was the injured person sent home with a chaperone or sent to the accident and emergency hospital department? Did the injured person simply remain in the studio to rest?
- The name of the person filing the report and any other people/assistants at the scene, for example, other teachers, choreographers or first-aiders. (An example of an accident report form can be found in appendix D.)

This type of documentation may seem excessive, but is necessary because it serves as a checklist of safeguards as well as a summary of previous actions taken (BAALPE, 2004). Accurate record

FIGURE 1.2

SAMPLE RISK ASSESSMENT FOR DANCE SESSIONS.

ACTIVITY		LOCATION		RISK ASSESSED BY (name)		DATE
Street dance class		Community Hall		D. Leader		01.01.14
IDENTIFY RISK Type of hazard	LIKELIHOOD Low (L), med. (M) or high (H) risk	PEOPLE Who is at risk and why	CONTROL Measures already in place	ACTION Further measures necessary	ACTION Responsibility (name)	DATE Action completed
Falls and trips	H	Dancers and leader: Dance floor is old and is curling at the edges.	Floor is retaped once every month by venue staff.	New Marley dance floor required	D. Leader to consult with venue manager	Ongoing
Slips: dirt and water on dance floor	M	Dancers and leader: Students use outdoor footwear for dance activity.	Participants asked to change footwear (into dance-specific shoes) outside in the communal area before entering.	Communicate to all participants necessity of separate dance footwear.	D. Leader	Ongoing (before each session)
Heating and ventilation system occasionally does not work: cold environment	L	Dancers and leader: Space is sometimes cold when entering.	Dance leader emphasises / conducts thorough warm-up before session and directs dancers to bring additional layers of clothing.	Maintenance and update of facilities	Venue manager, T. Boss	Planned for 02.02.14
REVIEW OF RISK Updated hazard status	LIKELIHOOD Low (L), med. (M) or high (H) risk	RESULTS OF ACTION AND CONTROL MEASURES			REVIEWER (name)	DATE
Heating/ventilation system occasionally out of order	L	Update and overhaul of system			D. Leader	02.02.14
Falls and trips	L	New Marley dance floor laid in Community Hall			D. Leader	03.03.14

keeping verifies that dance leaders have taken their responsibilities seriously, and it provides them with an opportunity to review and improve their own strategies.

SUMMARY

The fun and art in dancing is always paramount for professionals and recreational dancers alike. Dance leaders obviously also do their jobs for the love of dancing, but when it becomes their occupational responsibility, they have a duty to uphold standards and keep themselves and their participants safe and healthy while dancing, both physically and mentally. While the ideal surroundings, facilities and conditions for dance practice and performance may not always be available or achievable, with a knowledge and understanding of the factors that can affect where and how dance activities can be optimally conducted, dance leaders will be able to create the most supportive environment possible.

KEY POINTS

Dance leaders and managers should do the following:

- Carry out an health and injury status check before leading a dance session.
- Ensure their participants have suitable clothing and footwear for the activity.
- Endeavour to provide the appropriate facilities for safe practice and, as far as possible, maintain recommended standards in the space.
- Make themselves familiar with fire and emergency procedures and communicate these to their participants.
- Ensure first aid is available in the workplace at all times.
- Research national and institutional requirements for duty of care and safeguarding that are relevant to their individual context.
- Ensure that both they and their participants are protected through appropriate insurance policies.
- Understand the function and applicability of risk assessment.
- Maintain accurate injury reporting and recording systems.

chapter 2

Alignment

After reading this chapter you should be able to do the following:

- Appreciate the concept of ideal dance alignment and how it can theoretically be achieved.
- Understand how the aligned body works as a connected unit in dancing and how the disruption of one body segment can affect another.
- Recognise common deviations from efficient dance alignment, both structural and non-structural.
- Make informed judgments on individual alignment anomalies and adapt activities to minimise risk.
- Construct appropriate technical cues based on the anatomical relationships of bones, joints and muscles.

≡ Key Terms

agonist	hypermobility	neutral pelvis
antagonist	isometric contraction	planes of movement
bony landmarks	kinetic chain	plumb line
centre of mass	kyphosis	posture
concentric contraction	line of gravity	range of motion
core stability	lordosis	(ROM)
cues	movement	scoliosis
delayed-onset muscle	descriptors	stabiliser muscle
soreness (DOMS)	muscle imbalance	synovial fluid
eccentric contraction	muscle synergy	synovial joint
forces	neutraliser muscle	turnout

Good **posture** and alignment are the basis for dancing safely. The body's natural biomechanics (how it works as a whole unit in response to **forces** acting within and upon it) need to be maintained if it is to work efficiently. Deviations from the structural norm or ideal as a result of genetic malalignments or habitual adaptations inevitably have consequences over time for people who place increased physical demands on their bodies. This includes professional and student dancers who practise relentlessly or dancers who enjoy frequent recreational dancing. An awareness of good postural habits, in everyday life as well as in dance, will benefit all dancers and feed into their practice.

Many student and teacher training courses now cover anatomy and kinesiology (the study of human movement) as an integral part of dance learning and practice. A wealth of texts and interactive websites also enable dancers and dance leaders to self-study in order to improve their understanding. A good functional and working knowledge supports judgements about alignment.

Most academic sources agree on the principles that can promote good body organisation. The approach of this chapter is to collate and consolidate current knowledge and expertise on how to achieve effective alignment and to highlight the interacting factors involved. It begins by introducing direct information on relevant anatomical and kinesiological principles and terms, setting out the frames of reference so that the subsequent application to practice can be appreciated, before addressing common difficulties. The intention of this chapter is to promote awareness of the important elements that support a working understanding of alignment and movement potential with reference to safe dance practice. This awareness is necessary in order to be able to recognise and communicate efficient alignment and so minimise undue stress on the body, regardless of specific and individual dance style features.

The different components of this chapter will mainly help dance teachers appreciate the reasons why good alignment is crucial in helping to minimise injury, but choreographers, directors and other dance leaders who make or rehearse work can also benefit.

Dancers and dance leaders should be able to identify and locate specific reference points in order to appreciate individual physical differences in anatomical structure and successfully match physical expectations to individual performance possibilities. Teachers need to be able to visually appreciate good alignment and recognise deviations from it in order to give precise feedback to their students. Dancers need to develop the physical understanding to be able to kinaesthetically feel the relationships between specific body areas. Possessing the biomechanical knowledge to recognise inefficient patterns will enhance teachers' ability to provide effective feedback on adjustments and solutions. Dance leaders with a sound knowledge of the anatomical relationships that support good alignment will be able to instruct their dancers safely, avoiding detrimental yet still not uncommon practices that encourage reaching beyond individual physical limitations. Individual genres may require a specific physical organisation in their shaping or carriage of the body, but in all dancing, maintaining the natural connections between bones, joints and muscles leads to structural support and movement efficiency, not to mention safety and longevity in dance.

Dancers and dance leaders need to be able to locate specific anatomical reference points in order to appreciate good alignment and possible deviations from it. This implies a good working knowledge of the body.

To encourage and preserve effective stylistic alignment, good communication between leader and participant is essential. Teachers and dance leaders should try to focus on education rather than pure instruction to improve alignment, which implies that they have the requisite skills to be able to facilitate this. The communication of feedback on alignment through instruction and cues should be specific and logical. Most importantly it should provide dancers with solutions to their alignment issues. **Cues** are shorthand directions and reminders, both tactile and verbal, that contain anatomical and potentially corrective information that can help dancers access their kinaesthetic sensations.

Dancers in training frequently complain of chasing alignment corrections around the body—that is, trying to fix one part then causes problems in another. They become frustrated if their teachers' feedback does not provide them with a clear strategy as to how to make positive changes. Dancers' perceptions of their own alignment are not always correct. They may have trouble adjusting to new placement—their habitual misalignments feel natural and the suggested adaptations feel alien and even restricting. Using mirrors to reinforce alignment for beginners may initially be helpful, but it is more important that dancers learn how correct alignment feels. Experienced dancers almost unconsciously use an internal feeling (kinaesthetic awareness) to provide them with information about relationships within the body and in relation to space. Specialised sensory receptors send information about balance, effort, and muscle tone to help establish fine control (Batson & IADMS, 2008). This skill can be trained to refine the sensations of movement and improve alignment through exercises that enhance proprioception (see chapter 4).

Combining anatomical references with imagery is a technique frequently used by dance teachers. A detailed explanation of imagery with reference to psychological skills can be found in chapter 8, but in this chapter it is discussed in relation to movement cues that support effective movement execution. Imagined actions can promote increased efficiency of neuromuscular co-ordination (Sweigard, 2013). Both pictures and words in the mind influence the feelings in the body and provide constructive information to create powerful and dynamic alignment (Franklin, 2012). However, the success of the feedback depends on the accuracy of the cues. It is crucial that the images provided are based on a solid anatomical and biomechanical foundation so as not to induce incorrect movement patterns or strategies. Some cues that have been passed down as part of tradition do not stand up to kinesiological scrutiny; they may suggest that dancers try to do things that actually do not physically occur within a given movement (Clippinger, 2016), or because of a miscalculated use of language they may have the opposite effect of the teacher's intent.

Generic cues such as 'keep everything in a straight line' or 'lift up' do not provide clear reference points or direction for dancers, and may lead to confusion and the creation of inefficient habits. Common cues such as 'pull in your abdominals' or 'close your ribs' may produce better alignment from a visual, external perspective, but they can also lead to increased muscle tension and gripping as the dancer tries to engage particular muscles to arrange the skeleton into a correct position (Franklin, 2012).

> *Cues from the leader help dancers to work towards efficient alignment, so they need to be specific, logical and anatomically accurate. Unhelpful cues can confuse dancers, increase tension and actually create further problems.*

ANATOMICAL AND KINESIOLOGICAL TERMINOLOGY

To make it easier to discuss, compare and appreciate alignment issues, technical terms of reference that describe movement are useful. The information included in this section is intended to summarise these principles and briefly introduce relevant terminology.

Planes of Movement, Forces and Stress

Three-dimensional actions are usually explained by referring to **planes of movement**. These are imagined as three flat, level surfaces or axes that bisect the body in various ways, each having a right-angled relationship to the other two (see figure 2.1). The sagittal (or wheel) plane runs through the body from front to back, dividing the body into left and right sides. The frontal (also know as the lateral or door) plane runs through

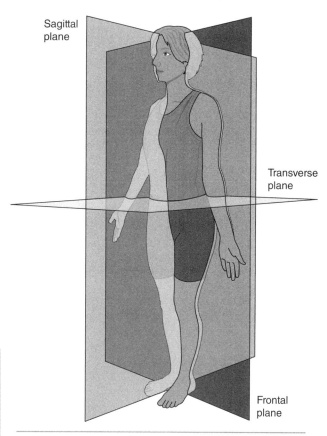

Figure 2.1 Planes of movement.

the centre of the body from side to side, dividing it into front and back sections. The transverse or horizontal plane (sometimes called the table plane) is usually depicted as cutting the body in two through the waist (approximately through the **centre of mass** of the body), dividing it into top and bottom halves.

The centre of mass (or centre of gravity when referring to the vertical direction) of the body is the point around which the body's mass is evenly distributed. Although the location of the centre of gravity varies with body build, age and sex (Luttgens & Hamilton,1997), dance kinesiologists refer to it as being located 'just in front of the second sacral vertebra and at about 55% of a person's height' (Clippinger, 2016, p. 12). The upright body must work against the force of gravity to maintain its alignment: the **line of gravity** runs through the body's centre of mass.

Forces act on the body, pushing or pulling to create, stop or prevent motion. Internal (muscle) forces cause differences in body shape and external forces (gravity, friction) cause displacement of the body (Luttgens & Hamilton, 1997). Stresses are naturally experienced in the bones as movement takes place. It is only when the mechanical balance is disturbed that the amount of stress becomes disproportionate, for example, when using inefficient weight-bearing and lifting techniques (see chapter 6 for more detail on preparing for lifting activities).

Tensile stress is produced in bones as muscles pull on them, and all bones experience compression stress when they are supporting the body's weight (Sweigard, 2013). However, these forces can be amplified through dance movements, leading to strains and sprains, injuries such as shin splints or metatarsal fractures, and damage or deformation at the site of the tendon–bone attachment in young dancers (Hamill & Knutzen, 2009). An example of this sort of damage is Osgood-Schlatter disease, an inflammation of the upper tibia at the site of attachment of the patellar tendon, resulting in a permanent bony bump under the knee that can cause problems in dance vocabulary involving kneeling.

Compression forces, while necessary for bone growth and development, can be excessive if the load applied is greater than the bone's stress limits. Some sites in the body are more prone to compression forces; in dance, relevant areas would include the patella (kneecap) and the lumbar vertebrae, especially if the spine is held in hyperextension, commonly known as *swayback* (see the section later in this chapter, Pelvis, Spine and Head). Shearing stress and torsion occur when forces cause one bone or section of a bone to slide (shear) over one another or when twisting or spiralling forces act on a bone. The risk of these stresses increases when the body is not in good alignment (Sweigard, 2013). For example, swayback positions in the lumbar spine and the knee make these joints susceptible to shear forces. Twisting forces can be experienced through the lower leg in forced turnout, when dancers anchor their weight to the floor by gripping with their feet, or when a sticky dance floor or inappropriate footwear prevents the foot from turning properly. Bending forces combine tensile, compression and shearing forces, and an increased potential for injury is due to the multiple forces applied at different points of the bone (Hamill & Knutzen, 2009).

Some traditional and regularly used dance movements subject the dancer's body to great amounts of stress. Dancers must be able to counteract these forces with good technique and alignment. As an example, moving in and out of the flat back position takes skill, co-ordination and a developed awareness of the neutral, flexed and extended positions of the spine. Therefore, this movement should not be repetitively included in beginner or recreational sessions and, for all

Stress and Forces in Dance Movements

Better biomechanical transfer of forces through the body reduces the likelihood of injury.

- Some common dance movements can result in detrimental force being applied to the body if the dancer does not have the strength and control to perform them effectively. For example, rolldowns and flat backs, included in many different genres, can place pressure on the spine if correct muscle activation is not understood, or if the movements are overemphasised in the class or choreography.

- These forces can be experienced during movements such as excessive hyperflexion in the cervical spine, repetitive flexion of the lumbar and cervical spine, excessive hyperextension of the knee, lumbar and cervical spine and increased rotational forces at the knee joint.

(Berardi, 2005; Clippinger, 2016; Franklin, 2012; Heyward, 2006; Kassing & Jay, 2003)

dancers, it should be preceded by a thorough warm-up of all the muscles involved. More detailed information on dealing with potentially contraindicated movements and actions in dance session vocabulary can be found in chapter 6.

Movement Descriptors

Basic movement in the three planes can be described according to the action on the joint. Understanding the directional capabilities of each joint and being able to accurately refer to their potential with terms called **movement descriptors** is helpful in improving dancers' alignment. *Flexion* and *extension*, in simple terms, the closing and opening of a joint, takes place in the sagittal plane (see figure 2.2a). *Hyperextension* creates an excessive movement in which a joint is opened beyond the normal **range of motion** and *hyperflexion* is bending to an extreme, such as in a deep knee squat. *Adduction* and *abduction*, movement towards and away from the centre line of the body respectively, occurs in the frontal plane (see figure

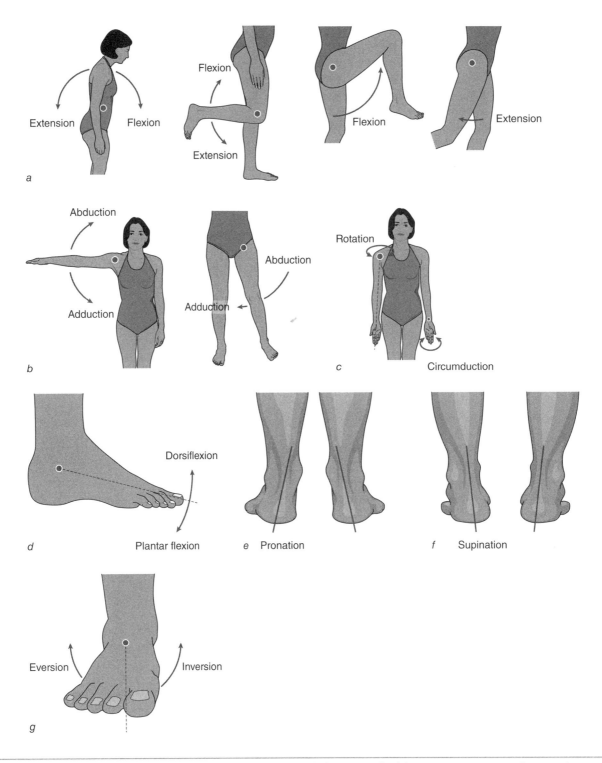

Figure 2.2 Joint movements: *(a)* flexion and extension, *(b)* abduction and adduction, *(c)* rotation and circumduction, *(d)* dorsiflexion and plantar flexion, *(e)* pronation, *(f)* supination, *(g)* eversion and inversion.

2.2*b*), and *rotation*, both medial (internal/inwards) and lateral (external/outwards), happens in the horizontal plane (see figure 2.2*c*).

More detailed actions include *plantar flexion* (pointing the foot) and *dorsiflexion* (flexing the foot; see figures 2.2*d-e*). These are actually movements at the ankle joint rather than the foot. The forearm and foot have specific movement terms to describe specialised actions. Inward rotation is termed *pronation* (turning the palm to face backwards or raising the outer edge of the foot; see figure 2.2*e*) and outward rotation is termed *supination* (the palm facing forward or the inner edge of the foot raised; see figure 2.2*f*). In the foot, these terms are sometimes used interchangeably with *inversion*, in which the inside border of the foot lifts up, and *eversion*, in which the outside border of the foot is raised (see figure 2.2*g*). *Lateral flexion*, otherwise known as side bending, is an action of the spine. *Elevation* is an upward motion and *depression*, a downward motion relating to the scapulae. *Circumduction* combines flexion, extension, abduction and adduction, for example, movement at the hip and shoulder joints, or at the wrist.

Types of Joints

Movement through the body is made possible by joint articulations. Varying amounts of movement are allowed by the structure of the different joints, defined as fused or immoveable (fibrous joints), semimoveable (cartilaginous joints, which allow movement to a limited degree) or fully moveable joints (**synovial joints**). The first two are respectively held together by collagen (a dense connective tissue) and cartilage, and neither have a joint cavity. Synovial joints are complex articulations, capable of withstanding increased amounts of wear and tear (see figure 2.3). The ends of the corresponding bones are protected by hyaline cartilage, which smoothes the articulating surfaces to reduce friction and absorb shock. A capsule containing lubricating **synovial fluid** surrounds the whole joint.

This fluid has a certain viscosity (consistency) that changes as the joint begins to move; when the joint moves slowly, the fluid is more viscous (thicker) and more supportive, but when the joint moves quickly, the fluid becomes more elastic and decreases friction in the joint (Hamill & Knutzen, 2009). This is why it is valuable to warm up before increased activity, to decrease the friction and stiffness in the joints, thus increasing lubrication and giving the joints more freedom in articulation (see chapter 3). The joint is bound (bone to bone) and

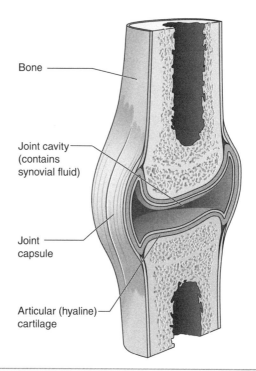

Figure 2.3 Synovial joint.

Bone

Joint cavity (contains synovial fluid)

Joint capsule

Articular (hyaline) cartilage

given stability by strong ligaments, which although pliable are not truly elastic. If stability of the joint is especially important, the capsule is fairly tight and thick and strengthened by numerous ligaments, whereas if mobility is more important for the type of joint, then its structure is wider and looser (Simmel, 2014). At the end of the range of motion, the compression forces in the joint are transferred into tensile loading of the ligaments as they tighten up to prevent further movement and align the structures within the joint (Simmel, 2014). If they are overloaded and subjected to repeated stress, the ligaments can be permanently lengthened, and therefore can lose their ability to protect the joint. This has particular relevance for dancers when they to attempt to push their range of motion to the limit, for example, in attempting to increase **turnout** or flexibility.

Differently shaped synovial joints serve a variety of purposes and are classified into types:

- *Hinge*. These joints permit flexion and extension in the sagittal plane, for example, the elbow or the knee (a modified hinge joint).

- *Pivot*. In these joints, a circular bone rotates on the axis of another bone, allowing rotation in the horizontal plane, for example, the atlas and axis in the cervical spine.

- *Gliding.* These joints involve one bone sliding past another, for example, the carpals in the hand and wrist or the sacroiliac joint.
- *Saddle.* This term describes the opposing concave and convex fit between two bones. It allows movement in two planes (excluding rotation), such as in the thumb (carpometacarpal joint).
- *Condyloid.* These joints have one oval surface that fits into another elliptical cavity, permitting movement in two planes, flexion and extension and adduction and abduction, for example, the joints of the fingers and toes (phalanges).
- *Ball-and-socket.* These joints have the most range of motion and allow movement in all three planes: flexion and extension, adduction and abduction and external and internal rotation, for example, the hip and shoulder joints.

While the function of these joints is the same in all bodies, individual bodies can have a wide range of variations in their structure due to genetic factors. Not all dancers will possess the same range

Understanding Joint Anatomy

By learning about the types of joints and their potential for movement, the dancer and dance leader will have an increased awareness of the strengths and limitations of each one.

- Knowing the neutral positions and the range of mobility in different joints can bring an understanding of how they can all work together and can help dancers and teachers to find a systematic way of addressing alignment issues.
- Attempting to stretch the ligaments is not a good idea because of their natural role in stabilising the joints. For example, the iliofemoral (Y-shaped) ligament across the front of the hip joint has a relative tautness, which varies in each individual dancer and will limit the potential range of turnout in each. Stretching it to encourage increased turnout is not an advisable strategy.

(Grieg, 1994; Kassing & Jay, 2003; Simmel, 2014)

of motion or have the same potential for achieving dance movement (Kassing & Jay, 2003; Kenney, Wilmore & Costill, 2012).

The preceding terms and descriptors provide a frame of reference from which to talk about alignment. A working knowledge of the movement potential at a joint—that is, how it functions anatomically and its individual range of motion, as well as how it may become susceptible to stress—will underpin safe practice for dancers and dance leaders.

SKELETAL AND MUSCULAR RELATIONSHIPS

In order to achieve good alignment, the bones and muscles interact to maintain a harmonious balance between the body parts. The relative relationship between different parts of the body affects how efficiently the joints and muscles work together to protect the body from injury: The less work the body has to do, the less tension is produced, and the less likely it is that injury will occur.

The relationships of specific body parts to each other and the counteractive response to the effects of gravity are usually described as posture. Posture can be defined as 'a position or attitude of the body, the relative arrangement of body parts for a specific activity or a characteristic manner of carrying one's body' (Smith, Weiss, & Lehmkuhl, 1996, as cited in Whiting & Rugg, 2006, p. 142). Poor posture is a faulty relationship of the various parts of the body that produces increased strain on the supporting structures (Kendall, McCreary, & Provance, 1983). Correct alignment in all dance techniques is key in preventing injury as well as improving performance because it minimises wear and tear on these supporting structures so that the bones, joints, ligaments, cartilage and muscles can work efficiently and for longer periods of time.

The body is a closed system, meaning all of its parts are connected. If one part is out of alignment, then the entire structure can be compromised. For example, badly aligned feet will cause stress in the hips and knees as well as the upper body (Watkins & Clarkson, 1990). The **kinetic chain** describes how forces are transmitted through the body from segment to segment. Joints in the kinetic chain are linked together, and the movement of any one joint affects how forces pass through any of the other joints. Therefore, the movement between all the joints must be co-ordinated to prevent each separate one, or the links between them, from becoming disproportionately loaded (Whiting & Rugg, 2006). Ideal standing posture and alignment minimises stresses through the kinetic chain by placing the relevant joints in vertical alignment such that forces and stresses are transferred directly through the joint centre (Ives, 2014).

> *All the parts of the body are interconnected through a kinetic chain. When one part of the body is out of alignment, other parts of the body are likely to be affected, subjecting all areas to increased forces and stress.*

Postural control must be learned. In the early and later years, in infants, children and senior adults, it is less effective because strength and co-ordination develop with the sensory motor system through childhood and decline with age; both age groups may have difficulties with balance and muscle control and increased risk of injury (Whiting & Rugg, 2006). For example, young children typically stand with their abdomen falling forward and a hollow lower back (Luttgens & Hamilton, 1997). Dance leaders selecting activities for these age groups need to take these challenges into consideration. Dancers of any age and level of ability should be mindful of the effects of poor posture, and teachers should aim to promote and develop good posture to maintain health as well as support the dance aesthetic.

Models describing standing posture always refer to the orientation of body segments in relation to one another, in response to and in counteracting gravity and ground reaction forces. Forces are also generated by the muscles and transmitted through the bones and joints to allow the maintenance of an upright body position and co-ordinated, controlled activity (Whiting & Rugg, 2006). In the standing position, the body is correctly aligned when its weight is transmitted down the skeletal chain to the floor through the centre of each joint, ensuring that the weight of the head is transferred though the appropriate vertebrae in the spine and that the weight of the upper body is transferred through the centre of the hip joints, then through the centres of the knee, ankle and foot (Whiting & Rugg, 2006; Watkins & Clarkson, 1990). The skilled dancer will be able to feel this distribution of weight internally; researchers suggest that dancers should develop their own kinaesthetic and proprioceptive sensations to maintain and fine-tune their alignment, as only then will

they know themselves when they are approaching ideal alignment, rather than relying too much on external feedback and regulation (Holt, Welsh, & Speights, 2011). However, standard external **bony landmarks** (identified in the next section) allow an observer to register how successfully the body parts fall in line with one another.

Plumb Line

Markers describing ideal alignment usually refer to a neutral base, with the body in an upright and stationary stance and the arms hanging loosely by the sides (anatomical position). Alignment can be appreciated three-dimensionally from both sides and from front and back. These four different views allow judgements to be made on possible genetic, functional or technical deviations from the ideal. Key reference points enable comparisons to be made.

The term **plumb line** is often used to measure alignment by observing how particular bony landmarks relate to one another along an imaginary vertical straight line (that is, the line of gravity) as observed from a side view of the body in standing position (see figure 2.4). Some researchers and practitioners suggest that the pelvis, as the near centre of the body, is the root of good or faulty alignment (Holt et al., 2011, Sweigard, 2013). Other authors have highlighted that the point from which a plumb line is drawn must be a standard fixed point, and in the standing position, the only fixed point in standing is the feet in contact with the floor. Therefore, the point of reference for the plumb line image must be the base (Kendall et al., 1983).

There are common guidelines for the orientation of the plumb line and details regarding its route through the bony landmarks (Franklin, 2012; Kendall et al., 1983; Sweigard, 2013; Watkins & Clarkson, 1990).

Other relationships of body parts are best viewed from the front or back of the body. A plumb line in this plane, seen from the front, would bisect the body through the tip of the nose, the centre of the sternum and the pubic bone and then touch the floor at a point equidistant from each foot. A secondary plumb line running through each leg would pass through the second toe, between the ankle bones, through the centre of the knee and the centre of the hip joint. Seen from the back, the main plumb line would pass through the centre of the back of the head, down the spine and touch the floor at a point equidistant from each foot. From both front and back views, the bilateral

Ideal Vertical Alignment

When a correctly placed body is viewed from the side, the plumb line passes through the following:

- The earlobe or centre of the ear
- The centre of the shoulder (the acromion process) if the arms are hanging in normal alignment
- Either through (or just behind) the cervical and lumbar vertebrae and slightly in front of the bodies of the thoracic vertebrae
- Slightly behind (posterior to) the centre (axis) of the hip joint (from the side view, the greater trochanter)
- Slightly in front (anterior) of the knee joint
- Slightly in front (anterior) of the ankle joint (the lateral malleolus)

The arms hang easily with the hand resting near the hip, the palms facing the body and the elbows slightly bent so that the forearms hang slightly forward.

Figure 2.4 Plumb line and ideal vertical alignment.

structures—the ears, shoulders and shoulder blades and crests of the ilia (tops of the pelvic girdle)—should be on the same horizontal level. The weight should be distributed evenly through the two feet (Franklin, 2012; Watkins & Clarkson, 1990).

In reality, the body is rarely static in the upright position, and an amount of what is termed *postural sway* occurs so that the body is always either slightly losing or regaining balance; dancers continually make small dynamic adjustments that require a degree of muscular effort (Franklin,

2012; Krasnow, Monasterio, & Chatfield, 2001). The dancer in motion needs to have an awareness of how the anatomical relationships are maintained when the body moves away from this semistillness. Every type of movement, from walking to jumping to the multiplanar activities of the dancer, involves continual changes in the position of the trunk (torso) and the relative placement of the extremities to maintain the equilibrium of the body (Whiting & Rugg, 2006). This 'ongoing process of neuromuscular postural responses' is called dynamic posture or dynamic alignment (Krasnow et al., 2001, p. 8).

Because of the huge variety in vocabulary, the inventive use of different bases of support or the combined alignment of the dancers in partner work or in lifting in different dance styles, the idea of registering a theoretical plumb line may be seen as irrelevant and actually not realistically or consistently achievable. Different dance genres and vocabularies can have their own stylistic posture or language that necessitates moving away from the recognisable upright stance described here. Nevertheless, being aware of stylistic or individual choreographic features that demand unusual physical organisation of body parts will help dancers counteract any negative effects. Returning to standard points of reference is extremely valuable for helping dancers aim for effective biomechanical relationships that could improve their dancing and prevent injury.

Muscle Action

Good body mechanics depend on effective skeletal alignment and appropriate muscle recruitment. This means that the range of motion at a joint should be adequate, but not excessive, with balanced amounts of flexibility and stability (Kendall et al., 1983). The action of the muscles on a joint determines how the dynamic alignment is attained and maintained.

Muscles are attached to bones via tendons, which transfer the tensile force produced by the muscular contraction to the bone. Therefore, they need a low degree of elasticity and a large amount of strength (Simmel, 2014). The contraction occurs in the centre of the muscle and pulls on both sides equally, with the attachment and path of the muscle determining its action (Kassing & Jay, 2003). Muscles cannot push—while most dance practitioners understand this concept, the cues and feedback they provide might not evidence this directly. One of the most cited examples of imag-

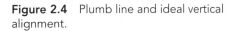

ery versus anatomy is the direction to lift the leg from underneath. This is impossible if examined physiologically, so when describing movements and stretches, teachers need to be careful that their instruction is supported by solid anatomical references. On the other hand, this cue is valuable in terms of imagery that helps to reduce excessive muscular tension and create beneficial movement dynamics. Clear explanation and a distinction between the use of anatomical direction and qualitative imagery will allow both approaches to increase movement efficiency, rather than indirectly encouraging ineffective muscle recruitment. An alternative and more accurate cue in this case might be 'lengthen through the back of your leg as you lift'.

> *Muscles can only pull, not push. Images for alignment and technique need to make kinesiological sense so that the dancer can access the necessary muscles that are required for the movement task.*

Dynamic (isotonic) contractions are either concentric or eccentric. Simply speaking, the first is a shortening of the muscle and the second, paradoxically, is a gradual lengthening of the muscle while contracting to control the resistance. **Eccentric contractions** are commonly used to control the effects of gravity, decelerate body segments and help absorb shock loads (Clippinger, 2016). This type of contraction involves higher maximal forces as compared to **concentric contraction,** and is particularly associated with **delayed-onset muscle soreness**, or DOMS (Koutedakis & Sharp, 1999; Kenney, Wilmore & Costill, 2012). DOMS is experienced as an acute stiffness and pain that appears a day or two after an exercise or dance session in which movements that rely on eccentric contractions have been overemphasised. Examples of these might be landings from jumps or supporting and lowering the upper body to the floor when falling onto the hands—any movements that involve 'braking' or decelerating. A typical everyday movement would be walking downstairs. In a third type of contraction, the **isometric contraction**, there is no visible change in length of the muscle; therefore this is often called a *static contraction.*

Individual muscles work co-operatively with others to produce three-dimensional movement.

This is called **muscle synergy** (Whiting & Rugg, 2006). The efficiency of the system needs each muscle to play one or more roles in different situations. Muscles can assume these roles interchangeably to function in a variety of ways.

- The muscle that contracts concentrically to actively control a single-joint movement is the **agonist.**
- The opposing muscle that eccentrically lengthens to allow this to happen is the **antagonist.**
- **Stabiliser muscles** mediate excessive contraction by the agonist or prevent both ends of the bones at a joint coming together when this is not required. In effect, they anchor a movement.
- Similarly, **neutraliser muscles** cancel out any unnecessary additional movement or force (they are sometimes also called *synergists*). These muscles smooth out and help to co-ordinate movement.

In most movements, several muscles act together as agonists, albeit with some playing a greater part than others. When both agonist and antagonist actively contract together, this is called *co-activation.* Sometimes beginner dancers will use co-activation unnecessarily if they are not able to identify the correct muscle to use. However, 'skilled performers of all kinds have the ability to recruit the appropriate muscles at the right time and with the right level of activation to produce and control movements of individual segments and the body as a whole' (Whiting & Rugg, 2006, p. 134).

Generally speaking, the muscles in the body have two broad functions: to move the body or to stabilise the body. The larger muscles tend to be the movers and the smaller, often deeper muscles tend to be the stabilisers. Their muscle fibre type defines their role as muscles, either working with high intensity for short periods or with low intensity for longer periods. Fast-twitch fibres are good for rapid movements and slow-twitch fibres are good for endurance. Postural muscles need endurance to continually maintain a low-grade contraction to ensure the body's alignment. Muscles that are used for bigger dance movements fatigue easily and therefore need good levels of strength to work at higher intensities. Researchers suggest that it is the goal of dancers to achieve smooth, easy movements with minimal effort but report that it is difficult to feel the effort of a low-grade contraction; the small amount of activity at a deep level to support alignment is influenced by proprioceptive input that needs to be reinforced and trained (Philips, 2005). Conflict arises when muscles designed for different roles are asked to change their function and perform actions for which they are not physiologically equipped, for example, using low-endurance movers to help maintain alignment, usually by superficial gripping and holding tension. This can be due to lack of understanding, inadequate technique, lack of specific fitness, unspecific or incorrect instruction or possibly because of adaptation to injury. Whatever the reason, the result can be movement inefficiency and potential injury.

Muscle imbalance can occur when one set of opposing muscles is stronger than the other. Muscles are negatively affected by improper alignment; conversely, muscles that are compromised can affect alignment because of changes in the direction or intensity of force that they exert, literally pulling a joint out of its normal position. A balance of strength and flexibility is needed to maintain the integrity of a joint and keep it centred in motion. If muscles become shortened, tight or weak, they are less able to meet the demands of dance movement and so become susceptible to injury (Watkins & Clarkson, 1990). Muscles can become imbalanced by habitual ways of using the body or performing a particular movement repetitively. Using muscles in a way that asks them to change the way they function best, as described previously, can also cause muscle imbalance.

Concentration on one type of activity provides a high potential for muscle imbalance; the nature of the activities and the time spent doing them are both contributory factors (Kendall et al., 1983). Dance leaders should manage the amount of repetition in their sessions and make sure that the choreography does not favour one side or direction so that their dancers do not overstress one muscle group. Choreographers could be mindful if they are creating material with their own preferred gesture or weight-bearing limbs so that their dancers find themselves working in predictable and limiting movement patterns. Teachers themselves could observe whether they always demonstrate on one particular side. Dancers who take part in competitive events will naturally opt for their best side to showcase their abilities (higher kicks, stronger leaps, better gymnastic or athletic elements and so on). Their teachers can be guilty of encouraging this practice to reap rewards for their schools, equating medals or trophies with good technique. More detail on how to avoid detrimental repetition and one-sided bias can be found in chapter 6.

The role of the muscles in stabilising the body is clear. How the body needs to be stabilised specifically depends on the style. The term *anti-gravity muscles*, normally those muscles maintaining a low-grade amount of tone to stand upright, takes on a whole new meaning when applied to styles requiring balance upside down. For example, participants in hip-hop or breaking genres require a great deal of strength and control to perform their movements and balances in asymmetric and inverted contexts. All dancers, whether belly dancers who can facilitate spinal undulations, ballet dancers balancing on pointe, Irish dancers controlling their upper bodies, jazz and street dancers working with precise isolations or modern dancers athletically combining a variety of movement vocabularies, must be able to manage their alignment in challenging situations. The centre of the body is the focus of this co-ordinated muscular control, referred to as **core stability.**

Core stability is a popular term in sports, fitness and dance training. The core is seen to play an important role in overall strength and stabilisation. It is actually a combination of various muscles that each plays a key role in organising and co-ordinating the body. The core incorporates the area between the sternum and the knees (Hamill & Knutzen, 2009), focusing on control of the spine and the pelvis, which stabilises the torso (trunk) and in turn co-ordinates movement of the limbs. In dance terms, this might be referred to as *connectivity* or *centring*. Core stability is essential for dancers. Effective body placement comes from being able to create strength and stability along the spine while keeping the natural curves intact (Haas, 2010). In dance, the torso is always moving off the vertical—flexing, extending, hyperextending, rotating, twisting and spiralling—while the limbs perform a huge variety of stylistic actions. This demands highly developed control of the muscles involved. Many people think of the core muscles simply as the abdominals and train intensely to gain a six-pack and the ripped appearance seen in magazines (this focuses on the more superficial rectus abdominis). For dancers, a deeper and more specific approach is needed. Dancers need not only education on which muscles to locate but clear instruction on how to do this. Again, cues used by teachers must be specific—the direction 'use your core' is useless unless the dancer knows what this involves.

The torso can be visualised as a cylinder, with the muscles at the top, bottom and sides contributing to the stabilisation (see figure 2.5). The pelvic floor muscles support the cylinder from underneath and the diaphragm provides support from the top, in conjunction with the abdominal group in the front and the deep muscles of the spine at the back. The pelvic floor is not always considered in training core stability, but an active pelvic floor ensures pelvic stability and facilitates balance while reducing strain on the back and abdominal muscles (Simmel, 2014). The multifidi muscles and the transversus abdominis are frequently identified as the key to lumbar stabilisation because of their short intervertebral attachments—they are the first to contract in order to stabilise the movement of an extremity (Kline, Krauss, Maher, & Xianggui, 2013). These muscles have a higher percentage of slow-twitch fibres, which are particularly important for sustained contraction to support alignment (Haas, 2010), and therefore need to have good levels of endurance. Additional local stabilisers that control segmental shearing forces are the psoas major, semispinalis and rotatores muscles, as well as the quadratus lumborum and the deeper erector spinae (Philips, 2005; Solomon, Solomon & Minton, 2005). Other muscles that contribute to core stabilisation include the internal and external obliques, the superficial erector spinae, and the latissimus dorsi. The work of the muscles that stabilise at a segmental level combined with the action of those muscles responsible for movement and directional control (the movers) is the key to controlling the movement of the spine and pelvis as a whole (Clippinger, 2016; Philips, 2005).

Every dance genre requires core control: performing fast footwork as in Irish dance or tap, sustaining spinal extension and rotation for ballroom and flamenco, performing isolations at speed in street dance or jazz, or connecting to and co-ordinating with each other's centres in the balanced partner work used in many dance styles. Working with equipment such as poles or wires and dancing on the hands or even the head requires enormous trunk stability in order to avoid accidents. Dance leaders working in all genres, with dancers at all levels, should focus on preparing and enhancing core stability to ensure that their participants can perform safely. Strength training is commonly advised for addressing weakness in the core, but an alternative conditioning focus, such as stability training, may be more useful.

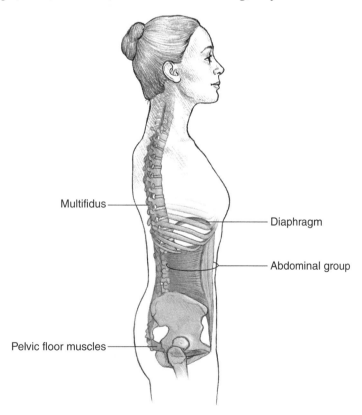

Figure 2.5 Core muscles.

This combines motor control principles so that muscles learn to work in synergy through effective agonist and antagonist recruitment and by encouraging endurance of the stabilising muscles. The technique is to work progressively from stable to unstable positions using specific movements with increasing complexity and speed with the help of equipment such as Swiss balls or balance boards (Philips, 2005). Further information on different types of strength and endurance training for dancers can be found in chapter 4.

DYNAMIC DANCE ALIGNMENT

Dance posture requires more aesthetic energy and presence than relaxed standing, and so generally involves more muscle activation. The body dynamically changes its position in multiple planes. Skilled dancers need to manage their dynamic alignment and return to neutral quickly, preserving the body's natural integrity (Clippinger, 2016). If a body is able to assume good basic alignment, then stylistic preferences can be overlaid on this foundation (Welsh, 2009). Different styles may require aesthetic adjustments to the neutral base. In each style, the most efficient way of performing the vocabulary should be identified. If dancers or dance leaders are not aware of ways in which their genre-specific placement can be safely achieved and if, or how, it may deviate from recommended neutral alignment, then they will not be able to regulate its effects. All dance practitioners need to understand how forces are distributed through the body in their own style. Providing detailed descriptions on the appropriate alignment in every possible dance style is beyond the scope of this book, but some examples in this section will help to identify some common alignment issues with reference to possible physical deviations from the norm.

For example, some flamenco schools ask for greater lift and arching of the upper back. Other styles, such as classical ballet and jazz, regularly use deep back bends. Each time the spine is extended in this way, the pressure in the rear of the intervertebral discs increases, and the facet joints in the spine are subjected to compressive forces (Simmel, 2014). Styles that require sitting on the floor, such as Graham technique and some jazz vocabulary, present specific challenges for alignment: The pelvis needs to maintain an erect orientation to lift the spine and prevent pressure

on the discs because of excessive flexion of the lumbar and thoracic regions (Clippinger, 2016). Other modern or contemporary styles (including Release and Flying Low) incorporate a developed use of the floor for support and inversion, quite literally turning normal alignment on its head, and require a development of upper body strength and alignment to move effortlessly between upright and upside down. Aerial or vertical dance and pole dancing require immense skill and control in defying gravity to extremes. Highly developed core stability and upper arm, forearm as well as finger strength are vital for maintaining safe biomechanical alignment. Breaking and hip-hop styles, in which the whole body weight is bearing down into the hands and wrists or even the head and neck, require significant amounts of strength in the muscles supporting these joints for distributing the loads and forces safely, not to mention an excellent ability to appreciate and control the unusual arrangements of body parts. In Irish dance, maintaining the upright posture is stylistically very important. The torso and arms need to remain stable but relaxed while the lower limbs complete fast, explosive and intricate movement. In order to achieve and maintain the posture, the core muscles must be strong and controlled. Similarly, tap dancers move their legs and feet at speed while holding their pelvis in balance. Belly dance might require increased elevation in the ribcage, and some African and jazz styles require an arch of the lower back, which could place added strain on the lumbar spine over time (Clippinger, 2016). Other tribal fusion styles might encourage lengthening of the lumbar spine, which could be misinterpreted as tucking if instruction is not clear. Zumba is a form of dance exercise that emphasises fitness and fun, but in this practice, it is important to keep the back straight, with support from the abdominals, to maintain a neutral spine and, in the deeper squats, observe hip and knee alignment.

Partner work in many traditional, social and competitive styles (such as ballet, ballroom, Dance Sport or tango) relies on individuals having a good awareness of alignment. In addition to this, the partnership has its own structural relationships that may need each dancer to veer from their own biomechanical security. Partner dancing is not necessarily symmetrical in a single body, but through two bodies joined through a base and frame; therefore weight balances and distribution may be different to normal (Lamberty, 2011). Techniques might be partner or gender specific. For example, there are many styles of competitive dance sport, with modern and Latin variations. A common trait in modern styles is for the female dancer to keep her upper body and head placed slightly back and left and to slightly elevate her arms and hands to correctly hold her frame. Researchers have found that the isometric contractions with a constant force output required for maintaining these positions through long hours of competition can lead to very specific neck injuries (McCabe, Hopkins, Vehrs, & O'Draper, 2013). Similarly, lifting techniques in ballet pose a risk for the male partner due to the lumbar stress forces, especially at the beginning of the lift as his partner leaves the ground. Dancers learning lifting and partnering combinations must rehearse carefully to ensure the correct positioning and distance from the partner (Alderson, Hopper, Elliott, & Ackland, 2009). See chapter 6 for more information on how to gradually prepare the body for lifting activities.

The point of these few examples is to highlight the diverse range of alignment requirements and to emphasise that safe practice in these styles requires appropriate training guidance. This will not be a problem for vocational and professional dancers who immerse themselves in their style and can securely embed the necessary technical directions. However, this must be taken into consideration in recreational settings if different forms of dance are experienced with less training and preparation. Similarly, even professional dancers who attempt new styles that are unfamiliar without adequate preparation could succumb to injuries due to different alignment requirements.

> *Being extra flexible (hypermobile) is not always an advantage, even in the dance population where good flexibility is an asset. Dancers with hypermobile joints may need additional strengthening work to stabilise the body and avoid injury.*

The next section deals with specific areas of the body and discusses the effects of deviations from recommended alignment. Before moving on, it is worth mentioning the issue of **hypermobility** because many of the deviations described refer to it. When a dancer has excessive range of motion at a joint (that is, beyond the normal range of motion), they are said to be hypermobile. In lay terms, this is sometimes called being double-jointed. It can often be seen as advantageous or aesthetically pleasing in some dance styles. Dancers can have individual joints that are hypermobile—it is not simply a matter of being globally loose. In effect, most dancers could be termed hypermobile because of their increased flexibility in relation to the general public, but the hypermobility seen in the dance population is usually more extreme. Healthy joints need a combination of flexibility and stability. With hypermobility, the supporting connective tissue (the tendons, ligaments and fascia) is less stable, leaving the joint more prone to injury. Dancers with this condition need careful training with knowledge and understanding of appropriate joint use and potential (McCormack, 2010). While stretching is important for all dancers, less emphasis on flexibility in both regular dance work and supplementary activities will help dancers with hypermobile joints to focus on training goals that encourage gains in strength and stability to control their range of motion.

Professional ballet dancers are often cited as examples, but some emerging street styles also require specific hypermobility. 'Bone-breaking' involves extreme distortion of the body and requires flexibility that very few recreational dancers will be able to achieve. Dancers attempting to learn this type of style through word of mouth or Internet tutorials should carefully heed any safety advice.

When performing lifts, dancers need to understand how they align efficiently with each other to minimise the effects of increased forces through their connected bodies.

Lower Body: Feet and Knees

The body's whole weight is distributed through the feet, ideally equally supported by the heel and the forefoot. The balance of weight is usually described as falling through three points of contact with the floor: the first and fifth toes and the heel, more specifically, the head of the first metatarsal, the head of the fifth metatarsal and the centre of the heel (the tuberosity of the calcaneus) with the toes spread and relaxed on the floor for balance rather than clawing to maintain a grip (Huwyler, 1999; Lewton-Brain, 2009; Watkins & Clarkson, 1990). A useful image to use here is that of the tripod. Dance leaders can direct dancers to consciously distribute the weight evenly through the feet (see figure 2.6).

Some dance styles (for example, ballet and jazz) require the weight to be shifted forwards slightly towards the balls of the feet. Often teachers will direct their dancers to be 'up on their feet or legs' or feeling 'ready to go'. It is reported that the use of the fully turned-out position of the legs supports and encourages a forward weight shift, consequently increasing mobility in the hamstrings, calf and back muscles. However, recommendations are that until young dancers develop adequate turnout, their teachers must not allow them to displace too much weight forward (Grieg, 1994). If the heels lose contact with the floor, there is an increased possibility of hyperextension in the knees and spine and increased stress in the metatarsals and

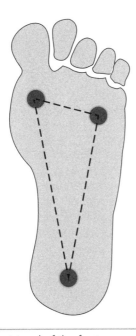

Figure 2.6   The tripod of the foot.

Common Lower Body Alignment Issues

- Feet: Flat or excessively arched
- Toes: Claw toes, hammer toes and *hallux valgus* (leading to bunions)
- Knees: Knock knees, bow legs and tibial torsion
- Swayback legs (knee joint).

balls of the feet, as well as for the plantar flexors, which could contribute to the incidence of shin splints (Watkins & Clarkson, 1990).

Correct knee alignment refers to the orientation of the kneecap (patella) and its relationship to the toes (or more specifically, to the second toe). In both parallel and turned-out dance positions, the dancer is directed to ensure that the knee maintains a straight line over the second toe, that is, the lower leg bones (the tibia and fibula) are in the same plane as the thigh bone (femur). An alternative cue would be to 'bring the toes under the knees', a direction that limits the likelihood of the dancer simply forcing the knees out to the sides. In the turned-out position, to avoid the dancer misinterpreting this cue by simply turning in more at the hip joint, the teacher should also encourage full access to the dancer's available turnout.

The longitudinal arches of the foot (both the medial and lateral that run along its length) should be in a neutral position in both bare feet and shoes, that is, with the weight evenly distributed along the central axis. Dancers who stand or work with the weight on the inside (medial) border of the foot are in effect flattening the longitudinal arch, pronating the foot, which is usually described as 'rolling in'. Less common is when the dancer stands or works with the weight shifted to the outside (lateral side) of the foot, lifting the arch, termed *supination* or 'rolling out'. Observing the Achilles tendon from the back view of the body can assess the extent of the roll. If the tendon curves in towards the centre (medially), then the dancer is rolling in; if it curves outwards (laterally), then the dancer is rolling out (see figures 2.2*e* and *f*). When the foot is pronated but not weight bearing, it is usually termed *winging*. The non-weight-bearing supinated foot is termed *sickling*.

The function of pronated and supinated foot and ankle positions becomes apparent in motion;

the relative positioning of the bones of the feet make the foot more or less stable. The more anatomically stable position (supination) is needed in propulsion for running or jumping and the more anatomically flexible position (pronation) allows dancers to adapt to uneven surfaces (Clippinger, 2016). This happens naturally in efficient movement mechanics, but too much movement in either direction contributes to stress on the joint and potential injury (Welsh, 2009). For example, if there is too much strain on the outside border of the foot when landing from jumps, this can overstretch and damage the external lateral ligament. Problems occur when the dancer has a specific structural foot deviation, or simply technically cannot control pronation or supination. It also happens when particular dance moves encourage weight bearing in these positions.

Several variations in foot structure affect the dancer; these are often not possible to change. When the inside border of the foot flattens, causing excessive pronation, this is termed *pes planus*, commonly known as flat feet. Although this type of foot may benefit from increased shock absorbency, there is also some evidence that it increases the risk of injuries such as shin splints, plantar fasciitis and metatarsal stress fractures (Clippinger, 2016).

Flat feet can be congenital, but excessive strain from dancing without adequate strength in the muscles of the foot can also cause fallen arches (Huwyler, 1999). The opposite is the excessively high-arched foot, or *pes cavus*, a rigid foot type that is not fully able to accommodate shock-absorbing pronation. This type of foot is often aesthetically appreciated in dance, but it is susceptible to injuries such as stress fractures, plantar fasciitis and metatarsal problems (Clippinger, 2016; Conti and Wong, 2001).

Other common foot alignment problems for the dancer are claw toes and hammer toes, in which the different joints in the toes are in permanent hyperextension or hyperflexion, respectively. *Hallux valgus*, where the big toe is displaced towards the outside of the foot, makes the joint at the first metatarsal head more prominent, leading to altered biomechanics and friction that can encourage the formation of bunions (Clippinger, 2016). These problems can instigate disturbances in balance and stability (Huwyler, 1999). Some conditions are genetic, but others can be caused or exacerbated by poor dance technique. Teachers can encourage foot and ankle strengthening exercises as both a preventive and rehabilitative measure and can point out weight-bearing issues to

Alignment Cues for the Lower Body in Dancing

Problems in the body

- The feet pronate or supinate as the ankles roll in or out.
- This could initially be due to the dancer forcing turnout with an accompanying forward tilt of the pelvis so that the plumb line is not transferring through the centre of the ankle joint.

Helpful and unhelpful cues

- Avoid simply telling the dancer to emphasise the opposite movement action (pronation or supination). For example, 'Put more weight on the outside of your foot' or 'Pull up your ankles.'
- Instead, highlight distributing the weight evenly through the foot's tripod and anchoring the ball of the big toe joint (first metatar-

sal) and the outside of the heel to improve stability. When standing, encourage dancers to actively engage the transverse arch from time to time to strengthen the intrinsic muscles of the foot.

Imagery tips

- Encourage dancers to imagine a fountain of water lifting the transverse arch from underneath.
- Dancers can try bending the legs and imagining each of the three points of the foot tripod moving away from one another, spreading the sole of the foot and widening the tripod, then straightening the legs and imagining the points coming closer together. (Do not use this image to initiate turnout from the feet.)

(Franklin, 2012; Grieg, 1994; Simmel, 2014; Sweigard, 2013)

Solutions for Hyperextended Knees

Rather than thinking of pushing the knees back when straightening the legs, the dancer can instead be directed to pull the knees straight up.

- Pulling up just below the back of the knee at the same time as the front of the knee can encourage a co-contraction of the hamstrings and the quadriceps femoris (the antagonistic pair of muscles), reducing the tendency to clench the quadriceps.

- As the dancer's own perception of straight is often distorted, using a mirror initially might help the dancer to understand how their sensations relate to the visual corrections.

(Clippinger, 2016; Grieg, 1994)

focus the dancer's attention on correct alignment. The importance of correctly fitting footwear to help prevent these conditions should be stressed.

Each dance style uses different and often unusual positions of the feet, especially in specialised footwear such as high heels (discussed later on), Irish dance shoes or ballet pointe shoes. The foot is susceptible to excessive pronation or supination in pointe work, and this can amplify the potential for injury (Grieg, 1994). While the sickled foot in ballet arabesque is often seen as an aesthetic benefit that enhances the line, the sickled foot in weight bearing on pointe is dangerous because the precarious balance predominantly on the big toe joint forces the ankle to fall inwards. The skilled ballet dancer must be able to understand the value of this ankle joint movement so that it is used only in gesturing.

As with the winged foot, the hyperextended knee joint can be seen as aesthetically desirable in leg gestures. Hyperextension of the knee (*genu recurvatum*) is often seen in dancers. It is also known as *swayback legs* because the legs appear to be curving backwards. The knee joint is straightened beyond the usual 180 degrees so that the weight of the body is no longer transferred through the centre of the joint, stretching the ligaments and affecting knee stability. This is particularly dangerous when landing from jumps.

Hyperflexion of the knee (*genu antecurvatum*), when the knee appears to be slightly bent, may be due to muscular and soft tissue restriction as well as or instead of joint mechanics. If this is the case, careful stretching (for example, of the hip flexors) may produce changes (Clippinger, 2016). This condition may not be frequently seen in training or professional dancers, but it can be more common in the recreational dancer.

The knee must be stable in both flexed and extended positions. When the knee is flexed, the collateral ligaments are relaxed, allowing a small amount of rotation to take place, so that the side-to-side stability of the knee becomes fully dependent on the supporting action of the surrounding muscles (Grieg, 1994). When the knee straightens, in the last 20 degrees of extension, the muscles and bones work together in a complicated process known as the *screw-home mechanism*, the point at which the medial and lateral condyles of the tibia naturally lock the joint, tautening the collateral ligaments (Hamill & Knutzen, 2009).

Dancers who push the knees backwards into hyperextension will reduce the stability of their knee joints, and dancers who do not fully straighten their knees when necessary will not allow the collateral ligaments to do their job efficiently. Cues given by teachers regarding how much to straighten the knee can be confusing for the dancer. Advice such as 'do not lock the knees' or 'keep the knees soft' are not particularly useful in supporting the necessary muscle activation to support a more effective alignment. The difficult job for teachers is to guide the dancer in finding the most appropriate use of muscle tension to pull up the front of the thighs and kneecaps, rather than pushing them back, while avoiding muscular overwork and gripping. A co-contraction of the hamstrings and quadriceps femoris could prove effective in this case (Clippinger, 2016). Dancers with hyperextended knees tend to work with their heels apart in (ballet) first position, which actually can make things worse. Teachers should not direct these dancers to immediately force the heels together, since this is difficult to control, and may spark other problems. Instead, teachers should encourage dancers to gradually bring the heels together over time in order to build the necessary strength for maintaining the position.

Dancers with various other misalignments of the knee have difficulty, first because deviations here are subject to increased stresses and forces in many usual dance movements and second because they are aesthetically less desirable

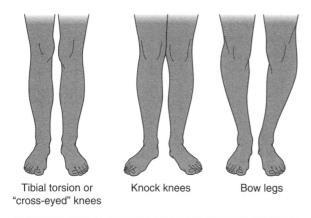

Tibial torsion or   Knock knees   Bow legs
"cross-eyed" knees

Figure 2.7 Misalignments of the knee.

(see figure 2.7). Dancers with tibial torsion have bowing or twisting along the length of the tibia. This manifests itself in a dancer whose lower legs bend outwards when standing in parallel position, causing more weight to be borne on the inside of the foot because the knees fall inwards of the plumb line. Its appearance is similar to but not the same as internal rotation of the knee joint, when the patella faces inwards. Tibial torsion is a distortion of the bone itself, and the teacher will not be able to correct this condition. Similarly, knock knees (*genu valgum*) and bow legs (*genu varum*) are not correctable, although their appearance can be minimised, and adaptations should be made for dancers exhibiting these conditions. In knock knees, the knees fall forward of the plumb line, causing compression stress on the outside and tensile stress on the inside of the joint. In bow legs, the knees fall outside the plumb line, causing tensile stress on the outside and compression stress on the inside of the joint (Franklin, 2012). Bow legs distort the line of the leg in parallel but are more stable than knock knees. Recommendations are that the dancer with knock knees should not be forced to stand in parallel with the feet touching, but instead stand with feet slightly apart to allow space for the knees (Sevey Fitt, 1996). These dancers should also not try to bring the heels together in the turned-out (ballet first) position, but should be encouraged to emphasise external rotation at the hip joint (Watkins & Clarkson, 1990).

Pelvis, Spine and Head

The position of the pelvis is very important in dance, and is said to be the key to good or faulty alignment (Holt et al., 2011). It is essential in dance activity to 'optimize lumbosacral and hip joint motions to minimize undue compression, tensile

or shear forces on spinal and neighbouring tissues' (Leiderbach, 2010, p. 116).

The term **neutral pelvis** describes the orientation of the pelvis that best supports efficient dance movement. When the pelvis is in a neutral position, the tissues are under the least amount of stress and are the most effective in supporting the spine. This orientation can be simply defined as 'balancing the pelvis on the heads of the femurs' (Deckert & IADMS, 2009, p.11), although this explanation does not fully describe what achieving neutral pelvis might entail. The pelvis has several bony landmarks (see figure 2.8): the anterior superior iliac spines (ASIS), otherwise known as the hip bones or frequently termed the 'headlights', the posterior superior iliac spines (PSIS), found as bony protuberances on the back of the pelvis or sometimes seen superficially as dimples, and the pubic bone (the pubic symphysis). The pelvis is in alignment when it maintains a vertical position with the ASIS and the pubic bone in the same frontal plane and the ASIS and PSIS in approximately the same horizontal plane.

From a front view, both ASIS are at the same horizontal level. Generally speaking, if the ASIS are considerably lower than the PSIS in the horizontal plane and forward of the pubic bone in the frontal plane, this is an anterior (forward) tilt. If the PSIS are lower than the ASIS and behind the pubic bone, this is a posterior (backward) tilt, commonly called *tucking*. Researchers report that measurements of pelvic alignment in the standing position reveal anterior tilt to be a common problem for

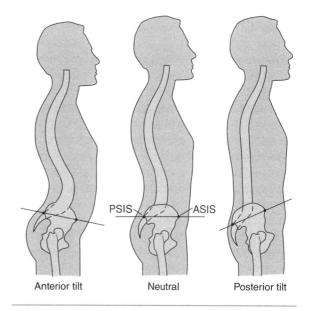

PSIS   ASIS

Anterior tilt   Neutral   Posterior tilt

Figure 2.8 Bones and bony landmarks of the pelvis.

Alignment Cues
for the Pelvis in Dancing
■ ■ ■

Problems in the body

- The dancer is working with an anterior or posterior tilt, and finds it difficult to release into a neutral position.

Helpful and unhelpful cues

- Avoid correcting one tilt by encouraging the opposite, for example, 'tuck your pelvis' or 'stick out your tailbone.'
- Instead, encourage activation of the pelvic floor, releasing (rather than excessively pulling) the sitting bones down towards the floor through awareness of the connection to the hamstrings and finding the vertical re-

lationship with the heels. Balance the ASIS and PSIS approximately in the same horizontal plane, and the ASIS and the pubic bone in the same vertical plane with the iliac crests level.

Imagery tips

- Encourage dancers to imagine heavy weights hanging from their sitting bones, like those hanging on a cuckoo clock.
- Imagine that the coccyx is extended into a dinosaur or kangaroo tail, reaching down into the floor.

(Franklin, 2012; Simmel, 2014)

dancers and non-dancers alike, with ranges of 1 to 23 degrees of forward tilt (Holt et al., 2011) and that pelvic alignment is different for each dancer, and can vary from day to day (Deckert & IADMS, 2009). Both types of tilt have negative effects on the body: An excessive anterior tilt puts stress on the facet joints in the spine and an excessive posterior tilt decreases the shock absorption in the lower back and decreases lower extremity strength, especially in the gluteus maximus and hip external rotators (Philips, 2005), with technical implications as described in the following section.

One difficulty in assessing the degree of pelvic tilt is that increased musculature around the pelvis in some body types (for example, a more pronounced gluteus maximus, or buttock muscle), can affect the accurate visual perception of neutral alignment; therefore using the bony landmarks described previously is recommended so that the dancer is not advised to use unnecessary compensations (Sevey Fitt, 1996; Welsh, 2009). In dynamic alignment, the pelvis should 'oscillate around a neutral position and certainly not be held there by voluntary muscle contraction' (Franklin, 2012, p. 260). In order to find a centred pelvis, the dancer and teacher could focus on finding the appropriate amount of contraction in the abdominal group, the lower fibres of the gluteus maximus and the upper fibres of the hamstrings to release the sacrum downwards and create the feeling of lift at the front of the pelvis (Grieg, 1994). Imagery

is very effective in visualising correct placement, and bodywork techniques such as Pilates can condition and enhance good pelvic alignment.

The structure and alignment of the pelvis is important for many dancers because of the implications for external rotation at the hip joint, otherwise known as turnout. Although not used in all styles, turnout is one of the most frequently misunderstood and misapplied aspects of dance technique, and the desire to achieve it is the cause of many poor alignment decisions that result in injury. Researchers report that poor technique in forcing turnout is the single largest contributing factor to overuse injuries of the lower extremity (Potts & Irrgang, 2001). Dancers and teachers therefore need to understand the mechanisms and limitations regarding how individual bodies can achieve turnout.

The potential for rotating the head of the femur in the ball-and-socket joint is limited by the bony shape of the pelvis and the relative tightness of the surrounding tissues. The orientation and depth of the socket (acetabulum) affects the degree of movement possible. The acetabulum may face farther forward or more to the side, and the angle of the neck of the femur relative to its long axis is also a factor: *Anteversion* (the angle turning forward) results in greater internal rotation of the femur and *retroversion* (turning backwards) results in greater hip external rotation (Clippinger, 2016). Basically, the more contact the femoral neck has with the edges of the acetabulum, the greater the restriction on the movement at the hip joint. It has been reported that the angle of the femoral neck may be altered as a result of the repetitive effects of training in turned-out positions in dancers who begin serious training before the age of 11 years (Solomon et al., 2005), but from then on, it is not possible. Clearly this does not mean that this is a feasible training goal, but simply that it is physiologically possible at this stage of physical development. Of course, it will be impossible for dancers and teachers to ascertain the bony structure without X-rays, although it has been suggested that there is a correlation between an observably narrower pelvic structure and a forward-facing acetabulum, so external rotation is more limited in these dancers (Sevey Fitt, 1996). The important message is that awareness of these structural variations should inform expectations for different dancers.

The iliofemoral ligament (the Y-ligament) is the strongest ligament in the body, and it limits how much the femur can rotate externally. Stretching of this ligament to achieve more external rotation may be possible in dancers under 11 years (as before, this is physiologically possible but not recommended), but other dancers attempting to do this can cause strains to the ligament and other soft tissues that can have permanent negative repercussions (Solomon et al., 2005; Watkins & Clarkson, 1990). The best way to improve turnout is to strengthen the external rotator muscles and to stretch the internal rotators; however, it is also important to keep a balance between the two. The muscles that play the major part in turnout are the six small deep rotators (quadratus femoris, obturator internus, obturator externus, piriformis, inferior gemellus inferior and gemellus superior) and, in addition, the gluteus maximus. The sartorius, biceps femoris and the adductors all assist. The gluteus maximus can often be the focus for teachers' direction regarding turnout but over-activating the bulk of this large muscle mostly causes a posterior tilt, which can actually inhibit turnout, stress the spine and create undue tension. Teachers should therefore emphasise the role of the six deep rotators and advise only a supporting mild (and often automatic) contraction of the gluteus maximus.

Forcing the turnout is common. This means that rather than relying on the available rotation at the hip, the source of turnout, dancers try to cheat by adding rotation through the knees and feet, often using friction with the floor to hold the position (Welsh, 2009). These joints are not designed for excessive twisting around a vertical axis. In a twisted position, the body's weight is no longer transmitted through the centre of the joints, but rolls in, making the knee, ankle, arch and big toe joints vulnerable to stress (Watkins and Clarkson, 1990; Whiting & Rugg, 2006). In addition, there is usually a forward pelvic tilt and hyperextension of the back. Likely injuries include chondromalacia, tendinitis, shin splints and stress fractures of the lower leg bones, but effects will be registered through the whole body (Watkins & Clarkson, 1990).

Having determined that turnout should come from the hip, researchers report that a substantial proportion comes from below the knee in many dancers (Welsh, Rodriguez, Beare, Barton, & Judge, 2008). Some suggest that between 60 and 70 degrees (of the perceived ideal 90 degrees) of turnout is contributed by each hip, with the lower leg adding between 10 and 35 degrees (Champion & Chatfield, 2008). It is also noted that some dancers

Cues for Effective Turnout

• Avoid focusing on the feet to initiate or hold turnout or to gauge the amount of turnout being used. If dancers use the friction of the floor to hold their turnout, the hip external rotators become weaker rather than conditioned.

• The cue to 'squeeze your glutes' is not helpful in encouraging the most efficient use of turnout. It is much easier to feel the gluteus maximus muscle working because of its size and superficial position, but its lower fibres should be activated only lightly. Beginners often overuse this muscle when trying to find turnout.

• Although they are more difficult to feel because they are underneath the gluteal muscles and their action is more sophisticated, the six small deep rotator muscles are the primary muscles used in turnout (with the assistance of others in various positions). Their fan-shaped arrangement pulls the greater trochanter backwards in external rotation.

(Grieg, 1994; Simmel, 2014; Staugaard-Jones, 2011; Welsh, 2009)

are not able to access their entire available turnout due to lack of strength and should be encouraged to condition their turnout muscles.

Dancers at all levels should remember that the notion of the perfect 180 degrees of turnout traditionally recommended (in ballet) is anatomically and biomechanically uncommon. Teachers should stress that this is not absolutely necessary for all styles or in all situations and that expectations should be realistic and context specific (Grossman, 2003).

Structural alignment of the pelvis is closely related to that of the spinal column. The spine is the connection between the upper and lower extremities, providing stability, flexibility and shock-absorbing potential. The spine has three natural flexible curves and one rigid section: (viewed from the side) a concave cervical curve, a convex thoracic curve, a concave lumbar curve and the convex rigid sacral curve (see figure 2.9). The curves are constructed by a combination of vertebrae, varying in shape from section to section, and by the intervertebral discs between them, which cushion and support.

The amount of curvature in these spinal regions is different from person to person. The relative weight of an individual, or the mass that is to be supported on the spine, can have an effect on the relative depth of the curves. It has been observed that a heavy person can have deeper spinal curves and a slight person, shallower curves (Sevey Fitt, 1996). For everyone, but especially for dancers, the variations in the depth of the curves may be genetically functional or may be detrimental to efficient posture and biomechanics. It is true to say that any exaggeration of these natural curves, as a result of genetic malalignments or muscular imbalances, will alter the resilience of the spine and will also have an effect on other parts of the body through the kinetic chain. If the curves of the spine are exaggerated, the column will be more mobile and if the curves are flat, the spine will be more rigid. The cervical and lumbar regions are the most mobile, and the pelvic regions more rigid. The junction where one curve ends and the next one begins is a site of increased mobility that is also vulnerable to injury (Hamill & Knutzen, 2009). When the curves are changed either through habit or by movements that repeatedly stress the spine, the weight of the upper body falls outside of the centre of the vertebrae and discs, potentially irritating spinal nerves, and the spinal muscles are stretched or contracted as they readjust their roles (Watkins & Clarkson, 1990).

Interesting points have been made regarding the effect of the time of day on the susceptibility of the spine (Berardi, 2005). Because of fluid shift and disc expansion that occurs during the night, dancers (as well as the general public) should avoid strenuous exercise just after getting up, especially movement that involves full spinal flexion or bending. Dancers should also be wary of these movements after prolonged flexion (for example, sitting on the floor in rehearsal), and might need to gently mobilise the spine again before recommencing activity.

The lumbar spine is a particularly vulnerable site for dancers. The lower part of the spine is specialised for transference of weight through the pelvis (Clippinger, 2016), and the joint between the fifth lumbar vertebra and the sacrum is frequently stressed in dance movement. The weight of the head, arms and torso pass through this area,

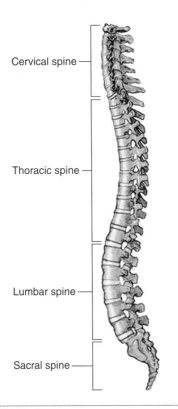

Cervical spine —

Thoracic spine —

Lumbar spine —

Sacral spine —

Figure 2.9   The four curves of the spine: cervical, thoracic, lumbar and sacral.

> *Strenuous movement just after getting up in the morning is detrimental to the spine because of the changes to intervertebral discs during the night. After prolonged sitting with the spine flexed, dancers should also gently mobilise the spine before recommencing activity.*

Common Pelvis, Spine and Head Alignment Issues

- Pelvis: Anterior (forward) and posterior (backward) tilts
- Spine: Hyperlordosis (lower back), kyphosis (upper back) and scoliosis
- Head: Forward head

and if the weight of another body is also added in partnering work, additional forces contribute to this stress, frequently resulting in problems such as stress fractures, disc compression or herniation, nerve irritation, ligament stress and tears, and muscle spasms and cramps (Gamboian, Chatfield, Woollacott, Barr, & Klug, 1999; Watkins & Clarkson, 1990).

In both anterior and posterior (as well lateral or side to side) pelvic tilts, the balance of the curves of the spine is detrimentally affected, particularly the lumbosacral spine, which is subjected to more wear and tear in the joints. An anterior tilt of the pelvis is frequently accompanied by increased arching of the lower back. The term for the normal arch in this area is **lordosis** (or the lordotic curve); therefore, the hyperextension here is technically called *hyperlordosis*, although frequently these terms are used interchangeably. It is also commonly described in dance as swayback posture. This hyperlordotic state can be seen in the dancer when there is a noticeably pronounced hollow in the lower back, which is associated with an anterior tilt and hyperextended knees, and the torso may either lean back behind the plumb line or be displaced forward (see figure 2.10). The appearance is of the tailbone flaring diagonally down and out behind the body. This type of posture is common in pregnancy when the body responds to increased abdominal weight and in the adolescent growth spurt (Whiting & Rugg, 2006; see chapter 10). Researchers report that there is a high incidence of anterior pelvic tilt and lordosis in dancers in training, and that the sliding loads on the intervertebral discs and surrounding structures are compounded when dancers are lifting and turning (Deckert, Barry, & Welsh 2007; Gamboian et al., 1999; Whiting & Rugg, 2006). In the hyperlordotic dancer, the iliopsoas, the back extensors and hip flexors are tight and the hamstrings are also likely to be tight, the back flexors and hip extensors are weak, and the gluteals and the abdominal muscles

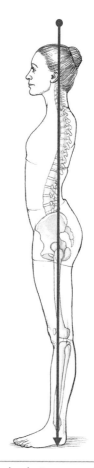

Figure 2.10 Hyperlordosis, or swayback posture.

may need further strengthening (Watkins & Clarkson, 1990; Whiting & Rugg, 2006). There might also be a consequential increase in the thoracic curve that causes the ribs to protrude, preventing efficient breathing (Grieg, 1994).

As every compensation in one part of the spine affects the posture of the rest, it is very important for the dancer and dance technique teacher to aim for a neutral pelvis whenever possible. A posterior tilt of the pelvis might be associated with flexion of the spine, seen as a decrease in the lumbar curve sometimes as a result of overcorrection of an anterior tilt (Clippinger, 2016). This is termed a *flat back*. As with any change to the curves, this reduces the spine's flexibility and shock-absorbing potential (Grieg, 1994). Researchers believe that this flattened spinal posture, as well as excessive curvatures, overworks and overdevelops the gluteal and quadriceps muscles (Deckert, 2009; Welsh, 2009) and also contributes to increased injury risk (McMeekin, Tully, Nattrass, & Stillman, 2002).

Further up the spine, **kyphosis** describes an increased thoracic curve, and it is often seen in combination with lordosis (see figure 2.11). Like lordosis, it is a natural position of the thoracic spine, but it becomes a problem if it is excessive. It manifests in a rounding of the upper back so that the posture is slightly hunched with a depressed chest. In normal life it can be caused by inefficient slouching positions, for example, in sitting or working at a computer, which results in an abnormal shortening of the muscles and ligaments at the front of the upper body. Kyphosis is common in young children and adolescents, with about 25 percent of these experiencing related difficulties. It is also seen more frequently in older adults, especially women, when it is linked to osteoporosis (Whiting & Rugg, 2006). For the dancer, kyphosis may be relatively more flexible and functional, but nevertheless it is accentuated by postural habits and weakness in the upper back extensors, or sometimes by the practice of performing abdominal work in a small range of motion without adding counteractive back extension exercises or stretching (Clippinger, 2016).

Kyphosis is often associated with the head being positioned too far forward in the plumb line,

considerably increasing the load on the cervical spine due the weight of the head being displaced. This is termed *forward head*, observed in dancers as a poking up or forward of the chin because it does not align with the rest of the spine. It also typically involves a depressed ribcage and raised shoulders that roll forward (Smith, 2005). Forward head is also associated with dancers carrying the arms too far back in (ballet) second position, which hyperextends the back (Watkins & Clarkson, 1990). The key to addressing the forward head is the re-alignment of the spine further down the chain (Sweigard, 2013).

Deviations in spinal alignment are due to either habitual posture patterns (non-structural) or to variations in bone structure (structural; Sevey Fitt, 1996). **Scoliosis** is an abnormal lateral (side to side) curvature in the frontal plane that can also involve some twisting of the spine. Although it is abnormal, it is not rare, and approximately 25 percent of the adult population exhibits it to some degree (Whiting & Rugg, 2006). It may be hereditary, and can be caused by differing leg lengths, pelvic torsion or muscle imbalance (Simmel, 2014). Everyone has slight degree of asymmetry, sometimes due to handedness preference and overuse of the muscles on one side (Watkins & Clarkson, 1990), but scoliosis is more pronounced. Viewed from the back, the spine deviates into a C-shape in either the thoracic (see figure 2.12) or the lumbar regions or in an S-shape if it occurs in both these regions, producing two different curves that bend in opposite directions to one another. Consequently, there is risk to the spine and the

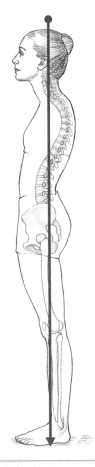

Figure 2.11   Kyphosis-lordosis posture.

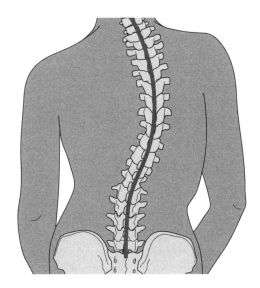

Figure 2.12   Scoliosis.

rest of the body because the vertebrae are not in alignment.

It is not uncommon to come across dancers who are dealing with mild cases of scoliosis in all types of training. It is suggested that this may be due to the general recommendation to take children who suffer from it to dance lessons to help them regain or maintain joint and muscle balance (Clippinger, 2016). In fact, scoliosis usually develops during the growth periods, especially during the second growth spurt in adolescence, as the vertebrae grow asymmetrically. The incidence of scoliosis is about the same in boys and girls, but severe cases are between five and eight times greater in girls (Huwyler, 1999; Whiting & Rugg, 2006).

Dance teachers can recognise the presence and effects of scoliosis by observing their dancers' alignment when standing and in motion. Possible signs are bilateral asymmetry, as with uneven horizontal levels of the shoulder or shoulder blades effecting the way the arms hang, different amounts of curvature at the sides of the waist and rotation of the ribcage and/or pelvis (Simmel 2014). In the more developed cases, structural alterations to the ribcage distort the ribs and form a hump on one side of the spine, and the pelvis may also tilt laterally (Huwyler, 1999). The forward bend test is often recommended to help dance teachers recognise cases of scoliosis (Clippinger, 2016; Watkins & Clarkson, 1990). The dancer relaxes into a forward bend, letting the arms hang, then as they roll up slowly, the teacher can make observations. Do the vertebrae fall in a straight line and do both sides of the spine appear equal? Is there a raised hump on either side of the ribcage or do the muscles appear to be more developed on one side? Is one shoulder blade more pronounced than the other? It is likely that dancers exhibiting most of these symptoms will already have received some medical attention, but if not, the teacher should refer them to a structural therapist. Moderate scoliosis with an evenly flexible spine does not prevent dancers from working effectively (Simmel, 2014).

Because scoliosis affects both upper and lower limb mechanics, dance leaders should be aware of adaptations that might need to be made for affected dancers in dance practice. Care should be taken not to overemphasise repetition on one side of the body in dance class or in rehearsing choreographic material. Choreographers should try not to get stuck in their own preferential working patterns that might transfer asymmetry to their dancers. This issue of lateral bias has many other implications, which are discussed further in

Cues for Managing Scoliosis

The mobility of the spine should be trained specifically where the curve or restriction is greatest. Actions that emphasise three-dimensional stretching and strengthening are beneficial.

- Mobilise the least flexible and stabilise the hypermobile sections to distribute the stress evenly across the entire spine.
- Stabilise the muscles of the spine through simultaneous contractions of the small muscles of the back and the transversus abdominis.
- When a strength-producing exercise is harder on one side, do more repetitions on that side. When a stretch is more difficult, stay with it for a longer period of time.
- Take care not to carry bags on the same shoulder all the time. Regularly switch sides or use a backpack worn over both shoulders.

(Clippinger, 2016; Sevey Fitt, 1996; Simmel, 2014)

chapter 6. Rebalancing and conditioning exercises will also be of benefit, especially symmetrical torso stabilisation through abdominal and back extensor strength exercises that emphasise rotation (Clippinger, 2016).

All of the preceding deviations represent a risk of injury due to structural factors. Stylistic factors dictating a distinctive or repetitive use of the spine also play a part. Some dance forms use prolonged lordotic postures and frequent back bending, resulting in back pain and a high incidence of spinal injuries (Smith, 2009). As before, this book cannot identify all the possible demands on the spine that are defined in every dance style, but some examples will help to illustrate what is involved and encourage genre-specific attention to preserving the integrity of the spine. For example, ballroom dancers maintain a beautiful top line, but this involves a strong rotation of the upper back, often maintained in one direction, especially for the female partner. Flamenco dancing requires that hyperextension be maintained in the spine. This distorted alignment of the spine affects the body's ability to effectively absorb the

Alignment Cues for the Spine in Dancing

Problems in the body

- In trying to find a sense of elongation to resist gravity, the dancer distorts the spine, becomes rigid, pulls the stomach in excessively and lifts the ribs and shoulders.
- The head is displaced forward, deepening the thoracic and cervical curves and producing tension.

Helpful and unhelpful cues

- Avoid saying, 'pull up', 'straighten your spine', 'suck in your stomach' or 'pull in your chin.'
- Instead, encourage a lengthening of the spine from coccyx to skull. Find a vertical connection from the pelvis, with the lumbar spine and sacrum elongating downwards towards the floor, while freeing the upper spine and head towards the ceiling and keeping the shoulders relaxed.
- A co-contraction of the back extensors and the abdominal group is necessary.

Imagery tips

Encourage dancers to do the following:

- Imagine the pelvis is weighted and the head is light and floating.
- Imagine a brush moving up along the front of the spine and another moving down the back of the spine. Try to visualise the two brushes working together in opposition.
- Visualise an imaginary line from the chin to the top of the sternum.
- Imagine the head balancing on a waterspout or fountain coming up through the spine.

(Clippinger, 2016; Franklin, 2012; Grieg, 1994; Kassing & Jay, 2003; Simmel, 2014)

whole-body vibrations from the percussive action of the feet and may lead to back pain (Pedersen & Wilmerding, 1998). Some teachers, therefore, attempt to prevent injuries caused by excessive lumbar lordosis by advocating a whole-body arch, beginning at the ankle joint and extending through the head and neck, while others suggest that the arch should occur primarily in the thoracic region, and that the lumbar spine should be maintained in the anatomically correct position to reduce the impact on the lower back.

Upper Body: Ribcage, Shoulders and Arms

The ribcage sits directly above the pelvis in efficient alignment. The shoulders should be horizontally level and relaxed, with the arms able to hang freely. On inhalation, the ribs widen and the abdominal muscles lengthen, and on exhalation, the ribs return and the abdominal muscles shorten (Haas, 2010). It is often difficult for dancers to understand how to find the engagement of the core muscles to provide support and keep the ribs relaxed—sucking in the belly too much leads to inefficient breathing patterns and tension in the ribcage. The stability of the shoulder girdle is essential for lifting and partnering activities. Dance styles that use balance in inversion or frequently support the weight through the arms should ensure a strong and secure upper body. Regardless of whether the upper body is used for weight bearing, every dance style incorporates a specific and expressive use of the arms, often with intricate choreography, such as in classical Indian dance and flamenco, which need control.

The thoracic and especially the cervical spine are vulnerable if not kept in alignment. Any weight bearing on the head and loading on this part of the spine is risky. General advice in sport is that overextension of the cervical spine can cause many problems, including compression of intervertebral discs and pinching of arteries and nerves at the base of the skull. However, full neck and head rolls, now seen as a contraindicated movement, are still included in some dance vocabulary. For example, whipping the head (and hair) is commonly seen in commercial and street dance choreography. Given the repetitive nature of dance training, the implica-

Common Upper Body Alignment Issues

- Shoulders: Rolled forward or elevated
- Shoulder blades: Winging out
- Ribcage: Lifted or protruding in front
- Arms: Held too high (lifted shoulders) or too far back

tions are obvious. Teachers and choreographers should seriously consider the use of head rolls in their vocabulary and should never use them in warm-up, substituting simpler up-and-down or side-to-side head movements instead.

When the shoulder blades (scapulae) wing— that is, the internal border can be seen sticking out away from the body—this is associated with muscle imbalance, especially a tight pectoralis minor and weakness of the muscles mentioned earlier that assist scapular stabilisation. The same can be said for protracted (rolled forward) shoulders. The shoulder blades should also not be pinched together. Ideally they should lie flat against the ribcage. The cue 'squeeze your shoulder blades together' to correct forward shoulders or kyphosis and to generally encourage upright posture or arm placement is unhelpful, and it can cause many repercussions in the upper spine. Another frequent misalignment is lifting the ribcage up and forwards, often as a compensation for an anterior pelvic tilt (Welsh, 2009). This can be a result of misunderstanding the cue 'pull up'.

Dancers need to be able to lift the arms without disturbing the centre, losing balance or increasing tension in the shoulder or back (Franklin, 2012). Each dance genre requires a specific and precise styling of the arms in space or strength and control

Alignment Cues for the Upper Body in Dancing

■ ■ ■

Problems in the body

- The front of the ribcage lifts up or pushes forwards and the shoulder blades pull back as the dancer tries to stand up straight. The abdominals cannot engage properly, and the dancer experiences difficulties with breathing effectively as well as reduced mobility and increased tension.
- The shoulders are raised and tense or rolled forward and the shoulder blades wing out.
- The arms are held too far behind the ribcage, causing excessive arching in the lower back and lifted ribs in front.

Helpful and unhelpful cues

- Avoid saying, 'open your chest', 'lift your chest', 'pull your shoulders back/down', 'pinch your shoulder blades together' and 'push your arms down in the back.'
- Instead, encourage dancers to relax the lower ribs so that the shoulder girdle sits freely on top of the ribcage. They should relax the shoulder girdle at a point close to the spine rather than forcefully pushing the outer edges of the shoulder down. Prompt them to release the shoulder blades downward and outwards, as the shoulders widen to the sides, emphasising the scapular adductors and the thoracic spine extensors. Direct dancers to lightly pull the arms down before they are raised. With the arms held out to the sides, if the shoulder joint is centred, the hands should be visible out of the corners of the eyes.

Imagery tips

Encourage dancers to do the following:

- Imagine the shoulders suspended from the neck like the sails of a ship, with the spine as a mast and the shoulder girdle as a crossbeam suspended from it.
- Imagine the shoulder blades sliding down the back and crossing into the opposite trouser back pockets.
- Imagine your armpits are deep and soft. They are filled with small balloons that inflate as you inhale and deflate as you exhale.

in weight bearing. As dance forms have developed, modern choreography has led to increased strain on the shoulders and arms, with the integration of more athletic and gymnastic movements and amount of floor work needing upper body support (Simmel, 2014). For many styles, the goal is to find a secure positioning of the arms in which the torso is also neutralised and stabilised (Clippinger, 2016).

One of the most common directions given to dancers is 'hold the arms on the back.' The meaning behind this is to encourage the most efficient muscular action to stabilise the arms, so the technical directions should explain how to do this effectively. If the dancer does not understand the mechanics, the primary result is tension in the upper body. The muscles that connect the arms to the back are concerned with scapular stabilisation (the serratus anterior, the rhomboids, the lower trapezius and the latissimus dorsi). It has been observed that dancers tend to be weak in these areas (Haas, 2010). A balanced use of these muscles makes the arms feel like they are coming from the back (Howse & McCormack, 2009). Problems arise when excessive tension and stress in the trapezius causes lifting of the shoulders (scapular elevation), which makes an efficient use of the arms difficult. If the arms are held too far behind the body when they are out to the sides (for example, in second position, used in many styles), this can cause excessive arching of the lower back and protruding ribs. If they are too far forward, this results in a closing in of the chest and a kyphotic posture (Clippinger, 2016).

To conclude this section on common deviations from ideal alignment, fatigue posture should also be mentioned. This posture requires less energy to stand than normal, and is a common unconscious adaptation in all dancers, even those who are highly experienced (Clippinger, 2016). For example, the dancer rests on the ligaments in the hip joints by pushing the pelvis forward considerably (increasing the posterior tilt) and hanging back in the upper torso (see figure 2.13). It is relaxing for the muscles, but puts a strain on the overstretched hip joints because the body's centre of gravity runs behind the pelvis (Simmel, 2014).

Similarly, it is quite common to see dancers alternating between different postures in a dance session, their everyday habitual stance and their dance alignment. Dance-specific posture is assumed during practice, but in the relaxed moments—for example, when listening to feedback, observing other dancers in class in

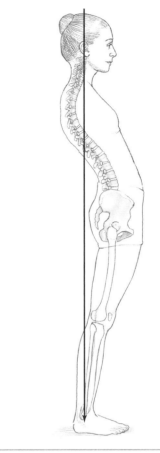

Figure 2.13 Fatigue posture.

moments of rest or even interacting socially in rehearsal—the dancer can slip into an unstable pose, reinforcing detrimental postural habits. This may involve sitting into the hips, leaning backwards in the upper torso, rounding the shoulders forward with the hands on the hips or shifting the weight habitually to one leg. Like all deviations, these habitual postures have detrimental effects. Teachers should bring these habits to the dancer's attention to encourage conscious employment of the necessary muscles (spinal extensors and hip flexors) at the appropriate level of contraction to remedy them. Conscious awareness of posture, even in normal movement such as sitting, standing or lying down, will help the dancer to maintain a healthy body that supports the demands of dance techniques more effectively.

It is also worth mentioning at this point that, for some dancers, regularly carrying their own kit and costumes in heavy dance bags can place added strain on the body, causing muscle imbalances and postural changes over time. Recommendations are to use bags that spread the load as evenly as possible, choose padded handles or shoulder straps

> *Dancers could be more aware of, and leaders should discourage, slipping into fatigue or relaxed posture, both in and out of the dance session. Slumping, sitting in the hips or habitually releasing the weight into one hip while resting places increased stress on ligaments and joints and does not support the development of good dancing alignment.*

or consider wheeled suitcases that allow a neutral standing posture to be maintained (SHAPE, 2002).

Effects of Footwear on Alignment

Deviations from efficient alignment are not always a result of intrinsic inefficiencies of the dancer's body, but can be imposed on the body. Many dance styles require the dancer, usually female but not always, to perform in heels of various heights. This will change the way the dancer can judge and achieve good alignment. Dancing in high heels is a necessity for ballroom, tango, flamenco and musical theatre dancers who need to accommodate full-body movement with limitations imposed by the shoes, including landing from jumps with a decreased ability to go through the full foot to reduce the impact. Reported side effects include stress to the balls of the feet and the lower leg as well as pain in the lower back due to the altered position of the spine (Kay, 2008). The use of high heels will substantially affect the biomechanics of alignment, as described in the previous sections of this chapter. Wearing heels alters the weight distribution in that the proportion of the weight on the ball of the foot increases with the height of the heel, increasing the load borne by the outer toes in relation to the first metatarsal head (Kendall et al., 1983). As heel height increases, a parallel position and in-toeing of the foot is encouraged (Kendall et al., 1983). The increased height not only disrupts the stability of the body by raising the body's centre of gravity (with the upper body becoming heavier), but also causes the lumbar flexion angle to increase significantly, creating additional compressive forces in the lumbar spine. There is also a compensatory increase in erector spinae activity to try to maintain normal posture, which can significantly affect fatigue levels (Lee, Jeong, & Freivalds, 2001). The foot is less stable in

heels because, in effect, the dancer is in constant plantar flexion, the degree of which depends on the heel height, putting a strain on the anterior structures of the foot and ankle. If the dancer regularly works in heels, the gastrocnemius and soleus muscles will be maintained in a shortened state for prolonged periods (Solomon et al., 2005), potentially making them more susceptible to subsequent injury. In the general population, the negative side effects of wearing high heels are reported as leg and lower back pain, a shortened Achilles tendon and a potential predisposition towards degenerative osteoarthritis in the knee (Lee et al., 2001).

It has been observed in some studies that wearers of high heels demonstrate lumbar flattening and posterior pelvic tilt, a reduction of the distance of the knee and ankle from the line of gravity and a posterior displacement of the head and thoracic spine (Opila, Wagner, Schiowitz, & Chen, 1988; see figure 2.14). However, several studies confirm that the use of high-heeled shoes is also correlated with increased anterior pelvic tilt and lumbar lordosis, especially in dancers with stiff hip flexors (De Oliveira Pezzan, João, Ribeiro, & Manfio, 2011; Smith, 2009). Studies have found that while younger women exhibited a compensatory increase in pelvic range of motion in the sagittal plane during walking in high heels as compared to low heels, middle-aged women did not. This may indicate that tissues in the lumbopelvic region, such as the erector spinae muscles, become more rigid with age and that the harmful effect of high-heeled shoes on posture and spinal tissues may be more pronounced with increasing age (Mika, Oleksy, Mika, Marchewka, & Clark, 2012). This may have an effect for older recreational dancers in social dance styles, such as ballroom, although it is likely that they will independently choose lower heels for comfort. If not, dance leaders in these styles should advise lower heels.

Researchers have also studied the effect of heel height on children's posture. For example, child flamenco dancers might be at an increased risk of injury because of the postural changes that accompany the frequent plantar-flexed position of the foot in this style. The recommendations, which can reasonably be translated into other genres that require young people to wear heels, are for teachers to comprehensively prepare students by increasing core stability and developing postural awareness and proprioception (Wilmerding, Gurney, & Torres, 2003).

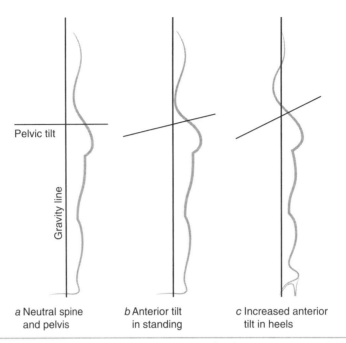

Pelvic tilt

Gravity line

a Neutral spine
and pelvis

b Anterior tilt
in standing

c Increased anterior
tilt in heels

Figure 2.14   Posture in heels: *(a)* pelvis in neutral without heels, full feet on the ground; *(b)* anterior pelvic tilt without heels; *(c)* accentuated anterior pelvic tilt in heels.

Heels obviously have limited shock-absorbing properties. Even styles with percussive stamping movements traditionally use shoes that have little capacity for shock absorption, for example, flamenco dancers (Pedersen & Wilmerding, 1998). Dancers in many styles prefer to practise and rehearse in sports shoes to protect their bodies from the repeated effects of rehearsing in non-supportive footwear. This is useful because athletic shoes provide lateral and hind foot stability, but they can cause problems in turning. When wearing athletic shoes for practice, turns should be avoided or adapted because the increased friction with the floor can cause twisting of the knees, potentially damaging the cartilage in the joint (Berardi, 2005). Inserting shock-absorbing insoles into running shoes has been found to reduce the load on the quadriceps and the erector spinae (Hong, Lee, Lin, Tang, & Chen, 2013), and this may also be beneficial for dancers looking for additional protection. Since neither bare feet nor dance footwear provide protection and support, the foot must have sufficient stability on its own (Simmel, 2014).

Some dancers would argue that practising in the correct shoes encourages the correct strengthening and conditioning of the leg in order to successfully perform in their dance style and allows them to acclimatise to the specific way a shoe affects their movement. However, dancers, as well as researchers, advocate preparing the body with supplementary exercises for foot and ankle

strength and core stability, because of the altered centre of gravity, as well as with rigorous stretching after rehearsals and performances (Kay, 2008; Pedersen & Wilmerding, 1998). Dancers could also perform the majority of their warm-up without heeled shoes, putting them on in the later stages to allow more genre-specific muscle activation. Similarly, the cool-down could begin with shoes on and then progress to removing the shoes, although care should be taken when stretching muscles in the lower leg that have been maintained in a prolonged contraction.

A combination of heels that are too high and too narrow means that the foot can slip forward in the shoe so that the toes are wedged in too small a space. A well-fitting shoe may help to offset some potential problems. For dance shoes, a deep and wide toe box and a wide heel, combined with an ankle or T-strap, as found in character shoes, is the best option for both support and stability (Kay, 2008). Normal fashion shoes that are pointed at the toes encourage the formation of bunions, and should be avoided by the dancer for everyday wear outside of their practice (Kendall et al., 1983).

SUMMARY

Many factors can contribute to poor alignment, including anatomical defects, muscle weakness

> *Dancers should take care of their feet by wearing supportive everyday shoes. Those worn for dancing need to fit properly, and they should be replaced when worn out. Shock absorption is not usually a feature of all dance shoes, so the foot needs to be strong and stable to cope with the demands of dancing in style-specific footwear.*

and imbalance, inflexibility, joint hypermobility and ligament laxity, fatigue and altered proprioception, as well as temporary body changes, as in pregnancy (Whiting & Rugg, 2006). Having established that postural control is necessary, regardless of the type and level of dance activity, dancers and dance leaders should always acknowledge poor postural habits. Dancers therefore need to strive for good posture. They should be able to maintain their functional alignment in their specific dance style in order to protect their bodies. If deviations from anatomically efficient alignment occur, either because of an individual's personal structural weaknesses or as a result of stylistic requirements that ask for special aesthetics, then the dancer and dance leader can be aware of how to combat them. While structural deviations cannot be changed, many alignment problems can be solved by improving technique or conditioning to correct muscular imbalances (Watkins & Clarkson, 1990). As well as physical conditioning,

for example, with different strength, endurance, stability or flexibility exercises, alternative methods such as somatic training involving anatomical imagery, relaxation techniques and mind–body integration can improve alignment (Berardi, 2005). Proprioceptive exercises can assist by improving kinaesthetic awareness. Suggestions for supplementary physical conditioning can be found in chapter 4 and details on imagery and relaxation can be found in chapter 8.

Teachers at all levels should understand the concept of ideal alignment and should be aware of common postural faults in their own genre and how to address them. The progression of exercises within the dance session should be built around promoting and integrating good alignment habits to protect the body while working in specific vocabularies.

Teachers must also have their own efficient movement mechanics in order to model and communicate good posture to others (Sweigard, 2013). It is clear that to avoid adding to alignment issues through the use of inappropriate cues that can contribute to muscle tension and imbalance, teachers could investigate their use of language and imagery and firmly root technical instruction in a solid anatomical framework. It is vital to understand how posture naturally changes from children to adults so as to adjust expectations accordingly. To underpin and reinforce good dance alignment, healthy postural habits should be encouraged in everyday life, not just in the dance studio.

KEY POINTS

- Efficient biomechanical alignment is necessary for preventing injury.
- Structural deviations and muscle imbalances can have a negative effect on ideal alignment.
- Dancers and dance leaders should have a working anatomical and biomechanical knowledge in order to communicate how to achieve efficient alignment.
- Dancers and dance leaders must be aware of the specific alignment requirements and challenges that are unique to their own genre.
- To promote healthy alignment and good physical function, engagement with conditioning or other bodywork techniques will help the dancer's body counteract alignment problems due to imbalance.

chapter 3

Warming Up
and Cooling Down

After reading this chapter you should be able to do the following:

- Understand the essential components of warming up and cooling down.
- Identify appropriate stretching modes for warming up and cooling down.
- Apply generic principles to specific genres and styles of dance.
- Differentiate between common misunderstandings and research-informed best practice.
- Advise participants on how to effectively warm up and cool down and explain why such elements are essential aspects of safe dance practice.

≡ Key Terms

autonomic nervous system	joint mobilisation	pulse reducer
cardiovascular stimulation	muscle lengthening	somatic nervous system
dynamic stretching	proprioceptive neuro-muscular facilitation (PNF)	static stretching
fast stretching	pulse raiser	stretch-shortening cycle

It is common knowledge that warming up and cooling down are an integral part of preparation for and recovery from any physical activity. However, these essential components of safe dance practice are frequently misunderstood and underutilised. Advice encouraging dancers to warm up is regularly vague and unspecific, such as 'stretch your muscles', 'loosen your joints' or 'do some cardio.' Therefore many dancers lack detailed understanding as to what a warm-up or cool-down should entail. In addition, research into what constitutes an effective warm-up and cool-down has developed significantly in the past decade, but the recommendations have yet to filter through to practice. As a result, all too often these essential components of safe practice can be superficial, inappropriate and potentially damaging.

This chapter intends to demystify warming up and cooling down for dance, focusing on the physiological benefits, in order to understand why it is advantageous to incorporate these aspects into daily practice. It emphasises the importance of correct preparation and recovery in relation to injury reduction and prolonged participation in dance. It also addresses the necessary content and structure of warm-up and cool-down and considers how to practically implement these fundamental aspects into dance sessions, regardless of dance style. In addition, it discusses the role of stretching in warm-up and cool-down in light of developments in research.

Prior to addressing the specifics it is worth bearing in mind the following points. A warm-up intends to gradually prepare the body for increased physical activity. Key terms here are 'gradually' and 'prepare'. Dancers often misinterpret the beginning exercises of class as the warm-up, ignoring the fact that preparations should be done prior to the first exercise in class (see also chapter 6). Similarly the cool-down is frequently ignored or it is hastily included as the dance leader and participants rush off to the next class, to catch the train, to get home to family or attend to other seemingly more pressing demands. As discussed in more detail in chapter 6, class or rehearsals often inappropriately finish at a high intensity, but dancers should be given time to wind down the body and mind before they transition to the next task of the day. If dancers and dance leaders fully understood the potential long- and short-term benefits of warming up and cooling down for both performance enhancement and injury reduction, would more time and space be ensured for such basic safe practice?

PRINCIPLES AND COMPONENTS OF WARMING UP

Dancers are more likely to warm up before a performance than before class or rehearsal (Laws, 2005). When dancers are anecdotally questioned on why this might be, they state that performing without having warmed up in advance is not something they would advocate. Most people seem to inherently understand that warming up helps dancers perform at their best. Why then, would we not want to perform at our best, our safest, at every opportunity? Warming up effectively is a simple method of supporting improved performance potential and decreased injury risk, and it is a fundamental aspect of safe practice.

It is generally accepted within existing dance and exercise literature that there is a relationship between an effective warm-up and reduction of injury incidence (Alter, 2004; Harris & Elbourne, 2002; Laws, Marsh, & Wyon, 2006; Malliou, Rokka, Beneka, Mavridis, & Godolias, 2007) and also between an effective warm-up and improved performance outcomes (Volianitis, Koutedakis, & Carson, 2001; Murphy, Di Santo, Alkanani, & Behm, 2010; Morrin & Redding, 2013; McArdle, Katch, & Katch, 2014; Young & Behm, 2003). Those who experience exercise-induced asthma will also benefit from completing a warm-up (Volianitis et al., 2001; see chapter 10 for more information specific to asthmatic dancers). But what does an effective warm-up entail?

Historically dancers have engaged in prolonged **static stretching** as the main, and at times the only, component of their warm-up. However, research in dance and exercise science is consistently evidencing that this practice is wholly inappropriate, ineffective and potentially hazardous. Instead, a combination of dynamic and brief static elements

is recommended for dance warm-up, particularly since dance often demands varied dynamic and explosive actions but also requires displays of static flexibility. For example, a warm-up consisting of the following elements has been shown to increase range of motion (ROM) for up to half an hour after the warm-up and to improve jump height (Murphy et al., 2010): 5 minutes of gradually increasing cardiorespiratory activity, followed by brief (up to 6 seconds per stretch) static stretches of the main muscle groups, then returning to approximately 5 minutes of targeting the cardiovascular system. A dance-specific study reported that doing 5 to 7 minutes of gradually increasing cardiorespiratory activity, followed by either **dynamic stretching** or a combination of both dynamic and static stretching, significantly improved performance variables such as vertical jump height and balance, with the combined stretching protocol also seeing significant improvements in ROM (Morrin & Redding, 2013). However, the same study reported that long-duration static stretching did not result in improvements in most of the performance variables assessed, except for ROM, and was in fact equivalent to not stretching at all. From these studies it can be concluded that an element of brief static stretching seems to be beneficial for ROM requirements, but **cardiovascular stimulation** and dynamic stretch activities are also necessary for preparing for the other demands of dance activity.

Research is highlighting that the relative duration of the warm-up is also a key factor influencing effectiveness. There appears to be an association between increased duration of warm-up and reduced injury rate. Insufficient warm-up is a common perceived cause of injury (Laws, 2005), and dance leaders who include a personal warm-up and cool-down before and after their classes have reported reduced injury rates when compared with colleagues who only warm up within the class time (Malliou et al., 2007).

Evidence is suggesting therefore that the relative intensity, duration and order of content are all contributing factors to the effectiveness, or otherwise, of a warm-up. These factors will of course vary depending on compounding considerations, including room temperature, the age of the participants, the purpose of the dance session (i.e., class, rehearsal, competition or performance) and the needs of the dance style. For example, a 20-minute high-energy performance with multiple jump sequences will require different warm-up considerations than a 1-hour seated creative dance class in an elderly care home. However, before considering any adaptations for specific situations, dance leaders should understand the fundamental principles of warming up: raising the pulse, mobilising the joints and lengthening the muscle fibres.

Raising the Pulse

The first component of warm-up involves increasing the pulse rate from a 'resting' or non-active state to approximately 50 to 60 percent of the dancer's personal heart rate maximum (HRmax; Volianitis et al., 2001; see key point). This gradual increase in heart rate and body temperature (by just 1 to 2 degrees Celsius; Murphy et al., 2010) is gentle; it should not be confused with a cardiorespiratory or aerobic workout. The intensity should be just enough so that dancers lightly perspire, but are still able to carry on a conversation. Using a scale to rate individual perceptions of exertion, such as the Borg scale (Borg, 1982), is another way to monitor appropriate intensity; the warm-up should be rated as 'very light' to 'fairly light'. The intention of this **pulse raiser** is to stimulate the cardiovascular system. The resultant increase in internal body temperature corresponds with capillary dilation, a reduced viscosity (thickness) of the blood and thus an increase in blood flow from core to periphery. The increased pulse rate promotes an increased breathing rate, which positively affects the oxygen-carrying capacity of the blood to the muscles.

When the cardiovascular system is stimulated, a transition in the focus and functioning of the nervous system simultaneously occurs. When the body is at rest, the nervous system is centred on

the **autonomic nervous system**, which is responsible for the involuntary inner functioning of the human body (e.g., digestion, regulation of pulse and breathing rates). When the body is voluntarily stimulated into action, the nervous system adjusts to become more responsive to external demands through the stimulation of the **somatic nervous system**. This shift in neurofunctioning stimulates increased mind–body interaction with both the activity and the environment being experienced.

A thorough pulse raiser should last approximately 5 minutes and should include easy movements that are comfortably within the capability level of the participating group. Examples of full-body, low-intensity actions are walking briskly around the studio space and gently rolling on the floor. Gentle changing of levels and vigorous body rubbing can also aid in increasing the pulse rate when used in conjunction with full-body movements. The intensity should gradually increase to include low-impact gallops, skips and jogging or an equivalent, depending on the group's needs. The movement does not need to be choreographed; participants should not be overly concerned with technical accuracy or movement memory. Awareness of both internal functioning and external environment should be encouraged.

Mobilising the Joints

A regularly overlooked aspect of warming up is **joint mobilisation.** This should not be confused with technical articulations or isolations, which are a specific component of some dance classes such as jazz or street dance (see chapter 6 for further clarification on the distinction between class-based exercises and warm-up exercises). Joint mobilisation is of particular importance in a dance warm-up due to the often exaggerated range of motion that the dancer's joints are required to perform. Although the full-body actions completed in the pulse-raiser phase of the warm-up will inevitably mobilise the joints, a specifically targeted joint mobilisation section is important. The intention of this phase is to focus on the range of motion that is available at a given joint and to prepare the joints for safe loading. Consider that the moveable joints engaged in dance practice are classified as *synovial joints* (see also chapter 2). This means that the joints are surrounded by nourishing synovial fluid, which aids smooth articulation and provides shock absorption. Focusing

Age-predicted heart rate maximum (AHRmax) can be calculated by subtracting your age from the standardised value of 220 beats per minute (bpm; ACSM, 2014). For example a 20-year-old dancer will have an AHRmax of 220 − 20 (years old) = 200 bpm. To work out what heart rate range represents 50 to 60 percent of that AHRmax, multiply 200 bpm by 0.5 (50%) and again by 0.6 (60%): 200 × 0.5 = 100 bpm and 200 × 0.6 = 120 bpm. This means that 100 to 120 bpm is the range of heart rate intensity during warm-up for a 20-year-old.

Dancers completing a group warm up prior to the beginning of class. Following the pulse raiser they are engaging with joint mobility and gentle dynamic muscle lengthening.

on joint mobility changes the viscosity of the fluid at the joint, which in turn increases range of motion and shock absorbency. A successfully warmed-up joint provides a cushion, efficiently distributing forces and impacts through the body with reduced negative effect. In addition, because range of motion is affected by both joint mobility and muscle flexibility, focusing on the range of motion available at each joint also gently warms up the surrounding soft tissues and lengthens the fibres of connecting muscles.

This section of the warm-up should last approximately 5 minutes and should focus on all the major joints to be used in the upcoming dance class, rehearsal or performance. This recommendation is based on a total warm-up duration of 15 to 20 minutes, which might be expanded as necessary for more intense performance needs or when the dance environment is less than ideal (e.g., hard flooring or cold temperature). Movements in this section of the warm-up should take account of the functional range of motion available at a joint; therefore dance leaders should understand joint movements and anatomical

planes of reference (refer to chapter 2 for images and definitions of these terms). For example, the knee (predominantly a hinge joint) should avoid rotation, especially in weight bearing, and merely flex (bend) and extend (straighten) in the sagittal plane (forward and backward directions). Also, movements should focus on the central articulation of the joint being mobilised (i.e., the space between the bones) rather than on the extremities of the limb. For example, when mobilising the ankle joint, dancers often complete ankle circles by transitioning the ankle joint through inversion, dorsiflexion (flexion), eversion and plantarflexion (pointing). However, completing this action with the intention of 'drawing circles with toes' often results in pointing of the toes and gripping of the foot and lower leg muscles. Instead, this action should attend to the joint articulations, or the spaces between the bones, resulting in a relaxed foot and toes, and promoting a gentler mobilisation within the joint. Similarly when performing circular actions with the shoulder's ball and socket joint, the emphasis should be on the centre of the joint, rather than drawing the circle with the finger tips reaching out to the edges of the circle.

Lengthening the Muscles

The phrase 'lengthening the muscles' distinguishes between the act of reminding the neuromuscular system of its safe functioning in anticipation of the upcoming dance session and the act of stretching with the intention of improving flexibility. Chapter 4 addresses the latter, but this section focuses on safe and effective methods of **muscle lengthening** in order to prepare the muscles for the range of motion required in the upcoming class, rehearsal or performance. Improvements in muscle flexibility can and should be targeted after the dance session, but during the warm-up, dancers should focus on reminding the body of the functional length of the muscles rather than working to train or improve flexibility (Alter, 2004).

Although dancers rarely need encouragement to stretch out, they may need guidance in choosing which of the multiple modes of stretching to pursue at which time. Developments in research and understanding in relation to the type, duration and intensity of stretch before, during and after activity should be carefully considered. The practice of dancers arriving in the studio, depositing their bag in one corner, adding layers of clothing and then commencing deep and sustained stretches is slowly being eradicated due to the increasing awareness of the needs for pulse raising and joint mobility before attending to the muscles. However, uncertainty among dancers and dance leaders still remains regarding the role of stretching in the warm-up.

Although static stretching is the most common and frequently used type of stretching, research has noted that it can change the contractile properties of the musculotendinous unit (MTU), thereby decreasing strength and power capabilities. The longer the static stretch is held, the greater the decrease in these abilities (Kallerud & Gleeson, 2013; Young & Behm, 2003; Tsolakis & Bogdanis, 2012; Hindle, Whitcomb, Briggs, & Hong, 2012). Therefore deep stretches, involving maximal eccentric contractions (see chapter 2) held for long durations are not appropriate prior to dance activity because they produce an overlengthening of the muscle fibres. This subsequently leaves the muscles less responsive to the **stretch-shortening cycle**—a quick succession of eccentric or lengthening and concentric or shortening muscular contractions—that is necessary for many actions

throughout the upcoming dance session. Deep stretches do have a purpose in other aspects of dance training (addressed in chapter 4), but the warm-up is not the place for them.

Research is repeatedly evidencing that the most effective mode of stretching before activity is dynamic stretching and brief static stretches (Samson, Button, Chaouachi, & Behm, 2012; Tsolakis & Bogdanis, 2012). One dance study recommended that dancers should move away from the 'exclusive reliance on static stretches in a warm-up and encourage the incorporation of Dynamic Stretch in addition to Static Stretch' (Morrin & Redding, 2013, p. 39). Brief static stretches targeting major muscle groups (such as gastrocnemius, quadriceps group and hamstring group) should be held for approximately 6 to 10 seconds. Static stretches during warm-up should be achieved with control and easily maintained without excessive tension. Dancers should aim to stay within their current capabilities. They should also mentally focus on the specific muscle group being lengthened and draw their awareness to their breath, making sure to breathe out during the lengthening phase.

Dynamic stretching, despite being the most recommended type of stretching, is not regularly used within dance warm-ups. Dynamic stretching involves repeatedly moving the limb, using gravity and momentum to assist, while also maintaining control as the movement progressively builds towards an easy (not forced) full range of motion. The emphasis should be on supporting the natural dynamic lengthening of the targeted muscle, while also ensuring that the speed and rate of increase of the range of motion are gradual. Remember that this is a preparatory act, not the full-out performance of a particular movement. An example would be a leg swing, where flexion and extension of the hip joint is supported by the momentum of the swing, with a focus on lengthening the hamstring muscle group and letting the limb gradually lift higher (through increased hip flexion, rather than increased extension at the knee) with each repetition. This mode of lengthening the muscles is known as an isotonic contraction, where the eccentric and concentric muscle contractions work together to allow for a contract–release lengthening and shortening phase to take place that mimics the muscle activation that occurs later in the dance class, rehearsal or performance (for more on muscle activations and types of muscle contractions, see chapter 2). In addition to targeting joint range of motion and muscle flexibility,

Note that dynamic stretching should not be confused with ballistic stretching (bouncing or bobbing in a stretch, at the end range of the joint mobility). Ballistic stretching, although it does serve a purpose immediately prior to jumps or dynamic leg kicks (Wyon, 2010b), is not suitable for the generic dance warm-up. It is more likely to cause injury than other stretching types if it is not carried out correctly (Critchfield, 2011). See chapter 4 for a further explanation of ballistic stretching.

dynamic stretching is aerobic in nature due to the repetitive action, which in turn maintains the increased body temperature that was achieved during the pulse-raising phase of the warm-up.

Following the pulse raiser, joint mobilisation and muscle lengthening, a fourth section of the warm-up should focus on the stylistic specific needs of the subsequent activity. For example, specific preparations for a ballet class, dancers could include focusing attention on core control, external hip rotation and load-bearing preparations for the knee joints; however, a jazz class might require more attention to spinal mobility, dynamic hamstring lengthening and neck mobility. It is also appropriate to mark through patterns or sequences that have been previously learned, working them at a low level of intensity.

A fifth, but equally important, element of the warm-up is psychological preparation. Going through the physical preparation process that has been outlined will also support mental preparation for the dance session. This mental preparation will help to bring dancers awareness into their bodies and increase focus and concentration throughout the class, rehearsal or performance (Taylor & Taylor, 1995). The heightened focus can support safe practice through increasing reaction times (for example, responding to external verbal cues from the teacher or having to swiftly avoid bumping into an oncoming dancer) and also attuning mind and body to internal kinaesthetic sensations. In performance or competition scenarios, mental preparation can be of particular importance in finding the self-belief to perform at one's best. Processes such as attending to the breath, using visualisation and focusing on positive self-talk can aid mental preparation (see chapter 8 for more details).

When preparing for a 90-minute dance session of medium to high intensity, effectively targeting all five components will result in a warm-up that takes approximately 20 minutes, with each section lasting around 5 minutes. Movement choices should always begin generally and become more specific as the warm-up progresses. If the joint mobilisation and muscle lengthening sections have caused the internal temperature of the body to drop, return to a brief pulse raiser before beginning the style-specific section. Similarly, if the style-specific section has caused a drop in temperature, and the beginning of the class is quite intense, insert a brief pulse raiser. Dancers and dance leaders should tailor the warm-up content with due consideration of areas that have been highlighted by the research as common sites of dance injury (see chapter 9). Individuals should give special attention to areas that have been injured previously, or feel particularly stiff. Leaders should additionally take account of age-specific, situation-specific and environment needs. Consideration of how to tailor

Benefits of Warming Up

Following these warm-up recommendations presented in this section will result in:

- A more effective dancing experience in the short and long term
- Heightened neuromuscular transmissions resulting in increased reaction times, which produce benefits in abilities to pick up and perform movement sequences
- Increased metabolic processes resulting in more efficient energy exchange, which limits strain on the body's energy production throughout class
- Joints that are effectively primed with their innate shock-absorption capacity, supporting short- and long-term well-being
- Muscles that are suitably primed for the shortening and lengthening dynamic contractions that they will repeatedly perform throughout the class
- Improved mind–body connections promoting enhanced mental focus and engagement with the subsequent activity

these generic principles to different situations is offered towards the end of this chapter, and is also addressed in chapter 10 in relation to specific population needs.

PRINCIPLES AND COMPONENTS OF COOLING DOWN

The purpose of a cool-down is to gradually return the body to its normal functioning; again the key word here is 'gradually'. Often the progressive intensity of a dance session means the highest physical intensity occurs at the end, which results in the dancer experiencing a high rate of blood flow around the body and a fast (sometimes near maximum) heart rate, with the metabolism and the nervous system in a heightened state of activity (see chapter 6 for more regarding the preferred versus the common intensities of session progression). To suddenly cease activity at this point is akin to slamming on the car brakes when you had been motoring along at full speed. Theory suggests that an effective cool-down can reduce injuries, in particular delayed-onset muscle soreness or DOMS (Harris & Elbourne, 2002; Laws, Marsh, & Wyon, 2006; Cheung, Hume, & Maxwell, 2003; Olsen, Sjøhaug, van Beekvelt, & Mork, 2012), and can promote enhanced performance for subsequent bouts of activity (Hindle et al., 2012; Rey, Lago-Peñas, Casáis, & Lago-Ballesteros, 2012). A focused cool-down is also thought to relieve any mental tension that may have built up during the dance session (Alter, 2004).

Regardless of dance situation (class, rehearsal, competition or performance), cooling down appears less popular than warming up (Laws, 2005; Koutedakis, Pacy, Carson, & Dick, 1997). Perhaps this is in part due to the limited amount of research that has been conducted on the benefits of cooling down and to the somewhat contradictory nature of the findings. Many of the research papers have focused solely on the stretching aspect of a cool-down. A 2002 systematic literature review noted that stretching after activity reduced muscular soreness for up to 72 hours after activity, although the authors comment that, due to a small effect size, these findings might not be strong enough to promote practical application (Herbert & Gabriel, 2002). A more recent review reported a literature consensus that static stretching post exercise can reduce muscle soreness for 24 hours after the

activity (Herbert, de Noronha, & Kamper, 2011). However, stretching is only one component of the cool-down. Other research has examined the positive effects of including an active element (e.g., a **pulse reducer**) to the cool-down, reporting beneficial outcomes for subsequent power activities (Rey et al., 2012).

Review papers continue to note that the effectiveness of a cool-down, as with warm-up, appears to depend on the intensity, duration and relative dynamic or static nature of the content, the order in which the sections are conducted, as well as the specificity of the cool-down content to the activity that has just been experienced (Herbert et al., 2011; Rey et al., 2012). Despite such inconclusive recommendations, a statistical relationship can be seen between injury rate and cool-down: For example, dancers who cool down after their sessions report lower injury rates (Laws, 2005; Malliou et al., 2007). These findings support common theories that propose that effective cooling down can bring multiple physiological, neurological and psychological benefits that promote reduced injury risk and enhanced performance.

In order to effectively recover from strenuous dance activity, dancers and teachers must understand the physiological demands that the dance session has just targeted. Therefore, when choosing the specific focus of the cool-down, they should consider the type, level of intensity and duration of the activity that has just taken place (for more on these aspects, see chapter 4). For example, an Irish dance class has quite a high physical intensity, and predominantly targets activation of the calf (gastrocnemius and soleus) muscle group. It also subjects the lower limb joints to repetitive impacts. In planning the cool-down, Irish dance teachers must consider how to counteract these actions in order to effectively balance out or neutralise the accumulative effects of the activity on the dancing body. However, similar to warming up, before considering such specificity, dance leaders must be aware of the general principles of cooling down. These principles include reducing the pulse rate, easing out the joints and stretching the muscles. Once teachers have understood these ideas, they can and should adapt the principles as the need arises.

Reducing the Pulse Rate

Transitioning from strenuous activity to a more neutral state targets similar components, but with the opposite intentions of what was recommended in the warm-up. The cool-down should begin with a pulse reducer, (decreasing pulse and breathing rates, and reducing internal body temperature), which will counteract the heightened cardiovascular stimulation that the dance session has promoted. As the pulse rate returns to a normal level, the nervous system and metabolism will also return to a more balanced functioning where the blood flow is redistributed to the vital organs. This supports a gradual elimination of by-products of exercise such as excessive build-up of lactic acid, which has been associated with DOMS.

Movements in this phase of the cool-down should gradually reduce in physical intensity. Teachers should promote general full-body actions, such as walking around the space, rather than technically challenging or detailed actions. In some instances this is an appropriate time to mark through movement sequences from class at a significantly reduced intensity (chapter 6 offers additional examples of how to end the dance session effectively). This will not only promote gradual temperature reduction, but also enhance movement sequencing and motor memory for subsequent dance sessions. For the majority of dance experiences, the duration of this section would ideally be 2 to 3 minutes, with the intensity of the movements decreasing gradually over time.

Easing Out the Joints

During dance sessions the MTU is repeatedly engaged in strength and stretching activities; as a result unnecessary tension can develop in the joint and the surrounding soft tissues. Returning to gentle joint mobilisation with the intention of rebalancing the soft-tissue activation and redistributing the synovial fluid balance is thought to support long-term health of the joint capsule and aid preparation for stretching, the next phase of the cool-down. This element is often not considered within the cool-down, yet it can be of great importance in releasing any stress or tension that might have built up in the soft tissues surrounding the joint.

Movements in this phase of the cool-down should focus on any joints that have been particularly targeted within the dance session. For example, after a breakdancing session where dancers have worked on headstands, they should focus on releasing the neck and shoulder girdle joints. Gentle mobilisation of the joints through their comfortable range of motion with limited tension and force is ideal. This phase should last approx-imately 2 to 3 minutes, depending on the intensity and duration of the preceding dance session.

Stretching the Muscles

The third phase of the cool-down is stretching. It is important to clarify the intention of stretching the muscles at this point in the dance session, since stretching after dance activity can have two purposes: for recovery (i.e., restoring the full functioning length of the muscle fibres, thereby reducing muscle aches and pains and ensuring a maintenance of current flexibility) or for improving flexibility. The stretch recommendations here are for recovery after dance activity, and they are recommended with the intention of releasing build-up of muscular tension and lengthening the muscle fibres to their resting length once again, so as to support a more effective return to activity at a subsequent date. Chapter 4 provides advice for improving flexibility.

> *Dancers should always practice stretching with care and control. Holding a stretch to the point of muscle shaking is not necessary, and it can be potentially harmful (see chapter 4 for more on this point).*

Stretching post activity is said to be of particular importance to people with short and/or tight muscles. Achieving prolonged benefits from stretching requires continual engagement with stretching for months or years. Hypermobile dancers, however, should place less emphasis on stretching and focus more on strengthening exercises instead, since they will not require the same extent of stretching as dancers who are tight (Critchfield, 2011). More information on specific considerations of hypermobile dancers is available in chapter 2. In considering which muscle groups to target, dancers should give particular attention to those that were dominantly used during the dance session. For example, if the session involved high-intensity or repetitive jumping, then dancers should stretch the calf muscle group (gastrocnemius and soleus) as well as the quadriceps muscle group (rectus femoris, vastus lateralis, vastus medialis and vastus intermedius).

Static stretching is appropriate in the cool-down. It may include, but is not exclusively related to, passive stretching, which refers to using an external force (such as gravity, a partner or an

A dancer engaging in static stretching as part of her cool-down after class. This is after she has completed the pulse reducer and joint easing sections.

external aid) to achieve the stretch. The mind–body connection and use of breath (exhalation) should be actively involved in static stretches. In addition, contrary to popular assumptions, static stretches can have a controlled active element. Reaching an immediate maximum stretch and holding that position often results in gripping, or unnecessary concentric activation of the muscle fibres (agonist and antagonist). Gripping results in greater difficulty and sometimes pain as dancers attempt to maintain the stretch for the desired duration. Instead dancers should engage in active-static stretches with mindful, controlled movement, working to gently and continually lengthen the muscle fibres with each exhalation and striving to increase space and range of motion (ROM) at the relevant joints for 30 to 60 seconds, depending on their flexibility. They can repeat stretches up to three times for each muscle group, and should prioritise the dominant muscle groups that were targeted during the dance session.

Example of Active-Static Stretching

■ ■ ■

Breathe in, breathe out and commence a stretch with control and attention, moving deeper into the position until the initial point of stretch sensation but not pain. Hold the position, mindfully relaxing any unnecessary tension, for around 10 seconds. Breathe in again. On the out breath, work to gently increase the stretch. Again hold this position for up to 10 seconds. If possible, gently increase the stretch once more on a third breath in and out. Using anatomical imagery can support an increase in ROM, especially if flexibility is currently restricted. Visualise making space in the joints and releasing the muscle fibres, even if no actual movement or increase in ROM is possible. Combining imagery with the breath helps reduce unnecessary muscular tension. Imagine increasing ROM and muscular length for the full duration of the stretch, even if you are not able to achieve any additional movement. Finish the stretch by maintaining the final position for approximately 20 seconds, and then gently ease the body out of the position.

Example of PNF Stretching for Hamstrings

■ ■ ■

Lie on your back. Breathe in, breathe out and flex at the hip joint, bringing the leg towards the ceiling and maintaining length at the knee joint. Go to the point of initial stretch sensation but not pain. Use a partner, your arms, or an external aid (such as an item of clothing or towel) to hold the limb in position. Once in position, actively contract the leg muscles, as if you are intending to return the leg to the floor. Your partner, if you're using one, will resist this action. Or if you are using an external aid like a strap, you will actively resist the leg from achieving this action. Contract the muscle (at approximately 70 to 100 percent of maximal contraction) for a maximum of 10 seconds (6 seconds has been shown to be most beneficial). As you come to the end of the contraction, breathe in. On the out breath, release the isometric contraction and allow your partner (or use your external aid) to passively increase the ROM at the hip joint, thereby elongating the target muscle group (hamstrings). Once you have reached a new position, take a moment to allow the body to register this new position before repeating the preceding steps. Three repetitions will likely suffice. Finish the stretch by maintaining the final position for approximately 20 seconds, and then gently ease the body out of the stretch and return to a neutral position. Use imagery and mindfulness to reduce unnecessary muscular tension during the lengthening (eccentric) phase of the stretch and to maximise the space and ROM at the hip joint.

A particular mode of stretching called **proprioceptive neuromuscular facilitation (PNF)** is also possible during cool-down, depending on the participant group. PNF involves isometric activation (maximum contraction, with no movement) of the muscle fibres against a resistance, followed by a passive repositioning of the limb. This active and passive pattern can be repeated up to three times, depending on the dancer's available range of motion. PNF can be conducted independently using an external aid for resistance, or with a partner. If working with a partner, dancers should exercise care and effective communication to ensure appropriateness and safety of the stretch. Dancers must be body aware when using PNF, since contraindications exist if due care is not followed. For more information on PNF stretching in relation to flexibility improvements, see chapter 4.

If time is limited, dancers may opt for a mode of stretching that has been identified recently. **Fast stretching** has been promoted as assisting a reset of the muscle's length post exercise (Wyon, 2010). Like static stretching, the stretch is held in a brief period of stillness, at full range of motion, for 5 or 6 seconds. As well as being a quick recovery stretch, this method can also be used during the dance session if the dancer experiences muscle tightness from excessive repetitions of concentric contractions, such as in the calf muscles following a series of high-intensity jumps. Unlike the active-static and PNF modes already mentioned, fast stretching is not known for contributing to flexibility improvements. Therefore, although this mode of recovery stretch is particularly useful if completing a quick cool-down before transitioning from one dance session to the next or from one performance repertory to another, the other two modes are preferable when time allows.

Mental recovery is also a purpose of the cool-down. Dancers might experience heightened psychological states following the class, rehearsal, competition or performance, such as frustration, elation or self-doubt. The process of conducting the physical transition can also support a mental transition, refocusing mind and body and returning both to a more balanced state. Other strategies for promoting a balanced state of mind are addressed in more detail in chapter 8.

Effectively targeting all sections of the cool-down will take at least 15 minutes in total: The pulse reducer and joint easing sections take approximately 3 minutes each, and the remainder of the time should be spent on stretching. Both individual stretches and the stretching section as a whole should last longer during the cool-down than in the warm-up. Dancers and dance leaders should also tailor the cool-down content with consideration of the common sites of dance injury (see chapter 9), targeting body parts that have been placed under particular strain during

Benefits of Cooling Down

Following these cool-down recommendations will result in:

- Restored cardiorespiratory, neuromuscular and metabolic functioning, which reduces likelihood of dizziness and blood pooling
- Reduced joint aches and muscle soreness following the dance session
- Effective recovery for return to subsequent activity
- Reduction in mental stress or tension that might have accumulated during the dance session
- Decreased likelihood of injury

the session. Individuals should give particular attention to any areas of previous injury. As with the warm-up, leaders should also account for age- and situation-specific needs. Consideration of how to tailor these generic cool-down principles is offered at the end of this chapter.

CONSIDERATIONS FOR VARIOUS DANCE SCENARIOS

The guidelines presented in this chapter cover the general principles of warming up and cooling down for dance. However, specific considerations are needed to tailor these guidelines to different situations, such as the age of the participating group, stylistic requirements, the nature of the dance session, dancer injuries and restrictions such as time and space. The following section offers examples that address these situations.

Age Group

Although specific research on the effects of warming up on different ages is not readily available, physiological understanding of the aging process suggests that older participants, and in particular participants who are both older and less active in their daily lives, require careful consideration

of warm-up and cool-down. The process for these participants should be more gradual and thorough. Warm-ups for a group of seated participants should still encourage a pulse raiser. Reaching the arms through space (up, down, around) and body rubbing can gradually increase the internal temperature and pulse rate. Mobilisation can include gentle arm circles, small spinal rotations, pointing and flexing the ankle and gentle leg lifts. Specific stretching exercises are not essential, but participants should be encouraged to extend their limbs towards their comfortable full range of motion.

Young children (pre-adolescence) respond more rapidly to warm-up activities. Often the challenge here is to continue to promote a gradual transition. Young dancers are the potential teachers and performers of the future, so instilling the importance of a gradual and thorough warm-up and cool-down will provide a lasting influence far beyond their personal well-being and longevity in dance. Note that children's bodies are not as efficient at temperature regulation as those of adults; therefore children should layer their clothing so that they can remove layers during the warm-up and then add them again during the cool-down.

Adolescents, especially those experiencing a growth spurt, should pay particular attention to the process of warming up and cooling down. Teachers should advise teenagers to practise gentle muscle lengthening because the adolescent skeleton is growing faster than its soft-tissue connections. Because the knee is a commonly injured area for this population, dancers should give particular attention to the knee joint, ensuring gradual mobilisation and preparation for weight-bearing movements. More specific considerations for different ages of dance participant are provided in chapter 10.

Stylistic Focus

Codified techniques have evolved through years of tradition. Therefore dancers and dance leaders infrequently challenge or question what the most effective ways of preparation and recovery are for their particular genre. While the generic principles outlined previously apply for all styles, each dance style also has its own particular needs when considering preparation for and recovery from the dance session. The fourth section of the warm-up should focus especially on these needs, and the cool-down should include elements that provide a counterbalance for particularly targeted areas.

A teacher leading young dancers through their warm-up activity. Young and inexperienced dancers will need guidance to ensure an effective warm-up.

• Dance styles such as aerial, breaking, pole dancing and physical theatre are likely to require a focus on the range of motion and strength of the core, upper body and upper limbs. Breakdancers should also pay particular attention to the wrist and neck by doing mobilising and easy weight-bearing actions before their session. During the cool-down, dancers should also focus on these areas, restoring mobility and stretching the muscle fibres for a safe return to functioning length.

• In styles that require specific footwear, especially heeled footwear or pointe shoes, dancers should complete the initial three sections of the warm-up without shoes and then introduce the footwear for the fourth section. Similarly, they should begin the cool-down wearing the footwear and then remove it toward the end of the session.

• In styles such as Irish, flamenco and Bharatanatyam, dancers should pay particular attention to weight-bearing preparation for the feet and lower limbs. In addition, Irish dancers should especially minimise static stretching in the warm-up and instead promote dynamic stretching to support optimum muscle activation for the explosive actions of the style. Flamenco and Bharatanatyam dancers should also focus on wrist, hand, and finger mobilisation, and a Bharatanatyam warm-up should additionally include eye and face mobilisation.

• Egyptian belly dance, salsa and rumba require a focus on pelvis mobility.

• Contemporary dance requires a particular emphasis on the mind–body connection, and it is likely to include some preparation for floor work, inversions or weight bearing in the upper limbs. Ballet requires a focus on feet, ankles and hip rotation, while jazz dance requires a particularly thorough full-body joint mobilisation section to prepare for the isolation exercises that are synonymous with that style. These similar areas should be targeted in the cool-down, with the intention of releasing rather than preparing.

• Creative dance or improvisational classes tend to naturally lend themselves to a gradual progression of activity; however, warm-ups and cool-downs should still be included. Creative tasks should be carefully considered and structured in such as way as to support the generic recommendations provided previously.

- Teachers of aerobic dance classes and dance exercise classes such as Zumba should remember that a warm-up should take place prior to the cardiorespiratory workout section of the class. They should also set time aside for a gradual decline in intensity at the end of the session.

Class, Rehearsal or Performance

Dancers should warm up and cool down before and after each dance scenario, whether a dance class, rehearsal, competition or performance. However, each of these elements demands different physical intensities; therefore leaders should adapt content, duration and intensity to suit each of these scenarios. Interestingly, research shows that dancers are generally more likely to warm up than to cool down, are more likely to complete a warm-up before a performance, rather than before class or rehearsal and are less likely to cool down after a performance than after class or rehearsal (Laws, 2005).

Rehearsals and performance schedules should allow time for appropriate warm-up and cool-down. Different members of the company might need to complete personal variations of the group warm-up, especially in the fourth activity-specific phase. The same is true for the cool-down, since the roles in the performance will call upon different physical demands from each individual. Also, the rehearsal and call times for cast members should consider whether all performers are needed simultaneously. There is little point in warming up a whole group of performers and then spending the next hour working with only a trio while the other dancers artificially cool down again (for more detail on the implications and methods of managing this situation see chapter 6). Theatres and venues should support the needs of dance groups and companies to warm up and cool down by providing a suitable space and factoring in time for these sessions, especially after a performance. Rehearsal directors and dance leaders should ensure that cooling down after performances becomes an integral part of the company or student ethos.

One touring company known to the authors conducted a group warm-up every evening before the show and also allowed time for personal warm-up needs following the group session. Despite being in a new venue every week, the company provided a specific warm-up and cool-down space, along with specialist equipment (e.g., blocks for stretching calf muscles, small weights, stretching bands, rowing machines). In addition, following the finale and curtain call, all cast members were required to exit the stage through the warm-up and cool-down area and complete their independent cool-down in this communal space for a minimum of 15 minutes before returning to the changing rooms to remove costumes and make-up. This is best practice, and it should be encouraged by all dance companies and performance groups.

Injury

During warm-up and cool-down, individual dancers and their dance leaders should allow additional time and focus for any previously injured areas. This might require an individual dancer to take longer mobilising a particular body part than others in the group do. For example, dancers should carefully mobilise a formerly sprained ankle and ease it into weight-bearing scenarios as appropriate, while also ensuring stability and control of the joint action. After the dance session, dancers should pay attention to easing any tension in the muscles surrounding the injured joint, as well as working on restoring any stability that may have been compromised during the session. Leaders should support dancers to include individual rehabilitation exercises as necessary, in accordance with advice from a healthcare practitioner. As with all aspects of dance activity, if any particular movements produce a sudden increase in pain or discomfort, then that action should be avoided until the discomfort has eased. However, dancers should tailor an appropriate, gradual warm-up and cool-down to ensure that these sessions do not induce any discomfort.

Time, Space or Environment Restrictions

If time restrictions prevent the recommended duration of warm-up from being performed, then dancers should undertake a condensed version instead, warming up for at least 5 minutes and including all three of the general warm-up components. If necessary, the pulse raiser and joint mobility sections could overlap to allow for a combination of both intentions. The muscle lengthening section should be dynamic. If time is limited to just 5 minutes, then dancers should build to higher intensities, such as 70 percent of maximum heart rate (Volianitis et al., 2001). They should also be sure to cool down, particularly using stretching elements that aim to restore the muscle length. Fast stretching or microstretch techniques are useful in time-constraint situations (Wyon, 2010b).

Space and environmental restrictions can also force adaptations. However, if dancers have enough room to stand or sit, then they have enough room to warm up and cool down. An on-the-spot warm-up can consist of repeated bouts of vigorous body rubbing that incorporates changes in level by reaching down along the legs to the feet, followed by gentle rebounding through alternating feet while swinging the arms across the body and then going through a full range of mobility actions, working through relevant joint segments and the relevant stretch requirements (brief static and dynamic stretches). A cool-down can include similar actions, but with the mindset and pace required to recover from activity rather than prepare for it. Environmental restrictions include elements such as hard or inappropriate floor surfaces, or room temperature or ventilation issues (see chapter 1 for more details). Adaptations here might include wearing protective footwear or avoiding actions that involve lying or rolling on the floor for the former, and wearing or removing layers as well as monitoring duration of rest phases or pauses within the session for the latter.

COMMON QUESTIONS

The following questions, frequently raised by both dancers and dance leaders, warrant response to clarify any remaining misunderstandings regarding the application of warm-up and cool-down principles.

Q - *Who is responsible for ensuring that a warm-up or cool-down takes place?*

A - This is an important question. The answer varies depending on the age and level of engagement of group. For example, a recreational dance class should include a warm-up and cool-down within the session time, but dancers in vocational training and professional dancers should be mature and responsible enough to complete their own. Ultimately, the dance leader is always responsible, either in leading the warm-up and cool-down for the group, or educating the group on how to warm

up and cool down on their own before and after the dance session. Of course, time and space should be provided for this to occur. Directors of companies and dance institutions should factor this into the daily schedule. The freelance dance teacher can find this balance a difficult one to get right, since space and time is always of a premium. However, warming up and cooling down are two of the most basic measures for safe dance practice, and their effects should not be underestimated. It is the dance leader's responsibility to lead by example. Therefore an effective warm-up and cool-down should be an integral part of every dance session, as well as the dance leader's personal preparation. Guidelines for structuring a dance session effectively to incorporate relevant aspects of warming-up and cooling-down are offered in chapter 6.

It is difficult to meet the needs of every individual, so leaders can encourage dancers who are more aware of their own body's needs to prepare and recover on their own. Dancers creating an individual warm-up and cool-down should adhere to the general recommendations within this chapter, including any adaptations that suit their personal needs, such as focusing on particular areas of tightness or giving additional time and attention to areas that have been prone to injury in the past. Hypermobile dancers, for example, should focus on proprioceptive elements of the warm-up. They will need to pay additional attention to strength and control excessive stretching. Combining personal needs with an awareness of the specific needs of the dance style is also important. Dance teachers should ensure personal time to warm up and cool down their own bodies and minds.

Q - *Is there anything I should avoid in the warm-up?*

A - It is difficult to rule specific movements out completely, since almost anything is possible if the appropriate physical precautions are considered. However, maximum-range head and neck rolls should never be conducted in the warm-up. Gentle neck mobility can take place if essential to the movement later in the sessions. The group should adhere to the following requirements: The pace should be slow and controlled, and the group should have sufficient strength and body awareness to manage this pace; the head should not be allowed to flop backwards and down onto the cervical spine (neck) during the backwards section of the roll;

and lateral (side to side) tilts and forward flexion motions should precede any head and neck rolls. This preparation should be included only if the head and neck will definitely be engaged in this motion during the session; otherwise, it is not an essential joint mobility action. Lateral tilts, rotations (looking right and left) and forward flexion that returns to an upright or slightly extended position will sufficiently warm up the neck area for general movements in this area. For more contraindicated positions that require careful consideration in session preparation and planning, see chapter 6.

Maximal or close to maximal power activities, such as jumping, should not be included in the warm-up. This type of action can have the opposite effect to what is intended in a warm-up and induce muscular fatigue or a shortening of the muscle fibres, which can reduce potential for the upcoming dance session rather than optimise it. Easy transference of weight between the feet on the spot or around the space should suffice. Similarly a full aerobic workout is not required, and it is likely to cause fatigue. As noted previously, long-duration (30 seconds or more), deep, passive static stretches should also be avoided. Contraindicated stretch positions are highlighted in chapter 4.

Q - *What is the difference between warm-up and the first few dance exercises?*

A - Dance students and teachers regularly refer to the first few exercises of class as the warm-up. However, these are often technique-specific exercises, and therefore the intention of these exercises is not to provide a general full-body warm-up. Instead they aim to provide technically specific movement patterning in preparation for more complex movement patterning later in the session. The recommendations provided in this chapter are for physiological preparation for dance activity. The technique-specific exercises at the beginning of class would therefore be the segue between the fourth component of the warm-up—the style-specific element — and the beginning section of class (as explained in more detail in chapter 6).

Dancers who are old enough or have sufficient experience and who have been educated on the components of an effective warm-up should complete up to 15 minutes of a general warm-up, following the recommendations previously mentioned, before the beginning of class. In this instance, the dance leader should also complete a personal warm-up before the dance session begins. Where a group are too young or space and time does not allow, the dance teacher should lead at least 10 minutes of generic warm-up before starting style-specific material. Chapter 6 covers how to integrate these principles within the planning of a dance session.

Q - *Is the pulse raiser an aerobic workout?*

A - Quite simply, no, it is not. The pulse raiser intends to increase the internal body temperature by just 1 to 2 degrees Celsius, reaching approximately 50 to 60 percent of maximum heart rate, which is categorised as 'light' or 'fairly light' intensity on a perceived exertion scale. In fact, higher warm-up intensity can have negative implications on performance outcomes, such as power. This is likely due to the effects of fatigue. Generic, whole-body movements that produce the required cardiovascular stimulation do involve a stimulation of the aerobic system; however, you are not aiming to provide aerobic training. If you are leading or attending an aerobics dance class, then you should complete a generic warm-up before commencing the class, and then begin the class with a pulse raiser that gently stimulates the cardiovascular system. Dancers and dance leaders who misinterpret the pulse raiser as an aerobic workout risk overstressing the cardiovascular system, therefore negatively affecting their energy levels and possibly inducing muscular fatigue, both of which can reduce performance capabilities for the subsequent dance session. Movements that are suitable to the pulse raiser section of a warm-up are outlined in the Principles and Components of Warming Up section of this chapter.

Q - *When is it most important to warm up or cool down?*

A - It is most important to warm up before any dance session, be that a class, rehearsal or performance. Similarly it is important to cool down after any dance session. Where multiple dance sessions take place in one day, such as in vocational dance training, then the warm-up before the first class of the day should be the most comprehensive, as should the cool-down following the last class of the day. In between classes the focus should be on the necessary stylistic transitions required of the different dance styles. For example, transitioning from a ballet to a contemporary technique class with just a 15-minute break in between does not require a comprehensive cool-down and then another warm-up. Instead dancers should focus on doing a brief cool-down from the ballet class, counteracting any joint or muscular tension that might have developed through repetitive or unfamiliar movement material, but avoiding deep and prolonged static stretches, since these would be detrimental to the performance needs of the upcoming contemporary class. Fast stretching is beneficial in this instance. They could follow this with a brief warm-up for the contemporary class, which would not require the pulse raiser, joint mobility or muscle lengthening sections, since they would already be primed from the previous class. Instead they should focus mainly on the fourth component of warm-up: the style-specific needs. Therefore the warm-up for a contemporary class that follows directly after a ballet class might involve actions that support a transition towards becoming more grounded, such as gentle floor work. Similar guidance can be transferred to a multiple performance bill, where each piece requires different physiological demands. The initial warm-up should be the most comprehensive; thereafter the preparation is transitional.

No more than 15 minutes should pass between completion of a warm-up and the beginning of the dance activity. When multiple dance sessions take place in one day, if there is a period longer than 30 minutes where no dancing takes place, such as lunch time, then dancers should repeat a more thorough warm-up before commencing dance activity again. Timing of warm-up and cool-down can become more of an issue during periods of rehearsals, or in choreographic classes, because any warm-up conducted prior to the session commencing can be negated due to the duration and intensity of activity often being sporadic in these situations. Similarly the stop–start nature of leading a dance session is also difficult. Wearing layers can be helpful in retaining the benefits of an effective warm-up. Leaders can try to remain physically active at low intensities throughout the duration of the session and refrain from stopping activity for a time longer than 15 minutes.

Q - *What about including other aspects, such as proprioception or strength, in the warm-up?*

A - Proprioception elements are useful to include in the warm-up, as are some strength elements. These would fall within the fourth component of the warm-up—the style-specific section. Proprioceptive elements could include conducting gentle movements with the eyes closed allowing a fine-tuning of the inner receptive senses, or body rubbing, where the hands are rubbed on the body's surface with reasonable vigour to heighten sensitisation. In relation to the inclusion of strength elements a careful consideration of the needs of the upcoming dance session is warranted. For example, a pole dancer would want to include actions that gently engage the core and also the upper body and adductors (inner thigh muscles), and perhaps practise relatively easy inversions using the floor instead of the pole. The ballet couple preparing for a *pas de deux* class should also include gentle, personal strength preparation exercises such as press-ups against the wall for arms and short-duration (seconds rather than minutes) plank positions for core. Remember that the intention of a warm-up is to prepare the body for the needs of the upcoming activity, not to train the body. Therefore specific exercises for training proprioception and muscular strength should take place at another time within the class or within a supplementary training session (see chapter 4 and 6 for more on these areas).

Interestingly, one study (Subasi, Gelecek, & Aksakoglu, 2008) examining the effect of different durations of a combined active and static stretching warm-up on subsequent proprioception and balance noted that the longer duration warm-ups (10 minutes, as opposed to 5 minutes, of aerobic stimulation and stretching) resulted in greater benefits in lower-limb proprioception, even though the warm-up protocols did not specifically target proprioception. Other studies examining the effects of warm-up on strength components noted that long-duration static stretching can have a negative effect on subsequent strength requirements, but that short-duration stretching, when combined with prior aerobic activity and followed by dynamic activity-specific actions, can have positive effects on subsequent strength performance.

Q - *I include yoga or Pilates exercises in my warm-up. Does this count?*

A - Yoga and Pilates exercises, along with any other exercises from somatic practices, or rehabilitation exercises that a health practitioner has recommended, can be included. However, dancers should adapt the order and intensity of the exercises as necessary and with consideration for the recommendations outlined in this chapter. Ideally such exercises would fall within the activity-specific section. Dancers often like to start their warm-up with a few yoga sun salutations, but this might not be appropriate. Walking a few laps of the studio while taking deep inhalations through the nose can fulfil the pulse raiser phase of the warm-up requirements, and this should be done before commencing sun salutations. The first salutation should be gentle and adapted to ensure that maximal muscle length is not reached on the first repetition, and each subsequent repetition should build gradually on the previous one. Again, remember that this is not a yoga session, but a preparation for a dance session, so the needs and intentions are different. Ideally such exercises would not take place until the activity-specific section of the warm-up.

Q - *The outside temperature is baking hot! Do I still need to warm up?*

A - Being warm due to external temperature is different to stimulating the internal physiological and neurological processes necessary for safely preparing for dance activity. Needless to say, on a warm day or in a warm studio, it will take less to successfully activate these systems and increase the internal temperature; therefore intensity and duration can be adapted. Moments allowing for hydration should be encouraged during the dance session, and rehydration should be prioritised after the session. Exposing areas of skin, such as arms and legs, will allow sweat to evaporate and will support a safe maintenance of temperature.

In contrast, a very cold day or a cold studio will require a more gradual and prolonged increase in intensity and duration to ensure an effective warm-up. Having multiple clothing layers will support achieving and maintaining the increased internal body temperature. On very cold days or in very cold studios, dancers must not do a cool-down that allows the body to suddenly drop in temperature. Instead, they should do a full cool-down, gradually decreasing pulse rate and adding clothing layers.

Q - *I take a cold shower. That works as a cool-down, doesn't it?*

A - In short, no, it does not. It is true that cold therapy (cryotherapy), such as immersing the legs in a cold or ice bath, is beneficial in reducing microswelling and damage in the muscle fibres following intense activity. However, cryotherapy does not support a gradual reduction in pulse rate or an easing of the joints and lengthening of the muscles that a thorough cool-down requires. Therefore dancers can follow a thorough cool-down with a cool shower, but they should not solely rely on the cool shower.

SUMMARY

The general consensus within the dance and exercise literature is that warming up and cooling down optimise performance and decrease injury risk when they include the appropriate intensity, duration and actions. The intentions of warming up, stimulating the body's systems for upcoming activity, and cooling down, providing a counterbalance for the activity just experienced, must be carefully considered so that appropriate general and style-specific choices can be made. Similarly, dance leaders should understand and apply updated guidelines on stretching. Sustained or long-duration stretches should be avoided before and during the dance session. After the dance session, the muscles and connective tissues are at their warmest. Therefore longer duration, deeper stretches are appropriate at this stage. Personal needs, such as attending to previously injured areas, should also be addressed within an effective warm-up and cool-down.

- A warm-up intends to gradually prepare the body's systems for subsequent activity, be that a class, rehearsal, competition or performance.
- A warm-up should include the following elements: pulse raiser, joint mobilisation, muscle lengthening and style-specific needs.
- Cardiovascular stimulation (e.g., pulse raiser) should not be confused with an aerobic workout.
- A warm-up should ideally last 15 to 20 minutes, with up to 5 minutes dedicated to each section.
- Appropriate stretching modes for a warm-up are dynamic stretching and/or brief static stretching.
- A cool-down intends to gradually restore the body to its balanced state following activity, be that a class, rehearsal, competition or performance.
- A cool-down should include the following elements: pulse reducer, joint easing and stretching the muscles.
- A cool-down should ideally last 15 to 20 minutes, with approximately 5 minutes dedicated to each section.
- Appropriate stretching modes for a cool-down are long-duration (approximately 1 minute) active-static stretching, PNF stretching and fast stretching.
- General components of warm-up and cool-down should be adapted to the specific needs of the dance style, the participating group and any environmental constraints.
- A break of more than 15 minutes between warm-up and activity will require an additional warm-up.
- It is ultimately the responsibility of dance leaders to either lead a warm-up and cool-down or support their participating group in understanding how and why to conduct these elements independently.
- Dance school and company managers and directors should ensure time and space in schedules and venues for warm-up and cool-down as standard practice before and after classes, rehearsals, competitions, auditions and performances.

chapter 4

Training Principles
and Supplementary Fitness

≡ Learning Objectives

After reading this chapter you should be able to do the following:

- Understand the principles of effective training.
- Apply training principles to improve dance performance and reduce injury potential.
- Advise dancers appropriately on supplementary activities that can provide additional physical conditioning.

≡ Key Terms

aerobic

anaerobic

balance

ballistic stretch

cardiorespiratory fitness

fast glycolytic system

FITTE (frequency, intensity, time, type and enjoyment)

individuality

muscular endurance

muscle strength

muscle power

muscle flexibility and joint mobility (MFJM)

overload

proprioception

rest

reversibility

specificity

stability

The physical demands placed on dancers by choreographers make physical fitness arguably as important as skill development, yet research states that dancers are not as aerobically fit as athletes in a similar physically demanding field (Twitchett, Nevill, Angioi, Koutedakis, & Wyon, 2011). If dancers are not fit enough to manage choreographic demands and workloads, they are more likely to suffer with fatigue and injury. It can also be suggested that improved physical fitness could support better dancing from both a physiological and an aesthetic point of view (Angioi, Metsios, Twitchett, Koutedakis, & Wyon 2009). The dance profession generates both physical and psychological demands that place an incredible amount of stress on the body. If not managed effectively, this stress can result in negative effects. If dancers are not physically or emotionally stable or strong enough to deal with these demands placed on them, decrement to performance or, in the worst case, injury is likely to occur, leading to short- or long-term damage. On the other hand, understanding and carefully managing these demands can positively influence performance, injury rates, longevity in dance and overall well-being.

There is a substantial difference between using dance as a recreational activity to increase fitness and using fitness to improve dance performance and help reduce risk of injury. Fitness is a state of health and well-being that helps us to achieve physical tasks, in the case of this chapter, the ability to dance effectively. In dance training, a common question is 'Isn't the dancers' training timetable enough to keep them fit?' The response is 'fit for what?' A dancer's training will provide the body with a lot of day-to-day repetition in order to improve skills, but in terms of physical training, similar activities that do not alter in demand will inevitably cause a plateau in fitness levels. Dancers need to incorporate change in the form of fitness and conditioning in order to improve their physical capabilities. This will help them achieve the demands of choreography at the intensity required of performance, without experiencing undue levels of fatigue that could increase likelihood of injury or cause a deterioration of the standard of artistry.

Some researchers have advocated supplementary sessions to take care of the dancer's broader conditioning needs. They suggest that the intent of a dance class is to develop the style-specific vocabulary and skills, which does not leave adequate time for the effective development of fitness parameters (Grossman & Wilmerding, 2000; Koutedakis & Jamurtas, 2004). Others surmise that elements of fitness could be incorporated into the dance class (Krasnow, 1997; Redding & Wyon, 2003). This advice has led dance teachers to investigate how to translate fitness into their sessions. If dance leaders include conditioning activities in the dance session, they must appreciate the physiological intentions of activities. For example, some leaders promote a cardio section in their warm-up, including vigorous activity and high-impact movement. This is a result of a misunderstanding of the pulse-raising recommendations (explained in chapter 3) as well as a misinterpretation of training principles, since excessive activity in warm-up unduly fatigues dancers, and cardiorespiratory improvements will only be gained with continuous moderate activity for 20 to 30 minutes.

With a key focus on the professional dancer and the dancer training for a performance career, this chapter explains the physiology behind improving fitness levels and suggests ways that dancers can make improvements. The general training and fitness principles addressed are pertinent to dancers of all genres.

COMPONENTS OF PHYSICAL FITNESS FOR DANCERS

The different components of physical activity are **cardiorespiratory fitness**, **muscle strength and muscle power**, **muscle flexibility and joint mobility (MFJM)**, **balance**, **stability**, **proprioception** and **rest**. All the components of fitness are inter-related, as seen in figure 4.1, and dancers should strive to achieve a balance of each one within their training.

Cardiorespiratory Fitness

For many dance genres, dance is classified as high-intensity intermittent exercise (Wyon, 2005). Usually the dance class or rehearsal has a start-stop nature so that dancers can incorporate the feedback and observation needed for skill acquisition and stylistic improvements. In fact, 85 percent of the technique class is not undertaken at the cardiorespiratory level required to match that of performance (Hamilton, 2009). This type of practice therefore will not stress the cardiorespiratory system for long enough to target **aerobic** fitness or to physiologically prepare the dancer for longer duration performances that utilise both the aerobic and glycolytic (**anaerobic**) energy production systems.

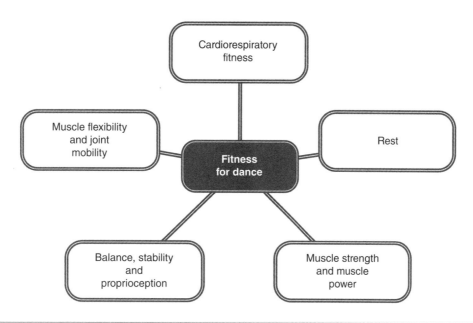

Figure 4.1 Components of fitness for dance.

Aerobic fitness is relatively low intensity compared to its anaerobic counterpart; therefore dancers can perform aerobic activity for a longer duration. Aerobic fitness is a key factor in dancing through full-length performances. Otherwise known as cardiorespiratory endurance, aerobic fitness relies on the heart and lungs to take in the required amounts of oxygen, which then travels to the larger muscle groups, allowing the dancer to perform for a greater length of time. The ability to keep going without suffering the negative effects of fatigue is just one of the positive effects of improved aerobic capacity. The professional dancer would often need to be able to do this in performance six to eight times a week for a full season at elite level. If dancers find that they struggle and become fatigued, their standard of performance may suffer. Fatigued dancers are more likely to sustain an injury than those who are more aerobically capable. Research has found a correlation between low levels of aerobic fitness and injury (Twitchett et al., 2010).

Another component of cardiorespiratory fitness is the **fast glycolytic system**, known by many as the *anaerobic system*. Generally in dance the aerobic system is principally working; however, when there are short burst of high-intensity activity resulting in a sudden increase in work rate, the anaerobic system will dominate. Both systems will be working at any one time, but it is the extent of which energy system is working at any given time that defines the difference in aerobic or anaerobic activity. 'Steady-state maximal exercise lasting more than 4 minutes at a time sees the aerobic system largely dominating in the provision of energy' (Wyon, 2005, p. 8), whereas short bursts of sudden high-intensity activity that can only be performed for a few seconds at a time require the anaerobic system to work at a greater ratio.

The human body is made up of both fast- and slow-twitch muscle fibres. Generally the slow-twitch muscle fibres predominantly work during aerobic activity, whereas the fast-twitch muscle fibres are recruited for anaerobic bursts. Every one of us has both fast- and slow-twitch fibres, the amount of which varies from person to person. Although we can cannot change the amount of muscle fibres we have they can be trained to improve their aerobic or anaerobic performance. Dancers should develop their aerobic foundation before progressing to training at anaerobic intensities or for muscle power (Wyon, 2005). This is because successful progression and development requires a gradual increase in intensity of training.

Improving Aerobic Capacity and Anaerobic Fitness

To train for aerobic fitness, dancers need to increase their lung capacity, which will allow them to take in more oxygen as the heart rate increases and to continue to work at an increased level. Dancers should engage in vigorous activity, enough to become short of breath and raise the heart rate to 70 to 90 percent of their maximal heart rate, for a duration of 20 to 40 minutes (Wyon, 2005). A simple and commonly used method of estimating maximal heart rate is the equation of 220 bpm (beats per minute) minus the dancer's age. This is called age-predicted heart rate maximum (AHRmax; also explained in chapter 3).

Dancers can achieve improvements in many ways, either using dance-specific exercise to improve aerobic capacity to support their dance performance, as recommended in recent research (Rodrigues-Krause et al., 2014), or with complementary fitness, which can support health, fitness and well-being overall. Both will benefit the dancer, and a combination of the two could be advised due to the general variation in dance choreography and stylistic demands. Popularised dance-specific workouts could include classes such as Zumba or aerobics, which use continuous dance moves over a period of time in order to improve fitness elements. The sense of familiarity of learning and repeating dance moves can be enjoyable for the dancer. A more technique-specific circuit could include dance activities like rolls to the floor and various types of jumps, depending on the dance style. Complementary exercise could include swimming, a good aerobic exercise that does not

Sample Calculation of Heart Rate Maximum

A 20-year-old dancer will have an AHRmax of 220 bpm – 20 (years old) = 200 bpm. To work out what heart rate represents 70 to 90% of that AHRmax, follow the formula below:

$$200 \text{ bpm} \times 0.7 \ (70\%) = 140 \text{ bpm}$$

$$200 \text{ bpm} \times 0.9 \ (90\%) = 180 \text{ bpm}$$

To train their aerobic system, 20-year-old dancers need to work their heart rate at between 140 and 180 bpm for approximately 20 to 40 minutes.

put pressure on the joints. However, the movement and stride of swimming is quite different to that of dance; therefore it may not actually help dancers' aerobic ability for their profession, but it will promote general health, fitness, well-being and relaxation. Running or jogging may be more suitable due to the dancer's upright posture travelling across and on or off stage; however, the implications of the increased repetitious impact on the joints needs to be considered. Appropriate footwear and some advice from a running expert would be beneficial. If receiving advice when participating in a fitness class, dancers should always make sure that the instructor has the appropriate qualifications, skills and expertise to give instructions for safe exercises. Other exercise could include using gym equipment such as a cross-trainer or rowing machine, which not only train aerobic fitness, but use muscle groups from both the upper and lower body simultaneously.

Once an aerobic foundation has been achieved, dancers can then look to anaerobic training. Interval training is recommended. First, the dancer trains at a high intensity (not maximum) for 3 to 6 minutes at a time, then has an active rest period (training at a lower intensity) before performing for another 3 to 6 minutes (Wyon, 2005). At this stage of training, the rest period should be the same duration as the exercise period. This is particularly useful for dancers who usually perform routines that are just 3 to 6 minutes duration at a time, which is common for dancers who perform in high-energy commercial or street dance routines.

Following this, interval training at a higher intensity, sometimes known as HIIT training (high-intensity interval training) can be introduced. This type of training, which is more likely to train the anaerobic system, is performed at maximal intensity for up to 30 seconds at a time. It is necessary to raise the heart rate substantially in a short space of time. It is suggested that dancers work at 90 to 95 percent of maximum heart rate, or higher, to stress the anaerobic system (Wyon, 2005). If heart rates cannot easily be monitored, using the Borg scale (1982) to measure rate of perceived exertion (RPE) can provide an indication of workload intensities. This system uses a scale from 6 to 20 for adults, with 6 measuring 'no feeling of exertion', 11 to 14 as 'fairly light' to 'somewhat hard', and 20 as 'very very hard'. A children's version can also be used with a scale of 1 to 10. When working aerobically, the dancer may describe the intensity as 'somewhat hard', but when working anaerobically, they may describe

it as 'hard' to 'very very hard'. HIIT training has become increasingly popular in the commercial fitness industry under many titles such as Tabata training, Insanity training and Metafit. This type of training is used as quick exercise, which is said to produce fast results for training the heart and lungs and for speeding up metabolism for a short time. In dance, this type of training helps dancers improve their ability to adapt to fast transitions, jumps and other explosive movements. A small circuit of high-intensity exercises like jumps or burpees (each performed for 20 to 30 seconds with a rest period of approximately 10 seconds in between) will train the fast glycolytic system if the dancer works with maximal effort. Dancers must stay active during rest periods between exercise bouts, but at a lower intensity than that of the exercises. This practice promotes recovery and prevents sudden drops in blood pressure, which can cause dizziness and further build-up of the lactic acid that causes muscle soreness (Wyon, 2005).

Muscle Strength and Muscle Power

Decades of research support the fact that muscle strength and muscle power are necessary for successfully performing sustained dance activity as well as explosive movements like jumps and lifts (Kirkendall & Calabrese, 1983), and reinforce the belief that strength training is beneficial for dancers (Kozai, 2012). Strength and power are distinctively different from one another, but they

Sample Circuit

Perform twice for a 4-minute anaerobic training programme:

20 seconds of burpees

10 seconds rest

20 seconds of rolling on the floor and jumping up

10 seconds rest

20 seconds of tuck jumps

10 seconds rest

20 seconds of power lunges/scissor jumps

10 seconds rest

Dancers can complement their anaerobic fitness by taking part in high-intensity fitness classes outside of their regular training.

are of equal importance to the dancer. Muscle strength has been defined as the maximum force that can be exerted in a single voluntary contraction (Koutedakis & Sharp, 1999). In dance terms, muscle strength is needed to lift partners and hold body parts in space, such as in a *développé à la seconde* in ballet. Muscle power is the ability to apply explosive force with strength, used substantially when performing jumping and travelling sequences or when pushing off the hands in acrobatic or floor routines.

As well as supporting performance ability, the importance of maintaining adequate muscle strength for the prevention of injuries cannot be overstated (Howse & McCormick, 2009). Research shows that low **muscular endurance** is associated with increased injury risk (Ambegaonkar, Caswell, Winchester, Caswell, & Andre, 2012), and that strength training can decrease injury and pain in dancers (Kline, Krauss, Maher, & Qu 2013). Strength training is also known to increase bone health and help in the prevention of osteoporosis in female athletes and dancers (Rafferty, 2010).

Despite this positive research, there seems to be a misconception that training muscle strength will result in muscle bulk and a reduction in flexibility. On the contrary, research data on both male and female dancers demonstrates 'that supplemental strength training can lead to better dancing and reduced incidents of dance injuries without interfering with key artistic and aesthetic requirements' (Koutedakis, 2005. p. 6).

Improving Muscle Strength

Dancers can improve muscle strength in many ways. The first is to use weights and resistance machines, usually found in gyms. Resistance machines help users focus on specific muscle groups by holding the rest of the body in a static position and therefore isolating the required muscles to do the work. If the rest of the body is held in a stable static position, technique is often controlled in a safe way. Another benefit of this type of training is that a trained instructor is often present who can advise dancers which machines to use and how to use them. With a specific aim

Sit-Up Exercises for Dancers

Aim for full flexion of the whole spine with the legs bent as it will engage the abdominals through their full range of motion, rather than lifting (or simply pulling) the upper back off the floor with the hands behind the neck. Maintain a scooped C-shape by sequentially flexing the spine and rounding forward to avoid stressing the hip flexors, and target the abdominal muscles with the desired overload for strength and endurance improvements (Clippinger, 2016; see figure 4.2).

Figure 4.2 Correct sit-up technique.

in mind, the instructor should be able to produce a targeted training programme. In this scenario, dancers must be aware that the instructor will probably not be a specialist in training strength for dance; rather, instructors will most likely work with the general public to improve overall health, lose weight or train to develop their physique. For example, exercises to improve abdominal strength for dancer may differ from the usual crunches used in sports training.

If dancers work with a trainer at a gym to support their strength training, they need to make their targets clear to the person they are taking advice from. In a studio environment, dancers can use their own body weight, performing exercises like press-ups, sit-ups, deep pliés (also see cautionary advice in chapter 6) and planks, or can carefully use a partner for resistance when performing weight-bearing exercises.

Some dancers may have access to free weights, which are provided by some dance companies or institutions. They can also use resistance bands to focus on strength training (see figure 4.3; Franklin, 2012). Training muscle strength will not reduce

flexibility if dancers perform recovery stretches after the workout to prevent shortening of the muscles.

Improving Muscle Power

Plyometric training, otherwise known as jump training, has been used for decades in sport, and it is now steadily being used in dance. Research advocates that plyometrics can increase both leg strength and power that are vital for dance performance (Brown, Wells, Schade, Smith, & Fehling, 2007). This same research has demonstrated that for substantial increases in muscle power, dancers need to take part in plyometric training only twice a week for six weeks. The Harkness Center for Dance Injuries in New York promotes plyometric training for dancers for a number of reasons, including reduction of injury, increased jump height and increases in muscle strength and power (Hewitt, Stroup, Nance, & Noyes, 1996; Harley, St. Clair Gibson, & Harley, Lambert, Vaughan & Noakes 2002).

Plyometric training is a form of high intensity exercise, therefore a dancer's readiness should be assessed. Apart from having a good aerobic foundation, adequate leg strength, and ability to perform jumps with correct technique and alignment, balance and proprioception need to be considered for safe practice. At a minimum, the dancer should be able to stand on one leg for 30 seconds with their eyes closed or for one minute with the eyes open. The dancer should also be able to perform a demi plié on one leg while maintaining appropriate alignment of the hip, knee and ankle. Both exercises should be competently achieved on each leg prior to commencing plyometric training. The airplane test, (described in chapter

Figure 4.3 Biceps curl with resistance band.

Plyometric Training

When the dancer has been assessed for their readiness for plyometric training, to practise the techniques, dancers should jump as high as they can, continuously for 20 seconds, then after a short recovery break, try a different type of jump for another 20 seconds. For example, dancers may choose to start with tuck jumps followed by power lunges, otherwise known as scissor jumps. After several weeks, dancers could then progress to more dance-specific jumps, such as *sautés* in first position and then *changement* or *pas de chat*. Over time the duration could be increased to 30 seconds or the type of jump could be made more technically advanced. A 6-week training plan should result in positive adaptation in jump power and height; however, plyometric training must be approached gradually and systematically to be performed safely with positive results.

10 – Assessments for Gauging Pointe Readiness) is another suitable exercise for considering readiness for plyometric training.

When muscular fatigue does start to take effect, correct alignment and technique can suffer, which must be observed and corrected (see chapter 2 for more information on safe alignment). Muscle power could also be trained in the upper body, particularly for those dancers who practise a great amount of lifts, floor work and acrobatic-type movements. Injury rates appear to be higher for breakdancers than for dancers in other styles, especially in the upper body (Bronner & Ojofeitimi, 2010). See chapter 9 for more details on injury patterns. To effectively improve upper body muscle power for performance and to reduce injury occurrence, dancers should gain strength first, for example, starting with exercises like press-ups against a wall, progressing to a modified (on the knees) position and then advancing to full press-ups on the floor. When substantial strength is achieved, they could then develop this exercise into travelling press-ups (move from side to side while pressing up) and then to jumping press-ups to develop muscle power. Correct technique and alignment must be sustained. Appropriate footwear with cushioning for shock absorption is a

necessity for all lower body plyometric training. An comprehensive warm-up and cool-down must always be performed (see chapter 3) for safe and effective training.

Muscle Flexibility and Joint Mobility (MFJM)

Muscle flexibility is crucial for complementing muscular strength, building efficiency in movement and co-ordination, and preventing injuries (Irvine, Redding, Rafferty, & IADMS, 2011). Without adequate flexibility, dancers are unlikely to raise themselves to professional standards (Deighan, 2005). It is clear then why some dancers might try to force their flexibility and range of motion (ROM) in excess of safe limits, but this practice is worrisome. When muscle is pushed beyond its normal active limits, a muscle or tendon with inadequate elasticity is at a higher risk of injury (Clippinger-Robertson, 1990). Tight muscles can also lead to compensation of another body part, causing malalignment and incorrect technique (see chapter 2). For example, tightness in the calf muscles (gastrocnemius and soleus) can cause pronation of the foot, which could result in tension of the knee during knee bends. Apart from muscle tightness, ROM beyond that of the average person is desired for many dance forms, and it is sometimes a prerequisite for success. ROM is a term that denotes the musculoskeletal articulation available at a given joint; therefore it relates to both the joint structure and the soft tissues (such as tendons, ligaments and muscles) that interact at the joint. Increasing range of motion is often a key ambition for the dancer, yet how to do this is often misunderstood.

Of the factors that limit range of motion, only 10% are muscular related; 85% are joint related, which is mostly hereditary, and the remaining 5% are due to other factors such as age, sex, and environmental temperature (Deighan 2005).

If a dancer has a joint restriction, range of motion will be limited by the joint structure rather than by the stretchiness of the muscle fibres; however, we can never be completely sure that we have reached our full joint potential. Therefore dancers will continue to work on the 10 percent of muscle flexibility available for improvement.

Improving Flexibility

To increase flexibility dancers must stretch; however, how and when they stretch will determine the results. There are multiple modes of stretching, and choosing which mode to pursue requires due consideration. Ask yourself, what is the purpose of my stretch? Are you about to perform sustained movements that require extensive flexibility and ROM? Are you about to bound across the floor in a series of high energy jumps? Have you just finished class, and are feeling tight in the muscles that have been repeatedly worked? Or are you aiming to improve your flexibility longer term? Each of these situations presents a different reason for stretching, and therefore will require a different mode of stretch. Broadly categorised, the two types of stretching are active (self-activated by muscle engagement, without external assistance) and passive (externally assisted). Active stretching is when dancers do the stretch by themselves, whereas passive stretching is when dancers use a partner, gravity or an external aid to facilitate the stretch. For example, consider stretching the hamstring muscle group by assuming the position sitting on the floor with one leg outstretched and the other leg flexed at the knee with the sole of the foot placed against the inside of the outstretched leg. This stretch is passive when the dancer simply relaxes over the outstretched leg and allows gravity to facilitate the stretch, therefore using little if any muscular effort in the hamstring to complete the stretch. The same stretch can be made active by purposefully engaging the quadriceps and focusing on a lengthening of the hamstring muscle group while actively moving the torso towards the limb.

Stretches can also be categorised under the following four methods:

• *Static stretching.* The static stretch is held in a still position. This is considered the safest type of stretch if the placement is correct, and it is one of the most likely modes for achieving long-term flexibility improvement. This stretch mode should only be performed when the muscles are warm; therefore it is mostly included after dance sessions (see the section Stretching the Muscles in chapter 3). As noted in chapter 3, if used within the warm-up, static stretches should be held for a maximum of 10 seconds. Any longer than this could reduce strength and power capabilities needed for the dance session. Longer duration static stretches can however be used effectively during cool-down to prevent sore muscles, as well as to target an increase in muscle flexibility.

If a muscle is stretched too much too quickly, the stretch reflex mechanism is instigated. When this happens the muscle spindles (sensory receptors) within the stretched muscle are stimulated by the sudden force. As a protective reaction, they cause the muscle to shorten and therefore tighten. This tightening is a warning sign that the stretch must be eased to prevent further damage to the muscle itself or the tendon (McAtee & Charland, 2013). It has been suggested that if a muscle shakes or spasms when being stretched, this is also a sign that the stretch is too intense (Wyon, 2010b), and must immediately be eased.

• *Dynamic stretching.* Dynamic stretching is performed while moving, usually as part of the warm-up (as explained in chapter 3) in order to gradually increase range of motion for the following dance activity. Range of motion should start small and progressively get bigger until full range of motion is achieved. Prior to dynamic stretching the heart rate needs to be gradually elevated to ensure increased blood flow to the working muscles and increased lubrication of the joints. Only then should dynamic stretching be used more intentionally to prepare for the upcoming dance activities. Due to its constant use of movement, dynamic stretching will also help maintain body temperature, supporting pliability of the muscles; however, it is not known for producing long-term gains in flexibility. For more information on dynamic stretching within the warm-up, see chapter 3.

• *Ballistic stretching.* **Ballistic stretching** involves a bouncing momentum. In this type of stretch, the end position is not held like in a static stretch, and the bouncing action involves greater speed and power than dynamic stretching. In the past ballistic stretching was practised as a powerful tool for increasing muscle length, yet we now know that this type of stretching is potentially dangerous if the muscles are not absolutely prepared, and it should be avoided when working with less experienced dancers. When the muscle and its surrounding tissues are rapidly stretched they are not given adequate time to adapt; therefore the muscle does not have time to safely relax into a lengthened state. This type of stretching can have immediate benefits for performing explosive actions such as high leg kicks or jumping, since it activates the stretch-shortening cycle (SSC). The SSC is activated when a muscle is contracted eccentrically (lengthened) immediately before contracting concentrically (shortened) to produce an explosive movement, for example, a plié before a jump (Critchfield & IADMS, 2011). However, long-term stretch gains have not been evidenced. Ballistic stretching remains one of the riskier modes of stretching due to its potential to cause muscle or tendon strain, since repeatedly bouncing into a muscle will not lengthen the muscle, but rather stimulate the firing of muscle spindles, causing it to tighten through the myotatic stretch reflex (Howse, & McCormack, 2009). It is therefore recommended that repetitive ballistic stretches are avoided, even though many dance moves are ballistic in nature.

• *Proprioceptive neuromuscular facilitation (PNF).* PNF stretching is the most effective type of stretch for increasing muscular length, and it has also been found to increase muscle strength (Deighan, 2005); however, it can be injurious if not performed correctly. PNF stretching involves a contract–relax stretch. Its focus is to produce an isometric contraction prior to the stretch to result in greater subsequent gains. This type of stretch has been shown to produce improvements in ROM and athletic performance when carried out post activity, but has decrements to maximal effort performances if carried out prior to activity (Hindle, Whitcomb, Briggs, & Hong, 2012).

PNF stretches must only be performed with experienced individuals, and the muscles must be fully warmed up and prepared for this activity. Some literature states that it should only be performed with a medical professional (Critchfield & IADMS, 2011), reinforcing that this type of stretch should never be performed on vulnerable bodies, for example, the muscles and tendinous units of adolescent students may be tighter than normal if they are experiencing growth spurts (see chapter 10). Additional information and an example of PNF stretching can be found in chapter 3.

Although dynamic stretching can be performed within the warm-up component of a dance session, long-duration static, ballistic (if at all) and PNF stretching should only be performed when fully warm. If dancers stretch occasionally (once a week, for example), their flexibility gains are more likely to last only for the short term, possibly even just a few minutes. If dancers were to undertake a multiweek stretch programme where they stretch regularly (a minimum of three times a week), the flexibility gains will last for much longer (Critchfield & IADMS, 2011). As with all training, rest and recovery periods must be included to avoid overstretching and therefore damaging the

muscle tissue. Correct technique and alignment are vital (see chapter 2), and some dancers may be tempted to cheat their stretches to make it appear that they are more flexible. Helping dancers to recognise good alignment in stretching will help them avoid injuries.

> *All stretches should be performed without pain in order to gain maximum benefits. If dancers experience pain, they will simply not be able to relax, which will cause muscles to tighten and not lengthen.*

Flexibility varies from one day to another, as it does from one person to another; therefore dancers must learn not to compare their flexibility with that of others, but to believe in the benefits of stretching long term on their health, mobility and performance. It is important to note that children often have a great range of flexibility until the ages of 11 to 15 when they experience the adolescent growth spurts. During this time flexibility training should not be pushed because the bones grow more rapidly than the muscular tissues; therefore the muscles, tendons and ligaments simply need to time to catch up. Any forcing of flexibility during this vulnerable time is likely to cause damage rather than positive progression. Instead it is advised that the session leader educate young dancers about growth spurts and explain that this sudden loss of flexibility is only short term. This is explained in greater detail in chapter 10. On the other end of the spectrum, as dancers reach an older age, they will also lose a degree of flexibility, which can increase risk of injury. The hypermobile dancer will also need to stretch, but with even greater care, and to ensure safe practice they will need to focus on strengthening specific muscles (hypermobility is addressed in chapter 2). These elements must be taken into account whether working with the professional dancer, the dance student in regular training, or the community dancer taking part in dance as a recreational activity.

Contraindicated Stretches

Some stretches may not have positive benefits. Even though they will lengthen specific muscles, they can also compromise alignment, bringing their effectiveness into question. Common contraindicated stretches include the hurdle or hero stretch, which involves lying on the back with either one or both knees fully flexed under the body and the lower legs flaring out to the side. This compresses the knee joint, particularly the medial ligaments, promotes knee instability and increases strain on the lower back if the dancer also lies back on the floor (Alter, 2004; Berardi, 2005; Heyward & Gibson, 2014; Kassing & Jay, 2003). The negative effects can be reduced if the body weight is evenly distributed on both ischial tuberosities (sitting bones), which is difficult for people with tight hip flexors, and the flexed leg is arranged with the shin parallel with the thigh and the foot pointed, so avoiding internal rotation at the hip (Alter, 2004; Krasnow & Devau, 2011). However, there are much simpler and safer alternatives that stretch the quadriceps and hamstrings such as a standing quadriceps stretch, simply flexing the knee and holding the foot behind you, and the seated hamstring stretch.

The traditional hamstring stretch performed at the barre has also come under scrutiny. Lifting the leg onto the barre and flexing the trunk over it stresses the lower back, and the effect of gravity produces additional pressure on the Achilles tendon. A safer option is to perform the stretch while sitting or lying on the floor (Dunn, 2014; Kassing & Jay, 2003). These are just two examples of stretches that can be detrimental, especially for dancers who are not highly trained.

Balance, Stability and Proprioception

Balance and stability are vital skills that dancers need to successfully maintain equilibrium while moving with grace and accuracy. The two main components to stability are passive stability, which is provided by the tissues surrounding the joints, and dynamic stability, which is provided by the interaction of muscular activity to provide smooth and controlled movements (Phillips, 2005). Because choreography is becoming more demanding, a greater range of flexibility can be expected; therefore muscular stability, both passive and dynamic, and control are paramount. Stability training, unlike strength training, is predominantly about motor learning, learning to use various muscle groups with minimum effort to control the skeleton. Dancers can do this by combining both their core stability training (see chapter 2 for details on core stability) with proprioception training. Proprioception may also be

known as *kinaesthesia* or as the dancers' sixth sense. It refers to the dancer's awareness of their body in space (Batson & IADMS, 2008). The greater dancers' use of proprioception, the greater control they will have over muscular effort and stability, either passive or dynamic, therefore lessening their chance of injury occurrence. When we walk, our body knows where to place the foot; similarly with dance our body knows where we are placing our body parts despite the increased complexity of the movements and positions that we are asking of our body. This knowing is especially honed in more experienced dancers. Dancers manage this because of their inner sense of accuracy, timing and placement, or their use of proprioception.

Proprioception training is not time consuming, and it should be included into the dancer's education or training regime. A range of techniques are available for training dancers' use of proprioception, many of which could easily be incorporated into a dance technique class, for example, motion-to-balance tasks such as running to suddenly balancing on one leg.

> *Dancers should be able to stand on one leg with their eyes closed for at least 30 seconds. This exercise could be included within the dance class at various points. Outside of class this could be advanced by rising on one leg or balancing on an uneven surface like a pillow or a wobble board, with eyes open.*

Other exercises could include positioning work where the dancers work in pairs: One dancer would close their eyes and allow a fellow dancer to move their limbs into positions. Keeping the eyes closed they must then accurately match this position with their second side. Another exercise could be to multitask with the eyes closed, for example, trying to walk in a straight line while counting back from 100 in threes (Batson & IADMS, 2008). As with all training, progression must be gradual. Dancers may find these tasks more challenging than they would have thought to begin with.

TRAINING PRINCIPLES

In order for improvements to be gained in any of the components of fitness mentioned previously, various principles should be taken into account.

These are broken down into four categories: **overload**, **specificity**, **reversibility** and **individuality**.

Overload

Overload can be defined as a positive adaptation to an increase in training load by imposing 'demands on the body or body-parts which are greater than normal' (Kent, 1996, p. 313). The principle states that training stimulus should be progressively increased because if the amount of stress remains constant, then the body will not adapt any further (Kenney, Wilmore & Costill, 2012). Therefore when the dancer trains, it is important that they regularly reach progressive overload for improvements in training to occur. For example, if aiming to increase muscular strength the load that the dancer is working with should gradually increase, stressing the muscles to a point of fatigue, allowing a period of recovery, and then increasing the load next time. Overload is also known as exercise-induced fatigue and should not be confused with the terms overtraining or overwork, which result in a negative response to training (explained further in chapter 5). Any well-designed training programme will need to incorporate the principle of overload, for positive adaptation to occur.

In exercise physiology, the recommendation is that exercise intensity should be at least 60% of maximum to stimulate strength development. For endurance gains, intensities as low as 30% of maximum can be effective but the muscle would need to be exercised to the point of fatigue (increased repetition) (Heyward, 2006). Overload could be achieved if the dancer were to increase the distance on a run, or decrease the time and run faster. Another example is if they were to lift a heavier weight than they managed in a former training session. In a dance specific situation, overload may be experienced when the dancer is performing a greater amount of strenuous jumps than they did the previous week or by holding an intense position for a longer duration than previously accomplished. The experience of overload, although it may feel tiring, will create positive adaptation to training physically when combined with effective recovery, and is likely to have a psychological benefit from the resultant sense of achievement.

Although rest and recovery are substantially covered in chapter 5, they must be addressed here because they are vital components in achieving effective overload. When dancers train for dance or fitness, they will undergo many repetitions of the same actions, which are intended to result in positive training effects. However excessive repetitions without sufficient rest or recovery time, both in between single exercises and between full workouts, will not support positive training effects. On the other hand, sufficient rest allows time for acceleration of muscle regeneration and promotes improvements in physiological functioning. During a workout dancers will need to have short rest periods in between exercises, for either a few seconds or minutes, to allow the body to recover and prepare for the next repetition. The duration of these rest periods may vary depending on the activity. For example, when performing interval training, the shorter the rest period, the more physically challenging the workout will be. However if dancers are spending a longer duration on a certain supplementary exercise, such as on a 30 minute bike ride, they may rest a few minutes rather than for seconds, before continuing with their next exercise. Dancers should always plan rest days into their training schedule to aid recovery and progression.

Specificity

The type of exercise must be specific to meet the aims of the dancer. For example, swimmers training to improve their front crawl would not focus on their diving, just like runners focusing on sprint speed would not practice distances. In dance, if the dancer's target is to improve jump height, a programme focusing on plyometrics, leg strength and core stability would be suitable, rather than an upper body strength programme, which would be more valuable for dancers who work in inverted motions or perform lifts. When preparing for a specific performance, appropriate supplemental training should be considered in order to for the dancers to be able to perform the work with physiological efficiency and minimal risk of injury. For example, if dancers will need to perform aerobically for 90 minutes, using both floor work and lifts, they should be participating in exercise that will train for this specific range of activity.

Reversibility

All training effects are reversible. The saying 'use it or lose it' is based on the training principle of reversibility, when gains are easily diminished or even lost if work is not maintained. If the dancer is to become injured or take time out for another reason, reversibility will inevitably occur. However, the rate of reversibility varies. Generally the longer dancers have been in physical training, the slower the rate of reversibility, and once they are back in training, the quicker they will regain their previous levels of fitness. For the less active individual, the rate of reversibility will be much quicker, and therefore regaining previous fitness levels also takes longer. Although reversibility may be a concern, this should not contradict the benefits of rest periods, which will actually support the dancer long term. Reversibility may occur when there is a decrease in training; however, if dancers are fit and well, they are likely to quickly regain their strength and possibly improve when they return to training after a rest period.

Individuality

Every dancing body is different. This is not simply dependent on age and gender, but on the individual's alignment, posture, physiological make-up, psychological stability and personal training targets. When training a group of dancers it may be difficult to meet each individual's specific needs, but adaptations should be available where possible. One training session may be too challenging for some participants, but may not be challenging enough for others. Therefore whether in fitness training or in the dance technique class, more advanced exercises or alternative options should be offered in order to help dancers reach appropriate levels of overload. This should result in all dancers being able to improve their fitness for performance without the unnecessary risk of injury.

When training for any activity, there are a number of aspects that need to be taken into account for achieving optimum performance and avoiding performance plateau. In order to effectively progress and reach the required overload, the following principles can be considered: frequency, intensity, time, type and enjoyment (FITTE). These terms have been used for decades in sport and can be used within a dance context also whether in a dance class, rehearsal or training for exercise outside of the studio.

Frequency

Frequency is how often the person trains or repeats a certain exercise. For example, dancers may do 15 shuttle runs rather than the 12 they managed the previous week. If they are participating in fitness training once a week, they could

then increase this to two or three times a week in order to continue to challenge themselves and improve. The capacity to do this, however, depends on the demands of their current dance schedule. For example, during an intense season, dancers may need to spend the majority of their training time in class, rehearsal or performance, with rest periods in between. In fact, it may be that the frequency they rehearse on a particular piece of work or dance technique is increased in order to aid progression within that context. However, out of season or during breaks from dancing, dancers may be able to train for fitness three or four times a week. More than this may not be beneficial; in fact, research into the general population suggests that people who exercise every day often give up due to fatigue or injury (Kenny et al., 2012). For the dancer, it is recommended that 'a workout frequency of one to two times per week for maintenance or three times per week for improvement is desirable' (Rafferty, 2010, p. 46).

Intensity

Intensity refers to training load, that is, the level of difficulty of an exercise. If dancers have been practising a modified press-up on their knees, they could make this more challenging by lifting the knees off the floor and performing with the full-body posture, therefore increasing the intensity. If dancers are doing weight training, they should gradually continue to increase the weight being lifted over time to continually build muscle strength. If resistance bands are being used, the band could be tightened, depending on the exercise, or a tougher band could be introduced. Intensity can also be increased when training cardiorespiratory fitness; by monitoring heart rate, the dancer could attempt work at a higher heart rate than a previous session. Once training has become comfortable, the intensity should shift up a notch in order to challenge the cardiorespiratory

> *Within the dance class, increasing the intensity of a particular dance movement or position could be practised, for example, holding the leg at a greater height or adding the weight of another dancer into a movement to create a weight-bearing exercise that can then be developed into a lift once strength and stability are achieved, if safe to do so.*

system again for a series of training sessions, for example, increasing workload to 80 percent of maximal from 60 to 70 percent and maintaining this until it becomes comfortable again, and a new increase is required.

Time

Time and intensity should be considered together. To reach training benefits, one or the other may be adjusted. The dancer can either work at a lower intensity for a longer duration or a higher intensity for a shorter amount of time. Each will have training benefits; therefore dancers should alternate between the two to meet the ever-changing demands placed on them, or focus on the one that most suits their current or upcoming dance work.

If focusing on increasing duration, the amount of time an exercise is performed could be extended in order to make an exercise more challenging. This being said, this should not compromise the length of other components, such as warm-up and cool-down, and the inclusion of rest phases, which are vital for safe and effective performance and progression.

> If dancers are holding a développé à la seconde for 10 seconds, they could then attempt to hold the position for 15 seconds. If performing a plank position, they could aim to hold the plank for 5 to 10 seconds longer than they did the previous week. Or if they currently run for 30 minutes a week, they could aim to increase the duration to 35 minutes, and so on. In the dance studio environment, the amount of time spent on specific tasks could be extended, or the length of time allowed for rehearsal of certain routines could be increased to allow for further repetition.

Type

Change can be incredibly beneficial for avoiding a plateau in fitness levels. By trying a new way of exercising, the muscles will need to work differently, therefore providing a new challenge for the body. Changing the type of training may require learning a new skill, which can also serve to develop motor learning. Even changing exercise positions slightly can activate different muscle fibres and can encourage increased benefits. Altering exercise type is useful for the dancer due to differencing demands across dance styles and choreography. Cross-training is becoming increasingly popular because it allows dancers to vary their workout. For example, they may combine a range of exercises for aerobic fitness, strength and flexibility within one training session or from day to day. By continuing to change the type of activity dancers will continue to challenge their fitness levels.

Enjoyment

Dancers must enjoy the activity they are participating in if they are to remain motivated to continue. This is pertinent to all dancers, whether using dance as a recreational activity or training for or within a dance career. Dance leaders should ensure that their classes are enjoyable and that the dancers taking part experience a sense of achievement. Dancers in training should partake in fitness activities that they find pleasurable in order to maintain motivation and commitment and subsequently enhance progress.

INCORPORATING FITNESS INTO DANCERS' SCHEDULES

Adding fitness training for dancers' schedules can be difficult due to their already demanding timetable, so it needs to be done with care to avoid negative effects of overtraining (discussed further in chapter 5). While dance classes can result in improvements in some of the components of fitness, this is not the aim of the sessions, and targeted fitness training is recommended for supporting the needs of the dance session. The freelance professional dancer should be able to train in between contracts and possibly during contracts, depending on the project. They may be able to substitute one weekly dance class for a conditioning session, which would support maintenance of their physical fitness without causing a negative effect on their artistic skills. Dancers with an established company may have access to fitness and conditioning facilities or may need to find time outside of their rehearsals for supplementary training. Some professional companies require their dancers to take part in supplementary fitness training as part of their company hours. For dance students, fitness and conditioning might be part of their course, or they may have to find the time to complete training outside of course hours. Many undergraduate and postgraduate dance courses now include lectures on dance physiology and fitness, with instructors encouraging the students to put this theory into practice.

Because of these varying situations, it is difficult to state one way that fitness should be integrated into a training programme. However, because 'reduced levels of physical fitness are associated with relatively high levels of injuries in dancers and may hinder their ability to perform to maximal potential' (Rafferty, 2010, p. 45), dancers are advised to explore ways to achieve supplementary fitness. For the full-time dancer a training plan incorporating all training formats, class, rehearsal, performance and supplementary conditioning is advised (see chapter 5 on periodization).

Fitness Training for Various Dance Genres

The focus of fitness for dancers will vary depending on their dance style or training. Similarly, how much and how often they train will also depend on their timetable and overall commitments. The following examples present ideas on how dancers can train to improve their fitness in relation to their dance style.

Full-Time Dance Students

The key here is variety. The full-time dance student in vocational training is likely to train in various dance styles, usually in a combination of ballet, contemporary, jazz, commercial and other dance practices such as choreography. This student will benefit from cross-training, therefore varying from aerobic to anaerobic exercise, as well as from strength training of both the upper and lower areas of the body as well as the core. Circuit training could be usefully incorporated into the weekly schedule. The student would need to include flexibility stretches regularly and could attend supplementary classes of yoga to support this. Finally proprioception exercises should be included to support increased balance and stability and reduce risk of injury.

Ballet Dancers

Fitness training for ballet dancers should include aerobic training in order to support their performance in full-length works, which can often last for hours. Swimming, running, or cycling could be useful for this. If dancers are not hypermobile or overflexible, they must also train their flexibility regularly to achieve challenging postures, so yoga or stretch classes could be advised. Stability and proprioception exercises should be practised regularly to support balance and control, and strength (resistance training) and core sta-bility training, such as Pilates, would be beneficial. These practices will support control around the joints and maintain leg height in various positions, and they are particularly useful for male ballet dancers, who need to perform traditional lifts seemingly without effort. Male dancers will benefit from resistance training, preferably under a personal trainer or exercise physiologist who understands physiology in dance. Dancers must not go on pointe until they have gained enough strength and accurate technique, particularly in the feet, ankles and core. Both male and female ballet dancers will benefit from well-structured ballet-specific plyometric training to improve jump height and ensure appropriate execution.

Breakdancers

Breakdancers will benefit from aerobic training as a foundation followed by interval training to support the short bursts of energy needed in break-dance. This should include frequent transitions and changes of levels, so could include exercises like burpees and floor exercises such as variations of squat thrusts and floor sprints. Breakdancers must complete regular weight-bearing and strength training sessions for the upper body (neck, shoulders, wrists and core) to safely practise, rehearse and perform traditional breakdance moves such as the helicopter, the six step, head stands and spins and inverted freezes. They must also focus on rest and recovery to avoid repetitive strain injuries.

Bharatanatyam Dancers

For this classical Indian style dancers should train their aerobic foundation to help prevent the onset of fatigue during training and performance. They

(continued)

Fitness Training for Various Dance Genres (continued)

must also train strength within the core, legs, ankles and feet to help control alignment and sustain dancing while executing deep knee bends that are often performed with the heels raised. They must be able to balance safely during routines; therefore training balance, stability and proprioception will help. Performing safe squats, knee bends in various positions (first and second positions) and rises onto the balls of the feet, and then carefully incorporating the rises and knee bends together, while ensuring correct alignment, would be a relevant way of training lower body strength for this dance style. Stability training and strengthening exercises for the hamstrings and quadriceps are key for safe execution. Using a resistance band to strengthen the feet and ankles could be beneficial. Regular exercises for the wrists, hands and fingers would also be useful due to the variety of hand gestures used in this style. Pilates could be advised to strengthen the deep muscles in the dancers' core to help with balance and control.

Pole or Aerial Dancers

Whether beginner, advanced or elite, pole and aerial dancers place challenging demands on their body. These dancers need to be strong enough to support their own body weight; therefore pre-strengthening and endurance training of the upper body are essential. Their adductors, quadriceps and hamstrings must be strong enough to hold dancers up in inverted positions. Dancers must strengthen the core (back, abdominals and pelvic floor muscles) to maintain postures and balance and support safe transitions. Aerobic training is recommended as a general foundation, but resistance training and Pilates will be valuable for these dancers.

Irish Dancers

Irish dance is mainly anaerobic, with short and repetitive bursts of muscular power being central to the style. Therefore plyometric training of the lower limbs, in appropriate shock-absorbing shoes such as running shoes, will be beneficial, along with strength and resistance work. The feet and ankles undergo much strain and repetitive impact. As a result, strength and balance and stability work for the feet and ankles will be especially important, along with mobility exercises for the toes and feet to counteract the strain placed on the feet while bound in the shoes. Active flexibility, especially in the legs, should also be targeted to aid in achieving the high leg kicks and front leg position in certain jumps. Core muscles (abdominal, spinal and pelvic floor muscles) require strength and control to maintain the upright posture without excessive tension. Pilates-based exercises could be effective for this. In order to effectively support the anaerobic requirements of the dance style, and in particular to support long days of class and rehearsals for competition or performance, aerobic training should be included. As with training in any dance style, swimming would be an appropriate option because it is not weight bearing and therefore does not add impact to the body. Swimming also provides some resistance work for the arms, which are often ignored in Irish training.

SUMMARY

Despite resistance from practitioners anchored in more traditional training regimes, it is now widely accepted that dance classes alone cannot provide all the conditioning needed for optimal fitness and injury-free performance. Therefore dancers are advised to supplement their dance skills training with separate activities that specifically develop their strength, muscle endurance and stamina, especially in low-level technical dancers who should try to improve their cardiorespiratory capacity (Malkogeorgos, Zaggelidou, Zaggelidis, & Christos, 2013). Conditioning is especially important for young dancers, who need to realise

early on that they need to take care of their body, which is the dancer's only instrument (Berardi, 2005). Recreational dancers and those beginning to dance for the first time, whatever their age, will also need to consider their physical readiness to engage in any type of dance activity in order to protect their body from the increased demands. All dance activity, even social, will ask more of the body than usual everyday actions. Dance leaders in recreational environments need to be careful not to overtax their participants, but should also help to prepare dancers with activities to gently increase their fitness capacities.

Dance leaders must ensure that the advice they give to participants is fully considered, appropriate and supported by research or expertise from a knowledgeable and appropriately qualified professional in that area. There are many training myths, and many teachers still deliver advice they were given years ago that is outdated and incorrect. The media also promotes many ideas that are not suitable for dancers of any particular age, level or ability. Dancers need appropriate, research-informed advice on how to train their bodies successfully for peak performance and prevention of injury. Dance providers should remember that 'to ignore the physiological needs in the training of today's dancers is to deny the development of the art form' (Rafferty, 2010, p. 48).

KEY POINTS

- An effective and appropriate warm-up and cool-down must always be performed when taking part in any physical training.

- Appropriate clothing and footwear must be worn so that alignment can be visible and that there is sufficient shock absorption through the lower limbs and spine if needed.

- If attending fitness classes of any type, make sure that the sessions are taught by an appropriately qualified and knowledgeable instructor.

- Always rehydrate regularly: before, during and following exercise. When the body starts to fatigue, continue with correct technique and alignment. If technique begins to suffer, dancers should stop or reduce the intensity until they can achieve correct technique.

- The traditional dance technique class is not designed to improve fitness for performance. Therefore supplementary fitness and conditioning need to be carefully incorporated into a dancer's schedule.

- Components of training fitness for the dancer include cardiorespiratory fitness, muscle strength, muscle power, muscle flexibility joint mobility (MFJM), balance stability and proprioception, and rest.

- Overload needs to be achieved for effective progression of training.

- Effective rest, recovery, nutrition and hydration are vital for successful training and progression.

- The training principles of specificity, individuality, reversibility and overload must be understood for effective training progression.

- Frequency, intensity, time, type and enjoyment (FITTE) must be considered for continuing training developments and avoiding plateau or boredom.

- Dance leaders should receive education on the importance of supplementary training and appropriate advice on how to integrate this into the dancer's already demanding schedule.

chapter 5

Rest and Recovery

≡ *Learning Objectives*

After reading this chapter you will be able to do the following:
- Understand the principles and the benefits of effective rest and recovery in training sessions and schedules.
- Recognise the physical and psychological effects of overtraining.
- Recommend strategies for applying periodization and tapering to dance practice.
- Promote rest and recovery as positive attributes within dance and physical training.

≡ *Key Terms*

active rest	distributed practice	periodization
burnout	fatigue	recovery
complete rest	massed practice	somatic practice
constructive rest	overtraining	tapering

With new and increasingly challenging choreography continuously being created, the demands on both professional dancers and dancers in vocational training are becoming more intense. Technical and physical expectations continue to push the boundaries of strength, flexibility, stamina and athleticism. To meet these requirements dancers need to adapt or increase their training, often resulting in longer working hours at a greater intensity. This increase, alongside the determination to get accepted into or remain in dance employment, can cause considerable negative effects on the body. If not well managed, this escalation may result in physical or emotional stress; however, if sufficient rest and **recovery** periods are scheduled and used effectively, the detrimental effects of **fatigue** can be reduced.

Exercise-induced fatigue, or overload, is needed for positive adaptation in physical training, as explained in chapter 4. The focus of this chapter, however, will be fatigue as a result of **overtraining** and insufficient rest. This type of fatigue is perceived to be a major cause of injury in dance, usually due to long working days and high physical demands (Brinson & Dick, 1996; Laws, 2005; Liederbach, Schanfein, & Kremenic, 2013; Twitchett, Angioi, Koutedakis, & Wyon, 2010; see chapter 9 for more on injury). Overtraining is a result of an imbalance of increased training and inadequate recovery, and is recognised when performers are not able to perform to the best of their physical ability due to chronic tiredness or exhaustion. It is both a physical and psychological issue that does not result in the positive adaptations seen with overload. On the contrary, it can lead the dancer on a pathway of reduced technical ability, lack of energy, emotional imbalance and increased risk of injury occurrence.

COMPONENTS OF REST AND RECOVERY

The components that contribute to effective recovery are quite simple: rest, nutrition and hydration. Rest can range from sleeping, to doing nothing, to reducing the amount of activity, to doing something different. Dancers need approximately 8 hours of sleep a night, although this will vary from one individual to another and will depend on the current intensity and duration of hours that the dancer is working. The National Sleep Foundation (n.d.) recommends 7 to 9 hours of sleep a night for adults, and more than this for those younger than 18. With appropriate quantities of sleep, **complete rest** helps repair damaged tissue and improves efficiency and performance output. Research suggests that a good night's sleep could improve motor performance, with another study stating that a lack of adequate sleep could be a risk factor for performance-related musculoskeletal disorders (Batson & Schwartz, 2007; Manchester, 2012).

Complete rest can also be interpreted as a day off away from any dance or physical activity entirely, or it could be a longer period of time away from training, for example, a summer break. During this time the dancer should be able to experience substantial recovery and soft-tissue repair. **Active rest** is when dancers have a break from dance but remain physically active at a less strenuous level than their usual vigorous training. For example, changing activity or attending a dance class of a different style without the training pressures that come with the original style may help dancers maintain their fitness levels as well as give them some physical recovery and psychological rest from their usual training programme. This is also a good opportunity for the dancers to experience other interests outside of dance, resulting in a break from their usual dance activity. A third type of rest that dancers can be encouraged to practise is **constructive rest**. Constructive rest utilises a biomechanically efficient position (see figure 5.1) that supports the body in releasing stress and tension, and it can include the use of imagery. Similar to the position often used in yoga, a pose in which dancers lie flat with the eyes closed and place the arms by the side of the body with the palms of the hands facing upwards can also allow for constructive rest.

Regular rest periods need to take place within the dance class or rehearsal (see chapter 6 for more information on effective sequencing of the dance class) as well as in between the dance sessions in the form of **distributed practice**. Distributed practice means spacing out periods of work with longer periods of rest, unlike **massed**

Figure 5.1 Constructive rest.

practice, which involves work periods that are very close together with either no break or only brief rest. Significant evidence states that leaving some time between practice sessions, even up to 48 hours, enhances learning (Batson & Schwarz, 2007). There are often concerns in dance practice that material already learned will inevitably be forgotten in the absence of short-term consolidation and that technical gains will be easily lost. Interestingly, research shows that while practice and repetition are necessary to secure movement skills, the effect of repetition is actually enhanced if the repetitions do not occur immediately, but instead are spaced apart. In fact, the spacing effect serves to enhance the memory, especially if there is some interference (another or different activity) occurring between those repetitions (Schmidt & Lee, 2011). These points have positive implications for dancers who cross-train, or work in different styles simultaneously.

Contrary to popular opinion, more does not always mean better. Therefore performing fewer repetitions with increased quality and clarity of purpose will provide considerably more benefits than performing unnecessary repetitions, which cause the dancer to excessively fatigue and pose an increased risk of injury and exhaustion. Of course dancers need to work to increase their fitness levels; however, there needs to be a balance of intensity of training and rest periods (see chapters 4 and 6). In chapter 6, it is recommended that a high-impact dance class lasts a maximum of 60 minutes and include regular rest periods. Further repetition without adequate rest can increase the risk of overuse issues, which can have injurious consequences. Dance teachers can adhere to principles of distributed practice within the class environment by creating opportunities for participants to perform their work in smaller groups so that others can rest while they learn by watching their peers perform. Brief rest periods can also be accompanied by water breaks, which additionally support dancers in remaining hydrated (see chapter 7 for more on hydration).

The benefits of scheduled rest periods in professional dance companies include increased cardiorespiratory fitness (Koutedakis, Budgett, & Faulmann, 1990); increased vigour, flexibility, anaerobic power and leg strength; and a decrease in fatigue (Koutedakis, Myszkewycz, Soulas, Papapostolou, & Sharp, 1999). More recently it has been reported that prolonged or excessive high-intensity exercise related to long hours of physical training, rehearsal and performance may lead to fatigue, psychological distress, performance decrements and injury (Murgia, 2010; 2013). We now know that the numbers of dancers experiencing fatigue, a major symptom of overtraining, could be decreased if effective recovery periods were put into place within the dancers' schedule. However, the opportunity to experience appropriate rest, and therefore recovery, is rarely supported. The need for rest should be highlighted and encouraged, particularly with dancers who are high achievers and with those who continuously work incredibly hard to please others or have unrealistic targets for themselves. Dance leaders should understand the importance of rest periods in improving performance potential and decreasing injury occurrence and should ensure effective application of rest periods in their dance sessions and personal schedules. Each type of rest mentioned will have its own benefits, but it is dependent on the individual's situation as to what type of rest is needed or for how long it should be experienced.

Rest periods can and should be sympathetically arranged within a dancer's schedule. Intelligent planning and managing of the dancer's timetable can provide significant opportunities for recovery. Professional dancers regularly work long hours when performing and touring, while vocational students have predetermined terms and semesters that have a variety of peaks in demand due to assessments and shows. These dancers need to have a supportive schedule. In the dance industry, rest has often been associated with weakness, yet rest should be encouraged as a positive element that increases the quality of performance within such a physically demanding field. Sleep, relaxation and recreation are important in recovering from intensive practice, and should be advised.

Balanced nutrition will also help the body to re-energise and repair damaged tissue. Drinking water will rehydrate the body, both supporting optimal recovery and improved performance. Nutrition and hydration are covered in more detail in chapter 7, but it is important at this point to recognise that recovery will only be successful with effective nutrition and that physical training can only have a positive result if recovery is integrated successfully into the dancer's life. The two possible outcomes for the dancer as demands become more intense are shown in figure 5.2.

In this diagram, 'training' consists of strength, stamina, flexibility, technique and choreography; 'rest and recovery' consists of well-balanced rest, sleep, nutrition and hydration. The scenario shown in figure 5.2*b* will help prevent the effects of overtraining.

OVERTRAINING AND BURNOUT

Overtraining is also known as *overtraining syndrome, chronic fatigue, overwork, staleness* and *chronic fatigue syndrome* (Koutedakis, 2000). Overtraining can be recognised when a dancer complains of reduced physical performance, suffers from constant fatigue or shows behavioural and emotional changes for no apparent medical or other obvious reason (Budgett, 1998). The condition is often associated with frequent infections and depression that occur following excessive training or competition. Of great concern for the dancer, teacher or choreographer is that symptoms are not always resolved despite adequate rest (Budgett, 1990). The effects of overtraining can include a decrease in performance levels,

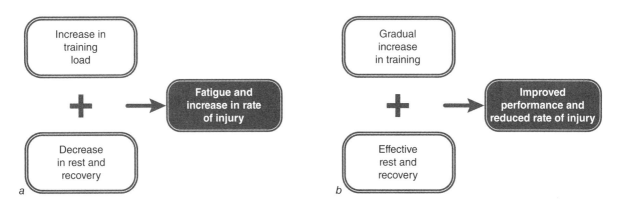

Figure 5.2 *(a)* Consequences of inadequate rest and increased training and *(b)* outcome with sufficient recovery periods.

change in mood states, fatigue, weight loss, depression, increase in resting heart rate, increase in resting blood pressure, disturbed sleep, painful muscles and decreased muscular strength (Budgett, 1998; Budgett, 1990; Kreider, Fry, & O'Toole, 1998; Koutedakis et al., 1999).

Literature to date is unsure of a confirmed cause; however, one frequently speculated is inadequate rest and recovery periods in relation to the intensity of training (Kentta, Hassmen, & Raglin, 2001). Research implies that individuals who are highly motivated suffer from overtraining because they usually respond to their lack of form by increasing the training load. This in turn can lead to a vicious cycle of fatigue and underperformance. It is proposed that if these dancers reversed this practice and increased their rest or recovery periods, they may well prevent underperforming (Budgett, 1990).

> Note that overtraining should not be confused with overload. Overload is a training principle that promotes positive adaptations. Overtraining has negative effects.

Burnout is regularly mentioned as an outcome of overtraining. Kent (1996, p71) describes it as a 'complex psychophysiological syndrome characterised by feelings of anxiety, tension, fatigue and exhaustion'. Williams (2006) states that burnout has been known to cause athletes to withdraw from their activity, and describes it as a psychological syndrome of emotional exhaustion, depersonalisation and a reduced sense of performance accomplishment. A combination of both physical and emotional effects could ultimately lead dancers to discontinue their participation in dance, either over the short or long term. By increasing awareness of the inter-related components of rest and recovery, overtraining and burnout and promoting effective use of the fundamental training principles (see chapter 4), dancers, dance teachers, choreographers and managers could dramatically reduce the negative physical and emotional outcomes of overtraining.

The following advice will help dancers avoid overtraining:

- Aim for one or two days free of dance training per week.
- Have interests or hobbies other than dance.
- Improve knowledge regarding the importance of rest and recovery for positive progression in dance.
- Regularly refuel and rehydrate.
- Gradually increase training intensity and alternate between work and rest periods.
- Aim to get adequate amounts of sleep every night to support workload.

Although dance leaders and managers can encourage the preceding guidelines, and should allow dancers enough time to cool down and warm up again without having to use their lunch break, they should also enable classes and timetables to be planned in a way that includes adequate recovery over time in order for dancers to progress in a safe and effective way (see the following sections for **periodization** and **tapering** principles).

Periodization

Periodization is used extensively in the training of elite athletes, but it has yet to be effectively adopted by dancers. At its most simple level, periodization dictates that working consistently at high intensities is detrimental to both physical and mental progression; therefore periods of training that include peaks and troughs in intensities are essential. The aim is to promote gradual and systematic progression of training through preplanned cycles that vary in intensity and volume, allowing recovery and avoiding overtraining of the body's systems. These cycles are usually scheduled across a year in order to achieve peak level of fitness for a desired event or series of events (Kenny, Wilmore & Costill, 2012). In sport this progression primarily leads up to competition, but in dance it could also relate to performances or assessments.

The theory of periodization explains that during the initial stage of training, athletes should develop their physiological foundation, but that any subsequent increase in training should be preceded by an unloading phase, in which they decrease the training level before implementing an increase (Bompa, 2009), shown as rest periods in figure 5.3. Following this they should then strive for improved performance standards in the later stages before a final short rest period (a tapering period as discussed later) towards the actual competitive phase or performance phase. However, periodization is more difficult to apply directly to dance because of the lack of consistent events. For decades, researchers investigating the potential for the application of periodization in dance have promoted the principle as a way to prevent overtraining, explaining that a consideration of training curves can be a way to set goals for continuous but gradual improvements (Clarkson & Skrinar, 1988). Rather than working at the same intensity and volume consistently, changes to the stimulus for training and varying the type of exercises can help dancers avoid becoming stale over time (Franklin, 2013; Heyward, 2006; Kenny, Wilmore & Costill, 2012). Application of the training principles to dance will involve examining how dance sessions and schedules are arranged over time. It should be remembered that the quality of training is more important than its length or quantity and that rest is a vital component (see chapters 4 and 6 for more information on rest as a supplementary aspect of fitness and as a constituent within the dance session). Figure 5.3 demonstrates that if training intensity is regulated over time

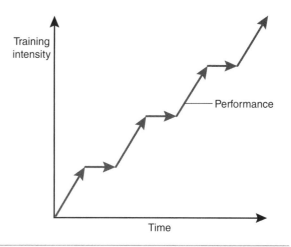

Figure 5.3 Effects of regulated training intensity on performance.

(combining periods of overload with periods of rest), standard of performance output should also increase.

These recovery periods should initiate a decrease in the risk of both physiological and

Periodization in Practice

- Avoid learning curves that are too steep. Not allowing the body to adapt gradually to an increased workload will usually result in injury or depreciation in performance.

- Be aware of sudden increases in activity and take steps to counteract this, for example, the period immediately before performance, when activity resumes after time off, or changes of activity context such as participation in summer schools, workshops or long audition processes.

- Dance schools could consider shorter training blocks throughout the year punctuated with frequent breaks rather than both extended training and holiday periods (for example, 6- to 8-week blocks followed by a 1- to 2-week holiday).

- At the end of a training break, remember that the muscles may be somewhat deconditioned. Take time to work back up to the usual intensity (up to 2 weeks), and avoid strenuous activities such as jumping during the first few days.

- Choreographers should aim to complete their work with time to spare before opening performances, reducing intensity during later stages so that dancers can prepare more effectively, reduce fatigue levels and become fit and ready. Look at reducing the workload just before performance to reduce physiological and psychological stress.

- Choreographers and managers could build in time to condition their dancers at the beginning of the choreographic process to help them prepare for changes in demands as well as use rehearsal to gradually condition their company. It is common for dancers to become fit for purpose by actually performing the work and only reach their peak specific fitness at the end of a tour.

- Dance leaders, managers and educational schools might consider applying distributed practice rather than massed practice schedules to allow for more rest and consolidation of learning.

(Clarkson & Skrinar, 1988; Bompa & Haff, 2009; Krasnow & Chatfield, 1996; Simmel 2014; Wyon, 2010a)

psychological fatigue, as well as allow the body to become fitter, stronger and more able to withstand the demands placed on it. With this in mind, when a dance student's annual timetable is produced, there should be an initial period intended for substantial physical preparation before technically and physically demanding choreography is expected. Similarly, the schedules of professional dancers should be designed with an initial period for preparation before they are expected to master extensive technical demands of choreography and performance. Recreational dance sessions and situations where a dancer has recovered and is returning from injury should also provide a gradual increase in intensity following a period of no dancing.

Tapering

Another method for incorporating rest and recovery into a dance schedule is to include a tapering period before important dance events. This area is connected with periodization. A tapering period is where dancers reduce their training to allow for healing of damaged tissues and for both physiological and psychological rest, in order for the body's energy reserves to be fully replenished immediately before performance or competition. The tapering period would be more readily applicable to professional dance companies, but it could also work with dancers in training and with amateur dancers working towards performance.

Currently many dancers are expected to rehearse 5 to 7 days a week up until the night before a performance. Often technical and dress rehearsals are scheduled on the same day as the premiere or opening night. The dancers are expected to perform at their peak throughout the rehearsal process and on into the performance season. With this intense preperformance schedule dancers could begin the performance season with fatigued or damaged muscle tissue and might already be suffering the effects of exhaustion, which means they cannot possibly perform to the best of their ability.

Therefore it is recommended that, especially when the dancer is working long hours or at a high intensity, a tapering period is endorsed before performances and competitions. Dancers should decrease training, for example, taking a day off to rest immediately before a show day or observing some rehearsals rather than physically participating in every session. Mental rehearsal, which incorporates imagery use, could also be taught and encouraged as an alternative element of the rehearsal period. This technique can be incredibly powerful at improving performance, and dancers who mentally rehearse their routines have a greater chance of achieving their optimum performance standard when they need it most (Budgett, 1990). Chapter 8 provides more information on using imagery for mental rehearsal. Rehearsals could be filmed so that the dancers can watch and make notes rather than rehearsing physically all of the time. Tapering periods have produced significant benefits, both physically and psychologically, in both sport and dance (Wyon, 2010a). Therefore, it is in the best interest of the dancers, dance leaders, choreographers and managers to plan carefully to allow for tapering in practice.

> *Educating dancers on the benefits of rest as a powerful tool for optimising performance could help prevent overtraining and reduce the risk of injury occurrence.*

INCORPORATING REST INTO DANCERS' SCHEDULES

We know the importance of rest, but putting it into a dancer's busy schedule can be difficult, especially when there are performances, assessments and other important dance events to consider. Therefore a dancer's annual timetable, as well as daily, weekly and monthly programme, needs to be organised with rest periods in mind, taking periodization or tapering into account. Depending on the type of dancer and the duration and intensity of training, the amount of rest will differ and the responsibility of who organises these rest periods will vary. The elite performer who works full time may need a tapering period before the performance season, whereas the recreational dancer who takes part in dance activity once or twice a week might not find this necessary. More specific examples have been considered in the sections that follow.

Whether dancers are participating in full-time vocational training or enrolled on a university degree programme, their training calendar often relates to a standard academic calendar, including half-terms and seasonal breaks, but this is by

Somatic Education in Dance

An effective way of incorporating components of rest into a dancer's daily or weekly timetable that is currently being practised in some dance institutions is to include elements of **somatic practice**. Key applications of somatic approaches within dance pedagogy are to reduce unnecessary or inefficient muscular effort and refine proprioceptive awareness for better co-ordination of motor action through finding a balance between rest and activity (Batson, 2009; Manchester, 2012), as well as to support recovery by allowing periods of non-doing. While some dancers will seek out specific somatic practices such as Alexander Technique, Body-Mind Centering, Ideokinesis or Feldenkrais, it is also common, especially within contemporary dance, for aspects of these to be integrated within the dance session. Research has found that dance students who took part in somatic sessions noticed numerous benefits, for example, dancing for longer periods of time with more efficiency and with less fatigue (Batson & Schwartz, 2007). Some students also said that they felt more relaxed and refreshed from the sessions.

consequence rather than design. When scheduling student dancers' timetable, consideration should be given to the following:

- Physically intense lessons should be followed by lessons of reduced physical intensity, or a low-intensity day following a highly physically demanding day, therefore allowing for effective recovery time and preventing overtraining of the body's systems.
- Appropriate recovery periods should be included each day, with suitable lunch breaks (a minimum of 1 hour) and time to transition between lessons.
- Somatic education sessions (see sidebar) could be integrated into the programme.
- Leaders should promote an ethos amongst staff and students that highlights the benefits of rest and recovery as integral and necessary aspects of training effectively and safely.

The dancer studying dance for a professional performing career is likely to be training long hours, often from 8 a.m. to 6 p.m., 5 days a week, with regular additional rehearsals in the evenings and on weekends. University dance students will often seek out additional dance classes and partake in dance societies within the wider student body. Trainee dancers are also likely to have employment in order to fund their studies and training, resulting in even longer hours.

Therefore it is the training institution's responsibility to highlight the importance of rest and recovery and to provide a curriculum that incorporates rest periods. Students must also plan their extracurricular activities to incorporate rest as necessary. They should use scheduled holiday periods to take enough time off to effectively recover from term-time training (4 consecutive weeks per year or a 2- to 3-week break, two or three times a year; Wyon, 2010a), while also gradually returning to physical capacity prior to recommencing dance training. When dance staff and students fully understand and recognise the benefits of rest and recovery and how their application positively affects the progression of dancers in training, these components will become commonplace, and will be naturally incorporated into their future professional dancing lives.

Recreational Dancers

In recreational dance, more young people are striving to excel, either working to progress into vocational training or competing in various dance competitions and examinations. In addition to their schooling and other extracurricular endeavours, the accumulation of these demands could result in physical and emotional stress for dancers. Consideration should also be given to external pressures from teachers, family members, friends or peers. Although these people are likely to mean well, their input could actually result in more psychological stress for the dancer. Reluctance to rest is often noticed in young dancers competing in events, those working at a higher technical standard or high achievers who are not willing to accept that they need a rest, therefore, the session leader must observe their participants carefully and make judgements as to when and how often to tell their dancers to rest, refuel and hydrate.

If participants are taking part in dance activity for exercise or enjoyment once or twice a week, then their recovery could simply involve an effective cool down followed by refuelling and

A Prevocational College Student's Schedule

Table 5.1 demonstrates the timetable of Sarah, a 16-year-old prevocational dance student studying dance at college full time. Her average week at college consists of 26 hours of dance before she attends her evening and weekend dance classes. She also goes to the gym and works a part-time job.

Sarah has approximately 12 performances scheduled with her college this academic year. Her college tutors actively encourage her to rest over her seasonal breaks (Christmas, Easter and summer). However, Sarah also competes in regular national dance competitions with her local dance school, which can minimise her opportunities for rest. There is little communication between the college tutors and her dance school teachers, so neither is fully aware of the extent of training that she is undertaking. Effective communication among Sarah, her teachers and her parents is necessary so that each party is aware of the cumulative effect of her activities, and can encourage Sarah to experience the positive aspects of rest and recovery.

Sarah is a common example of the 16- to 18-year-old dancer, working long hours in the hope of making it as a dancer. If she is accepted into full-time vocational training it is likely that her dancing hours will be increased, therefore she should be educated on the benefits of rest and recovery so that she can begin to implement it into her practice sooner rather than later to avoid the negative effects of fatigue and overtraining. A working week of 7 days is not advised for anybody. If this is the case, the dancer's participation should be evaluated and achievable rest periods should be arranged.

Table 5.1 Sample Timetable for a 16-Year-Old Preprofessional Dance Student

Day	9–11am Lesson 1		11–11:30 am Break	11:30am–1:30pm Lesson 2	1:30– 2:30pm Lunch	2:30–4:30pm Lesson 3
Monday	Ballet			Commercial dance		Contemporary dance
Tuesday	Jazz			Musical theatre dance		Stretching
Wednesday	Ballet			Latin American dance		Theory (Maths and English)
Thursday	Jazz			Commercial dance		Urban dance
Friday	Theory (Maths and English)	Rehearsal slot		Choreography		Choreography

rehydrating after the session (discussed further in chapter 7). However, recommendations will vary depending on the age and ability of participants. Older participants should take frequent but short rest periods within the dance sessions. 'Whilst it is good practice to encourage people to work at their own pace and take a break when they need one, some individuals do not realise they are becoming tired; others are reluctant to admit they need a rest' (Amans, 2013, p. 132). Elderly participants and young children may also need reminding to drink water, and short breaks from the dance activity will provide this opportunity (see chapter 10 for more age-specific recommendations).

Professional Dancers

The situation of the professional dancer varies substantially, from the freelance dancer working short contracted projects, often in various locations, to the full-time employed dancer with an established company. Either way, it is typically expected that at the professional level, dancers can train and care for themselves effectively in order to manage their dance employment. There may be exceptions at elite level where training coaches, nutritionists and dance scientists are part of the company, but often professional dancers must care for themselves. However, this should be supported by considered training and performance schedules, which often fall under the responsibility of the choreographers and directors. It is hoped, therefore, that within the training and rehearsal schedule there are days when not all dancers are called so that each individual can have at least one day to rest each week. During the performance season, where possible, there may be two casts, so that dancers can rest when they are not performing. This is also useful if a dancer were to become injured. Rather than trying to continue, which could be detrimental to that dancer's career, another dancer can take that role until the injured dancer has fully recovered.

Dance Teachers

Dance teachers should not be forgotten. There has been an upsurge of research into the training and performing dancer and the effects of fatigue and overtraining, but much less on the teachers who lead the sessions. Yet, frequently it is these leaders of dance who are working too many hours and not taking the time out that they need to fully recover for best practice. Independent dance teachers often work unsociable hours so that their students can train out of school or work time, which usually means working evenings, late nights and at the weekend. Teachers who work in dance education all too often spend the their time teaching long days, one class after another, with very short breaks, and they often spend the rest of their time completing lengthy amounts of administration, resulting in expanded working hours. In the nature of this type of employment, freelance teachers are often paid for the contact time with the learners only, resulting in extra pressure to teach more hours to earn a living, while having to complete paperwork and session planning in their own, unpaid, time. If dance teachers themselves do not take enough time to rest and recover, they might also experience the effects of overtraining, resulting in an increased risk of injury or illness.

SUMMARY

Whether dancing in the community setting as a hobby or at a professional level, the tendency to push too hard can be tempting. Dance schools and organisations, companies, choreographers and rehearsal directors should aim to implement periodization and tapering into their dance calendars, and should encourage effective recovery in practice. When scheduling rest periods, it is not just the dancers' term timetable or annual rehearsal and performance schedules that need to be considered. Rest is also of great consequence if dancers do not have short breaks during physically demanding sessions. We now know that rest is beneficial for the body to replenish and prepare for more challenges. If dancers are showing signs of fatigue in a dance session, they must be given time to stop, rest for a short time, rehydrate and then return to the dance activity. Additionally, dance teachers should also allow themselves time to rest and recover. It is important to remember that every dancing body is different. Whether professional, amateur or recreational, the dancer's need and duration of rest and recovery periods will inevitably vary.

KEY POINTS

- Rest and recovery consist of a decrease in or break from activity, sleep, nutrition and hydration.

- Effective rest periods can result in improved strength, mood, vigour, flexibility, energy levels, cardiorespiratory fitness and overall quality of performance.

- More does not always mean better—short rest periods should be included within high-intensity lessons and rehearsals to avoid fatigue.

- Fatigue is one of the most common perceived causes of injury, and it can be reduced with effective rest periods.

- Increases in training should be gradual and accompanied with rest and recovery to improve performance and avoid overtraining.

- Overtraining is a condition with many symptoms, including serious fatigue, illness, depression, low self-esteem and loss of physical ability to perform at previous standard. It is most common in high achievers, those with perfectionistic tendencies and those who are highly motivated.

- Rest periods should be scheduled within the dancers' daily, weekly and annual timetable using periodization and tapering periods.

- It is advised that dancers have another interest or hobby that is not dance related to allow effective time off.

- Dancers and dance leaders need to be educated on the serious effects of fatigue and overtraining, as well as the benefits of rest and recovery, in order to effectively understand these and apply them to their practice.

chapter 6

Sequencing and Progression

After reading this chapter you should be able to do the following:

- Appreciate how training, conditioning and motor learning principles inform the structure of a dance session.
- Understand the relationship and differences between learning physical skills and training the body effectively.
- Choose appropriate training content and place individual movements and exercises in a beneficial sequence within the dance session.
- Plan a sound, physiologically progressive dance session with the needs of specific participants in mind.
- Appreciate the value and detriment of repetition.
- Ensure that the demands encountered during the dance session are given adequate preparation and time for recovery.
- Make judgements on, manage and deliver common dance movements that may have contraindicated components.

≡ Key Terms

kinesiology	pedagogy	skill acquisition
lateral bias	repetition	transfer of learning
motor learning		

Dance sessions can have a variety of purposes. Dancers are trained in a specific genre to improve their skills, but the level of physical conditioning required and amount of **skill acquisition** necessary depends on their reasons for participation. Those who dance for recreational purposes may emphasise enjoyment and social interaction over technical skill acquisition, whereas dancers working towards professional performance need to explicitly develop their technical prowess. Other dance sessions might focus on exploring the creative aspects of dancing, while in a rehearsal context, the practice aim is mainly to develop and perfect choreographic material for performance. The structure of all of these sessions will differ according to their individual aims, but the balance of activities in each can be considered with attention to safe dance practice.

This chapter brings together many of the topics covered in other chapters and investigates how they might be absorbed into the dance session itself. The knowledge base accumulated throughout this book provides the foundation for making informed decisions on session content and delivery. Other chapters explain the principles that come into play when managing and sustaining training activities, but the predominant focus here is the planning of the single dance session and how it can be balanced to ensure effective integration of these principles. How can a dance session be designed and devised so that the activities within it logically fit together to promote safety and well-being?

This chapter may have most significance for teachers of dance classes, but it also provides applicable information for choreographers and rehearsal directors who construct schedules for dancers. The aim is not to provide detailed lesson plans for specific dance styles and for specific scenarios, but instead to prompt teachers or leaders to observe and examine their personal rationale in structuring their sessions in relation to safe dance practice guidelines. Chapter 11 also encourages ongoing evaluation and monitoring of session content and structure in personal practice.

FACTORS THAT INFLUENCE SESSION CONTENT, STRUCTURE AND DELIVERY

The terms progression and sequencing describe how the content, structure and delivery of dance sessions inter-relate and influence the way that dancers can gain skills and knowledge about a style through the manner in which the chosen activities are ordered.

Dance **pedagogy** (the academic appreciation of teaching in terms of educational theories) informs dance leaders on how to choose specific techniques and strategies to enhance learning. **Kinesiology** deals with the physiological, biomechanical and psychological elements of dance practice. Educational theory is extremely important, and it affects areas of safe dance practice, including the behavioural and psychological aspects discussed in chapter 1 and especially chapter 8. When leaders select appropriate material and use appropriate teaching methods, they create a positive learning climate (Kimmerle & Côté-Laurence, 2003). It is often difficult to separate out pedagogy and kinesiology, since good teachers are likely also to be safe teachers; therefore this chapter also introduces concepts of dance science that inform both teaching theory and physiological understanding, in particular, ideas from the field of **motor learning** (how movement skills are learned and developed). However, the main focus is on how to select methods and activities that avoid physically overstressing the body, help to reduce likelihood of injury, enhance performance and promote health and efficiency in dance practice.

Framed from a physiological or kinesiological perspective, the preliminary questions to consider for each session are as follows:

- How does the session prepare and warm up the specific muscle groups?
- How does it build up to full-body involvement?
- How does one exercise or activity link to the next?
- How much movement is involved, and how often are individual movements repeated?
- Are rest periods provided between exercises and activities?

- What is the appropriate pace and speed?
- How does the session help the dancer recover and cool down?

These factors all need to be considered in relation to their physical effects. Taking care to prepare the body and to avoid or counteract overwork for specific muscles and joints is part of teaching safely. **Repetition** is a necessary part of skill acquisition, but over-repetition can lead to fatigue. As chapter 9 explains, fatigue is a significant factor for injury risk (Laws, 2005). Making an informed judgement on how to balance practice benefits against physiological needs is a necessary skill for dance leaders. Leaders must assess the varying demands on the body during each phase of the session, from the warm-up into the preparatory exercises, to the peak of the actual dancing sequences and then the cool-down and recovery. Of course, it is not just teachers who have to balance their sessions. Choreographers, directors and company managers also make decisions about the amount, distribution and extent of their dancers' activities with some different constraints. In their eagerness to produce and complete work in short or perhaps expensive time allocations, they may not always be able to consider the structure of their sessions with physiological benefits in mind.

Dance Vocabulary

In addition to the physiological principles, other factors contribute to dance leaders' ability to make decisions on what they need to include. It goes without saying that they should have a good working knowledge of the stylistic vocabulary and how to technically achieve it. The vocabulary of the genre is the vehicle for communicating the essentials of the movement form, but simply reproducing vocabulary and using it to choreograph combinations is not the basis for constructing a sound dance session. Some styles have a recognised and translatable vocabulary (Graham or Cunningham technique, traditional Irish and Highland dance, classical Indian dance). Others are determined by cultural factors (folk dance) or prescribed by certifying organisations, as in aerobic dance, competition ballroom or Dance Sport (Gibbons, 2007).

Sometimes the dance technique teacher follows a series of predetermined arrangements performed in a set order (a syllabus), as is frequently seen in classical ballet classes. Other teachers working in newer hybrid styles will use their own personal references to different styles or their performing experience to build their own philosophy and language. Street styles originally arose by individual gangs or crews developing their own idiosyncratic vocabulary and passing it down hand to hand or by word of mouth.

While a knowledge of style-specific terminology is necessary for describing common movements in each genre, dance leaders must also be able to work out the physiological reasoning behind their material for themselves, so as to move beyond simply recreating steps. They have to analyse their own material and question the choices they make in order to train dancers effectively. Teachers often rely on replicating how they were taught themselves when making decisions on both the content and the modes of practice they employ (Rafferty & Wyon, 2006). This is called *inadvertent teaching*, and is based on principles that predate safety concerns in dancing (Gibbons, 2007). This type of approach can distract teachers from having to make personal decisions on the framework of their sessions. To ensure safety for all the individual participants, teachers must be ready to move away from any preconceived plans or syllabi in all settings if necessary.

Dancers will start by learning the vocabulary as the means for acquiring and developing the technical skills in their genre (Kassing & Jay, 2003). The challenge for technique teachers (especially if they practise in styles that are not universally formalised) is to build a clear set of principles underpinned by sound physiological understanding. A systematic delivery of vocabulary and concepts is necessary for safely communicating principles to others wishing to perform similar movement. This is not to say that the vocabulary and structure of traditional forms, even if they have been established for a long time, are not above scrutiny in terms of examining their safety and applicability. Scientific analysis has increased our understanding of the stresses placed on the body in physical activity, which in sport has improved training techniques, enhanced performance and helped to decrease the incidence of injuries. Developing dance science knowledge can now allow teachers to question dance practice more thoroughly than before. Specific movements have been the subject of sustained research in order to determine potentially detrimental biomechanical effects. Practical information on common contraindi-

> Creating a safe dance session depends on a systematic set of principles that takes into account the vocabulary, but does not simply rely on it. Dance leaders need to look beyond a syllabus to investigate the most physiologically sound way to thread activities together.

cated movements are outlined in the Contraindicated Movements and Actions section later in this chapter (see chapter 4 for information on contraindicated stretches), with recommendations for teachers and choreographers on what to minimise or avoid in practice and why.

Context

More important than the vocabulary itself is the context in which it is delivered. This has a major influence on the content, structure and progression of the session. The context includes the following:

- Purpose of the session (reason for participation)
- Ability level and experience of the participants
- Age and physical maturity of the dancers
- How each individual session relates to other training sessions
- Practice environment

Reason for Participation

The participants' reason and motivation for dancing have a vital role in deciding what to include in a dance session. Recreational and professional dancers take part in dance activities to serve very different outcomes. This chapter will have relevance for social and recreational dance but will have a strong focus on the more complex aspects of training and practice for the vocational student dancer and the professional.

Each genre has beginners and advanced dancers, and the dance material chosen for each will undoubtedly reflect their experience. The amount of work done in any one session depends on its purpose. The dance material, while following stylistic parameters, will vary in terms of the principles of training (as detailed in chapter 4) and in the way skills are learned and developed for each participant group. Dance leaders will need to evaluate the demands of their proposed content in a specific style and consider these in relation to the individuals in the class—this relies on their ability to make alternative on-the-spot decisions and adapt their material if necessary (Gibbons, 2007). If the practice environment is less than ideal, for example, if there is not much space, the floor is not sprung or the temperature is too cold, modifications to the content also need to reflect the conditions such as, increasing the warm-up time or avoiding jumping (see chapter 1 for more details on the characteristics of an ideal dance environment).

Managing Individual Sessions in Combination With Other Activities

Planning how much material to attempt in a single session in isolation is difficult enough when that session represents the only training vehicle for a group of dancers. Dance leaders should also consider how their material relates to other activities that same group of dancers may encounter. The detrimental effects of repetition can be cumulative within one session, between sessions or across sessions provided by different leaders. The individual session itself needs to be balanced, but it also needs to be seen in context with other activities so that overall demands are not excessive. (Chapter 5 discusses this in more detail when describing periodization.)

Material should always be targeted to the participants on any given day, time or in a particular situation. How does the session fit in with others? Is it one of many training or rehearsal sessions that day? Does it occur once a week? Does it represent the sole vehicle for training a group of dancers or is it part of curriculum? Its particular time of delivery can affect the content. Is it the first class of the day, the first class of a new course or term or the last in a daily schedule? The likely condition of the participants at these different contact points can influence their ability to meet the leader's expectations. For example, the first dance class of a new term or following a lay-off should be slower and less complex than usual to allow dancers to work back into their bodies. Intensity and more strenuous work should build up again gradually over the next few weeks (Krasnow & Chatfield, 1996).

Dance leaders are advised to limit the amount of sessions that address technical development and skill to 3 hours per day (Franklin, 2004), particularly if dancers also need to complete rehearsals, performance or supplementary training. Responses to the preceding questions will help leaders to determine both the length of the class and the amount and distribution of material it contains. Dance leaders often do not personally set the time frame for a session, but they can certainly modify the amount of activity within it. The necessity of proper planning should be highlighted but also the requirement for flexibility and adaptability in response to the needs of individuals and groups. Figure 6.1 provides points to consider when looking at the role of an individual session in combination with others.

DIFFERENTIATING AMONG LEARNING, TRAINING AND PRACTICE

The terms *practice* and *training* are frequently used interchangeably, but they have slightly different meanings. Practice can be defined as 'dedicated effort towards improving upon a skill or task' (Ives, 2014, p. 192), while training is aimed at 'improving physiological function and physical proficiency abilities' (Ives, 2014, p. 192). On the other hand, motor learning is concerned with how movement is learned as a result of practice or experience (Kimmerle & Côté-Laurence, 2003).

Training implies that there is a combination of physical conditioning and skill acquisition. Different types of sessions are constructed for different purposes, and might include varying degrees of skill learning or conditioning. Recreational and social dancers also train, but probably not to the same extent as the vocational dancer. Rather they will learn and practise sequences of movement either to gain more mobility and improve an aspect of fitness, or simply to be able to successfully dance with others. Student dancers in full-time training need to improve their physical capacities and their skills in tandem, with one supporting the development of the other. Professional dancers need to maintain their physical condition and reinforce their skills to support the learning and performance of new choreographic vocabulary. In all dance sessions it can be supposed that participants will be learning, practising and training, although the emphasis may differ. Looking at skills acquisition and conditioning separately will help leaders make appropriate judgements for the different groups.

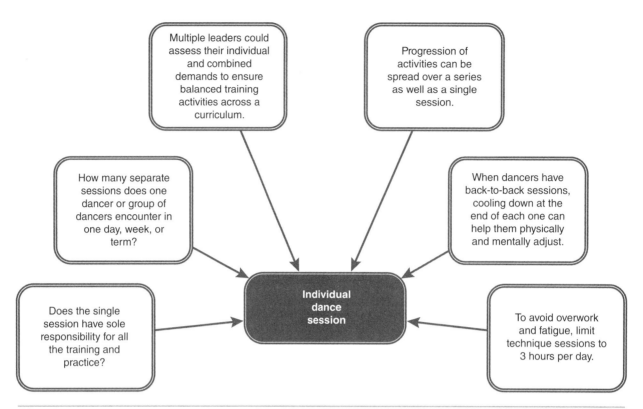

Figure 6.1   How the individual dance session relates to other sessions.

Franklin, 2004; Kassing and Jay, 2003; Krasnow and Chatfield, 1996.

All dancers want to improve their skills, but this is affected not just by their physical aptitude but also by their ability to learn. While this could be seen as an adjunct to safe dance practice, investigating the principles of **motor learning** can have benefits in preparing and delivering safe dance sessions.

Dance skills are specialised versions of simple motor skills, for example, turning, hopping, balancing and jumping. These are developed and filtered into specific stylistic interpretations, for example, a windmill turn on the upper back or head in hip-hop styles, the coccyx balance in modern Horton technique and the grand jeté in ballet. Skill learning is part of any dance style, and learners experience common difficulties across the dance forms, that is, how to sequence a series of dance skills in their own body, move in a particular way through space and adapt to different partner and group relationships (Kimmerle & Coté-Laurence, 2003). The relevance of motor learning for dance leaders is in what to expect from each participant group with regard to how they absorb information, assimilate and utilise that information independently and ultimately practise it successfully without detrimental effects. Understanding the different

stages of learning will help dance leaders to make appropriate decisions about what to include to match the learners' capabilities. In brief, these stages are as follows:

• *The verbal-cognitive stage.* The leader breaks down the material into small segments to introduce the dance vocabulary in manageable chunks and delivers it through demonstration and explanation. The student engages in consistent repetitive practice assisted by feedback from the leader. Correct preparation and technique at this stage of learning is important.

• *The motor stage.* The leader focuses on more specific problems with a more varied appreciation of the movement actions, which do not need as much input as in the previous stage. The student can independently manipulate and experiment with the vocabulary, and requires less feedback.

• *The autonomous stage.* The dance leader can rely less on visual cues and demonstration, instead using vocal reminders to encourage correct execution. Students have a more developed movement memory and can perform combinations of movements more accurately and automatically (Kassing & Jay, 2003; Kimmerle & Coté-Laurence, 2003).

Dancers at all levels can benefit from practising their genre-specific skills to improve both their understanding and their physical capacity. These student Irish dancers are working together to hone their footwork.

An understanding of these principles can help dance leaders assess the amount of instruction and feedback they need to provide for both teaching individual skills and working with specific groups, depending on the frequency of their contact time with them. Leading dance sessions and especially teaching dance technique classes effectively means that decisions on what to include and why must respond to the learners' capabilities. Dance teachers must recognise the different stages of learning at any one point in time in order to apply the most appropriate strategies. Some participants will have differences or difficulties in how to learn, and some may lack the physical ability to actually execute certain skilled movements. For example, dyslexic or dyspraxic dancers might experience disturbances with the planning, organisation and execution of movement (Gibbs, Appleton, & Appleton, 2007). See chapter 10 for more information for dancers with specific learning difficulties.

Younger children (under 8) are naturally unable to concentrate for more than 20 minutes at a time, and it is only in late adolescence that motor coordination stabilises (Kassing & Jay, 2003). When considering safety consequences, dance leaders inevitably are concerned with how dancers stay engaged with the session and how much information they can take on board in order to execute

tasks competently. With motor learning theories in mind, leaders can set appropriate material for the dancer's age, degree of maturity and skill level. More detailed information on the characteristics of different participant groups can be found in chapter 10.

Paying attention to the amount and quality of information provided in a dance session is the responsibility of both the teacher and the learner: Too much or too little information can reduce students' attention, and irrelevant or repetitive information can affect their span of attention (Gray, 1989). Overwhelming participants with an inappropriate level of stimulus will have negative effects, both mentally and physically. Learning motor skills effectively depends on how teachers are able to communicate the desired effects through the use of clear instruction and demonstration (their choice of appropriate language and their own technical ability and clarity of execution). If this is successful, students can develop correct technique from the outset, ensuring safe alignment and efficient muscle use. In motor learning, repetition of the specific skill reinforces the mastery of that skill. If the skill is incorrectly taught or is misunderstood, this version will then be more familiar to the student's body. The resulting inefficient movement patterns will then have to be unlearned at some point (Welsh, 2009).

Facilitating Motor Learning and Skill Acquisition

In terms of motor learning and skill acquisition, dance leaders are recommended to do the following (Kimmerle & Côté-Laurence, 2003):

- Appreciate the skills content of a good dance session.
- Understand the range of skills in each specific dance form.
- Identify and analyse the difficulty of specific skills.
- Organise a logical progression of skills, thinking about the relationship of one to another.
- Select age- and ability-appropriate skills for a session while still providing a learning challenge for participants

USING TRAINING PRINCIPLES TO CONSTRUCT A DANCE SESSION

A sound system of training is constructed by observing three basic principles (Bonderchuck, 1988, as cited in Bompa & Haff, 2009):

1. Knowledge of the theory and methods of training
2. Construction of the training methods
3. Constant evaluation of the system

Physical training in dance is often seen as a by-product of skill acquisition (Redding & Wyon, 2003; Wyon & Redding, 2005). In sport, the objectives of training include, among other things, multilateral physical development (general fitness), task-specific technical skills and injury resistance. Technical skills depend on both general and specific fitness, while injury resistance depends on the participants' physiological characteristics and their ability to endure training applications (Bompa & Haff, 2009). These objectives can be applied to dance practice, although how much dance training contributes to multilateral fitness has been questioned. It is undeniable that the skilled dancer needs strength, endurance, flexibility and co-ordination, but the extent to which the dance class, by itself, can contribute to the development of these components is debatable.

While including all of the training principles in the dance session might be unrealistic, certainly a better understanding of them will influence how leaders can select and arrange dance material to both support physical development and prevent injuries. Applying exercise physiology to dance training can enhance not only performance but also safety (Koutedakis & Sharp, 1999).

The relevant principles of training (see chapter 4) to bear in mind when building dance material are overload (related to intensity, volume, frequency and reversibility), specificity (and indi-

> *If physical training is the aim of the dance session, the dance leader must consider the principles that condition the body by integrating them into the selected activities. A well-prepared body will be able to work efficiently without succumbing to injury.*

viduality) and rest, but central to the application of these principles is the understanding of fatigue.

Fatigue is not just a matter of being or becoming tired. It is a complex notion that has repercussions for dancers in that it is one of the largest contributory factors to injury (Laws, 2005). It can be induced by an accumulation of workload over time, or can occur simply because one muscle group has been asked to do too much at a specific point. It is important to judge the value of performing single exercises or a combination of exercises so that fatigue is avoided.

For dance leaders, the difficulty is that if they want to train their dancers to improve their physical abilities within the style, they will need to find the balance between overload and fatigue, encouraging the former while avoiding the latter.

The sensation of overload is a slight discomfort in the muscles (Kassing & Jay, 2003), while fatigue is much more pronounced—the dancer will experience muscle weakness or even trembling. If this is in the legs, standing weight bearing will not be supported effectively. If fatigue manifests itself in the upper body, then dancers will not be able to support their own body weight in inversion or in lifting other bodies or holding onto equipment, both of which have obvious safety connotations. The dance leader must observe and appreciate the effects of fatigue on each individual dancer in order to be able to assess if their material is delivered at the appropriate level of difficulty.

Challenging the dancers' capabilities (increasing the difficulty of steps or asking them to repeat material more often in rehearsal) should be done gradually, working not at, but just above previous limits (Welsh, 2009). Using the weakest of the dancer's physical capacities rather than the strongest sets a realistic benchmark that is a guide to avoid progressing too quickly. Rapid progression leads to compensations in technique, usually negative, in order to match the demands (Welsh, 2009). However, the dancer must also be challenged: If dancers always do the same number of exercises (volume) at the same level of difficulty (intensity), they will not improve physically in terms of strength, flexibility or endurance, not to mention becoming bored and unfocused. This means that they will be able to meet only the demands of the material at a constant level, and will become injured if the demands are then increased for any reason. Similarly, excessive training at too high a volume or intensity produces no further improvement in capacity, but will have consequences

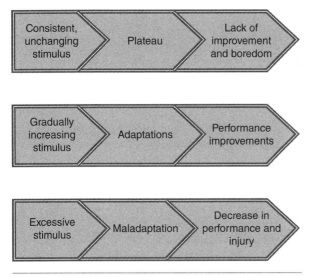

Figure 6.2 Effects of different work intensities on performance improvements.

in terms of chronic fatigue (Kenney, Wilmore, & Costill, 2012; see figure 6.2)

For dance leaders, an understanding of how to distribute the workload in class, training and rehearsal will only have positive benefits. Rather than having dancers consistently work at the same intensity and volume, changing the stimulus for

training and varying the type of exercises can help to keep dancers from becoming stale over time (Franklin, 2004; Heyward, 2006; Kenney et al., 2012). Manipulating the training principles in this way will involve examining how individual dance sessions and cumulative schedules are developed, progressed and arranged over time to achieve optimum results, ensuring dancers are not overworked, fatigued and injury prone.

As explained in chapter 4, the principle of specificity determines that the training for the dancing itself must stress the physiological systems that are essential for optimum performance in the given skill in order to achieve the necessary adaptations (Kenney et al., 2012). This means that the preparatory exercises should ideally involve the same type of muscle activity (for more on concentric, eccentric or isometric contractions, see chapter 2), the same ranges of motion and the same intensity, pace and speed as the activity to be performed (Heyward & Gibson, 2014; Schmidt & Lee, 2011). This concept is discussed further in relation to **transfer of learning** later in this chapter. An additional benefit from matching these preparatory training activities to skills necessary for dancing is that making the speed and power

Sequencing and Progression

■ ■ ■

A group of young dancers in training are studying with several teachers in different styles, working towards technical assessments as well as rehearsing for their end of year performance.

In their morning ballet class, their teacher is concerned that they are not able to jump accurately or efficiently, so resolves to help them improve with a targeted in-class conditioning programme for jumps. In their second class of the day, their contemporary/modern teacher sees that they are struggling with falling and recovering to and from the floor and decides to focus on these types of movements more specifically for a few weeks to improve their understanding and execution. The visiting choreographer working with the dancers for their end-of-year show is scheduled for an extended afternoon session five times a week for 4 weeks. He is making a piece that contains lots of hops and small jumps.

In each class, the teachers are careful not to overemphasise their specific focus, and the choreographer allows the dancers short but frequent breaks. In each individual session, the teachers attempt to reduce the impact of the increased specialisation, but inevitably, each leader spends a little more time than usual emphasising these specific areas as the assessments and performance approaches. The increased lower body focus fatigues the dancers' leg muscles more than usual, not because of the individual teacher's aims and good intentions but because of the cumulative effects and combined impact over a brief but intense period. Many of the dancers begin to show signs of overuse injuries, such as shin splints and tendinitis, which affect their ability in their technical assessments and compromise their performance in the final show.

Fatigue and Overload Within the Dance Session

- Repeating a single exercise or action too many times will stress and fatigue individual muscles.

- The greater the intensity (difficulty) and volume (amount) of work in each session, the greater the fatigue for dancers, and the more time they will need to recover properly for the next dance session.

- Overly long sessions create a large amount of fatigue, decreasing the quality of the training and affecting the dancers' ability to perfect technical skills.

- Increase overload in class by adding more difficult steps or performing a few more repetitions (see the sidebar Balancing Rest and Repetition in Practice).

- When student dancers change training styles and genres abruptly, they need to do a substantial amount of work to accommodate the new movement patterns. Some muscle groups may not have been subjected to the training overload in the previous style, and may be at risk of overwork in the new style. This can also apply to beginner social dancers who might not be used to an increased level of physical work.

- Dancers returning to work or class after a break, for example, following injury or pregnancy, must take care to slowly and methodically work up to the required level of intensity.

(Bompa & Haff, 2009; Clarkson & Skrinar, 1988; Grove, Main, & Sharp, 2013; Franklin, 2004; Kassing & Jay, 2003)

elements the same encourages the development of exercise economy (Bompa & Haff, 2009), an aptitude clearly seen in experienced dancers. Being able to work the body economically will obviously reduce the onset of fatigue. Remember that beginners and less experienced dancers who have not yet learned movement economy will tire more easily, and the volume of work will need to be reduced.

Related to specificity is the principle of individuality (see chapter 4), which means that each body is unique. Specificity might be different for each dancer because no two bodies are physiologically the same (Kassing & Jay, 2003). Not everyone will have the same capacity to adapt to exercise training, and the optimal amount of work may differ from person to person. Some people show greater improvement, while others show little change doing the same thing (Kenney et al., 2012). This has repercussions for the dancer and dance leader in terms of improving both fitness and dance skills for different individuals within a group. Having dancers grouped into levels of ability (beginners, advanced, improvers and so on) will help the dance leader to set appropriate limits for the majority of the group, but this is not always possible, for example, in community sessions or those that operate on a drop-in basis. Offering alternatives or adaptations to the move-

ment material might be necessary in order to allow all dancers to reach their potential. Individuality nevertheless needs to be taken into account when setting expectations and goals for any group. Including options to accommodate variations of ability (both increased and decreased) within one session will allow the leader to meet all the dancers' needs while challenging them to improve their individual skills (Kassing & Jay, 2003). Providing a choice for self-selection, rather than publicly identifying strong or weak members of the group, is likely to be the most psychologically sound way of approaching this strategy, but the leader should intervene and advise discreetly if dancers consistently demonstrate an unrealistic appreciation of their own skills.

Repetition

The number of times an exercise will be performed (**repetition**) and its level of difficulty determines the likelihood of fatigue occurring. It is a common assumption that professional and preprofessional dancers must prove themselves through relentless physical effort. The stereotype of the budding dancer working to exhaustion in order to make it in the profession is a popular media image. It is reported that rest carries the negative connotation of lack of dedication or commitment to being an

Specificity and Individuality in Practice

- Make sure that exercises that prepare the dancer to perform the stylistic sequences are specific. They should incorporate the same physiological elements as the dancing sequences, ideally using similar directions (not always facing one way or into a mirror), bases of support (sitting, standing or lying down) and static or moving contexts (use weight shift as well as on-the-spot exercises).

- Does the stylistic material unnecessarily isolate parts of the body by practicing only one leg or arm in gesture and support at a time? Consider how the class moves from simple bases of support (two feet) to more complex (one foot, hands or even head), and give physical indications of this transition before asking students to perform these actions suddenly in routines and combinations.

- In supplementary fitness activities, choose exercises that mimic the planes of motion, range of motion, intensity, timing and speed (with care) that are needed in your dance skills, and then apply the overload principle to make physiological improvements.

- Think about how each individual is responding to the material. Try not to expect the same rate of improvement from each dancer and avoid making comparisons or judgments of dancers who might respond differently at various points in their training. Offer adaptations for varying ability levels within one group if possible without singling out individuals or making them feel inadequate.

(Clarkson & Skrinar, 1988; Krasnow & Chatfield, 1996)

artist (Batson, 2009). However, excessive repetition also has detrimental effects.

Hard work is necessary, but how hard do different dancers need to work? Those who train less frequently, for fun or to participate in purely creative activities, will not need the same level of intensity in practice. Training towards being a professional dancer can be rigorous and consuming– the specific stylistic movements must be repeated over and over again in practice to become adept. It has been established that repetition is a necessary process for skill acquisition and a way to increase intensity and level of difficulty. It is essential both in order to perfect specialized motor skills and to build stamina, strength and flexibility to develop efficient neuromuscular pathways and kinaesthetic awareness (Gibbons, 2007; Kimmerle & Coté-Laurence, 2003). Under-repetition can lead to a lack of training effect and confusion over how to master skills but over-repetition and excessive practice can also lead to boredom, frustration and lack of attention (Gibbons; Gray, 1989). While it is a traditional notion in dance training that the more times a skill is performed, the better it will be, in most cases the opposite is true (Kassing & Jay, 2003). Effective practice is not about repetition after repetition until perfect (Ives, 2014).

If a muscle targeted in a particular exercise becomes overworked and fatigued, dancers often subconsciously shift the action slightly to take the stress off this muscle, which can result in the exercise being done incorrectly and potentially stressing other muscles (Gibbons, 2007). As discussed in chapter 2, inefficient alignment or physical limitations will already have an effect on the individual dancer's ability to work safely. Chapter 9 also explains that technical faults are a risk factor for injury. Both of these factors are further compounded by frequent practice and lack of recovery. Poor technical habits and less-than-ideal biomechanical relationships in the body are reinforced through the accumulated effects of repetition, contributing to overuse injuries (Berardi, 2005). The challenge for dance leaders is to balance out the benefit of repetition with the danger of fatigue and to recognise when repetition has served its purpose and has reached its limit. To counteract and mediate the effects of repetition, they must incorporate rest periods within the session. The principles of rest and recovery are covered in more detail in chapter 5.

Rest has distinct benefits for all levels of dancers, and it can be utilised in a variety of ways, for example, using teaching strategies that incorporate

> *Training hard does not mean working to excess. The activities during the session should be balanced, and should include strategic rest periods that allow for recuperation and reflection to benefit both training and learning.*

group discussion and observation, setting up an opportunity to refuel and rehydrate or simply taking a few minutes of time out for a comfort break. Researchers in somatic practice highlight the value of non-doing and indicate that personal options to consider the idea of rest might be deliberately assuming a resting posture (sitting or lying down), paying attention to breathing, or stopping to listen to the body's kinaesthetic sensations (Batson & Schwarz, 2007; Batson, 2009). Sitting down in dance class or rehearsal (during practice rather than in a designated break), at least for adult dancers, has long been frowned upon. As already mentioned, dancers may avoid sitting so that they are not seen as lacking commitment, but the main concern is that of cooling down. This can be a problem if rest periods are not clearly directed and integrated attentively. Cooling down can happen, for example, if some dancers are rehearsed for any length of time in separate groups while others are not used, if performers have to wait their turn to go on stage or if teachers talk too much and give excessive corrections in class (Berardi, 2005). Rest does not necessarily have to mean stopping completely—taking a few seconds to listen and observe or even practising at a lower intensity will have benefits.

Other options are to engage in brief recovery stretches (see chapter 3 and the discussion on stretching in class later in this chapter) to reset the muscle length following certain types of movement, for example, flexing the spine for a moment to ease out following prolonged arching of the back. Taking a short hydration break and listening to the music while mentally rehearsing the material are also useful. Alternatively, the length of the session itself could be adapted and varied. If one class works particularly on one movement skill or fitness component, the session the next day could be shorter and less intense, perhaps using a contrasting effort and energy level.

Some styles require a high volume of repetition of similar movements in their vocabulary, for example, the drilling of the heels in flamenco.

This is a necessary feature of the style that clearly needs to be practised, but in styles such as this that have comparatively less movement variability, strategic rest points will be very beneficial. Alternatively, the traditional patterns in some styles dictate the amount of repetition, for example, the *en croix* (cross) arrangement in classical ballet. It has been suggested that there is little justification in repeating the same material to the front, side, back, then side again, and that the repetitions in the three main directions will be enough for training purposes (White, 1996). Lateral equality is rightly seen as very important for muscle balance, but does each exercise have to be performed exactly the same number of times to each side in every dance class, or would it be possible to balance out the same activities over consecutive classes, concentrating on one side one day and the other the next?

Appropriate **pacing** is one of the most challenging aspects of teaching a dance class. It can have an effect on developing both the mastery of the skill and the psychological response of the participants, especially in terms of their confidence and self-esteem (Mainwaring & Krasnow, 2010). Dancers need to be able to push their limits to achieve overload, but should not be overwhelmed by material that is too fast and sessions that are crammed with too much information. If skills or concepts are introduced too quickly or new ones added on too frequently, little time is available to really practise, master or retain them (Gray, 1989).

The progressive flow of the activities in a session needs to be paced appropriately for each participant group. Too many long, complex exercises can have several negative effects: The dancer must focus more on remembering material than accurately executing it; the teacher has to demonstrate the material too much, which means the dancer might cool down; and the student might become saturated with skill demands and experience mental fatigue (Krasnow & Chatfield, 1996).

It has been suggested that the quality of a training session is more important than its length or quantity. Therefore, it is the responsibility of a teacher or rehearsal director to recognise the point at which the quality of the movement starts to become compromised. At this point, rather than encourage dancers to try harder, leaders should give them a break (Wyon, 2010a).

Research suggests that consistently high-impact dance classes and rehearsals should last a maximum of 60 minutes and should contain several rest opportunities: A suggested work to rest ratio is 1:3 to allow recovery from the high-intensity sequences and to avoid compromising movement quality, for example, in a rehearsal when a dancer needs to perform the same section of choreography several times in a row (Wyon & Koutedakis, 2013).

In companies, rehearsal sessions should be based on quality, not quantity because concentration and learning ability diminish after 30 minutes. Therefore back-to-back rehearsals are counterproductive (Wyon, 2010a). Shorter exercise durations have been suggested as a means of injury prevention (Batson & Schwarz, 2007).

This wide range of factors to take into account when planning sessions could easily overwhelm the dance leader. Clearly, the principles described so far in this chapter will have more or less influence on their working practice depending on the characteristics of their specific participants, as well as the amount of contact time with their dancers (how much time is allocated to one session and how much time passes between sessions). To reiterate, making informed decisions about the content and structure of dance sessions is essential in order to prevent overwork but also to safely encourage positive training adaptations. In both recreational and vocational settings, these are common aims. Even if there may be contrasting extremes in the type of workload depending on the nature of the session, dance is still 'a demanding and intricate form of movement which requires development of each of the components of training' to participate safely (Clarkson & Skrinar, 1988, p. 81).

STRUCTURE AND CONTENT OF INDIVIDUAL DANCE SESSIONS

Formal research on dance session progression and sequencing in general, let alone for specific genres, is comparatively limited, although class plans, guides to styles, vocabularies, glossaries and how-to tutorials are abundant, both in print and online.

The physiological or kinesiological viewpoint, as opposed to the skill acquisition emphasis, is not always taken into account. The components for each style may differ, but they all have (or should have) commonalities: warm-up and preparation, exercises that improve skills, specific elements that work towards dance movements in combination and attention to cooling down. In the recreational format, these specific parts might be less defined so that the focus is on having fun and enjoying the dancing (Kassing & Jay, 2003). In this case it is usual to see combinations of steps linked together to form longer sequences, practised in each session so that the learning time is reduced, and saving time for more doing. The variability for vocational and professional dancers is likely to be greater. In

Balancing Repetition and Rest in Practice

- Make sure the session progresses gradually, and is punctuated by periods of rest so that the body can regenerate physically and mentally from the stresses of style-specific training.

- Question the purpose of repetition for any given task and gauge the value in terms of learning and the likelihood of fatigue.

- Try to include different types of rest that can also help with teaching and learning strategies, for example, using peer-observation tasks, asking dancers to take a moment to reflect on feedback or marking through material for memory rather than dancing it full-out each time.

- If one day is particularly intense, lower the training intensity the next day.

- Avoid over-rehearsal of one specific piece of choreography to the exclusion of other activities.

- Take short refuelling (snack) and hydration breaks across the course of the day or during a rehearsal to physiologically support the dancers.

- Balance out the practice activities throughout the session and between a series of sessions to space out the workload effectively.

(Clarkson & Skrinar, 1988; Kassing & Jay, 2003; Simmel, 2014; Wyon, 2010a)

creative classes, the focus is more on exploration and discovery of movement potential through open tasks rather than on prescribed exercises.

In general, whatever the purpose of the dance session, progression can be thought of as the preparation, the practice or training and the recovery (see figure 6.3). Different types of activity can be inserted into this progression to ensure a logical arrangement that minimises stress on the body.

In all styles, the basis for the construction of a safe and effective session is a logical progression of suitable exercises and activities guided by a clear methodology. Dance leaders must have the ability to devise exercises that make sense and fit together (White, 1996). The template for dance leaders is based on movement principles that make anatomical, kinesiological and physical sense, and it is the leaders' responsibility to highlight these principles to their participants and indicate clearly how they should be applied (Berardi, 2005). Tradition has a substantial influence on methodology, particularly for the more formal, established styles. On the other hand, a word-of-mouth or mimicry (passing on by copying) type of approach can also communicate newer, less codified sub-styles.

Much of the research into dance class structure has been undertaken with classical ballet, precisely because it is one of the oldest, most recognisable forms, with little practice variation. Because of all the attention and the employment of new technology and physical assessment techniques, some of the actions that have long been an integral part of the ballet vocabulary have come into question. Examples of these are included in the Contraindicated Movements and Actions section later in this chapter. Although some of the most readily available dance science research is based on the classical ballet form, it is especially important for emerging styles to take note of any exploratory research in order to create viable, safe and effective training plans. Dancers, students and especially dance leaders in all genres should be open to new ideas and prepared to investigate their own stylistic vocabulary and session structure. Gaining knowledge in order to make informed decisions will help prevent risks and allow the styles to continue to develop safely.

The basis for determining the sequencing and progression of dance content is the choice of movements (vocabulary), the amount of repetition and the location of the specific movements in the scan of the whole session. Whether a class, rehearsal or supplementary workout, each session should be built on principles that progressively develop the dancer's technique, skills or fitness. A well-designed structure that helps dancers acquire both vocabulary and skills and improve physiological components is the key to training effectively (Kassing & Jay, 2003). An understanding of the energy systems required for performance in different dance styles would also be helpful (the mixture of aerobic and anaerobic demands). Certain skills are common to many styles, for example, alignment, motor control, co-ordination and balance. The foundation for the basic skills in each genre must be set in place before more complex and sophisticated vocabulary and combinations can be attempted (Mainwaring & Krasnow, 2010).

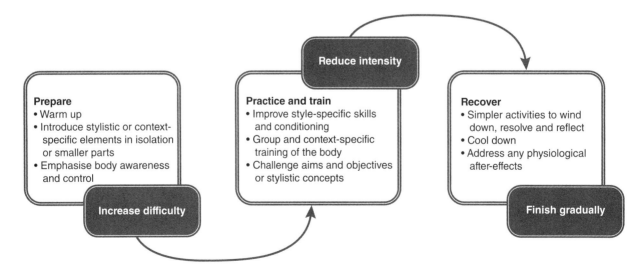

Figure 6.3 General dance session progression.

> *Each part of the dance session has specific demands. The selection of appropriate activities for each stage depends on the purpose, the skills to be learned and the people doing the learning.*

The structure of almost any dance class can be distilled down into the following template:

1. Generic warm-up, followed by a style-specific warm-up

2. Preparatory exercises to introduce and break down stylistic movement patterns, actions and sensibilities (often emphasising alignment and technical concepts)

3. Progressive exercises that specifically address dancers' physical capacities for that style (for example, the development of required strength and flexibility)

4. The actual dancing: combinations of movements that move through space, using different orientations, levels, speeds, intensities and dynamic movement qualities, and test the dancers' knowledge, understanding, adaptability and readiness for performance (which means ability to dance successfully in the style rather than being on stage)

5. Cool-down

However, this template needs to be applied by considering the context of the session. The first question to ask when planning a dance session is to determine its purpose. Is it a creative class, a recreational session, a rehearsal towards a performance, a warm-up or one of a daily set of training classes? The level of difficulty of material and the physiological demands to be made will need to be determined with this purpose in mind.

The priority in planning is to consider the participants: their reason for dancing, their ability level and their age. The key point to remember is not simply to teach the session effectively but to teach effectively to the specific people in the session. It is important not to judge all dancers by their ability to achieve perfect technique or their intention to work towards achieving it. For example, adult participants in social settings may consider enjoyment and interaction more important than achieving technical perfection in their motivation to dance, while children may be more

engaged by creative, expressive movement than formalised techniques (Gibbons, 2007).

Unique population groups are directly addressed in chapter 10, but there are broad theoretical questions to ask in determining the basic dance material (Gibbons, 2007):

- What is the aim of the session (training, social)?
- What is the ability level of the group (for example, in terms of degrees of strength, flexibility and cardiorespiratory capacity)?
- Are there unique considerations for the group (age, sex, life stage, ability or disability)?
- How does the class contribute to the overall amount of dance practice?

In planning their sessions from a physiological perspective, dance leaders could take the lead from sports and consider a training needs analysis (Kenney et al., 2012). This can be adapted to fit the dance session by asking:

- Which muscles will be used, or need to be trained?
- How will they be used or trained?
- Which energy systems (aerobic or anaerobic) are involved in the dance style?
- Which are the primary sites of concerns for injury prevention?

Depending on these needs, the dance leader then needs to logically select:

- The exercises that will be performed
- The order that they will be performed in
- The number of times they are to be repeated to produce a training effect and avoid fatigue
- The amount of rest between each exercise or set of exercises

Examination of the preceding questions and points will inform the overall structure of the session. This can be broken down into several stages: in very simple terms, the beginning, middle and end. While this seems quite obvious, there can sometimes be a blurring of activities that sit most comfortably and efficiently within each stage. The beginning of the session will include the warm-up and preparatory exercises and activities. The body of the class will increase in difficulty and demand to develop the specific skills for each style, working towards a peak of activity, the actual dancing, which brings together the preparatory and developmental work in combinations, sequences and routines. Following this peak, the demand will reduce and the material will focus on a cool-down and recovery. This pattern may be contrary to the structure of many dance sessions, where it is common to see a more or less gradual and consistent progression of intensity that culminates in a peak at the very end. Rather than sustaining or increasing the intensity throughout a session (see common practice, figure 6.4a), the dance leader could include periodic short rest and recovery periods, working towards the peak in activity (the big dancing combinations) before bringing down the intensity earlier in the session (recommended practice, figure 6.4b). A session that takes into account pacing and recovery by following the recommended pattern will be more beneficial for dancers. This is discussed further in the section End of the Session later in this chapter. The Repetition section earlier in this chapter provides some guidelines as to the type of activities that might be appropriate in order to follow this pattern.

Beginning of the Session

The beginning of the session is the introduction to exercising and to the style itself (see figure 6.5). It is 'opening doors to the work ahead' (Erkert, 2003, p. 86). Ideally, all the bodies physically participating in the session will be warm and ready to go—this includes the teacher and choreographer as well as the dancers. This cannot always be relied upon since not all participants will have the skills to understand how to warm up properly, for exam-

ple, beginners and children. For more experienced dancers and recreational dancers already familiar with the stylistic vocabulary, it is good practice to encourage them to prepare in advance for the session, especially before a rehearsal that does not have the same build-up as dance class. Although the dance class begins (or rather should begin) with focused, style-specific introductory movement, even the most experienced of teachers will not be able to design a specific warm-up to meet the needs of all the individual bodies in their class (Dunn, 2014), making self-preparation all the more important.

The preparatory stage of the session is often, confusingly, referred to as the warm-up. This is where the potential for injury becomes evident. A true warm-up means physiologically preparing the body for subsequent exercise (see chapter 3), but teachers frequently also label their stylistic preparations for later exercises as their warm-up. If dancers are told that the class begins with a warm-up section, they might assume that their leader will provide a physiologically based set of exercises that activates the cardiovascular system, raises the heart rate and brings heat to the muscles and lubrication to the joints. If this is not the case, and the teacher instead means that their warm-up comprises a set of introductory technical exercises, the dancer may not be sufficiently prepared for the style-specific movement patterns. To combat this, dance leaders could try to incorporate some general, physiological warm-up activities before, or in combination with, style-specific actions at the very beginning of the session. Preparing the body effectively means working progressively from using larger, more global muscle groups (warm-up) to smaller muscle groups that address the subtle

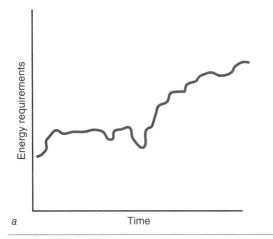

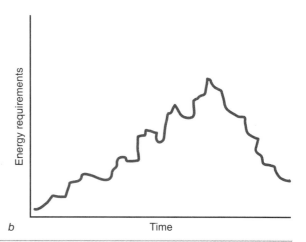

Figure 6.4   Common (a) and recommended (b) intensities during dance sessions.

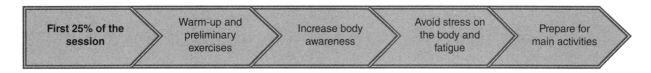

Figure 6.5 Beginning of the session.

and distinctive aspects of each technique and refine the neuromuscular co-ordination needed to perform style-specific vocabulary successfully and safely (technical preparation).

So, once the large muscle groups are warmed, it is wise to then focus locally on movements, breaking skills down so that the dancer is able to concentrate on fewer technical aspects to allow the body to acclimatise to the style more slowly. This also begins to activate muscle patterns that are inherent in the stylistic vocabulary. In many formal dance styles, a class will begin with more stationary exercises and work from a balanced base (two feet) to shift weight onto one leg, with or without turnout, using gesture and weight bearing to encourage balance, co-ordination and integration of the different body parts. These more straightforward movement activation patterns for particular body parts are then added together in combination. For example, a jazz class will perform isolations of different body areas, such as the head, ribs and hip, a belly dance class would begin with hip rotations and spinal undulations and a pole dance class will concentrate on basic connections with the pole before proceeding further. In classical ballet, this will involve practising alternating gestures and weight bearing on different sides of the body. In styles using inversion and upper body work, simple exercises to introduce upper body weight bearing, performed with low demand (less athletic or virtuosic emphasis), can be included. If the style requires the dancers to work in shoes, some introductory exercises to encourage acclimatisation to the altered balance and base of support will be beneficial (see chapter 2 for more on alignment and issues with footwear).

Often, the beginning of the session concentrates on creating the correct alignment and setting up efficient movement patterns that will inform subsequent dynamic actions. These preparatory exercises should minimise the stress on the body. If dancers are first given time to access their organisational and postural support through smaller, more focused and distinctive muscle activation and motor patterns (specificity), they can then effectively integrate these when actually danc-

ing, that is, when asked to use them in a more global context (Daniels, 2009). Proprioceptive exercises are useful at this point to bring greater kinaesthetic awareness to alignment and connectivity (see chapters 3 and 4 for more detail on proprioception).

Some styles use the floor to minimise the effects of gravity (lying down or sitting) or use equipment to provide support for the initial training exercises and before attention is given to translating the exercises to an unsupported context (for example, the ballet barre or floor work in Graham or Release techniques). Others need to build up the physical assurance first in order to safely transfer to equipment (for example, in vertical work such as wire, ribbon or pole). In styles that require close partner contact, introductory exercises and activities need to take into account not just individual readiness but also partner connection. Any session involving a couple working together as a unit needs to have some preliminary partnering activities that uses the very basic step patterns and brings awareness to the communication signals, for example, the understanding of following and leading roles. In social, ballroom, tango and some folk styles, good leading and following responses are very important for synchronising the rhythm, responding to cues and learning how to manage the shared weight and negotiate the foot patterns (Kassing & Jay, 2003). There needs to be a synergy between

> *Warm-up and style-specific preparatory activities are not the same. Warm-up physiologically prepares the body for increased activity, while introductory stylistic exercises introduce the concepts, vocabulary and specific co-ordination needed to practise.*

the two dancers so that couple can perform as a single body.

In this early stage of the session, the exercises should address each major muscle group and body part. The joints and muscle groups should be taken through their own full range of motion using multiplanar movements: flexion and extension in the sagittal plane (known as homologous movement), abduction and adduction in the lateral plane (homolateral movement patterns) and rotational or spiralling movements in the transverse plane (contralateral movements; Erkert, 2003). (See chapter 2 for more information on planes of movement and movement descriptors.) This provides the body with a good three-dimensional preparation. Excessively sharp movements and extreme speed should be avoided at this point.

The amount of time spent on this preparatory phase will depend on the total length of the class as well as its overall purpose: class, rehearsal, performance, competition or event. In general, it usually represents around 25 to 30 percent of the whole class time, perhaps a little more for beginners in formal styles. If the context is a rehearsal, this stage can be relatively brief as long as dancers are still prepared gradually to ease into the session, working towards the repertory using low-intensity impressions of the choreography to come. A choreographer could choose the least demanding section of the work to begin the session and work up to the more intensive excerpts. For example, marking through the first run would

help the dancers to engage with the material and concentrate on remembering their own roles, and would serve to raise ensemble spatial awareness in preparation for more full-out run-throughs.

A useful technique to maximise learning and practice time within a session is to consider a set introduction that does not need to be retaught every session. This will allow more time to focus on the actual integration of the elements in combination. It is also one way to effectively address a cardiorespiratory training element. To successfully support improvements in stamina, dance leaders could amalgamate the initial class-specific preparatory exercises to create a longer series that is familiar to the dancers. This section could then be conducted at a continuous (but moderate) pace for 20 to 30 minutes. The downside of this approach is that opportunities for feedback are more limited, but dance leaders could consider conducting this type of class on alternate days so that the focus of this stage of the class can be either predominantly skill learning or physiological improvements (White, 1996).

In competitive environments, such as aerobic dance, dance sport and freestyle events, it is important to find a way to safely and gradually

Dancers performing style-specific exercises in the beginning of class, following their preparatory warm-up

increase the level of activity before the performance. This may be difficult when individuals, couples or teams need to suddenly get on stage and perform energetically and athletically to their maximum. Dance leaders in these contexts must encourage their dancers to warm up thoroughly and stay warm before their appearance. Dancers should use gentle full-body movements to maintain mobility rather than sitting down and perhaps watching other competitors, wear additional layers of clothing and stay in a warm environment to ensure their body temperature remains elevated.

The Motor Learning Perspective

Once again, motor learning principles can inform the choices of material at this stage. A common technique for teaching motor skills is to break them down into smaller parts; that is, introducing movement actions in smaller components that can be learned before incorporating them into more complex movement patterns. Dancers, especially beginners and children, can benefit from learning how to jump, turn or fall safely before attaching style-specific requirements. This separation into achievable chunks would also help dance leaders explain how to do more unusual movement vocabulary that poses particular risks, for example, inverted material, one-handed balances or material with gymnastic or athletic content.

In terms of organising dance material, it is often assumed that beginners of any age need to work on more stationary material, such as static alignment, and are not ready to move dynamically until they have mastered the basics. However it is recommended that locomotor skills should be practised right from the beginning of training so that dancers can learn how to shift weight and adjust alignment, since these skills require different neuromuscular mechanisms (Kimmerle & Côté-Laurence, 2003). This aspect of learning has relevance to the choices of movement material for the different stages of the dance session.

Transfer of Learning

Considering the concept of **transfer of learning** can raise questions about how best to distribute activities throughout the session. Transfer of learning is defined as 'previous learning and experiences influencing the learning of subsequent motor skills' (Ives, 2014, p. 147). It enables individuals to take what is learned in one situation and apply it in another. The idea is that learning the smaller skill components will translate and inform the performance of the more complex combination of skills. However, there is also a concern that practising the isolated parts of the skill may actually change the motor programming so that it is no longer the same as it is in the context of the main skill (Schmidt & Lee, 2011). The success of the transfer depends on how similar the skills elements in each context are. Positive transfer occurs when there are very similar or identical elements between the two: This can happen when there is a progression of skill components from simple to complex, giving the learner a platform from which to advance by developing and refining the simpler patterns into secondary skills (Ives, 2014). Conversely, negative transfer interferes with this process because the skills in each context are too different. For example, research suggests that tasks with similar relative timing and sequencing will tend to transfer to each other positively, while two tasks that have similar sequencing but a different timing will tend to transfer to each other negatively. A task with neither in common will have little or no transfer effect (Schmidt & Lee, 2011).

What is the significance of transfer of learning to dance practice? Dance science researchers have suggested that teachers could look again at the connection between the warm-up and preparatory phases of the dance class and the motional work in the later stages. Once again, the classical ballet class has been the subject of much of the research, but examining this style can identify some key points that are applicable to other class structures. It has been proposed that the ballet barre (preparatory phase) focuses more on training the gesture leg, while the centre work (in the body of the class) emphasises the placement and stability of the standing leg, therefore the efficacy of the potential transfer in terms of progression might be questioned (Berardi, 2005). Similarly, the orientation of the barre work mostly asks the dancers to work sideways to a mirror, face one direction and work one arm and leg at a time, while their centre work usually requires them to face the mirror, frequently change direction and shift the weight from leg to leg (Clarkson & Skrinar, 1988). The potential effectiveness of the transfer of learning in this case has been questioned (Krasnow & Chatfield, 1996). How do the exercises at the barre contribute to dancers' physical understanding of how to work in an unsupported manner and three-dimensionally in space?

The point here is to stimulate dance teachers to investigate why they select certain movements in preparation for sequences or routines later in the session. They might ask themselves why they begin on the floor, which involves a different relationship to gravity, if the bulk of their dancing activity requires strength to work muscles against gravity? How might the most frequent base of support for the dancing style (weight exchange between two feet, the upper body, the whole body moving in and out of the floor) be introduced within this preparatory stage of the session? How does the play between standing on the spot, weight shift and variations in balance or centre of gravity translate into travelling through space in the particular stylistic idiom? Are the preparatory exercises performed only at slow speeds, while later in the class, the dancer is asked to perform the same skills at a faster pace? There may be very good reasons why dance leaders will work on similar movements in different contexts, for example, to be able to break down the action into smaller parts effectively or use the floor to access material from alternative perspectives, but they must be able to judge the benefits of each element rather than simply assuming that the actions will automatically transfer.

Specificity once again becomes involved. It is advised to use material in the preparatory stages of the class that is not too far removed from the dancing context. If the required muscle firing patterns are accessed earlier on, the muscle groups will be able to work synergistically (see chapter 2) while dancing to encourage specific strength and endurance and promote efficiency. Specificity and transfer of learning also have relevance in the design of supplementary conditioning programmes for dancers (see chapter 4). These concepts also affect the timing and setting of individual dance sessions and how they relate to one another within a co-ordinated curriculum (the choice and combination of complementary styles or activities to formulate overall training strategies), as in vocational training schools or studio programmes.

In the last part of the preparatory stage, when the body is woken up and ready for more, dance leaders should have identified the muscles they need to train for their dance style and begin to introduce more demanding training exercises. In the next phase leaders can implement specific solutions for strengthening the weaker muscles using the principles of training, so the end of the preparatory stage is a good place to think about changing gears.

Body of the Session

In some dance forms, it is difficult to ascertain where the beginning (style-specific preparation) ends and the body of the class begins, since these can often merge together (Kassing & Jay, 2003). In certain styles, it is very clear, as in the move away from the ballet barre, but in others the activity gradually metamorphoses from preparation to integration.

Tips for the Beginning of the Session

- Warm-up and preparation exercises are different. Dancers should perform a thorough general physiological warm-up (usually before the session begins), and then the leader will take them through graduated preparatory exercises. To be sure that all the dancers are warm, incorporate some general movements with the involvement of large muscle groups, using dynamic stretching techniques, during the very first exercises (see chapter 3).

- After the pre-session or generic warm-up, introduce movement actions in smaller components so that dancers can acclimatise to the stylistic vocabulary and concentrate on a few technical aspects at a time.

- Try to include some movement patterns that mimic the actual dancing part of your session. Performing similar movement patterns too statically, slowly or in a different orientation (sitting, lying down or in only one position) could interfere with transfer of learning.

- Avoid excessive speed at this point.

- Static stretching at the end of the first phase may be counterproductive if the session involves subsequent jumping activities.

- *Motor learning tip:* Include actions in the preparatory exercises that directly relate to the movements in combination, using as much specificity as possible to help transfer of learning.

Nevertheless, around the end of the preliminary stage is often a good place for a short rest or regrouping period. A drink of water would be a good idea here to rehydrate the dancers for the next, more demanding stage. Some styles traditionally use this natural pause as an opportunity for stretching. Opinion suggests that stretching at this point of class is beneficial for easing any muscular tension that might have built up during the preparatory work. However, research shows that stretching during the class is not always productive. Prolonged static stretches cause a decline in strength, power and endurance, although brief stretches of up to 15 seconds are unlikely to cause substantial deficits (Critchfield & IADMS, 2012; Wyon, 2010b). This is especially relevant if jumping activities are included in the body of the session. Questioning the reason for stretching at any point in the dance session should be encouraged, and the decision to include stretching should be founded on physiological understanding rather than a reliance on progressions based on tradition. Static stretching within a dance class should only be included when necessary and when productive, such as using fast-stretching techniques to counteract the repetitive concentric (shortening) muscle action of the calf muscles following a series of repetitive jumps. If controlled dynamic stretching has been used in preparatory activities as advised, then the body will be prepared properly (Critchfield & IADMS, 2012). See chapter 3 and chapter 4 for more information on these stretches in relation to warm-up and cool-down and flexibility training respectively.

Some styles also include an intermediate or transitional stage to add another step towards the main dance section. This could be the move from the barre to centre practice in ballet, or the point where the dancer leaves the floor and comes to standing work in contemporary techniques. This is said to be an opportunity to work the muscles closer to the bone (the postural muscles) and to expose the variety of co-ordination patterns that will be used in the longer movement combinations—in any case, the dancer should be thoroughly warm (Erkert, 2003). The function of exercises at this point is to develop unsupported balance and stability and to enhance functional strength. It is very important then that the dancer is adequately prepared for this phase. A common pitfall when progressing into more complex work is to jump (sometimes quite literally) into the increased intensity without physical warning. Perhaps a dance teacher has spent much of the class lying on the floor to engage her students' attention with deep movement patterns and body relationships, then will stand and immediately begin to move through space. This lack of build-up for locomotion will result in sudden activation and increased demand in different muscle groups, which may cause injury.

In most styles, the body of the session represents the main purpose of the class, that is, to actually be dancing rather than preparing to dance. All in all, it is generally longer in length than the preparation, and takes up approximately 50 percent of the session time. It is distinguished from the preparatory stage mostly by the amount of locomotion involved, using more spatially ambitious combinations of movements (see figure 6.6). It is usually the focal point of the class, but it should not be the sole point of the class. It has been suggested that perhaps too much emphasis is placed on combinations and routines and that 'a very good class may never get to the combination if concepts are followed through from the beginning to the end of the session' (Erkert, 2003, p. 87).

This stage can be used either as an introduction to a new sequencing of material (the way movement travels through the body) that encourages dancers to learn how to manipulate combinations of movement more independently, or as a review of previously learned steps or dances, such as in folk or social dance (Gibbons, 2007). The dancer definitely moves more in this portion than in the early stages of the class, and is usually asked to deal with material that is more complex, has more pronounced demands, and is conducted at a higher intensity and increased pace. There are distinct changes in effort, achieved through using different rhythms and tempo, and the material usually might move from the familiar to the unknown

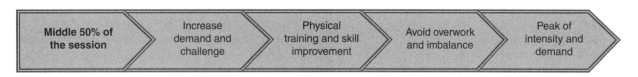

Figure 6.6 Body of the session.

(Gibbons, 2007). In some styles, this is often the reverse, for example, in recreational and traditional forms, when new elements are introduced early on and then added on to accentuate and develop previous sequences.

In this phase of the dance session, the workload needs to be balanced through the different muscle groups. Spending too long working on one action or choosing consecutive exercises that focus exclusively on the same muscle groups will cause fatigue. The order of exercises might be varied so that different body areas are tested alternately, much like a fitness programme. For example, it can be productive to alternate the work in antagonistic muscle groups, address upper and lower body stresses or left and right balance and emphasise strength, endurance or flexibility (Krasnow & Devau, 2011). This is easier said than done, since dance is a full-bodied activity, and it rarely relies on one body part or action over another. Nevertheless, if this is kept in mind, the stress on individual muscle groups can be minimised to a degree.

This is very achievable in rehearsals, when the dance leader can ensure that the same excerpt of choreography is not repeatedly or excessively performed. Choreographers whose dancers all succumb to the same injury in the same body part or show signs of imbalanced muscle development over time should question their own movement choices and rehearsal strategies.

Similarly, trying to consider the different types of muscle contraction will help to avoid muscle overwork. A muscle is able to produce more force in an eccentric (lengthening) contraction. This type of muscle work results in flexibility gains, but also produces more muscle soreness. To combat this, it is necessary to focus more on the lengthening phase of a movement, for example, taking more time coming up from a plié than releasing down into it (Franklin, 2012). Eccentric contractions help reduce the impact when weight is absorbed into the floor, either through the upper body, for example, falling onto the hands or lowering the body with the weight on the hands, or in landing from jumps, when the impact is managed through foot, ankle and lower leg muscles. Being aware of the potential for microdamage to the muscles from excessive eccentric work will prevent discomfort and pain.

Choosing activities that continue to train dancers from session to session is vital in avoiding stagnation or a plateau in development. As mentioned earlier, the overload principle needs to be applied to consistently challenge dancers. If the class always contains the same material, with combinations that are predictable and easily achievable, both professional and recreational dancers will lose concentration, focus and motivation. If this happens, they may become distracted and pay less attention to correct technique, becoming sloppy in their execution and perhaps increasing the likelihood of injuring themselves or the dancers they are working with. Similarly, some dancers can be fully conditioned for specific steps, and can perform them with minimal effort, but can also have an underlying lack of strength that causes them to succumb to overwork in other muscle groups. Problems arise when dancers are asked to move away from these strengths (Franklin, 2004). This can be seen when they change styles in training, work with a different choreographer or perform unplanned, arbitrary and disconnected movement sequences in class.

Combinations should be constructed by drawing together clear threads that have been laid out during the first phase of the class. Training programmes for dance teachers often emphasise the technique of working backwards from the combinations to the preparatory exercises so as to effectively plan dance material in terms of breaking down and building up skills. This concept can also be applied to the preparation of individual muscles and activation patterns that will be targeted in the movement combinations—the initial exercises can already have exposed the dancer to the required muscular connections.

The body of the class will contain most of the physically challenging material. Dancers will become increasingly warm as it progresses, but will also become more fatigued. Choosing the most productive time for introducing certain elements will increase their benefits and reduce their potential for injury. At the beginning of this phase, dancers still need to continue to work up to more demanding material, so leaders should gradually increase the effort levels and range of motion. Shorter combinations to first test balance, stability and weight shift are useful. Reviewing past steps in preparation for new ones or revising material so that more can be added is also positive. About halfway through the session, dance leaders can increase the pace and introduce faster combinations. It is still necessary to remember that too much speed can be overwhelming and detrimental to learning for those participants who are not ready for it or who are not physically able to cope with it. Concentration is stimulated when working at speed, which is positive for learning, but if the material is too fast, dancers may not gain depth of understanding (White, 1996).

Any movements that involve ballistic type lengthening of the muscles (high kicks, grand battements, bouncing, more explosive dropping and rebounding from the floor) can be included as this stage reaches its peak when the leader is confident that the dancers are thoroughly prepared. This type of work produces high muscle tension, and because of the element of speed, the movement is not easily controlled so there is potential to exceed the extensibility limit of the soft tissues very easily (Critchfield & IADMS, 2012). Hamstring injuries are often caused through not being sufficiently prepared for these types of movements. Dancers whose genre requires them to perform many high kicks and split leaps or to drop into splits or hurdle-shaped floor positions (one leg bent back and one leg fully stretched forwards, as seen in hip-hop and street styles) should make absolutely sure that they are fully warm before attempting material involving extreme ranges of motion performed at speed. When working with experienced dancers, teachers could include an incremental progression towards full range of motion for ballistic type movements in the first part of the body of the session by constructing exercises using mid-range movements performed at a controlled, moderate speed before gradually increasing the speed and range of motion (Wyon, 2010b). The exercises and routines in this main section should aim to challenge strength, endurance, agility and speed (if the aims include both training and conditioning) and, of course, further develop skill. However, speed and agility activities are taxing,

and they should only be practised for relatively short durations (Bompa & Haff, 2009).

Fatigue impedes the ability to learn motor skills, so teachers should include new material early in the body of the session (Bompa & Haff, 2009). As this section progresses, once leaders have thoroughly prepared dancers with progressive, supportive movement material, then they can incorporate intermittent, near-maximal (anaerobic) bursts of activity, again if training and conditioning are primary aims. (Clarkson & Skrinar, 1988). This would not be appropriate with less conditioned or recreational participants. However, some level of jumping activity will be beneficial for most groups, with the exception of older dancers, pregnant dancers and dancers recovering from injury.

Jumping is a very strenuous activity, and it needs very solid preparation. Therefore the most appropriate place to include jumps is towards the end of this stage of the session, when dancers are properly warmed up but are not yet overly fatigued. Preliminary footwork followed by small jumps is the way to prepare effectively for bigger, more explosive jumps. Care should be taken not to overemphasise the small jumps or repeat them too much so that participants are already fatigued before the peak of the class. It is inappropriate and unsafe to perform big jumps in the first stage of the dance session, and jumping should never be included in warm-up activities. This does not mean that dancers who are required to perform leaps should not try out a few jumps just before they go on stage. The message to dance leaders is to understand that performing impactive activities without adequate preparation is detrimental to the dancer's body. Many genres do have jumping as

Tips for the Body of a Session

- Gradually increase the level of difficulty and demand, aiming towards a peak as all the previous elements come together.

- Alternate the use of muscle groups and muscle actions wherever possible so that one particular group is not unduly fatigued.

- Avoid using high-impact activities (for example, jumping) too soon. These should be reserved for the latter half of this stage when the body is fully prepared, physiologically and technically.

- Additional weight-bearing activities, such as partner work and lifting, should be introduced only when preparatory exercises have been performed, and not after a break or rest period when the dancers have been sitting down.

- *Motor learning tip:* Make sure that both sides of the body are used equally and that lateral preferences and bias do not encourage asymmetry.

an integral part of their basic content. This is perfectly acceptable—the problem arises when dancers are asked to suddenly perform jumping movements if they have not been trained or prepared for them. In any vocational dance curriculum, jumping should be an integral part of the training but, conversely, the amount of jumping should be monitored across the full range of activities. A sudden increase in jumping activity is an injury flashpoint. In an educational environment, if every teacher is focusing on this at the same time or if students are working on a piece of choreography that contains demanding jumps, there may be an increase in overuse injuries such as shin splints (Krasnow & Chatfield, 1996).

Additional activities that vary the demands on the participant's own body might also be included in the body of the dance session, for example, when bodies begin to work together. In genres and contexts that involve weight sharing and lifting, the same principles of progression apply. Dancers should be thoroughly prepared for the additional effort that will be required, with partner warm-ups, less strenuous practice lifts or key exercises. This also applies to rehearsals.

With partnering and lifting, the two (or more) dancers should be prepared for the increased loading and stress that comes with an additional body weight. This means doing preparatory strengthening work in the first instance (preconditioning in advance of the choreographic process) as well as a targeted warm-up for the muscle groups involved. These would usually include the flexors and abductors of the shoulder joint, upward rotators of the scapula, all the muscles of the torso for stabilisation and the extensors of the knee and hip. Conditioning for special lifts should be done at the specific joint angle to be used, which implies that dancers and leaders should be able to recognise which of the muscles are involved (Fitt, 1996). Within the session progression, the spine should be prestressed and stabilised with light lifting and weight-bearing tasks, and rest periods should be included (Whiting & Rugg, 2006). Prior to actually executing the lifts, the biomechanical principles involved in the specific lifting technique should be introduced through a series of exercises that expose each of the components (Lafortune, 2008). In rehearsal it is important not to perform strenuous activities such as weight bearing and lifting following prolonged flexion (Whiting & Rugg, 2006). This means that these types of actions need to be approached when dancers are fully warm and

mobile, definitely not following a rest break when they have been sitting down.

Most styles that use specialised footwear will have dancers work continuously from the beginning of the session in their required shoes, although perhaps with some modifications (as discussed in chapter 2 with regard to alignment and in relation to warm-up activities in chapter 3). In the case of the ballet class, pointe shoes require an additional, more advanced set of skills. If pointe work is included in a normal class, dance leaders must consider the increased demands of working in the specialised shoes during their preparation and must progress through exercises that encourage the requisite physical conditioning that is absolutely essential to prevent injury (see chapter 9 for more information on what this entails), especially for dancers who are transitioning to pointe work. It is more beneficial for dancers to train for pointe work in shorter 20- to 30-minute segments during a regular class than in a single additional class once or twice a week because the latter will be a detrimental load. Dancers should also not be encouraged to wear pointe shoes all the way through the normal class because this increases fatigue in the legs and feet (White, 1996).

The Motor Learning Perspective

Motor learning principles can inform the dance leader as to how to maintain balance in this part of the session. In an ideal world, dancers should have the opportunity to perform dance tasks equally on both sides of the body (in standing and in gesture) to maintain a neutral instrument and encourage equality in muscle strength (Kimmerle & Côté-Laurence, 2003). This means trying to equalise the number of repetitions of sequences of movement on both sides. As discussed earlier, it may not be absolutely necessary to do this in every single session—the equality in repetition could be spread over more than one class. The concept of sides is different for every genre. In ballet and some other formalised modern styles, it is much easier to define because it is common to use the right side of the body for support while the left is gesturing and vice versa, and the exercises divide the repetitions of specific actions more or less equally. In styles that incorporate more three-dimensional actions and in more informal genres that take less account of which limb is taking the lead, it is much harder to interpret whether the movement patterns are equalised. Translating material to the other side of the body is spatially

> *Dance leaders can sometimes consciously or unconsciously favour sides of the body, using preferred gesture or standing legs to create movement material. Dancers can also be guilty of practising more on their best sides rather than balancing out the work evenly.*

and sequentially much more complicated. This brings up the issue of **lateral bias**.

Lateral bias is a complex issue, but is nevertheless important to consider because of its physiological effects. For example, if one leg is favoured frequently in a jump, more repetitions of the push-off into that jump will result in greater strengthening of the preferred push-off leg. Dancers often have inherent asymmetrical body structures as well as a preference for learning and performing specific skills on one leg or one side, but laterally biased dance experiences contribute to further asymmetry (Kimmerle & Côté-Laurence, 2003). In competitive dance, value and scores are given to proficiency of specific skills. It would make sense for dancers in these types of genres to select their best leg for kicks, splits and balances. Over time if preferences go unchecked, either individual ones or those imposed by the leader, then imbalance and limitations will inevitably occur, not to mention injuries if those preferences are suddenly challenged in different contexts.

To address possible bias in their own sessions, dance leaders could investigate dancers' personal or individual habits, and even their own preferences when demonstrating, to help free up any underlying bias. For example, does the class always start with the right hand on the barre? Do the exercises always start with the right foot? Or are dancers always allowed to choose their best side to demonstrate their skills? Do dancers in free or street styles ever try out moves in the opposite direction, or do they always follow the same spinning direction or use the same hand to balance? The application is endless, but the effect of biased repetition is the same: imbalanced muscles, some strong and some weak, that may ultimately contribute to overwork and injury.

In terms of learning time allocations, research suggests that the right and left sides of the body are not given the same amount of time in actual practice (Wilmerding, Krasnow, & IADMS, 2009). The first side, usually the right, is used for initial learning of the sequence, which is then trans-

posed to the other, usually the left, side. Although transferring the material to the second side does take time, the amount of teaching information and practice is likely to be more on the first side. The number of repetitions is therefore unbalanced. Dance teachers could try to use alternate sides to learn the original material. Different dancers may have different preferred sides, but varying the options will have benefits overall. In fact, evidence also shows that transfer of learning is enhanced if the exercise or combination is first learned on the non-preferred side, making it easier to translate the material to the second side (Wilmerding, Krasnow, & IADMS, 2009).

This phase of the class will have included most of the definitive elements of the style. Dancers should feel that they have actually been dancing rather than completing discrete exercises. The end of this stage probably represents the peak of the session in terms of intensity, effort and amount of learning. Note that about 20 percent of the session time still remains. The next phase can then focus on consolidation of learning and physiological recovery.

End of the Session

This aspect of the dance session is usually the least considered. Teachers can often conclude the class at its peak, ending with high-energy leaps and full-out combinations. While the cool-down should always be performed post session by the dancers themselves (see chapter 3), the dance leader could include a period of winding or coming down in the latter stages. This would be especially beneficial for less experienced dancers who might need more education, advice or supervision at this point. Cooling down is sometimes only an afterthought, but constructively incorporating activities that bring the body to rest will physically and mentally benefit all participants as well as the leader. There is often a pressure, particularly in commercial environments, to send the customer away with a buzz, feeling that they have been worked to the maximum. The heart rate during the last activities is likely to be at its highest point, and stopping immediately will have negative effects (as described in chapter 3). Ending on a high, with applause and sweating, out-of-breath participants can be perceived as evidence of a positive, successful session. Sometimes this is for the teacher's own satisfaction and ego. It is more beneficial to bring things to a close more gradually and progressively. This means reducing the intensity earlier

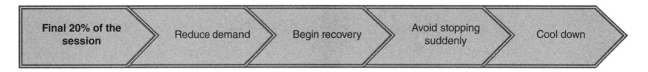

Figure 6.7 End of the session.

and allowing the body to ease out of the more physically demanding combinations to begin the recovery process (see figure 6.7).

As discussed earlier, recovery and rest do not automatically mean stopping altogether. Changing the dynamic, lowering the pace and speed and reducing the range of motion can help to reduce intensity. A new combination might be introduced here, but one that requires a slower, more controlled dynamic, so that dancers can continue to learn new skills but the leader can still be mindful of physiological principles.. Recapitulating movements that were performed earlier in the session at a slower tempo is also a good option (Franklin, 2004). This type of dynamic muscle work, involving alternately engaging and releasing the load, is said to allow the muscles to begin the regeneration process while still working; slower movements recruit only some of the motor units at a time, allowing others to briefly rest (Simmel, 2014). Reducing the intensity before the end of the session will promote more efficient recovery.

The dance leader might include some specific recovery stretches relative to the specific dance style at this point. These could be choreographed into a sequence and performed regularly without having to be taught each time. Directing participants through a structured winding down also reminds them to consider further cool-down activities for themselves (see chapter 3). The leader might provide advice on how to continue and extend the recovery activities after the session, for example, indicating specific body areas that may need more attention because they have been subjected to increased demands. Genre-specific knowledge is key to focusing this attention productively. What are the specific muscle groups that are frequently stressed? For example, Irish, Highland

or flamenco dancers are likely to need attend to the lower legs. Dancers in hip-hop, breaking and modern styles that use the upper body on the floor need to ease out their shoulder girdle and arms. Partner dancers might want to rebalance their individual bodies.

In rehearsals, choreographers could try to reduce intensity towards the end of a session so that dancers do not suddenly stop for a break. Schedules should include enough time so that the lunch break is not used for cooling down, since refuelling should be a priority instead. The body is likely to cool significantly during the lunch break, which usually lasts about an hour, so dancers should be given time both to recover after the first session and rewarm before the next session if necessary. (Chapter 3 explains that after just 15 minutes of inactivity, the body will have cooled sufficiently as to require warming up again, although the second warm-up will not need to be as rigorous.) Once again, fast-stretching recovery techniques (Wyon, 2010b) may be useful at this point (see chapter 3). Dancers should also take responsibility to avoid cooling down when they are not being used by a choreographer or director. As mentioned earlier, short rest periods are valuable for reducing the effects of fatigue, but suddenly starting or stopping activity can cause more stress on the nervous and cardiovascular systems than staying ready for peaks in activity (Franklin, 2004).

For managers and directors who provide company classes for their dancers, it will be unproductive to schedule a lunch break after class and before rehearsal if the purpose of the class is to warm up the dancers. Similarly, company warm-up for performance should end only a very short time (maximum of 15 minutes) before the actual performance. Dancers should not return to the dressing room after warming up to sit and put on make-up. Dancers should wear make-up and as much of their costume as possible during their warm-up; only last-minute adjustments will be necessary before they go on stage (Dunn, 2014). This also applies to recreational shows and student concerts.

Performers frequently omit the recovery stage. They may experience pressure to leave the per-

> *Rather than finishing on a high, dance leaders could begin to wind down their sessions towards (instead of at) the end, reducing the intensity to begin the recovery period earlier.*

Tips for the End of a Session

- Try not to end on a high in terms of effort and demand. Add some simpler movements that bring the heart rate back to normal, gradually becoming more stationary.
- Construct an additional sequence that reduces the intensity by performing it at a slower speed, or have the last run of rehearsal material performed at around 60 percent of maximum.
- Alternatively, repeat a combination that has already been used in the session, but this time employ an easier, more controlled

dynamic or have dancers mark through the transfer of material to the opposite side in preparation for starting on that side in the next session.
- Include, or give advice on, beneficial stretches for your style or those that will help to counteract soreness due to specific individual actions used in the session.
- *Motor learning tip:* During the cool down, try visualisation techniques that both enhance the internal processing of the skills just learned and help to reduce tension.

forming area quickly because of short theatre get-out times, travelling commitments or even socialising opportunities. It is even more important for choreographers and directors to allow time for recovery at this point since the physiological demands are frequently higher for performance than class or rehearsal. Dance educators and community practitioners should also encourage (and provide) a post-performance cool-down for dance students and recreational dancers before they leave the venue to meet friends and family. This requires determination and motivation for the leaders themselves—a longer performance day is an extended time commitment for them, too. In order to protect their bodies in both the short and long term, dancers should personally acknowledge the necessity of recovery at this point and resist the temptation to skip a cool-down.

The Motor Learning Perspective

Although motor learning is about engaging in the doing of the skill, an element in the process requires dancers to mentally process the input (Kimmerle & Côté-Laurence, 2003). While this usually happens as dancers attempt to physically describe the movement that they have been taught (input-processing-output), the learning value could presumably be improved by considering visualisation, a psychological tool frequently recommended to enhance and consolidate physical practice (Haas, 2010; see chapter 8). The end of the session, as dancers move into cool-down activities following the taught elements, might be a good

time to reflect on the activities worked on earlier, imprinting both the material and the results and getting them ready for continued work in the next class or rehearsal. Perhaps the final repetition of the last sequence could be a mental practice version to help reduce tension. Chapter 3 contains more detailed information about specific activities to include in physiological cool-down.

Each individual dance session needs to be designed around clear training or practice aims but inevitably all needs cannot be addressed in every single one. The information in the preceding sections is condensed into a set of guidelines for teachers to consider when planning activities for the different stages (see table 6.1).

OBSERVING AND OFFERING CONSTRUCTIVE FEEDBACK

The structure and content of the dance session lays the foundation for safe practice, but planning and programming are of little use unless the effects are monitored, both on the spot and over time. Constructive feedback that informs both individuals and groups can be formulated only by observing the participants dancing. Unsafe alignment or stretches can be addressed only if the leader is able to see them and has the knowledge to understand what must be corrected. It is important to identify which skills are present and which

Table 6.1 Breakdown of Activities in Each Stage of the Dance Session

Section of session	Type of activities	Application
Beginning 25–30% of session	• Physiological and style-specific warm-up and preparation • Minimise stress on the body in the early stages. • Focus on body organisation and alignment. • Address the main muscle groups and body parts to be used during the session. • Include proprioception to increase kinaesthetic awareness. • Introduce the fundamental skills and basic movement pathways for the style in isolation, but encourage positive transfer. • Include some introductory locomotor activities rather than simply standing on the spot to aid transfer of learning. • Consider specificity when choosing motor patterns to build preparatory exercises. • In rehearsal, make sure that the body is fully warmed, then initially run through the material with less demand (speed, effort, intensity) at first.	• For beginners or dancers learning a new style, this section can be longer (up to 35% of total time). • Vocational and preprofessional dancers will benefit from breaking down material at this stage. • Professional dancers may need less time to prepare for or achieve these elements. • In the rehearsal context, this phase can be shorter as long as the body is properly warmed up for the choreographic demands.
Middle 50% of session	• Incrementally progress the level of difficulty. • More complex material can present greater physical challenges. • Muscle work is deeper and addresses the conditioning or training aspects necessary to support the stylistic vocabulary. • The actual dancing features more complicated sequencing, combinations of steps and spatial demands. • Avoid prolonged stretching during this phase if power or endurance activities are to be included (for example, jumps). • Test balance, stability and weight shift. • If desired, increase overall pace and introduce speed and agility elements, but keep the exercises short and do not repeat them too much. • Introduce adequate preparatory work before jumping, and introduce the movement towards the end of this section. • Consider and recreate the aerobic and anaerobic energy demands required for performance in the specific genre. • Balance left and right sides in repetition. • In rehearsal, allow dancers to perform full-out runs, but vary phrases or sections of repertory to avoid overwork for specific muscles.	• The creative dance class has less focus on technical elements and so will focus on investigation and discovery at this point rather than conditioning and training. • All the elements in the column to the left can be applied to each age or ability level, but suitable activities must be gauged for particular groups and the level of complexity and demand adjusted to match their capacities. • If all the training activities do not fit into a single session, they can be spread out over a series, as long as the progression in each one makes sound physiological sense, and key elements are not frequently omitted or ignored.
End 20% of session	• Reduce pace and intensity gradually and begin to work towards winding down. • Reduce complexity, reintroduce simpler movement sequences or revisit known material at a slower speed. • Encourage reflection of what has been learned and experienced to aid retention of material for the next session. • In rehearsal, allow dancers to perform the last run at around 50–60% of normal intensity, productively using an alternative focus such as spacing or musical timing. • In cooling-down, attend to the body parts that have been worked and tested during the session. • If not included in the session itself, advise on appropriate stretching techniques to lengthen the worked muscles to their pre-activity state.	• Reducing intensity and demand gradually is important for beginners or recreational dancers who may not have the knowledge or experience to perform their own cool-down. • Advice on appropriate stretches is helpful for student and preprofessional dancers to focus their attention on recovery from style-specific muscle use. • In rehearsal and performance environments, time should be built into schedules to allow for cool-down.

are lacking so that whatever the dance form, the teacher can establish criteria for effective performance for each ability level (Kassing & Jay, 2003).

Observation is consistently highlighted as key to good teaching practice, but it is also very relevant to safe practice. Strategies that ensure effective learning also affect the creation of an optimum working environment. When delivering technical information, the orientation of dance teaching has a powerful influence on the learning process, and in most teaching scenarios the leader directly faces and observes the group (Gray, 1989). However, contrary to much of the traditional teaching pedagogy which encourages teachers predominantly to face their dancers and requires mirroring of taught actions, it is good practice to consider the needs of the specific group before relying on this positioning. The teacher's movement patterns might not use simple delineations of left and right, and could instead include diagonals and different facings in space throughout the class. This would support the notion of transfer discussed earlier in this chapter. In that case it is likely to be easier to follow the teacher's movements directly, facing the same way as them, to avoid confusion. This is helpful in recreational settings when the use of a mirror adds more information and allows the leader to see the group while facing away from them (Kassing & Jay, 2003). The teacher should aim to be very mobile around the space. In fact, it is good practice in general for teachers to change their position frequently so that they can see and be seen. This type of leader mobility will also greatly help dyslexic or dyspraxic dancers and partially sighted or deaf dancers, although leaders should speak with dancers with special needs about their preferences on positioning (see more in chapter 10).

It is sometimes difficult for teachers not to perform in class themselves. This may be due to inexperience, or may simply be a necessity if dancers need to consistently follow the leader because the material is not codified. This type of scenario is sometimes found in commercial master classes and dance fitness classes, which involve participants mimicking a cumulative arrangement of steps that continuously evolves. Obviously if leaders are dancing every exercise all the time, they cannot be directly engaged in error detection. They will also fatigue themselves. One or two demonstrations of the material should be enough to communicate the necessary skills, and will allow leaders opportunities to observe the dancers (Gibbons, 2007). On the other hand, leaders must stay warm so that they can demonstrate at various strategic points throughout the session without injuring themselves. They must illustrate the skills that they want to communicate to the best of their ability so that their participants can clearly appreciate what is being asked of them. This fine balance takes practice and experience.

In order to successfully progress their activities, dance leaders need to ask themselves if their participants have been able to meet the expectations of each set of exercises and of each whole session. The response of the participants acts as a marker to determine how quickly or slowly to move forwards (Kassing & Jay, 2003). Sometimes teachers leave out what they personally do not like (White, 1996) or have technical difficulty with themselves. This will only negatively affect dancers' progression of these particular movements or exercises. To be realistic, it is impossible for dance leaders to cover everything in a single session. Every practising teacher or choreographer knows when they have conducted a successful session, when learning and training have come together in a positive experience, but this might not be the case every time. However, if dance leaders feel they have disregarded any relevant aspect of the training, they should question and be able to justify why this might have been the case. If they are consistently omitting some elements, they will need to re-examine the session plan. To ensure balanced sessions, they must evaluate each session and series of sessions. Chapter 11 addresses the role of evaluation for safe dance practice.

CONTRAINDICATED MOVEMENTS AND ACTIONS

A contraindicated movement is an action that raises questions about its effectiveness or, more importantly, its safety. As discussed, the progressive structure of a dance session will have a great influence on the safety of the participants. In terms of content, some individual movements are associated with particular risks, regardless of the style. In many contexts, these specific movements come with warnings and advice to avoid them where possible. However, there is also a view that 'there is generally no such thing as an unsafe stretch or exercise, only an unsafe way of executing any movement for a specific individual at a specific time' (Siff, 1993, as quoted in Alter, 2004, p. 203).

The underlying purpose of this book is not to eliminate challenge and risk completely in pursuit of restrictive health and safety rules, but some movements are widely recognised as detrimental to the body, and it is necessary to highlight these where they appear in dance vocabulary.

How might dance leaders deal with contraindicated movements that are inherent to a particular dance genre? It is very important that they have the ability to assess the value of such movements as training tools, especially when working with different participant groups. It should be noted that some of the highlighted actions or exercises (see the following sections) may be deemed safe if performed absolutely correctly with excellent technique and appropriate physiological and biomechanical preparation. Some dance leaders are confident in using these actions with advanced dancers, individuals who are strong, flexible and kinaesthetically aware, while others stay within conservative guidelines and prohibit them across the board (Gibbons, 2007).

What types of movements are of concern? There are general actions through particular planes of

Caution Regarding Online Advice

Because of the increased communication and self-promotion opportunities that are provided by the Internet, it is now very common to find dance tips and technique sharing online. While a great many of the websites, blogs and vlogs do offer sound information and clearly promote good practice, it is of great concern that a huge amount of the so-called advice is misinformed and simply not safe. Particularly worrying are the comments from young dancers who clearly value some of the more extreme practices as goals to strive towards. Although this has already been stressed at various points in this book, once again, it is vital that dance leaders have the appropriate genre-specific knowledge and the experience to select, modify and deliver safe movement material and communicate any potential negative effects to their dancers. For the dancer, awareness and understanding of contraindicated movements and techniques contribute significantly to personal injury prevention.

motion that have detrimental effects on specific joints (detailed at the end of this section), but some dance-specific actions can be singled out as warranting more careful consideration for their repeated use. One of the most controversial is the deep knee bend to full flexion. For example, the grand plié in classical ballet, in particular, the full plié in fourth position, has been the subject of much interrogation. Many dance teachers have been resistant to objections regarding this traditional action in the ballet class, but the emergence of research techniques and technology that were not previously available have enabled this movement to be more closely examined. Clear evidence has emerged that the movement is potentially harmful to the knee due to the associated compressive forces, excessive range of motion and longitudinal rotations that occur at the joint (Barnes, Krasnow, Tupling, & Thomas, 2000). Some have argued that the grand plié is a necessary training device because it warms up the knee joint in preparation for the dance activity, but research has shown that the demi-plié can serve that purpose (Wilmerding, Krasnow, & IADMS, 2009). Fourth position full plié is cited as the most stressful deep knee bend, with a high risk-to-benefit ratio, and its frequent use has been implicated as a contributory factor to chronic lower-limb injuries (Barnes et al., 2000).

Because repetition is a necessary part of both strength building and skills learning, the cumulative effect plays a part in increasing the susceptibility of the knee joint to injury, so extra care must be taken not to rely heavily on the grand plié throughout the session. The case for its inclusion does have some merit, however. The fuller range of motion can be seen as key to developing adequate strength and the explosive power necessary for high-level performance. Grand pliés, as well as jumps and hinges, are among only a few exercises that include sufficient overload for effectively enhancing the quadriceps strength that may be required in the choreographic context (Clippinger, 2016). Similarly, if movements involving full flexion are to be used in performance, then it would be unwise to eliminate them completely from training (Barnes et al., 2000). The deep knee bend can enhance the flexibility of the hamstrings, calves and Achilles tendon, but if performed incorrectly, for example, at speed and without support or control, it can also compress the kneecaps and crush the menisci (Alter, 2004). Therefore, concerns need to be taken into account, especially when working with dancers who are not in the peak of fitness or do not possess a high level of technical strength and control. Recommendations are to limit active knee flexion (which also includes squats and lunges) to about 90 degrees or a position in which the thigh is parallel with the floor for beginners, recreational participants or deconditioned older individuals (Alter, 2004; Clippinger, 2016). The effect of excessive repetition of these types of movements will also have potentially significant negative effects on young dancers experiencing a growth spurt (Barnes et al., 2000; see chapter 10).

Full-knee flexion when bearing weight is also seen in contemporary or modern, jazz and street and commercial genres, in releasing weight to the ground, bouncing up and down in squats or even falling or sliding directly onto the knees. If dance leaders decide to include weight-bearing full-knee flexion in their sessions, certain strategies can minimise the potential negative effects to a degree. The first and most important is to ensure that the knee joint is very well prepared and warmed up. Second, leaders should ensure that the action is not frequently repeated. This implies that using the grand plié or a squat in a first or second preparatory exercise is unwise. However, using it later in the progression, especially with a barre for support, might lessen the effects of gravity and body weight and reduce the forces through the knees. Performing the full plié in the centre part of the class, especially in third or fourth positions, requires great strength and high skill levels to maintain turnout, balance and alignment, whereas second position is more stable, and it provides conditioning effects and avoids the longitudinal rotation at the knee joint (Clippinger, 2016).

Another recognisable dance action is the hinge, seen in jazz layouts, Horton and Graham techniques and street and commercial styles (the body leans backwards as the knees bend forwards, sometimes releasing the body all the way down to the floor; see figure 6.8).

Teaching this type of movement to beginners and dancers new to the styles should be approached with caution. Dancers should be prepared gradually until they have the necessary quadriceps strength to be able to control the body weight in the leaning position (Clippinger, 2016), as well as the requisite core strength to maintain the integrity of the spine.

Forward flexion from the hip joint while standing, for example, in the flat backs seen in jazz and Cunningham techniques (see figure 6.9), imposes large forces on the lumbar spine and requires very good control of the deep spinal and abdominal muscles, as well as strong buttock muscles and hamstrings to stabilise the movement (Clippinger, 2016; Simmel, 2014). If this is not the case, this type of movement may cause an extreme stretch of the hamstrings, hyperextension of the knee and increased pressure on the lower back (Kassing & Jay, 2003). If this movement is not integral to the stylistic vocabulary or essential for training purposes, the dance leader could question its use for dancers who are less technically able. The forces operating on the body in this situation are described in relation to alignment in chapter 2.

Full head rolls, extreme extension of the neck (dropping the head back and down) and rapid upper body twists, common features in jazz, street, commercial, freestyle and disco styles, can cause injury to cervical vertebrae, hyperextend the muscles of the neck and place pressure on the lumbar region and upper back (Kassing & Jay, 2003). Full head rolls should be practised only if they are an

Figure 6.8 Hinge.

Figure 6.9 Flat back.

essential part of the forthcoming choreography to be performed, and should not be routinely incorporated as a training tool or warm-up movement (see chapter 3). If preparation is needed, moving the head by looking up and down and side to side will help to prepare the muscles to control the action more effectively. Recovery stretches for the same muscles should be included post performance.

Some of the more everyday, even somatically informed, technical approaches are not without question. The hanging-over stretch with straight legs (in layman's terms, the *standing toe touch*) or the slow roll-down from the head, vertebra by vertebra, are extremely common in many contemporary, modern and jazz styles, and are frequently performed as the first preparatory exercise.

However, the flexion of the spine when leaning forwards increases the pressure in the front of the intervertebral discs—to protect the spine, the deep abdominal muscles need to contract to support the movement (Simmel, 2014). This movement may be unsuitable for anyone with a medical history of back (especially disc) problems or individuals with weak abdominals or tight lower back muscles. It can also encourage hyperextension in individuals with swayback knees (Alter, 2004).

To perform a roll-down (and return to standing) more efficiently, dancers should increase awareness of the lumbar–pelvic rhythm to reduce stress on the lower back (Clippinger, 2016):

- To minimise stress on the lumbar spine, rolling down sequentially should maintain the curve in the front of the body for as long as possible, delaying hip flexion rather than hinging or leaning forwards.

- In reverse, the pelvis rotates around the femur in the hip joint with the help of the gluteus maximus. The hamstrings should also engage to help to draw the sitting bones (ischial tuberosities) down to bring the pelvis to an upright position (Clippinger, 2016).

Alternatively, dancers can approach the position from a squatting position, then carefully release the body forwards while slowly straightening the legs (Alter, 2004). Dance leaders can consider limiting the amount of time spent in the relaxed hanging-over position with the legs straight if it is not stylistically necessary or does not have clear training value, as well as reducing the number of roll-down repetitions.

Yoga-based movements are frequently amalgamated into contemporary and release-style preparatory exercises. Yoga plough-type positions, lying on the back with the legs over the head, or rolls across the back of the neck, are some of the most controversial and potentially dangerous positions. They may induce pressure on the vertebrae and nerves because of the increased compressive forces on the cervical spine (Alter, 2004; Berardi, 2005; Kassing & Jay, 2003). There will be an added impact if dancers already have less-than-ideal thoracic or cervical posture (kyphosis or forward head). These types of movements need to be carefully assessed for their training benefits and used sparingly, if included. Once again, if dancers have adequate strength to support the body's weight, and learn and practise the movements in sequential stages, they will be able to limit the negative effects, but these movements are particularly risky for children and dancers of advancing age (Alter, 2004). Refer to chapter 10 for concerns within specific populations.

Balancing and spinning on the upper back, neck and head will clearly have potentially negative outcomes if dancers repeat these movements too much, or are not physically equipped to manage the forces they create. Strengthening and conditioning for the neck, upper back and shoulder girdle is advised for all dancers who practise these types of movements within their genre-specific vocabulary. Individual dancers who attempt to learn and replicate such material themselves via online tutorials without the guidance of a specialised teacher are at considerable risk.

Full sit-ups, usually included as a means of strengthening the core in both dance and fitness contexts, stress the iliopsoas and can increase back pain (Heyward & Gibson, 2014; Kassing & Jay, 2003). Dance leaders sometimes use continuous, fast-paced and highly fatigue-inducing sit-up combinations in an attempt to condition their dancers, which may do more harm than good. Repetitive crunches, especially at speed, will not effectively target or condition the vital deep core muscles that dancers need to support their specialised technical movements. Correct and efficient technique is essential for gaining benefits and avoiding detrimental effects.

A discussion on the meaning of functional core stability and which muscles are involved can be found in chapter 2 and a beneficial dance-specific technique for performing sit-ups can be found in chapter 4.

In terms of stretching, whether this is incorporated into the dance material, included in the cool-down or observed by the leader in the dancer's own practice, certain actions could also be of concern. For examples of contraindicated stretches, see chapter 4.

Many of these exercises and stretches are considered to be potentially damaging because they do not allow for individual differences. Some may actually be supportive if they are modified or supervised carefully (Berardi, 2005). Because choreographers may ask dancers to perform these or similar movements in performance, it makes sense for the dancer to prepare and condition the body to attempt them, even though the potential for risk remains. The dance leader's responsibility is to suggest adjustments where necessary and the dancer must be able to apply the original movement or its variation to suit his or her individual body. Having said this, children and less-experienced participants will need the teacher to take the lead and offer clear and sensible adaptations or modifications when required. Knowledgeable dancers also have the choice to refrain from performing any movement they feel is detrimental, or will cause them injury. In both cases, these decisions should be supported by evidence-based knowledge of the risks rather than speculation or guesswork.

Although the preceding list is not exhaustive, it represents some of the recognised movement language encountered in a range of genres. Some

Movements that can have potentially detrimental effects should be assessed for their training potential. Some of these may be suitable for strong, knowledgeable dancers, but not for inexperienced dancers. It is important to understand the physiological forces, and their repetitive effects on joints and muscles, to be able to make an informed decision on whether or not to include certain movements in the stylistic training vocabulary. Leaders should not simply reproduce movements because they are traditional or choreographically interesting. Knowledge informs judgement, and good judgement protects participants.

more general movement actions that should be questioned across a range of styles can be found in the following sidebar. The message is that extreme contraindicated movements or stretches are best kept for experienced dancers who are used to taking direction and who understand instructions clearly and have a good anatomical knowledge of the body. Alternatives should be sought to gradually increase both vocabulary and flexibility in beginner and recreational dancers, and outcomes must match the requirements of the style and the context. An informed and rational assessment

Types of Movements to Minimise or Avoid

- Repetitive flexion of the knee beyond 90 degrees (deep lunges, full squats and grand pliés, especially in fourth position)
- Rotational forces in the knee (twisting or rolling movements around the joint)
- Hyperextension and hyperflexion in the neck (head rolls, throwing the head back, whipping the head and rolling through the neck from headstands)
- Excessive hyperextension of the knee, lower back and neck, especially at speed
- Excessive repetition of flexion of the lumbar and cervical spine, especially at speed

- Movements that cause excessive compression of spinal discs
- Stretches in which the effects of gravity cannot be controlled
- Stretches in which an additional weight (or another body) is used to forcefully increase flexibility
- Fast twists or uncontrolled swings of the upper body, especially in combination with jumps

(Berardi, 2005; Clippinger, 2016; Heyward & Gibson, 2014; Kassing & Jay, 2003)

of whether to include these types of movements with specific populations is essential. For example, it is very likely that any of the movements mentioned here would be unsuitable for use with inexperienced young dancers or elderly bodies. There is also no point in including controversial movements within the dance session if they do not serve any genre-specific purpose or support the performance of the stylistic vocabulary.

SUMMARY

The structure of a session has a major influence on the degree of safety in dance practice. Knowing how to successfully progress dance activities depends on awareness of the capabilities of the learners, informed choices regarding content and the ability to thread this content together with both skill learning and conditioning aims in mind. The vocabulary used, whether formalised or uncodified, should always be assessed for its training value and suitability for each participant group.

When delivering their sessions, dance leaders should be wary of crowd-pleasing, that is providing an exciting and full-on experience that supports their own desire for recognition and appreciation at the expense of the needs of their participants. Leaders should have the experience to know what is best for each of their participants, and should not succumb to pressure to provide a popular but superficial class that relies on tricksy choreography and emphasises high-intensity work, encouraging sweat and fatigue to prove that they can work their dancers hard. To push technical limits, improve skills and encourage innovation safely in any genre requires knowledge and considered application of the different principles and perspectives discussed in this chapter. Leaders in both traditional and newly formed styles can learn a great deal from science-based research, and they should continually question the content and structure of their session based on training principles, rather than simply relying on an arrangement just because it has always been done that way.

KEY POINTS

- Dance sessions should progress logically from beginning to end, using appropriate activities and exercises at each stage.

- Activities should be selected according to the purpose and context of the session and the level of ability of the participants.

- Dance leaders should plan their sessions effectively, but be prepared to spontaneously adapt and modify their material in response to the needs of the group or individuals.

- Repetition of dance material within a session has both positive and negative effects in terms of learning skills and training the body.

- Periods of rest and recovery within the session can help to counteract the effects of fatigue and overuse.

- Pace and speed can affect the ability to learn and perform dance movement safely.

- Some common dance movements may have potentially harmful effects. Using these movements knowledgably for different levels of ability will help to prevent injury.

- Just because a particular movement has been traditionally taught in a certain way does not mean it should be exempt from regular appraisal for its value in dance training and performance.

Nutrition and Hydration

After reading this chapter you should be able to do the following:

• Understand the importance of healthy nutrition for dance practice.
• Know which food groups make up a balanced diet for dance practice.
• Know what to advise dance participants on nutrition and hydration for healthy dance practice.

amenorrhoea	hydration	nutrition
body mass index (BMI)	macronutrient	osteoporosis
calorie	micronutrient	protein
carbohydrate	minerals	vitamins
fat		

The importance of good **nutrition** and **hydration** for the dancer cannot be overstated. A diet that is high in essential nutrients will assist in the repair of muscles and other damaged tissues, provide the body with energy, promote efficient recovery, reduce risk of overtraining (see chapter 5), help the dancer to ward off illness, prevent bone damage, maintain a healthy body weight, and ultimately achieve best performance (Bean, 2009). Preparing for and recovering from dance sessions by fuelling the body properly is a key aspect of safe dance practice. For example, not having enough energy to complete the activity effectively contributes to fatigue, a major reason for injury occurrence (see chapter 5 for more information on fatigue and chapter 9 on how it contributes to injury). The aims of this chapter are not to provide the reader with a comprehensive knowledge of nutrition theory, but to provide information on the importance of healthy eating for dancers and to enable an understanding of what makes up a good well-balanced and functional diet. It will demystify what dance leaders should and should not be promoting as healthy nutrition for the participants in their dance sessions to be physiologically ready for dance activity, regardless of the dance styles being practiced.

NUTRITION FOR DANCERS

Many dance institutions now include modules on nutrition and hydration within their training, and many professional companies have nutritionists and dieticians as part of the health team. Despite this, studies have shown that adult dancers ingest fewer **calories** than are generally recommended for health and well-being, and therefore worryingly fewer than what they need for the physical demands of dance (Benson, Gillien, Bourdet, & Loosli, 1985; Clarkson, 1998; Clarkson & IADMS, 2003).

A report found that just 11 percent of subjects took their nutrition advice from a registered dietician, 11 percent from their GP (doctor), 34 percent from school staff, 30 percent from friends and 40 percent from media or literature (Laws, 2005). A further 14 percent was from other sources such as family members. Much of this information (particularly from friends and the media) is probably not research informed, and could be providing inappropriate or misleading information for the dancer.

With the pressure to achieve an ideal body, the dancer often faces challenges to attain a body shape that could result in more harm than good to health and performance. If they do not consume enough nutrients, female dancers are at risk of **amenorrhoea** (absence of periods), a component of the female athlete triad. This condition leads to the female athlete or dancer suffering from a combination of low energy availability (with or without eating disorders), menstrual dysfunction and low bone mineral density (ACSM, 2011). **Osteoporosis**, for example, a condition of low bone mass resulting in weakened and fragile bones, could be prevented if dancers were to consume more calcium at a young age, particularly up to the age of 20 (Sayce, 2012). These issues can have long-term negative outcomes for female dancers, such as more frequent bone injuries or serious disordered eating habits (explained later in this chapter). Finally, injury rate is higher in dancers who do not consume sufficient nutrients for the demands of their practice. A study found that 80 percent of dancers with recent stress fractures weighed less than 75 percent of ideal body weight, demonstrated a tendency towards eating disorders, and consumed a lower fat intake and a higher intake of low-calorie food (Frusztajer, Dhuper, Warren, Brooks-Gunn, & Fox, 1990).

It is important therefore that dancers and dance leaders understand the health and performance benefits of effective nutrition, rather than following the overemphasised and overgeneralised approach that calories must be reduced. Energy from food is measured in calories and is needed for basic physiological functions such as breathing, digestion and everyday physical tasks, let alone dance, exercise and performance. The important message is that the body needs calories, but it is the type and quality of calories that will determine how the body functions. But how many calories per day does the dancer need? Our basal metabolic rate (energy required for the body to function at rest) is at least 1,200 calories, so ingesting much more than this is needed to undergo any physical activity effectively (Hamilton, 2008). Generally it is reported that, when active, the female dancer needs 2,000 to 2,700 calories a day and a male dancer needs 2,200 to 3,000 each day (Hamilton, 2008) for enough energy for practice and performance, and to avoid weight changes. It is suggested that dancers burn between 300 and 480 calories per hour during dance practice (Mastin, 2009), so if they are dancing numerous hours each day, they must increase their calorie intake to meet these demands. Participants who take part in one or two dance classes a week for exercise or enjoyment also need to consider effective nutrition before and after the dance session, so their diet allows best practice and promotes effective recovery. A healthy, well-balanced diet must consist of an appropriate combination of both **macronutrients** (**carbohydrate**, **fat** and **protein**) and **micronutrients** (**vitamins** and **minerals**), as well as plenty of fluids.

Macronutrients

Macronutrients are the main sources of fuel for energy and repair, and consist of carbohydrate, fat and protein. Figure 7.1 demonstrates the amount of macronutrients needed each day for best performance.

Carbohydrate

Carbohydrate is our main fuel source for physical activity. Once broken down it is stored in the liver and muscles as glycogen. The glycogen in the liver will maintain blood sugar levels and the glycogen in the muscles will provide fuel for dance or exercise. As a general rule more active people may need a higher percentage of carbohydrate within their diet. 'A high muscle-glycogen concentration will allow you to train at your optimum intensity and achieve a greater training effect. A low muscle-glycogen concentration will lead to early fatigue, reduced training intensity and suboptimal performance' (Bean, 2009, p. 21). Once glycogen

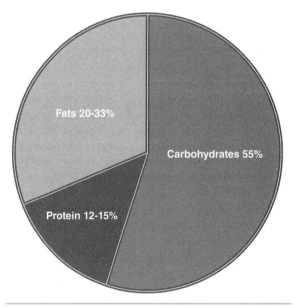

Figure 7.1 Percentage of daily calorie consumption of each food group needed for effective performance and recovery.

> *A dancer who eats 2,500 calories a day would need between 1,375 and 1,625 calories from carbohydrate. Dance participants who take part in one or two recreational dance classes a week as general exercise would not need as much, but they should still consider a carbohydrate-appropriate meal 2 hours, or a snack up to 30 minutes, before class and as soon as possible afterwards.*

stores have been used up, they need to be replaced to refuel the body for further activity or exercise. Glycogen stores in the body will provide energy for 90 minutes of intensive activity (Challis, 2009); therefore a dancer will need to refuel with carbohydrate regularly to replace energy lost. Ideally, dancers should eat complex carbohydrates 2 to 4 hours before physical training (Bean, 2009) and as soon as possible after. Although a principal role of carbohydrate is energy production, other functions include helping to burn fat when exercising, preventing the ineffective use of protein (protein can be used more productively for muscle recovery rather than as energy), and providing B vitamins that boost metabolism (Mastin, 2009). Due to these benefits, 55 to 60 percent carbohydrate of the dancer's daily calorie intake should be made up of carbohydrates, and up to 65 percent on more physically intense days (Clarkson & IADMS, 2003).

What foods contain carbohydrate? Carbohydrate can be classified as *simple* or *complex*. Simple carbohydrates are generally referred to as sugars and complex carbohydrates as starch. For longer lasting energy, dancers should aim to prioritise complex carbohydrate (for example,

whole wheat bread and whole wheat pasta). The foods that have a significantly high level of simple carbohydrate (sugars; for example, sweets) should be consumed the least. Fruit is an exception. It is high in natural sugars (fructose), and therefore is often termed a simple carbohydrate, yet fruits and vegetables should be encouraged as a main component of any diet due to their high levels of fibre, vitamins and minerals. With regards to fruit juices and smoothies, options that do not come from concentrate contain more substantial nutrients than the concentrated choices. However when fruit is juiced, most of the fibre is removed, allowing the more concentrated sugar to enter the bloodstream more quickly causing a spike in blood sugar levels. Juice is best diluted with water and recent recommendations suggest ideally limiting it to one glass per day (HSPH, 2015). Examples of foods higher in each type of carbohydrate are listed in table 7.1.

Wholegrain products such as brown pasta, rice, bread and cereals contain less processed sugar than the white alternatives, and therefore are recommended. These also contain higher quantities of fibre, also present in fruit and vegetables, which is beneficial for a healthy digestive system.

Protein

Protein is made up of amino acids, some classed as essential and some nonessential. The essential molecules cannot be produced by the body, and therefore must be consumed through the food that we eat. Nonessential amino acids can be manufactured from the body's carbohydrate and fat sources as well as from other amino acids in the body. In total 22 different amino acids make up the body's protein, of which at least 8 are considered essential (Bean, 2009).

Table 7.1   Foods With Carbohydrate

Foods high in complex carbohydrate	Foods high in simple carbohydrate
Pasta	Sugar
Rice	Jam and marmalade
Potatoes	Soft drinks
Bread	Ice cream
Couscous	Yogurt
Flour	Jelly
Unsweetened cereals	Sweets and confectionery
Pulses or legumes	

Adapted from Mastin 2009

Protein is often associated with muscle mass and bodybuilding, yet protein is incredibly valuable for the dancer due to its many benefits, such as repair of damaged tissues, and its supporting role in gaining muscle strength (which is not necessarily synonymous with muscle bulk), helping to prevent water retention, supporting healthy hair and skin, regulating metabolic pathways and helping to transport oxygen around the body (regulating blood flow). Protein can also be used as energy once carbohydrate sources have been exhausted, although this is not recommended since it would restrict the use of protein for muscle growth and repair. Adequate supply of protein is essential for the body to function, and it should be consumed to support overall health and performance.

For the dancer consuming 2,500 calories in a day, 300 to 375 calories should be from protein. For the average person 0.75 grams of protein per kilogram of body weight are sufficient; however, for the dancer or athlete, this should be increased to 1.2 to 1.4 grams per kilogram of body weight (Clarkson & IADMS, 2003). Therefore a dancer weighing 55 kilograms would need approximately 66 to 77 grams of protein per day, much of which should be unsaturated.

Although dancers do not need as much protein as they do carbohydrate, they do need more than the general population. As with carbohydrate, the more intensely dancers train, the more protein they will need for muscle repair. Whether dancing for recreational exercise or as a full-time professional, the best time to refuel the body with protein is as soon as possible up to 2 hours after finishing the training session. This is when dancers' muscles and damaged tissues will mostly be in need of recovery. However this does not mean that protein supplementation is required, simply that dancers should space out their daily protein (Bean, 2009). Recommendations are that dancers consume 12 to 15 percent of their daily calorie intake from protein (Clarkson & IADMS, 2003).

High quantities of protein are found in animal products such as meat, fish, milk, cheese, yogurt and eggs, meaning that the vegetarian dancer needs to be more creative in accessing sources of protein. Protein from meat contains all essential amino acids, yet vegetarian foods do not (with the exception of quinoa and soya protein). Therefore vegetarian dancers should vary their sources of protein and ensure that they are consuming enough. Some non-animal foods that contain protein include beans and pulses, rice, corn, couscous, wheat, chickpeas, nuts and seeds, soya, tofu and Quorn products. Consuming a wide range of protein is beneficial and non-vegetarians could also look beyond the animal products listed here for their protein intake.

Dietary Fat

Although it is assumed that dancers need a low-fat diet, they do still need to consume essential fatty acids for health, well-being and performance. Deficiency of these can lead to health problems including poor circulation and hormone imbalance (Challis, 2009). Fat provides warmth and protection for the organs and helps the body absorb vitamins. Fats in the diet do not equate to fat on the body. In fact a diet that combines high amounts of sugary products (simple carbohydrates) with saturated fat is more problematic for weight gain.

Dancers are often surprised that the recommendation for fat consumption is 20-33 percent of their daily calorie intake, although no more than 10 percent should be from saturated sources (Bean, 2009). This equates to 1.2 grams of fat per kilogram of body weight (Clarkson & IADMS, 2003).

Unsaturated fat and the fat-soluble vitamins A, D and E (explained later in this chapter) are important sources of energy for exercise. They can help increase the delivery of oxygen to the muscles, improve endurance and speed of recovery, and reduce inflammation and joint stiffness (Bean, 2009). Polyunsaturated fat, monounsaturated fat, Omega-3 and Omega-6 are all classed as healthy unsaturated fat, and should make up most of the recommended amount in the dancer's diet. These can be found in vegetable oils, nuts, seeds, oily fish, peanut butter and avocado.

Saturated fat, which is found in highly processed and fried foods provides little to no positive benefits. Many of these foods are also high in sugar, such as biscuits, cakes, pastries and other foods often known as junk food. These should be avoided for peak performance. Animal products such as dairy, eggs, and meat also contain saturated fat; however, these additionally provide a useful source of protein and, in the case of dairy products, calcium. Lean red meat is a valuable source of iron. It is important not to exclude these products from a healthy diet on the grounds of saturated fat content, but to be mindful that these products should be consumed within balance and that unsaturated fats should make up a larger portion of the fat intake within the dancers diet.

> One gram of fat contains 9 calories. If a dancer consumes about 2,500 calories a day, approximately 500 to 825 of that calorie intake would come from fat, with fewer than 200 from saturated sources. A 55-kilogram dancer would consume approximately 66 grams of fat per day.

Micronutrients

Although macronutrients provide the body with energy, micronutrients, which include vitamins and minerals, are also of great importance in anyone's diet. We may need only small quantities, but our bodies would not function effectively without these essential nutrients. Although there is a huge market for vitamin supplementation, it is possible to gain all the vitamins and minerals we need from food, and too much of any one vitamin or mineral in isolation could do more harm than good. Excessive intake of certain vitamins can interfere with the absorption of others, and in some rare cases consuming too much can cause stomach upset and kidney stones (Challis, 2014). More is not necessarily better, therefore supplements should only be used if a deficiency is diagnosed or if recommended by a medical practitioner, such as iron for the anaemic dancer or folic acid for the pregnant dancer (see chapter 10 for more information on safe practice for the pregnant dancer).

Vitamins

Vitamins can be broken down into two categories: water-soluble and fat-soluble. Vitamins B and C are water-soluble and vitamins A, D, E and K are fat-soluble. Each type has its own benefits and functions, yet each one helps another vitamin to operate effectively. B vitamins are particularly good for energy production, production of red blood cells and metabolism of protein. Quite simply, a lack of B vitamins can impair performance. A variety of B vitamins can be found in wholegrain rich foods such as bread, cereals and brown rice. Vitamin C provides benefits for the dancer due to its role in the formation of connective tissue and in repairing overstressed muscles. It can be found in most fruits and vegetables. Both vitamins B and C should be included in the dancer's daily diet, but because they are water-soluble, if too much of these particular vitamins are consumed, they will simply be excreted in urine.

Fat-soluble vitamins can be stored in the body. Vitamins A and E have a similar function to vitamin C, repairing damaged muscular tissue. Vitamin A can be found in cheese, eggs, low-fat spreads and yogurts, and vitamin E can be found in nuts, seeds and cereals. Vitamin K is important for building connective tissue, strengthening bones, and for helping blood clot and wounds heal quickly. It can be found in green leafy vegetables, cereals and vegetable oils. The other fat-soluble vitamin is vitamin D. Research has demonstrated that the incidence of vitamin D deficiency is becoming more common for dancers, which is a concern because it can potentially lead to osteoporosis, stress fractures and rickets, among other medical pathologies (Shah, 2010). Vitamin D is vital for bone formation, and it supports calcium absorption, another essential ingredient for healthy bones. This fundamental nutrient can be found in dairy products, fish, cereals and margarine. Vitamin D can also be produced in the skin by exposure to sunlight. Dancers who are indoors all day every day may have difficulty in achieving adequate exposure to the sun. Just 10 to 15 minutes a day of partial exposure to sunlight are needed to make high amounts of vitamin D in the body (Robson, Chertoff, & IADMS, 2010).

Minerals

Minerals, just like vitamins, are essential for our body's processes. A variety of minerals, each having varying functions, can be found in animals and plant sources and water. These are split into macrominerals (calcium, phosphorus and magnesium, with daily consumption of more than 100 milligrams per day required) and microminerals (trace elements, with daily consumption of fewer than 100 milligrams per day). Calcium is one of the most valuable macrominerals. Along with vitamin D, calcium plays a vital role in the formation and strength of bones. Sufficient calcium intake will help dancers avoid brittle bones, bone fractures and osteoporosis, any of which can be detrimental to their careers. Higher levels of calcium are associated with greater bone mineral density (Yannakoulia, Keramopoulos, & Matalas, 2004); therefore calcium should be included in the dancer's diet. Worryingly, dancers sometimes avoid dairy foods because of the fat content, but lack of calcium can be damaging. If fat content is a concern, the dancer could try reduced-fat milk (skimmed, semi-skimmed or light) since it has similar levels of calcium as whole milk. A safe upper limit for daily calcium intake is 1500mg (Bean 2009). Literature has reported low calcium intake in both female dancers and athletes (Clarkson, 1998; Bean, 2009). Other research has reported that the average iron, phosphorus and calcium intake in female ballet dancers is 15 to 33 percent lower than the recommended daily allowances (Koutedakis, 1996). High quantities of calcium can be found in dairy products, fish, root vegetables and dark leafy vegetables such as kale and cabbage. However, the calcium in vegetables is less easily absorbed by the body. Sports nutritionists recommend two to four portions of calcium-rich foods per day (Bean, 2009).

The two other main macrominerals are phosphorus and magnesium. Phosphorus, like calcium, is essential for strong bones and teeth, but it is also a supporting element for metabolising carbohydrate, synthesising protein, and transporting fat. It is easily consumed because it is present in a wide variety of foods. The best sources are found in high-protein foods such as meat, fish, poultry, eggs and milk, but grains, nuts, seeds and beans also provide sufficient amounts (Rinzler, 2011). The average person needs about half the amount of phosphorus than calcium. The main functions of magnesium are to support bone structure, regulate nerve and muscle action, and enable food to turn into energy, which will support the use of carbohydrate (Rinzler, 2011; Koutedakis & Sharp, 1999). Green vegetables, milk, meat, nuts and bananas all contain generous amounts of magnesium.

Microminerals, otherwise known as *trace elements*, are also of great importance, but are needed in smaller quantities. The two most important are iron and zinc. The main roles of iron are to form haemoglobin and produce red blood cells and to transport oxygen to the working muscles. A lack of iron can cause headaches, depleted energy and feelings of dizziness and irritability (Mastin, 2009), any of which will negatively affect a dancer's ability to perform. Despite this, research states that many female dancers and athletes do not consume enough iron and are iron deficient (Clarkson, 1998). This is not to state that male athletes have better diets, but that more research is needed to assess the nutrition status of the male dancer. The recommendations for zinc are 7 milligrams per day for women and 9.5 milligrams per day for men (Bean, 2009). Dancers most likely to experience deficiency are those who experience heavy menstruation, restrict calorie intake or avoid red meat (Mastin, 2009). Red meat, liver and egg yolks supply high quantities of iron that is easily absorbed. Non-animal sources of iron can be found in beans, dried fruit and dark green leafy

vegetables, but they are present in lower quantities in these foods, so vegetarian dancers need to include great variety in their diet and endeavour to consume enough of these nutrients.

Zinc is part of the enzymes that are used to metabolise food. It protects nerve and brain tissue and boosts the immune system, and it is essential for growth (Rinzler, 2011) and important for production of energy and red blood cells. Yet just like iron, female athletes and dancers do not consume enough zinc (Clarkson 1998). The recommendations for women are 7 milligrams per day (Bean 2009) 1. This is not to state that male athletes have better diets, but that more research is needed to assess the nutrition status of the male dancer. Recommendations for men are 9.5 milligrams (Bean 2009). Zinc is also found in red meat; therefore it is not surprising that if dancers lack iron, they also lack zinc. Other foods containing zinc are oysters, liver, eggs, nuts, beans, seeds, wholegrain products and vegetables such as spinach. Again, like iron, zinc is better absorbed from animal products rather than plant sources.

If dancers, whether they are training, working professionally or taking part in dance as a recreational activity, do not consume sufficient amounts of vitamins and minerals, preferably from foods rather than supplementary products, they are likely to experience negative effects on their physical performance. However, if they follow a healthy, well-balanced diet, they should be consuming enough vitamins and minerals to avoid these negative effects.

HYDRATION FOR DANCERS

Hydration is just as important as nutrition. When advising dancers on healthy nutrition, dance leaders should remember that water is also considered a macronutrient. Our bodies are made up of 50 to 70 percent water (Rinzler, 2011). The body cannot live without water, and it will function less effectively if it does not receive enough of it. Those who participate in dance, sport or exercise will need more than sedentary people. The body does not store water: It is lost when we breathe, perspire, urinate and defecate. When we exercise, we create heat; this stimulates the body's cooling system, otherwise known as sweating. Sweat evaporates from the skin to cool the body down. The more we sweat, the more we need to drink to replace lost fluid. If the body does not have enough water it is more likely to overheat, which can cause dizziness and nausea, two effects of dehydration.

When dancing in extreme heat, for example, when in hot and humid environments, the dancer will need more water for hydration (see chapter 1 for temperature effects in the dance environment). If the body becomes dehydrated, this will inevitably affect its ability to operate. In dance, this can result in impaired performance and mental functioning, affecting the dancer's ability to pick up choreography at speed and to perform work at required standards. Dehydration can result in decrements in short- and long-term memory capabilities, as well as impairments in their ability to perform at anaerobic intensities,, and because of the early onset of fatigue there may also be a reduction in quality of skills, postural stability and balance (Spampinato, 2011). As is frequently stated, fatigue can be a risk factor for injury occurrence, or result in decreased skill quality and stamina. Water will also help the body to digest food, carry away waste products, regulate body temperature and lubricate the joints (Rinzler, 2011). Joint and muscle soreness as well as muscle cramps are associated with poor fluid intake and dehydration (Mastin, 2009).

The best option for hydration is water, rather than tea, coffee or carbonated drinks, but how

Caffeine is a known stimulant and is found in coffee, tea, some carbonated and energy drinks. It encourages fluids to pass through the body more quickly, contributing to dehydration. Some of the effects of caffeine may include nausea, headaches, increases in anxiety, inability to sleep, and a decrease in bone mineral density, any of which will increase the risk of injury and will impair performance.

much water should the dancer drink? The saying goes that 'if you're thirsty, you are already dehydrated.' If you are thirsty you should drink, but this should not be the only clue. 'Even a 2% fluid loss of total body weight reduces the dancer's ability to regulate heat loss and cope with the physical demands of dance' (Mastin, 2014 p1). However, to accurately follow these amounts dancers would need to weigh themselves before and after the dance activity, which should certainly not be advised in such a weight-conscious environment. Experts suggest that the average adult needs approximately 2 litres of water per day (Mastin, 2009); therefore dancers will need

Recipes for Homemade Sports Drinks

Drinks for Hydration and Refuelling (Isontonic)

Recipe 1:
40–80 g sucrose
1 L warm water
1/4 tsp salt (optional)
Sugar-free squash for flavouring (optional)

Recipe 2:
200 ml fruit squash
800 ml water
1/4 tsp of salt (optional)

Recipe 3:
500 ml fruit juice
500 ml water
1/4 tsp salt (optional)

(Bean, 2009, p. 96)

Drinks for Fast Absorption (Hypotonic)

Recipe 1:
20–40 g sucrose
1 L warm water
1/4 tsp salt (optional)
Sugar-free squash for flavouring (optional)

Recipe 2:
100 ml fruit squash
900 ml water
1/4 tsp salt (optional)

Recipe 3:
250 ml fruit juice
750 ml water
1/4 tsp salt (optional)

(Bean, 2009, p. 96)

more than this to replace fluid losses through sweat. In fact, some research states that dancers can lose up to 2 litres of water in 1 hour of intense class or rehearsal (Clarkson & IADMS, 2003), which clearly supports the needs for more fluid intake. This same literature suggests that 250 millilitres of fluid should be consumed every 15 minutes within these dance sessions. However, this is in reference to very high-intensity sessions, and practically it may not be possible or necessary in all dance situations. Dancers should drink water before and after dance activity, and take opportunities within the session to sip water (not gulp) to rehydrate when possible.

For effective hydration, and due to increasing demands of energy, dancers might choose to include sports drinks within their fluid intake however this is not recommended for children. Isotonic sports drinks contain carbohydrate and sodium, which will rehydrate the body (Mastin, 2015), and replace electrolytes lost through sweating. Dancers should be vigilant, though, since many products labelled as energy drinks also include high levels of caffeine (which can reduce the body's ability to hydrate) and other additives that will not have a positive effect on the body. Therefore, an isotonic drink or hypotonic drink is recommended for rehydration. Sports drinks should not be consumed as a substitute to water, but as an addition if the dancer is working long hours or completing physically demanding training. Hypotonic drinks, otherwise known as sports waters, have fewer calories because they contain less carbohydrate than isotonic drinks yet still contain sodium electrolytes. Dancers can make either type of sports drink at home following published recipes (Mastin, 2009; Bean, 2009). If dancers like what they are drinking, then they are more likely to drink it. If the dancer at any age is more likely to drink diluted squash than water, then this is better than not drinking any fluids at all.

An easy way to check whether the body is hydrated is to check the colour of urine; clear to pale yellow urine means the dancer is hydrated, whereas yellow to dark yellow signals dehydration. This is a simple test that dance teachers can encourage their participants to do to ensure that they are drinking enough fluids.

Tips for hydration:

- Always have a bottle of water in your kit bag.
- Always start dance class hydrated.

Water is the most recommended drink for maintaining hydration and dancers should drink sufficient amounts before, during and after their dance session as necessary.

- Drink small amounts of water at regular intervals within the dance session.
- Rehydrate immediately after dance or exercise activity.
- A sports drink may be more suitable than water, or to drink alongside water in longer or more intense sessions.
- Avoid too much caffeine. It may make you feel more alert instantaneously, but can result in increases in anxiety, insomnia and calcium loss, and can possibly risk fracture.

EFFECTIVE FUELLING FOR DANCE-SPECIFIC ACTIVITY

Each food group has essential nutrients for health and performance. The amount needed will vary depending on age, sex, height, weight and physical exertion, among other factors. Dancers should

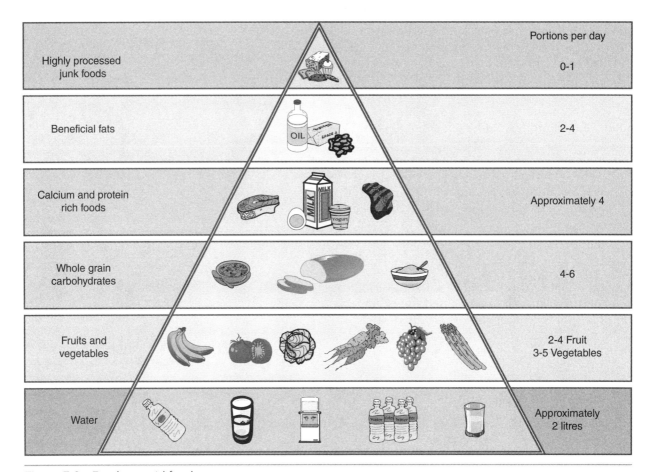

		Portions per day
Highly processed junk foods		0-1
Beneficial fats		2-4
Calcium and protein rich foods		Approximately 4
Whole grain carbohydrates		4-6
Fruits and vegetables		2-4 Fruit 3-5 Vegetables
Water		Approximately 2 litres

Figure 7.2 Food pyramid for dancers.

Adapted from Bean 2009

follow the guidelines within the pyramid shown in figure 7.2.

The food groups in figure 7.2 have been divided into water, fruits and vegetables, complex carbohydrate, dairy and protein, healthy fat and finally junk foods at the top. Quite simply dancers need more of the foods at the lower part of the pyramid and less of the ones at the top. This particular pyramid is designed for healthy adults who exercise on most days, totalling 5 or more hours per week. Therefore if the dancer is exercising more than this, quantities may need to be increased. When not dancing, such as during holidays, in the off-season or when injured, carbohydrate intake can be reduced slightly since there is not such an immediate need for fuel, and protein intake can be increased (for recovery and restoration). When not exercising so much, focusing on protein intake without exceeding the daily recommendations can reduce the need for snacking, because protein helps you feel fuller for longer. The junk food or sweet and salty snacks at the top of the pyramid should only be consumed in moderation because they do not provide any health benefits. In fact eating too much of these foods can result

Daily Consumption for Dancers

Following is the recommended daily consumption of macronutrients for the professional or preprofessional dancer:

Carbohydrate
- 55–60% of daily energy consumption
- 6–10 g per kg of body weight

Protein
- 12–15% of daily energy consumption
- 1.4–1.6 g per kg of body weight

Fat
- 25–30%, with less than 10% coming from saturated fat
- 1.2 g per kg of body weight

Example: Following these guidelines, a dancer weighing 55 kg should consume approximately 330 to 550 g of carbohydrate, 77 to 88 g of protein, and 66 g of fat each day for best practice (Clarkson & IADMS, 2003).

Sample Food Diaries for Dancers

■ ■ ■

Food Diary for an Employed Male Professional Dancer on a Performance Day

8:00 a.m. Breakfast

Scrambled eggs and tomato on wholemeal toast

1 glass of fruit juice (not from concentrate)

10:30 a.m. to 12:00 p.m. Company technique class

12:00 to 1:00 p.m. Lunch

Small ham salad baguette and piece of fruit

Cottage cheese and crisp-bread or cracker

1:00 to 3:00 p.m. Warm-up then company rehearsal or choreography with breaks included

Isotonic drink during this time, snack on nuts and fruit on breaks

3:00 p.m. Time given to cool down and stretch

Break and snack

Banana and milk-based drink

4:30 p.m. Preperformance dinner

Wholemeal pasta with tuna and vegetables

6.30 p.m. Dancers called to get ready for performance and complete warm-up

7:30 p.m. Performance

9:30 p.m. Light recovery meal

Beans on wholemeal toast or jacket potato

Yogurt or glass of milk

Water throughout the day and before, during and after dance activity

This food diary is purely an example. If you have any food allergies or special requirements seek advice from a nutritionist, dietician or medical practitioner.

Food Diary for an 18-year-old Female Full-Time Dance Student on a Training Day

7 a.m. Breakfast

2 poached eggs on wholemeal toast or porridge with fruit

1 glass of orange juice (not from concentrate)

9 to 10:30 a.m. Ballet class

10:30 a.m. Snack

Banana

11:00 a.m. to 12:30 p.m. Jazz or contemporary technique class

12:30 to 1:30 p.m. Lunch

Jacket potato with tuna and salad

Apple

1:30 to 3:30 p.m. Choreography or rehearsal

3:30-4:00 p.m. Snack

Isotonic or milk-based drink

Piece of fruit and handful of nuts

4:00 to 5:30 p.m. Academic session

7:00 p.m. Dinner

Chicken with rice and vegetables

Yogurt for desert or glass of skimmed milk

Water throughout the day and before, during and after classes.

This food diary is purely an example. If you have any food allergies or special requirements seek advice from a nutritionist, dietician or medical practitioner.

in weight gain and health problems such as type 2 diabetes (see chapter 10 for more information on the diabetic dancer). Overall the more intense or longer duration the activity, the more calories will be used up, therefore more need to be replaced.

When to eat is just as important as what to eat. There would be no physical benefits from eating a meal high in carbohydrate 5 minutes before performing, as this could cause nausea and discomfort. Yet research has concluded that eating carbohydrate before exercise results in improved performance when compared with exercising on an empty stomach (Bean, 2009). As mentioned earlier, active people should eat a meal high in carbohydrate 2 to 4 hours before exercise to allow time for food in the stomach to settle. Clearly for the full-time company dancer or students in training, who have prescribed breaks, this is not always possible. These dancers should eat smaller meals or snacks more often so that they can regularly refuel to meet the demands of dance activity and delay the onset of fatigue. Dancers should always begin the day with a good breakfast rich in carbohydrate, and following exercise or intense dance sessions, they should refuel for effective recovery. Suitable choices for recovery include:

- carbohydrate and protein rich foods
- sports recovery drinks containing a blend of carbohydrate, protein, salt and sodium,
- homemade smoothies with fruit and milk or yoghurt.

Dancers should aim to eat as soon as possible after exercise so that the food has time to be absorbed and digested before their next physical session. Refuelling within 45 minutes is best but up to 1 hour - 2 hours post physical activity will also be beneficial for muscle recovery and for the body to re-build energy stores. Even if dancers finish late following an evening performance, they should still refuel and rehydrate to aid muscle repair and recovery. This is not to suggest that they should go to bed on a full stomach, which would affect their ability to gain a good night's sleep, but if it is late they should still have a light meal to aid recovery. Throughout the day dancers should consume healthy snacks which include complex carbohydrate and protein, dairy, and fruits and vegetables rather than high-sugar alternatives such as chocolate bars or products high in saturated fat like crisps. Examples of effective meal choices have been included in table 7.2, and two food diary examples have been included in the fol-

Table 7.2   Examples of Appropriate Nutrition Choices for Pre, Post and During Dance Activity or Exercise

Breakfast	Throughout the day	Lunch options	Following dance activity	Evening meal
Wholemeal toast with eggs or beans Porridge with milk and fruit Wholegrain cereal with milk or yogurt Toast with Marmite or peanut butter	Snacks could include fruits, vegetable sticks, granola or alternative nut bars, wholemeal sandwiches (varying fillings such as egg, cooked meats, cheese or tuna), nuts and seeds, yogurt Isotonic drinks Milk drinks	Jacket potatoes Wholemeal sandwiches, wraps or baguettes Salads (varying content: tuna, chicken, ham, pork or cheese) Sushi Omelette	Sports recovery drink (made with carbohydrate- and protein-rich ingredients) Fruit smoothie Homemade milkshake Yogurt Wholemeal sandwich, wrap or baguette filled with lean protein Fruit Dried fruits and nuts Wholegrain cereal or porridge Eggs	Lean meat, potatoes and vegetables Pasta with tuna in a tomato-based sauce Jacket potato with lean meat or bean chilli, tuna or low-fat cheese and salad Homemade pizza Fish with rice or potato and salad or vegetables

Fluids should be consumed regularly throughout the day.

Table 7.3   Average Calorie Requirements Up to the Age of 18

Age range	Male	Female
1 to 3 years	1,230	1,165
4 to 6 years	1,715	1,545
7 to 10 years	1,970	1,740
11 to 14 years	2,220	1,845
15 to 18 years	2,755	2,110

Dare and O'Donavon 2009

lowing case study. It must be stated that these are merely examples, and that dancers could consume many alternatives. A nutrition intake record has been included in appendix E for dancers to assess their own nutrition consumption to make further improvements for health and performance.

Younger Dancers

The importance of encouraging a healthy attitude towards food cannot be stressed enough. Where possible, meal times should be a happy social time for family or friends to come together and enjoy food. For all young people the issue of body shape will inevitably arise as they grow, develop and experience puberty. For young dancers, this can be an even more concerning matter if their dream career depends on an aesthetically pleasing physique. Confidence in both body shape and eating well should be encouraged at an early age to help in supporting healthy attitudes towards food. Much of dance nutrition research has been based on adult dancers but a study focusing on dance students reported that lower levels of nutrition knowledge were related to dancers with disordered eating, and the study recommended that the eating attitudes and BMI of female students should especially be monitored during periods of adolescent development (Wyon, Hutchings, Wells, & Neville, 2013).

Although the general principles remain the same for all ages, there is some additional advice to take into account for young dancers due to the rapid growth that is occurring as they develop into young adults (see chapter 10). For example, adequate intakes of calcium and vitamin D are of utmost importance for the young dancing body, in order to ensure effective growth of a strong skeleton, which will be the foundation of a healthy adult skeleton. Growing dancers should consume three or four portions of dairy products a day (if tolerated) in order to support the body's demand for calcium, but caution is also advised against

excess intake of non-dairy protein because these are thought to be associated with reduced bone development (Burckhardt, Wynn, Krieg, Bagutti, & Faouzi, 2011). Specific calcium and vitamin D intakes for young people are as follows:

- Calcium: Between 500 and 1,000 milligrams per day for children aged 1 to 9 years; between 1,000 and 1,300 milligrams per day for children aged 9 to 11 years; 1,300 milligrams per day for children aged 11 to 18 years (International Osteoporosis Foundation, 2014; Australian National Health and Medical Research Council, 2006)

- 600 IU of vitamin D per day for adolescents (The Society for Adolescent Health and Medicine, 2013). The young dancer must also aim to consume enough essential fat (where possible, unsaturated) to support hormonal changes and the onset of puberty.

- Up to the age of 14, in most cases, the young person will not need to consume as many calories as the active adult. Although the energy levels of most young children may seem higher, their body mass index will be lower; therefore they need fewer calories. Table 7.3 demonstrates the average calorie intake needed for the general population at various ages.

These amounts are based on the average person, yet are the same as what is advised in dance literature (Mastin, 2009). As with anyone in more intense or athletic training, these quantities could be increased as necessary to meet the demands of dance training. Although these amounts are slightly lower than the active adult intake, percentages of intake remain similar; approximately 50 to 55 percent carbohydrate, 15 to 20 percent protein and 30 percent fat (see figure 7.1). There are some key pointers, however, that should remembered for the younger dancer:

- Avoid giving children sugary drinks and snacks, particularly before dance activity. Consuming these foods will cause a large increase in sugar, followed by early onset of fatigue.
- Avoid giving children carbonated energy drinks at any time. These often contain high levels of caffeine as well as other chemicals and ingredients that can cause an unnecessary increase in heart rate and anxiety, fluctuations in energy levels, difficulty in sleeping, and can have a negative impact on bone health.
- Encourage fruits and vegetables from an early age so that these become a common component in their diets.
- Avoid giving children fast foods and highly processed foods. These foods can contain high levels of saturated fat, sugar and alternative ingredients with little nutritional value.
- Encourage children to drink water. Children often fail to recognise thirst, so they are more at risk of overheating or dehydration. Although the young dancer will not need the full 2 litres of water that an adult needs, 1 to 1.5 litres daily is recommended (Mastin, 2009).
- Encourage calcium intake to promote healthy joints and bones, which will particularly help in later life.
- As with dancers of any age, avoid fad diets. These are usually quick-fix plans to lose weight, which will inevitably restrict essential nutrition consumption.

Older Dancers

Just like young people, older dancers will also experience changes in their bodies that are unavoidable. Not only can physical abilities deteriorate, such as the ability to retain or learn new skills and the amount of flexibility and mobility one has, but older dancers will also experience reduction in strength and stamina, possible joint problems and a slower rate of recovery (see chapter 10; Amans, 2013). Required reduction in exercise intensity can result in weight gain and health concerns due to the decrease in the ability to exercise and burn calories. For this reason, table 7.4 demonstrates that older dancers need fewer calories than they consumed at an age where they were more active.

Unless there are any health issues, for example, diabetes (see chapter 10) or high cholesterol, older dancers can remain on the same healthy diet as advised previously, but they will possibly need slightly smaller portion sizes. There are, however, a few key points to bear in mind:

- Calcium levels in the bones reduce as we age, and the older body is not as efficient at absorbing calcium; therefore older people should consume higher levels of calcium in the diet.
- As with young people, older adults are at greater risk of dehydration due to reduced thirst recognition. They should drink water before, during and after dance activity.
- Older participants should follow nutrition advice from their own medical practitioner rather than from the dance leader. This is because of individual health issues. For example, one participant may be told to cut out bananas due to the high level of potassium, whereas a banana would normally be a healthy snack for dancers.

With dancers of any age the dance leader should encourage plenty of fluids and a positive attitude towards healthy food. Dance leaders should lead by example, since they are often seen as a role model in the profession. Therefore if they are seen to prefuel and refuel, following a well-balanced healthy diet, their dance students are more likely to follow suit. More detailed advice and guidance

Table 7.4 Average Calorie Requirements

Age range	Male	Female
19 to 50 years	2,550	1,940
51 to 59 years	2,550	1,900
60 to 64 years	2,380	1,900
65 to 75 years	2,330	1,900
75+ years	2,100	1,810

Dare & O'Donavon 2009

about specific dietary needs should be taken from a nutrition or medical expert.

DISORDERED EATING IN THE DANCE COMMUNITY

The pressures to attain the perfect dancer's body can result in restricted nutrition intake or other disordered eating habits. The aim of this book is not to provide a comprehensive study on eating disorders in dance, but to draw awareness to disordered eating within the dance community and to address how the dance leader should approach such a sensitive issue.

In many cases the dancer is expected to sustain a low body weight and perform with a lean physique that is capable of both elegance and athleticism. The desire to gain this aesthetic can inevitably create pressure on some dancers to be unhealthily thin. Consequently it is not surprising that research finds that a high percentage of dancers have low levels of body fat and that the demands of dance might cause a dancer to experience health-compromising behaviours to stay slim (Wilmerding, McKinnon, & Mermier, 2005). A study published in 2005 found that 40.6 percent of the dancers who took part had a **body mass index (BMI)** between 14.5 and 19.99, and 9.7 percent of these dancers had a BMI of less than 18 (Laws, 2005).

BMI is a calculation of body mass relevant to height and is used to measure whether or not a person is within healthy ranges. A healthy BMI is generally reported to be between 18 and 25, with lower than 18 being classed as underweight and higher than 25 being classed as obese. However, some very healthy people with a high BMI may be classed as overweight due to the amount of muscle mass, and some active people who have a BMI of lower than 18 are able to maintain a healthy balance of fat and muscle mass with the support of a health care team. A considerable amount of international research into dance nutrition frequently suggests inadequate nutrition consumption, low body weight and disordered eating habits or eating disorders occur in dance within a range of genres, particularly when compared to non-active individuals (Frieson et al., 2011; Ribeiro & Veiga, 2010; Nazarewicz & Babicz-Zielinska, 2000; Lopez-Varela, Montero, Chandra, & Marcos, 1999; Mihajlovic & Mijatov, 2003). Research on professional dancers found a significant decrease in body weight and body fat post performance season, and

stated that dancers often limit caloric intake to maintain their desired appearance (Micheli, Cassella, Faigenbaum, Southwick, & Ho, 2005). This attitude does not solely affect the adult dancer; studies researching body composition found that young female dancers were significantly leaner than a non-dancer control group of the same age, with some reporting significantly low body mass index, lower percentage of body fat, later age of menarche (first period), and a lower calorie and fat intake in young dancers than in non-dancers (Kadel, Donaldson-Fletcher, Gerberg, & Micheli, 2005; Yang et al., 2010). This research is of great concern because of the problems that can arise due to malnutrition.

An eating disorder and disordered eating are two different things. Disordered eating arises when dancers experience a range of eating habits that result in them not obtaining a nutritionally sound, balanced diet. Habits could include skipping meals, eating quick and easy junk foods or ready-made snacks, cutting down calories, worrying about food, or trying fad or roller-coaster dieting. Any of these habits will affect the dancer's ability to sustain effective energy levels for dance, and may also result in weight changes, mood swings and emotional imbalance. Even though this is not always dangerous, it is not good practice, and those who display disordered eating habits are said to be more likely to develop a clinical eating disorder (Dyke, 2001). An eating disorder is a medically diagnosed condition either from serious food restriction resulting in severe weight loss, which negatively affects one's health (anorexia nervosa), or by fluctuating between food restriction, binging and induced vomiting (bulimia nervosa). Either condition will have damaging effects, both physically and psychologically, and can be detrimental to general health and a dancer's career.

One of the many outcomes of restricted calorie intake for women can be amenorrhoea (absence of menstrual periods). One study in particular found that 69 percent of the adolescent female dancers taking part in the study had an irregular menstrual cycle as well as significantly low body mass index, lower percentage of body fat and a later age at menarche. They also reported a lower daily calorie and fat intake than those reported in the control group (Yang et al., 2010). In the female general population, prevalence of amenorrhoea is between 2 and 5 percent, but in the ballet community it is 6 to 71 percent (Chartrand & Chatfield, 2005). This is not to say that the phenomenon occurs only in ballet dance, but that more studies are needed to assess this concerning area in other genres of dance. Likewise, it should not be assumed that nutrition research is only relevant to female dancers, since male dancers experience similar pressures. However, studies are currently limited in this area.

GIVING NUTRITION ADVICE TO DANCE PARTICIPANTS

Whether in the dance profession, training, education or in a recreational dance setting, it is the dance leader's responsibility to encourage healthy food choices and endorse the importance of well-balanced and necessary nutrition for best practice and overall health. On the other hand, the person providing the dance activity will most probably not be a registered dietician, so any advice provided should be research informed and appropriate. Education on nutrition is key, but where this education comes from is of equal importance. Research into ballet, jazz and modern dancers reported that, worryingly, many gained their nutrition knowledge from printed media such as magazines (Stensland & Sobal, 1992). It is recommended that nutrition advice comes from a specialist in dance or sports nutrition, a medical practitioner or suitable up-to-date published resources, rather than the fad diets that are promoted in so many magazines. If dance leaders have concerns about a participant and potential eating disorders, they must not ignore the issue. The dance leader should approach the situation with sensitivity and, if a young person is involved, speak to their parent or guardian. If the person is aged 18 or over, the dancer should be consulted in confidence and advised that help is available from a medical practitioner. Dancers with disordered eating should be advised to talk to someone they feel comfortable with, such as a doctor, friend, family member, teacher or counsellor. Addressing the situation is the first step to recovery, and it could save a dancer's career and prevent serious health issues.

Dance Training Environments

Within dance education and training, the organisation should provide their students with nutrition advice and guidance from a registered nutritionist who specialises in the dance field or a dance scientist with a sound knowledge of the principles covered in this chapter. Ability to provide this education will vary depending on the funds available, for example, the institution could pay for a specialist to deliver a guest lecture at the start of their students' training, focusing on advice and guidance on healthy nutrition for dance practice. Ideally a dietician could be employed to work within the training environment and meet dancers on regular intervals throughout the training year to assess and improve personal nutrition for best practice. This could begin with nutrition screening which should be delivered by a specialist in dance nutrition. This will determine any concerns within the dancer's diet and eating patterns, which can then be addressed as appropriate to the individual cases. Another method could be to incorporate an educational intervention programme into the dancer's timetable, which could consist of lectures and instructional videos to expand the dancer's knowledge in this area. This idea has been tested, and it was effective at increasing dancer's nutrition knowledge and improving dietary intake (Doyle-Lucas & Davy, 2011). It would be useful for institutions to assess the food that is sold or provided at their establishment and for their facilities to serve appropriate menus for dancers rather than inappropriate snacks. Finally an on-site counsellor would be of benefit for those needing further psychological support.

Professional Companies

Within the professional dance company, the ideal scenario would be a nutrition specialist working with the dancers, just like in high-level sport. However, this is not often the case, due to either financial cost or unrecognised importance. All too often seeing a dietician is not advised until a dancer experiences health problems or a decrease in performance ability due to weight loss and insufficient calorie consumption. The company should require their dancers to practise effective nutrition for the demands of choreography and to sustain a healthy lifestyle. Like the educational institution, the company could invite a specialist to educate their dancers or provide a screening programme. If this is not possible, dancers should be encouraged to research effective fuel for performance and take responsibility for eating a well-balanced diet. It is expected that the dancers' schedules should incorporate appropriate lunch breaks and time for rest and recovery (see chapter 5).

Recreational Dance Environments

For people who take part in dance as a hobby or as exercise, the methods mentioned previously would not be viable. More appropriate would be for the dance leader to give general advice to support effective performance in their session and post-class recovery.

Advice could include the following:

- Drink water before, during and after the dance activity.
- Aim to eat a meal with healthy complex carbohydrate 2 hours before the dance session.
- Consume a combination of healthy carbohydrate and protein as soon as possible after the session for ultimate recovery.
- Eat a well-balanced diet that combines a variety of fruits, vegetables, complex carbohydrate, protein and healthy unsaturated fat sources.

Finally smoking should be discouraged completely due to its serious health concerns. More specifically smoking affects one's ability to achieve ultimate cardiorespiratory fitness for dance activity. Research has recognised smoking as a contributing factor to injury (Brinson & Dick, 2001), as well as inhibiting recovery from injury. Dancers should be educated on the effects of smoking from a young age. Similarly, alcohol should be consumed only by adults, in moderation and in accordance with standardised guidelines. Alcohol should be avoided on the day of and the evening before dance class, rehearsal and performance due to its potential to dehydrate the body and cause headaches and fatigue, which will result in impaired performance ability and increased injury potential. If alcohol replaces food within the first 2 hours after dance activity, glycogen refuelling cannot occur; even if food is subsequently consumed, the refuelling process will be less effective (Challis, 2014).

SUMMARY

Although dance leaders are most probably not nutrition specialists, they can still encourage healthy nutrition and hydration to support safe and effective dance practice. Various difficulties may come into play to hamper dancers' ability to consume sufficient energy for class and performance, including touring, travelling across time zones, heavy scheduling of classes, lunch breaks immediately before practical lessons and long training hours, to name a few. However, if dancers are well educated on nutrition they can make better choices about food, and will therefore be able to plan meal times and snacks more effectively. The message is that dancers of all levels should be properly fuelled to dance, and should recognise that eating well following exercise will help the body to recover. A healthy attitude towards food and body image needs to be promoted from a young age so that dancers can appreciate food and use it as a tool to help them in achieving peak performance or simply enjoying their dance activities.

KEY POINTS

- A healthy well-balanced diet consisting of a balance of macronutrients (water, carbohydrate, protein, fat) and micronutrients (vitamins and minerals) can improve performance and reduce potential injury as a result of fatigue.

- Active adults should consume at least 2 litres of water each day.

- Young people and elderly dancers should be reminded to drink water regularly to avoid dehydration.

- A healthy attitude towards food and body image needs to be encouraged in dancers from an early age.

- Dance teachers should lead by example and should also consume a well-balanced diet for their own health and performance.

- Fuel and hydration are important before, during and after dance activity.

- Educating dancers about healthy nutrition is key for best practice.

- If there are concerns regarding eating disorders the issue should not be ignored.

- Smoking should be discouraged and alcohol consumed by adults in moderation only.

chapter **8**

Psychological
Well-Being

≡ Learning Objectives

After reading this chapter you should be able to do the following:

- Understand the importance of promoting a healthy and positive psychological learning environment.
- Create a predominantly task-involving environment.
- Understand the relationship between positive psychological environments and the enhancement of autonomy, belonging and competency.
- Provide positive and effective feedback.
- Apply psychological skills strategies such as goal setting, self-talk, imagery and relaxation.

≡ Key Terms

autonomy

basic psychological needs

belonging

competency

ego-involving

goal setting

ill-being

imagery

instructional feedback

psychological environment

psychological skills

relaxation

self-talk

task-involving

well-being

Research has identified specific psychological variables that are associated with **ill-being** and injury occurrence, such as stress and anxiety (Krasnow, Mainwaring, & Kerr 1999; Patterson, Smith, Everett, & Ptacek, 1998; Laws, 2005), neurotic perfectionism (setting excessively high standards and being overly critical to the point of never being satisfied with yourself; Krasnow et al., 1999; Carr & Wyon, 2003), low levels of self-confidence or a sudden drop in confidence (Laws, 2005), and emotional and physical fatigue (Quested & Duda, 2009; Laws, 2005). Where a dancer is repeatedly exposed to negative **psychological environments** these unhealthy traits are exacerbated and injury vulnerability, or likelihood of ill-being, is increased. On the other hand, positive psychological environments can mediate against such negative feelings, and therefore attenuate injury vulnerability and promote more healthful attitudes to dance practice. In a culture where the pressure to excel can be crippling, working though injury is commonplace, and unhealthy attitudes towards self, one's body and nutritional intakes are prevalent, it could be argued that creating a healthful and supportive learning environment is a vital component in implementing safe practice.

The relevance of psychology to safe dance practice lies in the importance of understanding how to provide an appropriate psychological environment for experiencing dance, and how dance leaders' behaviour and ability to communicate help establish positive dance experiences. While physical elements of dance participation are naturally considered within the realm of safe practice, psychological considerations are not often featured. Perhaps the tendency to shy away from this aspect is connected to a somewhat negative association or misconception of the term *psychological*. In the past, fellow dance leaders have expressed to the authors that **psychological skills** appear beyond their area of expertise, and instead they feel that such components should reside firmly with trained psychological experts. One study investigating teachers' perceptions and use of psychological skills supports this anecdotal finding, noting that many teachers and coaches did not engage with the psychological aspects of training due to a perceived lack of experience or expertise; however, there was a desire for increased knowledge and education in this area (Klockarea, Gustafsson, & Nordin-Bates, 2011). Professional dancers and teachers alike acknowledge that despite having experienced high standards of physical training, psychological components had not been given the same attention (Nordin & Cumming, 2006a; Walker & Nordin-Bates, 2010; Klockarea et al., 2011). These observations allude to the fact that education on positive psychological approaches is not commonplace during dance or dance teacher training. Therefore this chapter presents fundamental psychological theories and principles relevant to creating positive dance experiences. Strategies for how dancers and dance leaders may deal with these concepts in everyday practice are provided, so as to support a safe social and emotional environment.

Like the body, the mind is a complex entity. Without formal training dance leaders should not assume the role of psychologist. However, in the same way that dance leaders can learn about best practice in minimising injury without actually treating the injury, they can also learn about how and why to promote mental and emotional **well-being** in their dance sessions, in order to support reduced injury occurrence and improved performance potential. The individual dancer can also afford to learn strategies that can be personally applied to support psychological well-being. Additionally, in both cases, knowing personal limits of promoting psychological well-being is also important, and the option of referral to a psychologist or counsellor for professional support should be considered where relevant in the same way that referral to a physical therapist is considered in the instance of chronic physical ailments.

CREATING AN EFFECTIVE PSYCHOLOGICAL ENVIRONMENT

It is said that the development of an appropriate learning atmosphere is the most important factor for influencing learning satisfaction (Pan, 2014). Research in multiple domains has highlighted that effective participant engagement occurs when the learning environment is supportive but also appropriately challenging. Additionally, the psychological environment can have positive and negative effects on the health status, including injury vulnerability, of participants. Much of the research regarding learning environments within educational, sports and dance contexts promotes creating an appropriate motivational setting, which supports positive attitudes towards participation and as a result increases healthful, rather than harmful, practice. This means that the group dynamic and overall atmosphere of the dance class, performance, competition or rehearsal setting can affect individual and group feelings towards themselves, the given situation and the other people present. In other words, a psychologically safe dancing environment is created when positive attitudes towards self, fellow dancers and the act of dancing are fostered. Although everyone engaging in the dance session will contribute to the psychological environment, the dance leader has the greatest influence (Carr & Wyon, 2003; Norfield & Nordin-Bates, 2012; Miulli & Nordin-Bates, 2011). Negative teaching behaviours, such as expecting dancers to work with a serious injury and publicly humiliating dancers by making inappropriate comments regarding their body shape or their inability to pick up material, result in significantly more incidences of performance anxiety, overuse injuries and thwarted career aspirations (Hamilton, 1999). A common personality type in dancers, that of high achievers who frequently seek perfection at any cost, can compound the negative effects of such inappropriate teaching behaviours. In the case of the recreational dancer, enjoyment of and adherence to dance activity will be affected. While dance leaders cannot change the personality traits of their participants, they can certainly adopt positive teaching behaviours.

> *In order to provide an appropriate setting for any dance experience, dance leaders need to be aware of how their behaviour and words can contribute to creating a positive and safe learning experience that promotes healthful engagement.*

In theoretical terms there is a continuum of psychological environments, ranging from **ego-involving**, also referred to as performance-orientated, to **task-involving**, also referred to as mastery-orientated (see figure 8.1). In basic terms, task-involving environments are created when there is an emphasis on individual effort, self-referenced progression and understanding that mistakes are part of the learning process. At the other end of the spectrum, an ego-involving environment is dominant where progression is measured through comparison with others, talent or ability is exulted over effort and mistakes are not acceptable. The most effective psychological environment for well-being, and also for fulfilling optimum performance potential, is one where task-involving features are dominant. According to literature, when participants perceive their environment to be predominantly task-orientated positive adaptations are seen, such as increased satisfaction and enjoyment, increased effort, increased creativity, high levels of intrinsic motivation, high levels of self-esteem, low levels of neurotic perfectionism and decreased anxiety. In contrast, ego-involving climates report issues with poor concentration, decreased self-esteem and perceptions of competence, increased feelings of anxiety and worry, negative associations with body image (which can lead to disordered eating patterns) and emotional and physical exhaustion (see Carr & Wyon, 2003; Quested and Duda, 2009; Redding, Nordin-Bates, & Walker, 2011; Miulli & Nordin-Bates, 2011; Nordin & McGill, 2009). In addition, ego-involving climates are associated with increased risk of dropping out of an activity (Quested and Duda, 2009; Walker, Nordin-Bates, & Redding, 2011). The connection between mind and body should not be underestimated because almost all of the negative outcomes of an ego-involving environment are also associated with increased injury risk. The message therefore is that a dominant task-involving environment provides a safer, but no less rigorous, experience for all. The days of the stereotypical autocratic dance tutor are diminishing. Safe and effective dance leaders will skilfully engage their participants by creating a positive and interactive environment that meets **basic psychological needs**.

MEETING BASIC PSYCHOLOGICAL NEEDS

Psychological theory purports that human beings have three basic psychological needs: the need for **autonomy**, the need for relatedness or **belonging** and the need to achieve **competency** (Deci & Ryan, 2000). These needs are termed the ABCs in more recent applications of the theory to dance and sport settings. Crucially, in creating a task-involving climate within the dance session, these three basic needs will be supported, thereby promoting healthful rather than harmful experiences. As noted previously the dance leader plays a key role in meeting these needs; however, the wider social community, such as parents, siblings and peers can also contribute towards facilitating or thwarting these needs. The following sections provide brief explanations of each of these elements and offer examples of how to apply them within a safe and appropriate psychological learning environment.

Autonomy

Often referred to as a sense of voice and choice, autonomy is supported when the dance leader recognises that each participant is an individual, and will have an inner desire to have some sense of control or ownership over his or her actions, even when those actions are in response to requests from others (i.e., the dance leader or the parent). Dance leaders can promote autonomy in the following ways:

- Allowing participants to ask questions
- Asking questions of the participants
- Allowing for a degree of variability during the dance session

For instance, the dance leader might suggest an alternative variation or modification of a particular dance move within a sequence and allow the participants to choose which one they complete: 'The jump can have the arms out to the side, or the arms reaching towards the ceiling' or perhaps 'The roll to the floor could be a step-turn-around instead, if you are unable to get into and out of the floor today.' Alternatively the dancer could contribute towards decision making in relation to the choreography or the dynamic phrasing of

Ego-involving climate	Task-involving climate
- Comparison with others	- Self-referenced progression
- Skill is exulted over effort	- Improvements require effort
- Mistakes are not acceptable	- Mistakes are part of learning

Figure 8.1   Comparison of ego-involving and task-involving climates.

> The dance leader can help dancers returning from injury by giving them some autonomy in relation to variations or adaptations to class material. Allowing dancers to participate in whatever way possible, even if this is seated on a chair, until they can return to full practice again will support recovery processes, decrease feelings of being left out of the group and decrease the likelihood that they will feel pressured to push beyond their capability level and risk re-injury.

the movement routine. Each of these situations provides opportunity for and places value on participant contribution.

Supporting autonomy by allowing voice and choice is not synonymous with letting the participants rule the session, and dance leaders should maintain a balance of authority and autonomy. They must remain in control of their session, ensuring skill learning and development is taking place in a progressive manner (see further considerations for session progression and sequencing in chapter 6). A careful balance of presenting opportunities for participant involvement while maintaining clear boundaries is important. Note that the examples offered earlier regarding alternative choices within a dance sequence provide options with limitations: either option A or option B. It is of course possible to provide free choice such as 'The jump can be anything you like!' but often participants (and teachers) prefer some guidelines, and these guidelines are often put in place to support physical safety or effective progression of movement learning or movement creation. Even improvisational dance classes will frequently offer some framework by which to adhere.

The opportunity for participant voice and choice should always be incorporated according to appropriateness for the age range and ability of the participating group. For example, an adult experienced dancer would be expected to be given more autonomy relative to a child novice. Similarly the nature of the dance session, such as a creative dance class versus an audition or competition setting, will also naturally require different emphases on the level of autonomy provided. Although auditions and competitions are not the most autonomous of situations, supporting a sense of autonomy in the dancers during the preparations

for these events will foster positive motivation and personal investment in the material or the event, which will make the dancing environment more healthful in the long term.

Belonging

In a dance context, belonging (often termed Relatedness in the theoretical literature) means having a sense of social belonging within the dance class, having a good group dynamic and feeling connected to the dance activity itself. Dance, although regarded as an individual activity, is often experienced in groups. Therefore the group dynamic can be key to having a healthful or harmful practice. Creating a cohesive environment provides a sense of safety and security, which supports increases in self-confidence (Klockarea et al., 2011). The dance leader can facilitate a sense of belonging among the participating dancers in the following ways:

- Promoting peer support and co-operation
- Avoiding promotion of unhealthy rivalry or displays of overt favouritism
- Arranging alternative or flexible groupings within the class situation

Flexible groupings promote positive group dynamics. Where smaller groups are created within the larger group, dance leaders should consider how these are formed. Putting all the best dancers at the front in every class can place pressure on those dancers and can disappoint the dancers who are frequently placed at the back. Of course, in vocational training situations the dance classes are often levelled to support effective learning and teaching with groups that are of similar abilities. However, even within these predefined groups, some individuals will be more advanced or capable than others in the group, depending on the task. Strategies to foster a sense of relatedness include the following:

- Asking dancers to change places in the room after each exercise
- Creating a buddy system where those who are more confident with a particular dance phrase can, for a short period within the dance session, work with a fellow student who is less confident
- Combining dancers who have a natural fluid quality with dancers who have a sharper quality so that they can feed off each other and collaborate to find a new

quality or dynamic phrasing within the movement

- Allowing dancers to choose their pairings or groupings from time to time

In dance styles where partnership is central to the genre, fostering relatedness between the two dancers is especially important. One paper discussing ballroom dance noted that increased communication between partners is often an element that benefits from psychological support (Tremayne & Ballinger, 2008), because the pair needs to have a sense of connection and relatedness in order to perform safely and effectively, with minimal muscular tension and increased confidence. This article also noted the importance of finding a compatible partner, not just in terms of technical proficiency, but also relating to the connection between the two dancers.

> *Injured dancers must maintain a sense of belonging to their group and to the act of dancing, despite being physically incapacitated. If the dancer is continuing to attend classes but is observing only, then the dance leader should encourage engagement with the dance class by providing appropriate tasks such as offering verbal feedback and observatory comments. Dance leaders should take care to encourage the injured dancer to provide feedback in a positive manner, following the guidelines that are outlined later in this chapter.*

Competency

For dance participants feeling competent is a balance of appropriate challenge and the belief that, with practice, the movement can be achieved. Feelings of competency are often affected by the tasks we are expected to complete and the feedback we receive as we work towards mastering the movement. Competency can be perceived by outdoing others (a quality of an ego-involving climate) or by working to better ourselves by personal mastery of the task (a quality of a task-involving climate; Morgan & Kingston, 2010). In creating a healthful learning environment dance leaders should encourage participants to better themselves rather than strive to outdo others. Although this might appear contradictory to audition or competitive settings, research shows that

in learning and training situations self-referenced improvement is preferable because it relates to positive and more realistic appraisals of the self and minimises catastrophising when success is not achieved in a given situation. On the contrary, if a dancer's level of ability is constantly in reference to others then mistakes or minor flaws in performance can become amplified and threaten the dancer's feelings of self-esteem and self-worth (see Carr & Wyon, 2003; Quested & Duda, 2009). Over time, these negative emotions can affect health and injury vulnerability as a result of pushing harder to please others or eliminate mistakes, often prompting dancers to work beyond their capabilities, leading to potential overwork or burnout (physiological strategies for preventing overtraining and burnout are addressed in chapter 5).

Because the tasks experienced in a dance session can influence dancers' sense of their own ability, when planning the class leaders should carefully consider the appropriate level of physical and mental challenge for both the whole group and the individual dancers within the group. Where possible the exercises and movement material that the participants are expected to complete should be varied, personally challenging and, with hard work and effort, achievable. Awareness that every dancer will accomplish mastery of any given task at different rates is also important. Leaders should emphasise encouraging dancers to be the best that they can be and should acknowledge and affirm their efforts to progress in this manner. Therefore the dance leader's approach to providing feedback is a vital element in creating and supporting feelings of competency and self-belief in the participants.

Dance leaders should aim to praise all dancers for their efforts, but should also carefully consider the effect of public recognition. It is difficult to offer individual recognition for each participant in every session, but across a series of sessions all dancers should feel like they have been noticed, and have received **instructional feedback** and acknowledgement for areas of effort and progression. Dance leaders should avoid singling out participants in order to highlight their lack of ability in any area, but should also avoid placing any one dancer on a pedestal. Of course, at times it is beneficial to have a student demonstrate to the group, but care should be taken to ensure it is not the same student on each occasion. While being used as a positive example every now and again can boost a dancer's confidence, if this becomes a frequent affair the dancer might feel pressurised

Restoring feelings of competency in the dancer returning from injury or ill-health is particularly important. Discouraging peer comparison and emphasising self-referenced improvement will be even more essential for this dancer. A careful balance between efforts to return to full capacity and gradual progression within current limitations should be supported through appropriate feedback. In addition, awareness that this dancer might require more emotional as well as technical support will be necessary.

to maintain such high levels and feel disappointed if (or when) the attention passes to someone else. Alternatively the rest of group might resent that dancer for being the teacher's star pupil, which can also diminish feeling of relatedness and contaminate positive group cohesion. Further points on positively framing feedback are offered later in this chapter.

Conclusions

The relative importance of autonomy, belonging and competency can depend on the situation. For example, in a recreational dance class, the need for relatedness is more important than in an audition setting. Similarly, the level of autonomy expected from a novice group of children will be different to that of a group of professional dancers. Or, as identified, when a dancer is returning to class following absence due to an injury or ill-health, leaders may need to consider these areas more for that person than for other dancers. Dance leaders who work with very mixed ability groups, or in community settings, are often adept at supporting

Issues Within the Learning Environments

Lucy began her dance participation as a hobby when she was very young. At the age of 12 she was chosen for a specialist training school. The training ethos at this school was very ego-involving. Mistakes were not tolerated by any of the teachers, comparisons were constantly being made between the dancers, and public comments were frequently made in relation to body shape and size.

One dancer in particular, Mia, was clearly the teacher's favourite. Mia was always picked out as the example of how things should be done. Even Lucy's parents would comment that it was Mia who always had the lead role in the summer shows. Lucy began to feel that she was no longer good enough. Initially Lucy thought Mia was unhealthily thin, but then Lucy began to think, 'if I were just a little thinner perhaps I would get more attention'. Lucy started to restrict her nutrient intake and do extra training in any spare moment. Her weight loss got her more attention from worried parents and friends, and teachers also seemed to be paying her more attention, but Lucy craved more.

One day Stella, a teacher and pastoral adviser for Lucy's year group, spoke with Lucy, expressing concerns about her well-being. Stella noted that the current situation seemed to be limiting Lucy's potential to progress in her training and preventing her from reaching performance standards that she had previously been capable of achieving. Stella explained that as her teacher and pastoral adviser she had a duty of care to do what she could to help, and made it clear that she would need to have a conversation with Lucy's parents about these concerns. Stella advised that Lucy and her parents seek professional support from the counselor connected to the school and also see a nutritionist and a medical practitioner (such as her family physician or GP). Lucy took time out of her training to seek care. During this time Lucy realised that although she wanted to dance, this particular learning environment had removed the joy and had caused her to regress instead of progress. Ultimately that dance environment was too stressful for Lucy to continue her training in a healthful way.

In this example the pressures and stresses of the learning environment coupled with Lucy's eagerness to excel resulted in a spiral of events that culminated in Lucy dropping out of dance training. Initial support from this one teacher was key to Lucy seeking the professional help that she needed.

these components through a task-involving learning environment (Norfield & Nordin-Bates, 2012), but performance and competitive settings seem to remain dominant in ego-involving traits, which it could be argued perpetuate increased likelihood of ill-being and injury risk in some dancers within these settings.

Many dancers and dance leaders are resistant to embracing dominant task-involving environments, despite the fairly conclusive evidence that this type of environment produces healthier and happier dancers, as well as better performance outcomes. Arguments against a task-involving approach include 'The professional dance world is a competitive world. We need to prepare our dancers for this harsh reality. If dancers can't cope with the stress, they are not designed to be in the profession' or 'Task-involving is too soft! Wrapping dancers of any level in cotton wool and protecting them from the facts that they have many areas to improve upon will just not work. I cannot ignore mistakes, poor technique or inappropriate behaviour' or 'My teenage youth dance group will totally take advantage of me if I do not lay down the law from the outset.' However, these comments are a direct result of a miscomprehension of what is meant by a dominant task-involving climate, therefore the message must be completely clear.

First, the key word is 'dominant'. Elements of the environment might still be categorised as ego-involving; for example, a study on young dancers on a gifted and talented prevocational training programme reported that these dancers perceived their learning environment as increasingly ego-involving as they got closer to leaving the scheme and attending full-time vocational training, however crucially they still perceived the overall environment to be mainly task-involving (Redding, Nordin-Bates, & Walker, 2011). Second, creating a dominant task-involving learning climate is not being soft. It is, in fact, the opposite. It is being strict and providing definite boundaries and high expectations. Dance leaders do this through clear and inclusive communication, verbalising and explaining the goals of the session, providing constructive feedback, accounting for individual differences and encouraging participants to be the best they can be at all times.

Of course other key individuals within the social network of the dance participant, such as parents, siblings or peers, will also influence whether the dancer's psychological needs are effectively met. Almost every dance teacher has experienced the pushy parent, the unhealthy sibling rivalry or the cliques among peers that cause obvious divisions within the participating group. These situations undoubtedly provide additional challenges to fostering positive dance experiences. On the other hand, supportive parents, siblings and peers can be crucial to compounding safe and healthful dance practices. In an ideal world fellow dance participants, parents and dance teachers would all work together to promote a task-involving approach to dance practice, however, the dance leader who succeeds at creating such an environment despite the contribution of others will provide the most beneficial and psychologically supportive dance experience.

> *Task-involving features should be included in all dance training and learning and movement creation sessions, not only to ensure a healthy psychological experience, but also to challenge participants to be the best they can be in a safe and effective manner.*

APPROACHES TO FEEDBACK

As highlighted in Chapter 2, providing detailed feedback and monitoring subsequent adjustments are essential in minimising repeated incorrect execution, which otherwise would perpetuate poor biomechanical efficiency and alignment, thereby increasing injury risk. From a positive psychology perspective and in accordance with promoting task-involving features, approaches to providing feedback are integral. Telling dancers their performance of a particular routine left a lot to be desired can be done in a number of ways. Honesty is essential, but so is encouragement. Positive reinforcement is a proven means of improving individual performance and promoting desired attitudes and behaviour towards self and learning (Klockarea et al., 2011). Feedback should always be instructional, rather than judgemental. Dance leaders should be aware of the wording, the tone of voice and the use of hands-on feedback when providing corrections, since each of these can influence how the feedback is received (see chapter 1 for more on the possible sensitivities to providing hands-on feedback through touch). Feedback should be used to reinforce positive performance outcomes or behaviour, and not just to correct.

Self-referenced progression should be promoted by acknowledging the dancer's efforts. The most healthful way is to be honest, specific, instructional and encouraging with word choice and tone of voice.

For example when providing positive feedback, saying 'Good!' after a dance phrase might reinforce general feelings of competency, but it does not provide the dancer with an understanding of what was good, and therefore they might not understand how to replicate what they were doing right when repeating that movement or sequence of movements, or how to transfer what was good to another sequence of movement. Instead, offering more specificity would be beneficial to the dancer, such as saying 'Good, I can really see the extension in your limbs. It contrasts very well with the more compact movements—more of that, please!' This version of feedback provides affirmation of what was effective and encourages dancers to continue to work on it, rather than just assume that they have it and will never need to think about it again. Research has demonstrated (Rafferty & Wyon, 2006) that effective leadership provides both training and instruction, plus positive feedback. Additionally, providing more detailed feedback can minimise repeated incorrect execution that perpetuates poor biomechanical efficiency and alignment (see chapter 2).

Corrective feedback should acknowledge efforts despite any inaccuracies, and use constructive wording. For example, 'OK, I see that you are trying, but it is not quite working just yet. You need to work on extending your limbs away from your centre even more. Can you imagine that you are a starfish with all your limbs extending to the edges of the space?' This approach to corrective feedback clearly acknowledges that efforts are being made and the movement that can be worked on. Although the dancer is not currently executing the movement correctly, the dance leader has given this person a strategy for the next attempt. In addition, depending on the dancer's age and the appropriateness of the situation, some kinaesthetic (hands-on) feedback could be included, giving the dancer the inner sensation of what is expected by gently pulling on each limb to support the full extension. Although this approach is more time consuming for the dance leader, it will produce much more rapid and effective outcomes than simply shouting, 'No! No! No! More extension!' and then leaving the dancer to figure out what this means. Such negative feedback can leave the dancer feeling deflated, incompetent and more

A teacher providing hands-on feedback in a constructive and engaging manner is more likely to promote positive motivation towards improvements.

> *Providing detailed feedback and monitoring subsequent adjustments are essential in minimising repeated incorrect execution, which otherwise would perpetuate poor biomechanical efficiency and alignment, thereby increasing injury risk.*

anxious about completing that movement again, and therefore feeling that any efforts to improve are worthless.

All too frequently dance teachers offer feedback, but then do not follow up on whether or not the dancer has understood and applied that feedback. In the case of the need to improve limb extension, with the next few attempts the dance leader should offer follow-up feedback to the dancer: 'Almost…it is getting there! Keep imagining the length…' or 'Now you have it! Try to retain it and find this quality straight away next time—well done.' As identified in chapter 2, following up on feedback can be of particular importance when it relates to promoting safe alignment and anatomically sound execution.

In situations where grades or scoring are commonplace, such as in an academic context and competitions, the criteria for feedback and evaluation should be made explicit. In competitive settings, scores should be transparent so that judges can be held accountable for the result (Tremayne & Ballinger, 2008). In educational settings grading systems should be clear and individuals should be encouraged not to compare their personal grades with their peers. Tutorials or qualitative reports should also accompany grades in order to identify areas of competency and provide direction for areas requiring improvement. Peer evaluation can also be employed with guidance from the dance leader, being careful to avoid being judgemental, but to offer positively worded instructive and constructive feedback instead.

Tips for Giving Feedback

- Be instructional.
- Be specific.
- Be encouraging.
- Be honest.
- Acknowledge effort.
- Acknowledge the individual dancer.
- Consider the tone of voice.
- Focus on what dancers can work on and how they can work on it.
- Focus on helping dancers better themselves rather than outdoing others.
- Focus on factors that are within the dancer's control.
- Include kinaesthetic feedback through hands-on feedback, as appropriate.

PSYCHOLOGICAL TOOLS AND STRATEGIES

Psychological skills are useful mental tools and strategies that a dancer or dance leader can employ in order to foster positive approaches to dance practice and to increase and maintain healthy motivation. Motivation is often considered as either present or absent, but in fact there are different types of motivation, such as intrinsic (self-motivation fuelled by an inner desire) and extrinsic (motivation that is fuelled by eternal drivers or rewards). While participants may have multiple motivations for engaging with dance or any other activity, fostering intrinsic motivation leads to prolonged engagement, increased persistence and positive well-being. A combination of task-involving learning experiences, appropriately framed feedback and application of psychological skills will promote intrinsic motivation. Popular psychological skills include **goal setting**, positive **self-talk**, **imagery** or mental rehearsal, and **relaxation**. The dancer and dance leader can incorporate these aspects into their dance sessions and daily life as relevant. These strategies support feelings of autonomy, belonging and competency and contribute towards features of a task-involving environment. These skills can also be of particular benefit to the injured dancer during rehabilitation and when returning to dance activity. As with any skill more frequent practice will produce greater benefits.

Goal Setting

Goal setting can be led by the teacher or the participants. For example, the dance leader might have a clear goal for the session or across a series of dance sessions. By making this goal public knowledge the whole group becomes aware of the targeted learning outcome and can effectively work towards it together, supporting group cohesion (Klockarea et al., 2011). In addition, setting session goals can contribute to effective planning and subsequent evaluation practices for the dance leader (see chapter 11 for more on evaluating practice). Alternatively in aiming to promote greater autonomy, the dance leader can encourage participants to set their own goals for each dance session or series of sessions. Research has highlighted that setting class goals in collaboration with the students supports a task-involving climate and therefore increases the students' healthful motivation and the likelihood that the goals will be achieved (Klockarea et al., 2011). In addition, allowing time for participants to share their individual goals with the dance leader can help the dance leader provide more targeted feedback to individual group members. Effective goal setting, which supports feelings of competency and encourages healthful means of striving for improvement, should follow the guidelines in this section.

While goals are useful tools to direct attention and encourage healthy motivation when aiming to reach a particular level of proficiency, research has shown that simply having goals does not ensure performance improvements; therefore specific principles need to be applied in order to achieve effective outcomes (Weinberg, 2010). Goals can be classified as process orientated (focusing on a particular task or skill), performance orientated, or outcome orientated. In dance, process- and performance-orientated goals are closely related, for example, a performance-orientated goal might be to improve balance, whereas the related process-orientated goal would be aiming to balance on one leg with eyes closed for 1 minute. An outcome-orientated goal would be aiming to get into a dance company or win a competition. Excessive focus on outcome goals would be a feature of ego-involving environments; therefore the emphasis should be on process goals because they nurture intrinsic motivation, leading to prolonged engagement and enhanced well-being (Klockarea et al., 2011), while naturally contributing to achieving outcome goals in the longer term.

Goals can also be short or long term. While long-term goals provide direction, short-term goals are like stepping stones that allow for incremental improvements (Weinberg, 2010). Where goals are being devised for a partnership, such as in ballroom dancers, shared process goals should be mutually agreed on, along with any individual goals that might be necessary (Tremayne & Ballinger, 2008).

Clear recommendations are helpful for creating effective goals:

- All goals should be worded positively—'I will stay focused during dance class' rather than 'I will not get distracted during dance class'—since keeping a healthy mindset requires positive reinforcement.

- Documenting goals in a journal helps to keep track and monitor progress and, if necessary, provides the opportunity to re-evaluate the nature of the goals.

- Detailing the specific steps dancers need to action in order to achieve their goal is vital.

- Identify who within dancers' social networks might be helpful in supporting them to achieve their goal, such as a teacher, a fellow student or their parents.

> *A goal for a dancer returning from injury might be 'I will get back to dancing fully, in time', but unless dancers address how they will get back to dancing fully, the goal will not be as effective. Identifying steps such as seeking treatment from a health practitioner, completing the recommended exercises as directed, remaining fit and healthy by working on elements of strength, stamina or flexibility that are not affected by the injury, fuelling the body appropriately and ensuring enough rest will provide a more strategic and targeted return to practice.*

In addition to the preceding generic pointers, goal setting should follow the **SMART** acronym:

Specific. Be specific with your goal. Aiming to improve flexibility is a noble goal, but it is very broad. What particular muscle or muscle group does the dancer wish to target? Is this person mainly working towards active or passive flexibility? Being specific allows dancers to create a step-by-step action plan that they can follow in the pursuit of their goals. If dancers are aiming to improve one or more of the components of physical fitness their action plan should follow appropriate training principles (refer to chapter 4).

Measureable. Tracking the progress of goals is important for monitoring improvements or re-evaluating the nature of the dancer's goal or the time frame in which it is to be achieved. Some goals are more straightforward to measure than others. For example, improvements in jump height can easily be measured through recording the height that dancers can jump before starting training and then continuing to measure it at regular intervals during their training according to the time frame that they have set for themselves. Other goals are more difficult to measure through quantitative means, such as improving self-confidence, but dancers can monitor or observe through qualitative means such as keeping a written reflective journal. By making note of times that they felt increased confidence dancers will be actively tracking more frequent occurrences of positive self-confidence and therefore reinforcing such feelings.

Achievable. Setting goals that are achievable is important in order to maintain motivation and experience a sense of accomplishment that will inspire dancers to continue to set goals. Aiming to accomplish five pirouettes in a 2-week time frame when a dancer has only recently managed to complete one pirouette successfully is simply not achievable. Setting such goals can result in negative thoughts and feelings that can be detrimental to a dancer's performance progression and well-being. In addition, if dancers lack underlying strength, control or flexibility it can be unsafe for them to work beyond their physical and technical capabilities. Of course dancers should also bear in mind that some outcome goals, such as being successful at a particular audition for a school or company, are not wholly within their control because the outcome relies on the selection panel's decision. Keeping goals in context will be important for avoiding negative feelings of stress, tension and failure.

Realistic. Closely related to setting achievable goals is the need to set realistic goals. As noted previously, goals should be challenging but achievable, and they should take account of a dancer's current status or ability. It is also important not to set too many goals, since this can be daunting, and it is unrealistic to work on achieving all of them at the same time. Having one or two medium- to long-term goals, that each have no more than

three process goals within them, will suffice. As dancers review and track their progress they will find that goal priorities will shift; once certain goals have been fulfilled, new goals can take their place. Setting an appropriate time frame will also be key.

Time frame. In order to effectively track the progress of their goals, dancers can create a timeline. This should include moments of checking in, which encourage evaluation and re-evaluation of the nature of the goal, as well as setting an end time by which they hope to have achieved the goal. The time frame dancers set should also be realistic and achievable.

Self-Talk

A review of self-talk research in sport and exercise settings has reported beneficial effects on cognition and behaviour, as well as cognitive anxiety, self-confidence, and performance (Tod, Hardy, & Oliver, 2011). Considered one of the most effective psychological strategies (Hamilton, Scott, & MacDougall, 2007), self-talk is the monologue inside our heads, where we evaluate and instruct ourselves. It both informs and is

A dancer should use her thought-log journal to encourage positive-self talk, framing her feedback and corrections in a positive manner, and reinforcing her sense of progression and competency.

informed by our perceptions of past, present and future experiences. Depending on the nature of the self-talk, it can be either beneficial or detrimental to performance outcomes and well-being. In general it can be categorised as positive or negative; however, our individual interpretation is what determines the facilitative or debilitative nature of this inner voice. Ruminating on the negative, such as thinking we cannot pick up the movement material, or we will fall out of the balance, or while injured we will regress so much there is no point on ever returning to dance, can be debilitative. Negative self-talk is associated with increased tension and stress levels, which can result in increased physical and mental exhaustion (Quested & Duda, 2009), ill health (Lench, Levine, & Roe, 2010) or injury (Krasnow et al., 1999). However, in some instances, research has actually noted improvements in performance where the interpretation of the negative talk was perceived as challenging and motivating, rather than debilitating (Hamilton et al., 2007). Therefore being aware of and identifying the nature and interpretation of our self-talk is necessary, so that we can aim to increase the instances of positive or challenging interpretations.

In addition, self-talk can be either instructional (focusing on technical or kinaesthetic aspects), or motivational (promoting increased effort, self-confidence or positive moods; Tod et al., 2011). Different situations, such as class versus performance, as well as different actions, such as an on pointe balance versus a physically dynamic phrase, will lend themselves to different uses (Hamilton et al., 2007; Tod et al., 2011). In learning, competition or performance situations, it is easy to let repeated corrections, comments and scoring fuel a negative view of ourselves. Learning to control debilitative thoughts and reframe or refocus these towards facilitative thoughts can favourably affect self-belief and promote a problem-solving attitude, directing our attention and expectations through positive reinforcement. Implementing positive self-talk could result in more rapid skill acquisition, increased and longer duration motivation, improved feelings of self-confidence and more rapid performance increases (Hamilton et al., 2007). It can also enhance concentration and enjoyment levels in performance situations (Klockarea et al., 2011). Dance leaders can influence self-talk by providing effective feedback and encouragement (see previous section on providing feedback), but dancers can also regulate self-talk themselves.

> *Injured dancers can benefit from self-talk strategies, in particular through the use of thought logging. Common emotions accompanying injury include stress, frustration, anger, guilt and fear (see chapter 9). It is easy to allow these feelings to create a negative state of mind that can hinder the recovery process. Dancers should acknowledge when negative thoughts occur and work to reframe them. For example, 'I will never get back to my pre-injury status' can be reframed as 'If I continue with my exercise prescription and work on other aspects of my training in the meantime, I can return to my former level, in time.'*

A common method of strategically applying self-regulated self-talk is through thought logging. This refers to documenting our current thoughts in a journal and practising ways to encourage more positive thoughts. Where frequent negative thoughts arise or negative interpretations of feedback occur, these should be reframed as challenging, instructional or motivational thoughts (see table 8.1 for an example). When reframing thoughts towards the positive, dancers should remain realistic. For example, it is not very purposeful to change 'I am terrible at picking up movement' to simply 'I am great at picking up movement.' Instead, the thought might be reframed as 'OK, so I need to work on improving my ability to pick up material. I can do this by positioning myself nearer the front and focusing initially on the first 8 to 16 counts of movement.' Note that this new thought acknowledges an area that requires improvement, but also comments on a strategy for addressing such an improvement. Often when dancers are struggling to reframe their negative thoughts it can be helpful to get them to think about what advice they would give to their friend if their friend were having these negative thoughts.

Of course, a dancer's current thoughts might already be positive, such as 'I am good at picking up movement material.' Logging these thoughts can reinforce this ability and also identify ways to build on this potential by adding 'Now I can work on achieving the movement quality by applying imagery.' Similar to goal-setting strategies, self-talk should be realistic and specific. Indeed both can be wonderful complementary tools that allow for identification of positive aspects of performance, as well as areas for improvement, and provide

Table 8.1   A Thought-Logging Table to Aid Positive Interpretation and Reinterpretation of Feedback

What was said:	'You keep falling off balance in your turns. You need to stay upright!'		
Current situation		**Reframed situation**	
Record your thoughts after receiving the feedback	I am terrible at turning. I can't do it!	Record a new thought that reframes the feedback	I need to work on maintaining my balance during turning. I know I can balance and I know I can turn, but I need to work on combining both. I should practice balancing with my eyes closed for 30 to 60 seconds. I should also practice imagery, such as imaging I am a spinning top, and positive self-talk to help remain calm and confident when turning.
Note how this thought made you feel	Negative towards turning. Fear of falling off balance again.	Note how this new thought makes you feel	Empowered to progress
Note how this thought affects your dancing	Tension when sequences include multiple turns. Fall off balance more frequently.	Note how you think this thought will affect your dancing	I will improve my balance ability and eventually will be able to maintain it while turning.

clear methods with which to identify steps for addressing changes or further improvements, while maintaining a positive attitude and supporting healthful and safe behaviours.

Self-talk cues are another useful way to apply positive self-talk to override negative thoughts or feelings of anxiety (Tremayne & Ballinger, 2008; Taylor & Taylor, 1995). Positive feedback that has been received from the dance leader or noted in the thought-log journal can be converted into one word cues that will, over time, trigger positive thoughts and enhanced mood states. For example, angry thoughts relating to a peer in the group who is considered the star student could be reframed using the cue 'zone in', which refers to focusing on self-improvement rather than being distracted by angry thoughts about someone else in the class. Each time these negative thoughts creep in, dancers can use the cue words.

Remember self-talk is a skill, and it takes practice before becoming an automatic part of the mental training and performance experience. It is a way for the dancer to try not to be so mentally hard on themselves and to keep negative mental thoughts from disrupting training, performance or personal well-being. Encouraging participants to effectively use self-talk can support their feelings of autonomy and competency, thereby promoting positive psychological behaviours and safe psychological learning environments.

Imagery

Although chapter 2 includes imagery as a strategy for promoting efficient alignment and providing useful feedback cues, imagery has many other uses in dance. It is frequently used as a means for imbuing emotion and supporting particular dynamic qualities of performance. Strategic and systematic use of imagery as a mental skill, however, is less common (Hanrahan, 1996; Nordin and Cumming, 2006b, 2006a ; Tremayne & Ballinger, 2008). Imagery as a psychological skill can be used to do the following:

- Mentally prepare for a dance situation (e.g., class, rehearsal, audition, competition or performance), reducing feelings of anxiety and increasing self-confidence, focus and concentration.
- Mentally rehearse previously learned dance movement material, allowing for ongoing practice and rehearsal without physical exertion, thereby contributing to rest and

Coping With Stress and Anxiety to Avoid Injury

Injury caused by stress and anxiety prior to an important situation such as audition or competition is a common occurrence. Chantel is 17 years old, and has been dancing in her local dance school for 10 years. She is about to audition for a place in a prestigious dance school for full-time professional training. As part of her audition she needs to perform a solo. Chantel has always shown perfectionistic tendencies, and tends to get very stressed about pressurised performance situations such as these. In the past she was so anxious about a performance that she pushed herself so much she got injured. Fortunately Chantel has a supportive dance teacher and peer network who have been working with her in preparation for this audition. Along with offering guidance on the creative and technical aspects of her solo, they have been helping her with maintaining a positive mindset. The latter is almost more important for Chantel.

In the weeks and months leading up to the audition Chantel's teacher has advised her to keep a thought-logging journal where she can acknowledge any negative thoughts and actively convert these into realistic, positive self-talk. She has also been noting all the positive feedback she has been receiving in class from her teacher and from her peers so as to reinforce feelings of self-confidence.

In addition Chantel, with the help of her teacher, has found out as much as she can about the location of the audition, and has been using imagery to mentally place herself in the audition situation, visualising herself feeling positive and confident. Her teacher has also recommended that Chantel does not physically practice her solo when she is overtired and instead has suggested using mental practice, rehearsing her solo in her mind while listening to the music accompaniment. Chantel finds that these strategies are helping her to feel confident, prepared and able to effectively perform at the peak of her ability. Chantel knows that she can only do her best and that, regardless of the outcome, her teacher, parents and peers will be proud of her for trying.

In this example Chantel has received suitable support from her teacher, who has also encouraged support from Chantel's peers. The suggestion of using a thought log gives her some autonomy in changing her negative and stressful thought pattern to a positive one. Overall Chantel feels less negative stress, tension and self-doubt as a result of these strategies. Mentally rehearsing also reduces excessive physical practice, decreasing her risk of injury due to physical fatigue.

recovery processes and reducing physical fatigue.

- Reinforce positive experiences and visualise improvements in movement sequencing, supporting feelings of competency and self-confidence that can, in turn, feed into the first two points.

Dancers have experienced many beneficial outcomes of utilising imagery skills for these purposes including decreased debilitative anxiety symptoms, especially cognitive anxiety (i.e., negative thoughts) prior to and during the dance situation (e.g., class, rehearsal, audition, competition or performance), increased confidence in themselves through a sense of already having been there and done that, and an improved distribution of practice due to a reduced need for excessive physical practice, which can lead to

fatigue, a common cause of injury in dance (see chapter 5 for more on physiological strategies to combat fatigue). Dance leaders can and should apply imagery as part of the warm-up, to mentally prepare dancers for the upcoming class, rehearsal or performance situation, or as part of the cool-down, to reinforce learning or positive experiences and to allow for mental relaxation. During dance class the teacher can allow time for visualisation between repetitions of exercises or the choreographer can lead a mental run-through of the piece partway through the rehearsal (see chapter 6 for more detailed guidance on balanced session planning and progression).

A combination of mental and physical practice is said to be as effective, if not more effective, than physical practice alone. Evoking an image stimulates the nerve centres in the brain and sends messages to the relevant senses and muscles in the body, usually without movement or action taking place, thereby training neuromuscular pathways and supporting ongoing training of mind and body without additional physical execution. Imaging can also evoke thoughts, feelings or emotions associated with the situation being imaged. If negative, these thoughts can be altered to create more positive feelings. If positive, they can be reinforced to promote further benefits. Consider for a moment a recent dance class that you experienced. What comes to mind? The physical space, the people present, what you were wearing, the music, how you felt, what you thought, the movement material? From what perspective are you seeing your surroundings? Are you looking out, as though looking through your own eyes, or are you seeing yourself as though looking at a video image or in a mirror? When you imagine the movement material, are you sensing it happen internally by feeling it kinaesthetically, or are you seeing yourself do it from more of an external audience's viewpoint? All of these thoughts, images and sensations can be systematically channelled to promote positive training and performance environments, as well as control feelings, emotions and behaviour.

Imagery has also been championed for use in rehabilitation settings (Dickstein & Deutsch, 2007), such as when recovering from an injury. Injury rehabilitation could be more effective if the exercises prescribed by the health practitioner were accompanied by imagery. Completing a few additional exercises using imagery alone would also allow for increased engagement with the rehabilitation process without risking physical fatigue of the area. Alternatively, imaging themselves successfully completing a movement that was not possible when initially injured, such as a single-leg relevé balance following a sprained ankle, can help dancers gain confidence and alleviate fears for when the time comes to physically complete that movement again.

In order for imagery to be most effective, images should be clear, vivid and controllable. It is said that dancers who are more experienced are better able to use imagery (Nordin and Cumming, 2006a, 2006b). Advice for dancers who have difficulty imaging is to begin simply, with familiar movements or situations, in order to increase vividness

and self-awareness (Tremayne & Ballinger, 2008). Strategies for systematically employing imagery as a psychological skill include creating imagery scripts. Personal scripts can be created by the individual dancer for any situation, or group scripts can be created by the dance leader, especially in situations such as rehearsing for assessment, competition, audition or performance. For dancers, reading their personal script into a voice recorder and listening back to it at opportune moments will be especially beneficial.

In creating and utilising effective imagery scripts leaders should consider the factors coined in the acronym PETTLEP, which refers to physical, environment, task, timing, learning, emotion and perspective (Holmes & Collins, 2001).

Physical. When dancers are imaging movements or situations, having a previous physical experience of these will support images that are more real. Therefore any imagery script that is designed in relation to known movement actions or experiences will be more effective. It is still possible for dancers to imagine themselves completing a whole dance sequence from a performance that they have only witnessed, or completing four turns in succession when at the moment they can accomplish only one, because the movement actions contained within this aspirational imaging would be familiar to the dancer.

Environment. When practising imagery it should, where possible, take place in the setting or as close to the setting where the actual movement will be subsequently experienced, recreating as much of the environment as possible, such as clothing or costumes, sounds and music, and so on. If it is not possible for dancers to actually be in the setting, then imaging the setting as vividly as possible will be beneficial. Of course, having a previous physical experience of the setting will also result in a more vivid and therefore effective imaging experience.

Task. When imaging, task familiarity is most beneficial. The movement and the setting being imaged should be appropriate to the skill level and experience of the dancer. In other words imaging movement material or actions that dancers have not physically experienced or that is far beyond their current level of physical ability is not as productive as being familiar with the movements being imaged.

Timing. Imaging should be completed in accordance with real-time actions. This is especially important for mental preparation and mental rehearsal. Imaging to the soundtrack that dancers will eventually perform with will be valuable. When mentally imaging in order to perfect or improve a movement or in order to retain newly learned movement the material might need to be slowed down so as to support improved subsequent physical performance.

Learning. This component refers to the fact that as dancers become more practised, both physically and mentally, at the situation or movement that they are imaging, they should adapt the image as necessary. Referring back to the recommendation made earlier, those who are less experienced with imaging should start with a simple and familiar task or setting and work towards including more complex detail about the movement (task) and the setting (environment), as they progress.

Emotion. When imaging it is useful to tune in to the emotional responses that the image creates, or to consciously reinforce a desired emotion. For example, if the preferred emotions that dancers wish to feel when mentally rehearsing prior to an assessment, an audition, a performance or a competition are feelings of calm and confidence, but instead feelings of debilitative anxiety begin to surface, then they should tailor an imagery script that promotes the desired emotion. In dance, some movement phrases are choreographed to express or convey a particular emotion. The imagery script could include cues to support this.

Perspective. This final component refers to which viewpoint dancers image from, either feeling and registering themselves doing the task from the inside, often referred to as kinaesthetic, or watching themselves doing the task as an observer, possibly as a reflection in a mirror or a video-recorded image, often referred to as visual. There is no consensus on which is most effective, and it is assumed that different tasks will require different perspectives. Being able to alter between both perspectives, as necessary, is likely to be most beneficial.

Although imagery is common within dance practice for creating movement, for providing feedback cues that guide movement quality (such as 'melt into the floor') and for adjusting alignment (see examples in chapter 2), strategically using imagery as a psychological skill requires more attention. From a safe practice perspective, this specific use of imagery can contribute towards dancers fostering positive psychological attitudes and behaviours towards themselves and the upcoming dance experience, as well as supporting effective distributed practice (see chapter 5), which can reduce injuries associated with fatigue and overwork, anxiety and low self-confidence. As with goal setting and self-talk, imaging should be realistic and specific. Combining imagery, goal setting and self-talk is also possible.

Relaxation

Relaxation may not appear to be a skill, but being able to physically and mentally relax is essential for a balanced body and mind. For many dancers this skill requires some practice. Dancers are notorious for being high achievers and pushing themselves physically and mentally to extremes (Hamilton, 1999). This drive can lead to excess stress and anxiety, as well as physical fatigue and exhaustion, ultimately culminating in injury or other health issues. As presented in chapter 5, taking time to rest and recover has multiple training and well-being benefits, including reduced feelings of anxiety, increased energy levels and improved skill learning and development. The many methods of seeking relaxation include complete rest, constructive rest, active rest and distributed practice. From a psychological perspective, purposefully taking time out to relax and enter into a positive state of mindfulness is important. It provides an opportunity to destress, allowing for a moment of whole body and mind recalibration. Relaxation strategies can be employed in the lead-up and immediately prior to stressful events such as performances, auditions, competitions or assessments. Improved focus and concentration, as well as reduced muscle tension, mean that relaxation strategies are also beneficial in any dance situation and for any level of engagement in any dance style. Injured dancers can also address negative feelings and physical or mental tension through relaxation techniques, thereby supporting the recovery processes.

From standing, sitting or lying in a constructive rest position (see image in chapter 5) dancers should focus on their breathing, taking slow deep breaths that expand the ribs laterally on the inhalation and releasing any stress or tension with the exhalation. Breaths can begin in counts of 4 (4 counts in and 4 counts out) and can slowly build to 8 counts for the in breath and 8 counts for the out breath. Slowing of the breath pattern in this way is said to access the parasympathetic nervous system, which allows the body to enter rest mode, slowing down the heart rate and promoting digestive activity and physical and mental restoration. When combined with other psychological skills, relaxation can further support and reinforce positive mental attitudes. For example, a combination of imagery and relaxation can transport the dancer to a beautiful sandy beach (see relaxation transcript that follows). By listening to a recording of positive self-talk affirmations dancers can reinforce positive thinking and behaviours while in a relaxed and receptive state.

Dance leaders can include relaxation periods during the cool-down section of the session, especially if this is the last physical session of the day. Dancers should also take it upon themselves to factor in specific times throughout their week that are dedicated to purposeful relaxation. Of course dance leaders should also take some personal time

in their week to focus on relaxation and care for themselves, rather than always thinking of their participant group. As with imagery scripts for mental rehearsal, dancers and leaders can tailor the relaxation session to personal preferences by creating a personalised relaxation script such as the one outlined in the sidebar and recording it on to an audio device. Before commencing, participants should make sure that they are in a comfortable position (e.g., constructive rest pose or a suitable modification; Sweigard, 2013) and should take time to focus on their breath, drawing their attention from the outer world to their inner being.

The relaxation script in the sidebar is merely a brief example. Other scripts can focus simply on the breath, incorporate anatomical imagery or include competence-reinforcing statements. As with the guidelines for imagery usage, include as much vividness of sensations (colours, smells, tastes, sounds or feelings) as possible. Additionally, if guiding a group of dancers through a relaxation experience, give participants the opportunity to remove themselves from the visualisation at any time that they feel uncomfortable with the situation. For example, if a participant has a fear of floating in water, then elements of the script in the sidebar will invoke fear rather than calm.

Sample Script for Relaxation Exercise

As your mind relaxes begin to visualise yourself lying on warm, soft sand in a beautiful sheltered cove. This might be a place that you have visited previously, or it might exist solely in your imagination. It does not matter—this is *your* cove. Allow yourself some time to familiarise yourself with your surroundings. See the colours, such as the clear blue sky. Feel the warm, soft sand. Listen to the gentle lapping of the crystal-green water on the shore. Taste the salty air. Sense the warmth of the sun in the sky above you. You feel comfortable. You feel calm. You feel safe. Attend to these positive feelings, letting any potential distractions just fizzle away with the out breath. . . [Pause.]

As you lie on the sand you feel the gentle lapping of the warm water at your feet. With each ebb and flow of the gentle tide the water creeps up behind your legs, pelvis, spine, shoulders, arms, neck and head until you find yourself buoyant in the shallow, warm, crystal-clear

waters. The sun continues to warm your front as you float weightlessly in the shallow waters . . . calm, comfortable, safe and at ease. . . [Pause.]

When you are ready, feel the water slowly ebb away from underneath your head, neck, shoulders, arms, spine, pelvis, legs and feet, until once again you sense the warm, soft sand moulding around your body as you sink into a deeper state of relaxation . . . feeling calm, comfortable, safe and at ease . . . letting your mind and body recharge. . . [Pause.]

When you are ready, prepare yourself to return to the physical place where you are actually lying. As you begin to bring your attention back to your breath and your real surroundings, remind yourself that this peaceful cove is a place that you can come to at any time you wish. As you gradually draw away, take with you the feelings of calm, of comfort, of safety and serenity. You feel relaxed, refreshed and revived . . . ready to continue with your day.

For the injured dancer relaxation strategies can aid in combating feelings of fear and stress associated with being temporarily incapacitated. It can also support a balanced return to physical practice, where gradual increases in training and participation are supported by appropriate rest and relaxation, aiding speedy mental and physical recovery.

Including the descriptors 'clear, warm, shallow water' should minimise this occurrence, but none the less, participants should be told that they have ultimate control over the mental journey they are about to experience.

Other more immediate relaxation cues that can be used across a variety of participating groups include 'Take a few deep breaths and imagine your body is full of clean, fresh water, washing away any tension' or for younger dancers, 'Let's imagine being wrapped up in a warm blanket and feeling very calm' or immediately prior to performing or competing, 'Breathe in . . . Breathe out . . . Relax, be confident, enjoy, let go. . .' Whether using brief cues or more strategic and guided scripts, the benefits of relaxation in a culture notorious for believing that more is better should not be underestimated and should be championed as a vital aspect of safe and effective mental and physical practice (also see chapter 5 for more on the role of rest and recovery in training).

Figure 8.2 illustrates the relationship between the principles and strategies addressed in this chapter. It highlights that striving for a positive task-involving learning environment supports the fulfilment of the three basic psychological needs. Strategies that can be employed to promote psychological well-being and reinforce feelings of autonomy, belonging and competency are the identified psychological skills of goal setting, self-talk, imagery and relaxation. An additional compounding factor is approach to feedback. Paying attention to behaviour, language use and tone of voice, for example, can go a long way to achieving positive learning environments.

SUMMARY

Psychological factors are as important to safe practice as physical factors, although they are possibly applied more indirectly than directly. Given the inextricable connection between body and mind, a healthy mind will inevitably support a healthy body and vice versa. The skills and strategies included in this chapter are important for both dance leaders and dancers. As a dance leader, knowing how and why to create a psychologically supportive learning environment can result in reduced prevalence of psychological variables that are known to relate to injury occurrence, unhealthy eating practices and dropping out of dance activity. In addition, dancers have responsibility to take ownership of their own

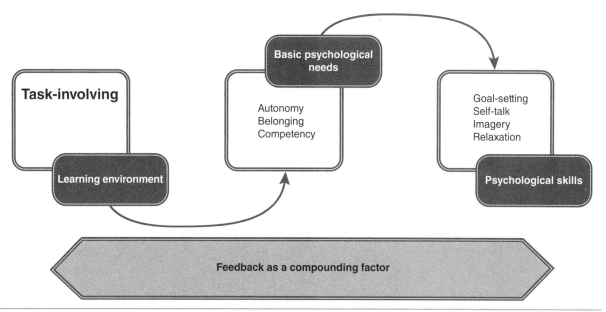

Figure 8.2 Related characteristics of an effective psychological environment.

well-being through engaging with psychological skills that can assist in maintaining healthy attitudes towards their dance experiences, in particular if their personality type is susceptible to feeling psychological pressures or if the dancing environment that they are experiencing is not as supportive as they would like. Dance leaders must not act as psychologists, and both dancers and dance leaders should be aware of when professional help is needed, and seek referrals. In the meantime ongoing safe practice will be promoted through engagement with and application of the strategies and recommendations within this chapter.

KEY POINTS

- A positive psychological environment is important for ensuring safe psychological and emotional practice.

- Dance leaders have the most influence over the type of psychological environment created.

- Environments that are dominant in task-involving features (using self-referenced progression, acknowledging efforts, seeing mistakes as part of learning) are most beneficial for participants of all ages and levels of ability.

- Task-involving environments promote positive feelings of autonomy, belonging and competency which support healthy motivation and contribute towards overall safe psychological practice.

- Dance leaders should pay attention to their language and behaviour, as well their tone of voice and their overall approach to providing feedback.

- Dance leaders should acknowledge the needs of individual dancers, and should be aware that learning is not a linear experience.

- Psychological skills (goal setting, self-talk, imagery, relaxation) are useful strategies for maintaining intrinsic motivation and healthful dance practice.

- The injured dancer often requires particular consideration in the application of the principles and strategies outlined in this chapter.

chapter **9**

Injury Awareness and Management

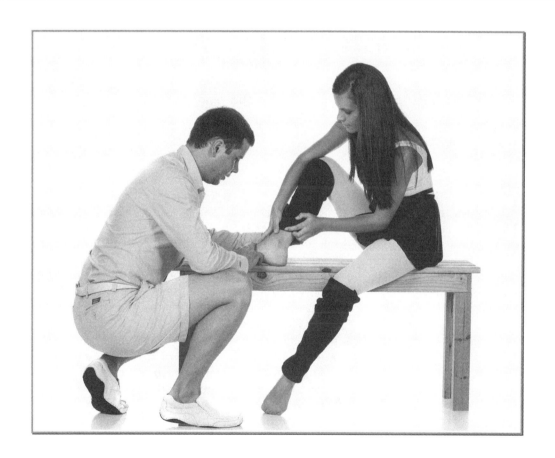

After reading this chapter you should be able to do the following:

- Recognise physical, psychological and environmental risk factors in your activity.
- Create strategies to minimise risk factors.
- Deal efficiently and appropriately with the occurrence of injury during your dance session, including relevant documentation.
- Apply recommended procedures for immediate injury management.
- Advise participants how to return safely to participation in your activity following an injury.

≡ *Key Terms*

documentation of injury
extrinsic risk factors
HARM (heat, alcohol, running and massage)
intrinsic risk factors

overuse injuries
PRICED (protection or prevention, rest, ice, compression, elevation and diagnosis)

primary injury
rehabilitation
secondary injury
traumatic injury

Activities that challenge the body inevitably include an element of risk. The mixture of environmental, physical and psychological factors affecting dancers increases the risk of injury (SHAPE, 2002). The exposure to risk might intensify with higher levels and frequency of participation, but for all types and level of dancer, increased risk leads to more likelihood of injury. The focus of this chapter is not to overemphasise injury or deter dancers by highlighting the extent of its occurrence but to raise awareness of the inherent concerns and common problems so as to protect dancing bodies as fully as possible. Knowledge and application of the safe dance practice components contained in this book will go a long way in helping to reduce injury occurrence and minimise its long-term effects. Injuries will still happen, despite the best efforts of all concerned, but learning from emerging trends in dance science literature and feeding this knowledge back into training and practice will ensure enhanced performance and prolonged participation.

As a population, dancers are susceptible to injury due to the physiological and psychological demands placed on their bodies. Research over-

views show that in groups of dancers studied across a range of genres and skill levels, between 42 and 97 percent have experienced injuries in dance (Russell, 2013). Ultimately, injury management and **rehabilitation** is the remit of professional therapists in consultation with individual dancers, but dancers themselves, their teachers and all those who manage and direct them in practice, training and performance should be aware of how they each can individually contribute to injury prevention. Dancers need to personally recognise and accept the symptoms of injury in order to take appropriate action to address pain and limitations early on. They should understand the consequences of ignoring injury warning signs and should fully engage with rehabilitation plans to counteract possible **secondary injury** and avoid longer-lasting damage. Dance leaders need to ensure that the activities they devise and deliver are considered in terms of the impact on the body and potential for injury, as well as take control when an injury occurs in their session. Following an injury, their assistance in helping a dancer return safely to full dance activity is vital.

DANCE INJURY PATTERNS

Exactly what constitutes a dance injury has been described in a variety of ways. An amalgamated definition would incorporate the following terms: a need for medical assistance for a physical complaint resulting from, and subsequently restricting, participation in dance activity (Bronner, Ojofeitimi, & Mayers, 2006; Krasnow, Mainwaring, & Kerr, 1999; Potts & Irrgang, 2001). However, this definition may not fully describe an individual dancer's experience of the negative effects of exercise on their bodies. Some injuries are not considered significant (or even regarded as an injury) because they do not, or are not allowed to, disrupt the dancer's activities. Dancers often ignore warning signs, such as pain signals. Failing to acknowledge an injury (and avoiding seeking help) may be due to a variety of reasons. Dancers exhibit higher pain thresholds and tolerance than non-dancers and frequently do not seek medical attention until dysfunction or a long-standing medical condition has developed (Howse & McCormack, 2009; Krasnow et al., 1999; Mainwaring, Krasnow, & Kerr, 2001; Potts & Irrgang, 2001; Russell, 2013). Nevertheless, pain is the body's mechanism for alerting us to injury, and it should not be dismissed. In order to deal successfully with injury and to avoid repercussions, the signs and symptoms of injury should be addressed as soon as possible.

The approach of 'no pain, no gain' may still be embedded in dance training culture. Dancers continue to push through pain and injury, although experienced dancers are more likely to seek treatment, possibly because they are increasingly aware of what constitutes an injury (Thomas & Tarr, 2009).

Dancers report that they worry about the reactions of parents, teachers, choreographers and other dancers, or feel pressure (real or perceived) from others and often themselves to continue to train, rehearse and perform while injured (Mainwaring et al., 2001). For example, a student in training might worry about the consequences of lack of attendance in class, a professional dancer could be nervous about losing a role to another dancer or financial loss and a recreational dancer may not want to miss out on the social aspects of regular participation. All of these are also influenced by a lack of either time or money to care for their injuries (Liederbach, 2000). Dancers tend to self-diagnose and self-manage, often because they have the perception that they understand their bodies

> *Dancers of all abilities are often reluctant to seek treatment for their injuries for different reasons, and can be prone to self-diagnosis and avoiding professional intervention. If even small but nagging injuries are ignored, the chances of them developing into something more serious, reoccurring at a later date or contributing to other related injuries are much greater.*

better than a doctor or therapist, who has less experiential understanding of the nature of dance activities, and they doubt physicians' abilities to help them recover (Lai, Krasnow, & Thomas, 2008; Liederbach, 2000; Shah et al., 2012). As well as a lack of trust in the capacities of the medical professional, this often comes about due to a lack of understanding as to the extent of the injury on the dancer's part. Therefore it is imperative that dancers of all abilities are made aware either directly or indirectly of how to recognise and prevent or rehabilitate injuries appropriately.

Much of the research on injury patterns and rates has focused on students in vocational training (preprofessional) and professional or elite dancers, but it also provides evidence regarding children and young people participating in dance activities. A long-term study on dance-related injuries in the United States reviewed 17 years of National Electronic Injury Surveillance System data to show that over this time, 113,084 injuries affected young individuals ranging from age 3 to 19 (Roberts, Nelson, & McKenzie, 2013).

The growing popularity of different dance forms as recreation means that this context is also receiving more attention. Concern regarding injury prevention during dance activities that are not housed within professional and vocational training curricula is leading to more observation and injury monitoring.

Dance activity is associated with a wide range of injuries to different sites in the body. Specific parts of the body can be affected more than others, with particular emphases depending on the style and genre. In general, research reveals that lower extremity injuries seem to be the most prevalent, accounting for between 58 and 88 percent of all dance injuries regardless of dance style, with the hip and back also featuring prominently (Liederbach, 2000; Potts & Irrgang, 2001). A review of 29 separate studies supports these findings, showing a high prevalence of lower extremity and back injuries, primarily sprains, strains and ten-dinopathies of the soft tissues (Jacobs, Hincapié, & Cassidy, 2012).

As concern has grown over the extent of injury, surveys to investigate dancers' health have been conducted. Two of the first and most notable were the Dance UK Fit to Dance 2 report (Laws, 2005) and Ausdance Safe Dance volume 3 (Crook-shanks, 1999). These reports provided a clearer picture of how dancers were affected by and responded to injury and identified causal factors. In the Dance UK survey, it was reported that 80 percent of dancers consulted had suffered at least one injury each year that significantly affected their ability to perform. Similarly, in the Ausdance report, it was found that 48 percent of responding dancers had sustained a recent or acute injury occurring in the previous 6 months and that 50 percent had sustained an injury that continued to affect their dancing in some way. Although similar larger-scale surveys have not yet been repeated, more recent studies and reviews of the literature suggest even higher injury rates (84 to 95 percent) if individual dancers' injuries are taken into account over their whole career rather than only the previous year (Russell, 2013; Thomas & Tarr, 2009).

Dance as an art form and as a social, recre-ational and competitive activity continues to develop. As a result, the more familiar or expected patterns of injury also continue to change. Statis-tics and trends for widening participation in new and developing dance styles are emerging. Many dance forms are exploring new ways of using the body, relying on the knees, upper extremities, spine, neck or even the head as transitory bases of support, presenting a whole new challenge to dancers and a new class of injury risk (Lieder-bach, 2000). The specific physical requirements of different genres may dictate injury location as a result of different methods of weight bearing and support or partner or equipment interac-tion. Some studies have been able to link the sites of injury to specific movement vocabulary or types of movements, but others discuss the combination of factors that might make dancers in specific styles vulnerable to injuries in certain areas, including frequency of performance, type of environment and the enormous diversity in choreographic interpretation of stylistic material. However, research detail regarding different styles has produced a map of injury sites. Professional ballet dancers mostly succumb to foot and ankle injuries, while contemporary or modern and jazz

dancers injure the knee, ankle, thigh and back (Campoy et al., 2011; Jacobs et al., 2012; Shah et al., 2012). Dancers performing in West End shows are mostly affected by injuries of the lower back, ankle and knee, but dancers in Broadway shows predominantly suffer back injuries (Harkness Center for Dance Injuries. n.d.). Although the reasons for injury are multifaceted, the extreme range of motion required to practise and perform in these styles, the instability of working in pointe shoes and heels or the experimental nature of modern techniques and choreography all have a major effect.

In other contexts, it may be easier to determine cause and effect. In styles with significant repeti-tion of percussive movement patterns, such as the stamping of the feet in flamenco, the predominant site of injury is the foot (Pedersen & Wilmerding, 1998), for example, stress fractures and sesamoid-itis (irritation surrounding the sesamoid bones on the sole of the foot), but vibration patterns can travel through the body to produce impact at the hip joint, back and neck pain and even produce urogenital disorders (Beijani et al., 1988). Similarly, the explosive bouncing on the balls of the feet in Highland dancing and the use of the on-toe posi-tion in Irish dance can make these dancers suscep-tible to lower extremity injuries, particularly at the ankle, and stress fractures of the lower leg and the sesamoids (Henderson & MacIntyre, 2006; Noon, Hoch, McNamara, & Schimke, 2010; Trégouët & Merland, 2013; Walls et al., 2010).

Tap dancers are also affected, in the main by ankle (30 percent of injuries assessed) and knee injuries (Campoy et al., 2011; Mayers, Judelson, & Bronner, 2003). There is a similarity here with ballroom dancers, who report mostly ankle, foot and toe injuries (35 percent of injuries assessed; Kuisis, Camacho, Krüger, & Camacho, 2012). Ballroom dancing has seen a recent resurgence in popularity, and is diversifying into a discipline known as Dance Sport, an activity that requires precision and power as well as endurance to meet the demands of practice, competition and exhibitions (Tsien, & Trepman, 2001). In addition to the stresses of frequent rotation and extension of the upper spine in this style, the requirements of internal rotation at the hip joint in combination with forces produced in partnering, if the foot is firmly in contact with the floor, can cause partic-ular strain on the knee. Investigation into Indian classical dance is limited, but Bharatanatyam dancers have been shown to exhibit lower body muscle tightness and, like many other dancers, succumb to knee and ankle injuries (Anbarasi, Rajan & Adalarasu, 2012).

Zumba is a form of dance exercise that has gained great popularity worldwide with people seeking a way to improve their cardiorespiratory fitness in a recreational environment. At present there are limited studies in this style, but reporting of Zumba-related injuries is becoming more common. Researchers suggest that new participants attracted to these types of dance exercise may be more susceptible to injury because it may be their first form of physical activity for some time: The most common site of injury is the knee (42 percent), and injury rate increases with more frequent weekly participation (Inouye, Nichols, Maskarinec, & Tseng, 2013). Because of the twisting motions in the lower leg, wearing sports shoes with treads rather than softer dance shoes can cause friction with the floor and invite injuries such as meniscus tears and ankle sprains. More advice on suitable footwear for Zumba sessions could be provided by dance leaders (Inouye et al., 2013). Similarly, the belly dance community discusses potential injuries due to shoes that grip the floor too much when pivoting or spinning, but dancing barefoot also presents certain dangers, for example, on dirty or unsuitable floors (Shira, n.d.).

Research on a variety of street and hip-hop styles (breaking, popping and locking and new school) suggests that dancers practising in these genres experience more injuries overall in than other dance styles (Ojofeitimi, Bronner, & Woo, 2012). Because of the extreme demands of the acrobatic moves, there is a greater frequency of injury to the upper limbs in contrast to other dance styles, particularly of the wrist and elbow. Breakdancing could be considered a high-risk dancing sport in which professional breakdancers may be more prone to injury than amateur dancers (Kauther, Wedemeyer, Wegner, Kauther, & von Knoch, 2009).

With the exception of the latter, the common factor in most of these styles is the incidence of lower-extremity injuries (see table 9.1). The reported incidence of injury in the upper extremity has historically been much lower, but these types of injuries are on the rise because of the increased partnering demands for both men and women, the inclusion of more floor work requiring support from the arms, and the more athletic

Table 9.1   Comparison of Common Injuries in Different Dance Styles

Dance style	Most common sites of injury
Classical ballet	Foot and ankle
Contemporary/modern	Foot, ankle, lower back and knee
Jazz	Foot, ankle, lower back and knee
Ballroom	Foot and ankle
Broadway (commercial)	Back
West End (commercial)	Lower back, ankle and knee
Irish	Ankle and lower leg
Highland	Ankle and lower leg
Tap	Ankle and knee
Flamenco	Foot
Zumba	Knee
Bharatanatyam (classical Indian)	Ankle and knee
Pole dance	Wrist, elbow and shoulder
Aerial (wire, silk/ribbon)	Wrist, elbow and shoulder
Hip-hop (breaking, popping and locking, new school)	Wrist and elbow

and gymnastic elements in modern choreography (Clippinger, 2016). Injury statistics in some of the newer dance disciplines that place the greatest demands on the upper body (as well as the core) are not yet widely available. For example, vertical and aerial styles that work with a pole, wire, silk or tissue are extremely upper body intensive. Anecdotal evidence and dedicated blogs suggest that, as expected, they can result in shoulder, back, wrist and elbow injuries.

Whether amateur or professional, for leisure or as a vocation, dance activity does have its risks, which should not be underestimated. A devastating injury during a pole dancing class in the UK, in which a recreational dancer was permanently paralysed (Blake, 2010), has brought the importance of injury awareness and prevention very much to the fore. While dance science research is providing a more detailed injury analysis of a wider range of styles, the advice for everyday practice is simple. For every form, genre and level of participation, recognition of the likelihood of injury, understanding of the circumstances in which it could happen and knowledge of how to mediate the effects are essential.

INJURY TYPES, CAUSES AND RISK FACTORS

All dance participants should aim to minimise risk of injury, so reducing injury occurrence. As well as applying the principles and guidelines addressed in other chapters, knowledge of the types of injury that can affect dancers, the most frequent causes and attention to the risk factors involved will help them attain this goal.

Dance injuries can range from relatively minor to career threatening. Injuries that may be initially superficial can be judged as comparatively trivial, but nevertheless, they can affect the dancer's ability to function effectively. These include problems such as blisters, friction burns, bruised or ingrowing toenails, corns and calluses. This type of injury is avoidable with care, but should they occur some basic treatment options can limit pain and infection. The advice is not to pierce small blisters but to protect them so that they do not grow bigger. For very large blisters, use a needle sterilised in alcohol to release the fluid. The area should then be cleaned and treated with antibiotic ointment (not alcohol or iodine) and then protected with an adhesive bandage, also using a foam pad with the centre cut out to relieve pres-

sure where necessary (SHAPE, 2002; Peterson & Renström, 2005). If the blister becomes infected, check with a doctor. Ideally all equipment that has the potential to cause blistering should be specifically designed for the dance activity and checked before use. Tight footwear can cause overcrowding of the toes, encouraging ingrowing nails, so shoes should be fitted to the individual and worn in where possible. Corns and calluses will also affect the dancer's capacity to work barefoot or in shoes. Any restricting injuries should be treated by a chiropodist.

While the preceding conditions can be uncomfortable, they do not significantly affect dance practice in the long term. More serious for the dancer are soft-tissue injuries, fractures, dislocations and neurological complaints. Other non-recurrent, accidental incidents such as concussion also need to be considered. These injures can be divided into two types: traumatic or acute injuries and overuse or chronic injuries.

Traumatic injuries happen spontaneously, and are the result of a specific event that causes the sudden excessive stress on the body, such as sprains, strains, fractures, lacerations or concussions. The incidence of contact injuries, as seen in many sports, is comparatively infrequent in dance activity, although the risk may be underestimated because of this. For example, dancers may experience concussion without recognising or reporting it. Without an actual loss of consciousness, they would likely attempt to dance through attributable symptoms. Causes of concussion across different genres have been identified as unintentional drops by a partner, falls in acrobatic-type movements, being kicked in the head or hit with a stage prop, slips and falls and even repeated whipping of the head and neck as part of a choreographed routine (Stein et al., 2014). The authors of this cited study warn that concussion must be taken seriously because dancers can put themselves and others at risk if their balance and reaction time are impaired.

More common in dance are **overuse injuries**. It is reported that 60 to 75 percent of all dance injuries are due to overuse (Potts & Irrgang, 2001; Thomas & Tarr, 2009). Overuse injuries develop over time as a result of repetitive loading that causes microdamage to the musculoskeletal system. These injuries are often long standing, and they reoccur as a result of an ineffective healing process. Seemingly inconsequential individual injuries can build up, through lack of treatment or by continued exposure to the causal factor, to chronic injuries that eventually compromise performance. Unsurprisingly, these chronic injuries tend to be more common in older dancers (Potts & Irrgang, 2001). Dance participation is interrupted most often due to overuse injuries and inadequate prevention strategies. Lost time is extremely frustrating to choreographers, teachers and dancers but, if attended to in the appropriate way, chronic injuries can be managed more wisely.

In a number of dance styles, the most common cause of both injury and subsequent worsening symptoms is excessive use and repetition of activities. Early treatment of acute injuries should be emphasised so that the injury does not progress to a chronic and recurrent condition (Campoy et al., 2011; Simpson, 2006). Dance practice necessarily requires repetition in order to perfect movement, but it is loading beyond the capacity of the individual body that brings about the damage. A relationship exists between loading (resistance) and frequency that affects the possibility of injury occurring: Risk increases with a normal load at high frequency (many repetitions), with a heavy load at normal frequency and especially with a heavy load at high frequency (Peterson & Renström, 2005). Chapter 4 discusses these concepts in considerably more detail.

Disregarding early warning signs can affect the potential severity of damage, thereby contributing to both cause and risk of further injury. These signs might include discomfort (pain or numbness) when dancing, general weakness and stiffness, loss of co-ordination or control and limitations in usual range of motion. Postural changes might also signal an injury, for example, tension patterns such as rounding or elevation of the shoulders, regardless of the actual injury site (Luke & Micheli, 2000). Inexperienced dancers sometimes have difficulty distinguishing between pain due to injury and muscle aches resulting from a sudden increase physical activity or unaccustomed muscle recruitment. This then affects their ability to make decisions whether or not to continue with dance activity. Muscle stiffness can peak 24 to 36 hours after strenuous activity (known as delayed-onset muscle soreness or DOMS), and is a normal physiological response that eases in a few days (a good cool-down can help to offset DOMS—see chapter 3). Pain due to acute injury usually appears more quickly, while pain due to overuse injury can be niggling and constant, becoming more intense as the injury worsens: The pain from these injuries has different characteristics when compared to stiffness (SHAPE, 2002). Pain description guidelines refer

to types of sensation that can help to recognise potential injury: A sharp pain may point towards a mechanical cause and an ache suggests inflammation; a deep pain may signify that a bone or joint is affected, whereas a more superficial pain might relate to muscle or connective tissue; a throbbing pain could be vascular in origin and pins and needles, numbness or sharp shooting pains may be nerve related (Simpson, 2006). While these indicators are useful for highlighting the possible onset of injury, dancers must not use them to self-diagnose, but rather to describe their symptoms to a qualified therapist when taking precautionary measures.

> Dancers appear to sometimes ignore or disregard pain. Pain is usually a warning sign, and it should always be taken seriously. Pain from injury comes on quickly and does not go away without attention. Pain from stiffness is a result of unexpected, unprepared or increased activity; it comes on more slowly but subsides after a short time.

Risk factors for injury are said to be either intrinsic or extrinsic, and these may be physical, psychological or environmental. **Intrinsic risk factors** can be defined as those that remain relatively constant, and are inherently related to the characteristics of the individual dancer. Extrinsic factors can negatively affect the function of the dancer from a more external perspective. Some of the causes of injury are common to all dance activities, but it is not always easy to pinpoint one single cause that has initiated the problem. The fact that there is frequently an interplay between these intrinsic and extrinsic factors should be kept in mind at all times (Caldwell, 2001; Conti & Wong, 2001; Howse & Mc Cormack, 2009; Motta-Valencia, 2006; Sevey Fitt, 1996; Shah et al., 2012; Thomas & Tarr, 2009).

Intrinsic Risk Factors

The body is the dancers' tool for their craft. If it is not in an adequate state of readiness to meet the demands to be made on it, then inevitably it may succumb to the physical pressures. In the professional setting, selection has usually determined those bodies that are naturally more able to progress to an elite standard. However, 'because of the range of demands on the professional dancer,

Risk Factors

Intrinsic Factors

- Physique and anatomical restrictions
- Inefficient alignment and posture
- Inadequate or defective technique
- Overwork and fatigue
- Age
- Sex
- Previous medical and injury history, including menstrual history for females
- Psychological state

Extrinsic Factors

- Insufficient warm-up
- Unskilled or inefficient teaching
- Overuse and excessive repetition
- Type and intensity of training: imbalanced schedules and training plans, unrealistic demands
- New or unusual choreography
- Lifestyle factors: diet, sleep, smoking
- Environmental conditions, unsuitable facilities and equipment

include *pes planus* (common name flat feet), *pes cavus* (exceptionally high arches in the feet), *genu valgum* (knock knees), *genu varum* (bow legs) and *hallux valgus* (bunions). Scoliosis (varying degrees of side-to-side curvature of the spine) affects the dancer's ability to fully achieve some aspects of dance movement and aesthetics. Conversely, hypermobility, often regarded as a positive attribute in some dance styles, also has many training and performance repercussions. Chapter 2 looks at these conditions and safe alignment in greater depth.

Inefficient alignment and posture as a result of genetic conditions, muscle imbalances and tightness or lack of strength and control are a contributory factor to injury risk because the body will not be working optimally, and may have to compensate for less than ideal skeletal relationships and weakened muscle groups, resulting in uneconomical movement patterns. Good biomechanics will encourage effective muscle balance and promote joint protection as well as enhance performance.

In the same way, inadequate or defective technique that is unable to support specific dance movements will increase the likelihood of injury. Beyond the actual physical execution, a lack of technical understanding and application of knowledge is also a risk; therefore dancers and, more specifically, teachers must set appropriate challenges in the development of skills. If an injured dancer resumes activity and simply repeats previous technical mistakes, the injury is very likely to reoccur. Teachers must have the requisite knowledge to be able to recognise faulty patterns in individuals and give precise technical feedback to counteract incorrect execution. Efficient biomechanics should be considered and managed within every style of dance vocabulary. Common examples of technical weakness in many styles would be pronation (rolling in of the feet in weight bearing), supination (sickling or winging of the foot in weight bearing) and lack of understanding of the mechanics of creating and maintaining turnout.

no single performer is equipped with the "ideal" body to meet all the requirements of their art. Each dancer must confront their own technical weaknesses with self-discipline and dedication' (Potts & Irrgang, 2001, p. 51). It is highly unlikely that everyone participating in dance activity will have the perfect body structure or attributes to achieve the ideal. All will have a specific anatomical composition that makes them unique, and will need to deal with the genetic limitations that restrict their range of motion. Working intelligently and realistically will allow each body to achieve its potential. Pushing the body beyond its genetic and functional capabilities is seen as a major contributory factor to injury: One of the most common examples of this is the inappropriate forcing of turnout and over-rotation of the feet beyond natural limits, the single largest contributing factor to overuse injuries of the lower extremity (Potts & Irrgang, 2001).

Other structural differences also present challenges to the dancer and teacher: These might

Everyone's unique anatomical composition means that each dancer can be susceptible to injury in a variety of different ways. The combination of the individual body's structure, its physiological readiness and the technical demands of the style collectively influence the likelihood of injury.

Dancers are all individual. If they understand the limits of their own body, they can minimise injury risk while enjoying energetic, athletic and exciting choreography.

Through a lack of specific conditioning, dancers may not be fit for purpose, apparent in unsatisfactory levels of stamina, strength, flexibility, power, co-ordination and control, which do not support technical efficiency. Much research supports the idea that dancers are not necessarily physiologically equipped for the demands made on them and that dance class and training do not automatically prepare dancers for performance. It has been suggested that reduced levels of general physical fitness are associated with relatively high levels of injuries in dancers, and may also hinder their ability to perform to maximum potential (Brown, Wells, Schade, Smith, & Fehling, 2007; Krasnow & Chatfield, 1996; Koutedakis, 2005; Koutedakis, Cross, & Sharp, 1996; Koutedakis & Jamurtas, 2004; Koutedakis & Sharp, 1999; Koutedakis, Stavropoulos-Kalinoglou, & Metsios, 2005; Wyon, Redding, Abt, Head, & Sharp, 2003). Some researchers have identified a lack of strength in relation to flexibility and weakness in core strength and stability as potential causes (Comfort & Abraham, 2010; Luke et al., 2002; Koutedakis & Jamurtas, 2004; Koutedakis & Sharp, 1999; Koutedakis et al., 2005; Poggini, Losasso, & Iannone, 1999; Wyon et al., 2003). Dancers working at an intensity that requires a degree

of physical fitness are therefore at a greater risk of injury if they are not able to meet the physiological demands. Chapter 4 discusses ways that dancers can improve their physical conditioning to reduce injury potential and enhance their performance.

Even if dancers do possess a good technical foundation and fitness level, the effects of overwork, fatigue or lack of recovery time can still negatively influence their efficiency. Incorrect execution of dance movements can actually be a result of tiredness rather than inability. Research shows that fatigued muscles demonstrate a reduced ability to generate force (Comfort & Abraham, 2010); therefore maintaining unrealistic intensity levels will inevitably result in shortfalls in muscle response. In dance settings, some of the principles of training are often overlooked in the construction of sessions, schedules and curricula, including periodization, specificity, overload and overtraining. All of these training principles are discussed at length in chapter 4 and applied to dance session structure in chapter 6, but in terms of injury, it must be stressed that they have a real influence on the body's ability to limit negative effects. For example, overload involves imposing loads on the body that are incrementally greater in order to make physical improvements, and specificity means that these loads mimic the physiological demands of the relevant activity. However, in applying these principles, this does not mean that the body has to be overworked. Chapter 5 explains that periodization takes into account the dancer's total effort exposure (Liederbach, 2000) through a gradual cycling of specificity, intensity and volume of training (Kenney, Wilmore & Costill, 2012) therefore assisting in managing the loads to reduce the overall and cumulative demand by considering rest as a counteractive measure. The inclusion of rest opportunities within the dance session is advised for all participants, but will be especially beneficial for recovering dancers in order to avoid repetitive stress and fatigue (Potts & Irrgang, 2001). For specificity in injury rehabilitation, the stresses must specifically address the demands of the pre-injury activities, including environmental working conditions (Liederbach, 2000).

Physiological differences due to age and sex are seen as risk factors. Young dancers in particular are susceptible to the effects of dance activity if their specific age-related characteristics are not fully understood. The main risk factor for overuse injuries in children and adolescents is the musculoskeletal changes during puberty and the growth spurt. Because of the effects of growth, children suffer particular injuries to bone, and the lower extremities and spine need special consideration (Luke et al., 2002; Poggini et al., 1999). See chapter 10 for particular issues regarding this age group.

Young dancers have a greater tendency to succumb to hip and back injuries, while older dancers are more likely to incur leg, ankle and foot injuries (Motta-Valencia, 2006). In the professional context, some studies have found that older dancers have an increased risk of injury, but this is possibly due only to the fact that experienced performers are given the more demanding roles; other studies suggest that young dancers experience greater injury occurrence (Campoy et al., 2011). Male and female dancers have different physiological attributes, especially in terms of strength and flexibility, and dance activity leaders should try to take this into account where possible. Female dancers also deal with issues surrounding disordered eating, menstrual irregularities, calcium intake and bone health (see chapter 7) that affect their likelihood of injury (Luke et al., 2002). Male dancers may have more demanding tasks in some styles, for example, traditional lifting and partnering roles, which may require aspects of strength and power training to be appropriately designed and implemented.

A dancer with a previous history of injuries may be more likely to suffer from a subsequent injury. As discussed earlier, injuries at the same site can be recurrent, especially if not fully healed at the first incidence and if appropriate conditioning practices are not undertaken to further strengthen susceptible areas. An injury to one body part may cause compensatory movement patterns, and consequently begin to affect a different muscle group or joint. Similarly, a dancer in a reduced state of general health for any reason may also be more prone to injury. While people who regularly exercise at a moderate intensity can reduce their risk of respiratory symptoms, they should not engage in intense exercise before or during viral infections (Martin, Pence, & Woods, 2009). Dancers who have recently had a viral or respiratory tract infection, including colds and high temperatures, should be wary of participating in physiologically demanding dance activity.

Psychological, as well as physical intrinsic factors can contribute to injury risk. Mood, state of mind and particularly stress can influence dancers' ability to fully focus on their execution. Lapses in concentration through worry or fatigue can detract from correct technique. The pressure to excel, often self-imposed, is recognised as a driving force for dancers, and can cause them to disregard injury (Shah et al., 2012). Certain types of personality can predispose individuals to injury, for example, dancers with competitive traits and achievement motivation (Liederbach, 2000; Mainwaring et al., 2001). It is reported that 'accumulation of life stressors can tax an individual's coping resources, increasing his or her susceptibility to fatigue, illness or injury' (Krasnow et al., 1999, p. 52). Examples of these life stressors include major life events but also general, day-to-day stressors, which for dancers could mean difficult relationships with their leaders or excessive time demands in training. As highlighted earlier, a culture that is believed to be prevalent in dance tends to embrace discomfort, pain and tolerance of injury, which can contribute to the likelihood of dancers to continue to work through injury. In psychological terms this is related to the concern over the 'disruption of self' that initially comes from registering the existence of injury, which is then heightened through the resulting absence from practice (Mainwaring et al., 2001, p. 105).

Dance leaders could examine their expectations and goals for their participants and guard against promoting an excessive drive to excel or encouraging overexertion and increased effort to please.

Ineffective Risk and Injury Management

Zoe is a young dancer (11 years old). She is attending a street dance class in her local church hall, which has lots of boys and girls of different ages taking part. All of the dancers are keen to show what they can do, and the environment is a little competitive.

The teacher demonstrates a movement that involves sliding and spinning on the knees followed by a spring back onto the feet. Zoe is not very good at this movement, but she keeps trying and hopes that because it is part of a routine that will be practised for a performance, she will get better at it.

Over the weeks, Zoe's knees begin to hurt. She tells her parents and her teacher, but both think the discomfort is perhaps due to growing pains. In one rehearsal, Zoe is very uncomfortable, and asks that she might be excused from performing this particular movement for a while. The teacher's response is that she will then have to do something else at the back instead. Zoe does not want to be seen to be second best or to lose her prominent place in the group on stage. She pretends that she is fine and carries on with the rest of the group.

At the end of the year, Zoe's knees continue to be troublesome. Her parents take her to a therapist, who explains that Zoe has been experiencing the beginning of her adolescent growth spurt, leaving her knee joints vulnerable and leading to some damage. He advises that she does not participate in this type of dance activity in the future.

The dance teacher has no further communication with Zoe's family and so does not receive valuable feedback on the detrimental effects of the vocabulary she continues to use.

If teachers and choreographers are able to recognise when dancers' physical and mental limits have been reached, dancers are less likely to feel pressure (whether genuine or interpreted) to push themselves beyond their capabilities (SHAPE, 2002). Leaders can reduce stress factors related to performance and ability by promoting a safe and supportive learning climate (see chapter 8).

Extrinsic Risk Factors

Extrinsic risk factors arise as a result of stresses outside the body that are not usually directly under the dancer's control. One exception, an extrinsic risk factor that dancers can personally address, is preparation.

A lack of preparation for dance activity is cited by dancers as one of the main causes of injury (Shah et al., 2012; Laws, 2005; Motta-Valencia, 2006). It is essential to follow recommended warm-up and cool-down procedures in order to allow the body to meet an increase in physical demand and to promote concentration and focus. Both dancers and dance leaders should take responsibility for ensuring that these procedures are followed, and their necessity should be encouraged from an early age or during initial participation in dance, as well as continually rein-

forced for all dancers, including professionals. If dancers are not able to independently understand and perform a warm-up and cool-down on their own (for example, beginners and children), then the dance leader should always include these sessions. Comprehensive guidelines for effective warm-up and cool-down can be found in chapter 3.

Insufficient knowledge, inexperienced teaching and misinformed strategies can lead to a range of potential risks: These might include a lack of understanding of individual limitations and physiological and psychological vulnerabilities, excessive focus on particular muscle groups and overly ambitious choreography. It is the dance teacher's responsibility to provide biomechanically sound training and to manage appropriate levels of intensity that can support technical gains and ensure training improvements, while still reducing impact and physical stress. Injury flashpoints often occur when there is a sudden change or rapid increase of exercise volume or intensity. There is a need to distribute the workload through muscle groups as much as possible, taking the stylistic objectives into account. Sessions should be designed according to the participant group's ability and structure them so as to meet training needs but also avoid overwork. Repetition is necessary in dance skill learning and for rehearsing material to appropriate standards, but overly repetitive actions are counterproductive, and they emphasise particular muscle groups with increased frequency, leading to fatigue and overuse injuries. The effects of repetitive high-impact movement such as jumping and percussive actions should be monitored to avoid overexposure. See chapter 6 for recommendations on session structure.

Dance leaders must set realistic and appropriate targets for their group of dancers. Professional schedules and training curricula that involve too heavy a workload can infringe on dancers' well-being in relation to their ability to eat properly, get enough sleep and allow the body to recover so that it can maintain its resiliency. Situations where dancers are asked to change styles or suddenly attempt different movement patterns required by a choreographer are injury flashpoints. Time for adaptation and preparation should ideally be allowed in order to minimise the risk of injury to muscles and joints unaccustomed to the new material. Training towards the performance of specific repertory and in preparation for the creation of new choreography should be progressive, although in practice this is very difficult to achieve because choreographers often create original vocabulary on the spot or rely on the creativity and individualism of their dancers to produce raw material. However, some advance planning to ensure that dancers are injury free and fit and then to prepare them properly by warming up for the specific activity will help to limit negative effects, as will cooling down, taking time to stretch and allowing the body to rest to encourage effective recovery (see chapters 3 and 5).

The majority of soft-tissue injuries occur in rehearsal or during performance (SHAPE, 2002). The run-up to competitions and shows, especially if dancers are subjected to a heavy combined workload of classes and rehearsals, is a time that makes dancers more vulnerable to injury. By considering other potential contributing factors (for example, that dancers may push themselves more in performance, that they could experience increased physical and mental anxiety at this point, that there could be temperature fluctuations or unfamiliar floor surfaces in different venues), dancers, choreographers and rehearsal directors could increase their awareness of heightened risks (SHAPE, 2002; Campoy et al., 2011).

Lifestyle factors and choices have an effect on the healthy functioning of the body and on the readiness of the body to respond to the demands of dance activity. Healthy nutrition to support the

> *Most injuries happen in rehearsal or performance rather than the dance class. Preventive measures can often be disregarded when time is short and the workload is heavy in preparation for shows and concerts. Extra care needs to be taken to prepare and recover properly during stressful periods.*

energy requirements of the activity and education regarding disordered eating and menstrual health are advised. Dancers should get adequate amounts of sleep to provide energy and reduce fatigue. Smoking, excessive alcohol intake and drug use all have influence over the likelihood of injury and have consequences for successful recovery. Chapter 7 looks at positive nutrition practices for dancers.

Environmental characteristics and inappropriate facilities can contribute appreciably to injury risk. Chapter 1 provides greater detail on how negative aspects of the dance environment, such as an unsuitable floor structure and surface or inappropriate room temperature, may contribute to injury risk, and also raises awareness of the associated effects of costume, clothing and footwear. It highlights how a risk assessment and a checklist for safe dance practice, identifying and evaluating potential risk factors in the dance workplace, especially for new environments, can contribute significantly to reducing these effects and promoting sound injury management. In conclusion, to ensure that they are not overlooked or underestimated, dance leaders should regularly review all extrinsic risk factors.

EFFECTIVE INJURY MANAGEMENT

As previously mentioned, the expertise to diagnose and treat injury should primarily come from qualified therapists. There are also statutory regulations regarding first aid in the workplace, which depend on the work activity and the number of employees, such as provision of qualified first-aiders with valid certificates of competence to attend to injuries. If employed by an organisation, dance leaders should ensure that they comply with first aid policies. Self-employed dance leaders should carry a first aid kit. Greater detail on health and safety regulations can be found in chapter 1.

However, dance leaders can and should assume certain responsibilities in order to support immediate injury management. They must assess the situation quickly, prevent the injured dancer from returning to activity and be in charge of the situation until the dancer is handed over to a suitably qualified person. Dance leaders and dancers can follow simple recommendations that can successfully mediate the immediate consequences of acute injury. Implementing the correct treatment procedures without delay will also influence the rate and quality of recovery.

Immediate treatment relates to the first 48 to 72 hours following the injury. Studies suggest that this acute care can be divided into three stages: emergency (involving cardiopulmonary resuscitation [CPR] or transport to hospital), immediate (from the time of injury to 12 hours afterwards) and transition care (from 12 hours to 4 days post injury; Comfort & Abraham, 2010).

In urgent injury situations, the emergency services should be called immediately. Examples of injuries requiring emergency treatment are as follows (Caldwell, 2001; Peterson & Renström, 2005):

- Any injury in which there is major concern over its severity
- Unconsciousness
- Suspected fracture or dislocation
- Breathing difficulties, nausea, vomiting, pains in the neck or dizziness after a head injury
- Severe eye injury
- Deep wounds with bleeding
- Abdominal pain or blood in the urine following the injury
- Suspected cardiac arrest

Treatment procedures for the immediate and transitional stages of acute soft-tissue injury are easily followed using the simple mnemonic RICE (rest, ice, compression and elevation), which can be expanded to **PRICED** or PRICES with the additions of *protection* or *prevention* and *diagnosis* or *stabilisation*. Some research suggests that the use of RICE may be more valid in the treatment of injuries to the less metabolically active tissues of ligaments and bone (Comfort & Abrahamson, 2010). However, most general guidelines advocate the use of the PRICED system.

In more detail, protection or prevention involves removing the injured dancer from the possibility of further risk. This could mean stopping other

PRICED

P Protection/prevention

R Rest

I Ice

C Compression

E Elevation

D Diagnosis or **S** Stabilisation

dancers from continuing their activity in the vicinity, or actually removing the injured person from the main dancing area and making him or her comfortable in a non-weight-bearing position. If there is any doubt or concern regarding potential spinal injuries, the dancer should not be moved. Similarly, rest involves ceasing movement and withdrawing from any activity that might aggravate the condition. This could mean complete immobilisation or simply stopping particular movements that cause pain. Any ongoing movement of the injured body part at this initial stage may cause further damage to the tissue and, in the subsequent days, result in an increase in the amount of scar tissue that is formed (Howse & McCormack, 2009). When resting, muscle has the capacity for rapid regeneration (Comfort & Abraham, 2010).

Ice, or cryotherapy, is widely recommended, although firm evidence of its benefits and effectiveness is actually limited (Russell, 2010). However, it can have a number of effects. When an injury occurs, the usual physiological response to the trauma is inflammation of the affected area, characterised by redness and heat as the blood vessels dilate to increase circulation.

Bleeding into the surrounding tissues, which produces the increase in temperature, is due to the rupturing of local blood vessels. Although inflammation is a natural part of tissue repair, it is believed to be necessary to limit a prolonged or excessive response. The accumulation of fluid causes swelling and increased pressure around the site, resulting in pain, all of which impair function.

The first priority in soft-tissue injuries is to control the bleeding. Application of ice can contribute to this by constricting the blood vessels and so reducing blood flow, but it also limits fluid pressure, helping to contain the damage. Ice cools the temperature of the injured tissues and has a pain-relieving (analgesic) effect due to the reduction of the speed of pain signals conducted via the affected nerves (Russell, 2010). Because the injured dancer usually needs to sit or lie down to administer ice therapy, this is also an incentive to rest (Caldwell, 2001; Comfort & Abraham, 2010). The recommended techniques for application are consistent: Ice below 0 degrees Celsius should be wrapped in cloth before being applied to the skin to avoid cold burns, continued for between 5 and 20 minutes, leaving 60 minutes between applications. This practice gives a chance for the blood supply to return to the tissues, rewarming them and bringing nutrients to the site, and uses venous return to help to drain excess fluid from the area. This process can be repeated for up to 72 hours (Howse & McCormack, 2009; Comfort & Abraham, 2010). Real ice, as opposed to single-use or reusable gel packs, is preferable, since it maintains a colder temperature for longer. If no ice is immediately available, as an emergency measure a cloth soaked in very cold water can be used and changed frequently. Alternative forms of icing (sprays or rubs) are not generally recommended because they cool only the superficial layers of skin, and do not effectively penetrate deeper into the injured area. Dancers should never ice an injured area and then return straightaway to the dance activity (SHAPE, 2002). It is worth mentioning that although ice can also help to alleviate discomfort due to chronic overuse injuries, dancers should not use it to numb pain in order to continue with their usual practice.

Compression refers to the external application of pressure to an injury through the use of elastic or crepe bandages, usually applied, not too tightly, in a crosswise manner. It is included in many injury care recommendations for the potential to promote lymphatic drainage and assist in venous return to remove excess fluid from the site. Compression should not be confused with taping. Caution is advised because taping an acute injury while swelling and bleeding may still be occurring could result in an impairment of the circulation (Peterson & Renström, 2005). Taping, when performed by a qualified therapist, is helpful in rehabilitation to temporarily improve stability while the dancer regains strength and control, but it is not seen as a long-term solution. Compression using an elastic bandage may be beneficial when used intermittently with ice during immediate injury management (Comfort & Abraham, 2010). Research sources also advise that, if possible, the elastic bandage should be kept in place for up to

two days after ice treatment has been stopped (Peterson & Renström, 2005).

Elevation is one of the simplest treatments to implement, obviously depending on the injured area. As with ice application, it is conducive to encouraging rest. Raising the injured body part uses gravity to help drain away blood and fluid from the site to reduce swelling. It also restricts blood flow into the injured area, reducing further bleeding. Dancers should elevate the injured body part for as much time as possible during the initial injury management stage, otherwise reduction in swelling may be limited (Comfort & Abraham, 2010).

Diagnosis or *stabilisation* refers to the importance of seeking professional treatment for an injury. The correct diagnosis will focus on more specific treatment and accelerate recovery. To prevent prolonged weakness or future susceptibility to injury reoccurrence, dancers should guard against self-diagnosis, and are advised to present to a qualified therapist to manage any injury that prevents them from dancing, even if it is initially short term. The wider availability of insurance plans for dancers makes this financially more realistic. Dance leaders should resist speculating on the nature of a participant's injury and instead advise that care and professional attention is required.

Another easily remembered mnemonic, **HARM (heat, alcohol, running and massage)**, directs dancers and leaders on what to avoid in first 36 hours following injury, particularly to ensure that the beneficial physiological effects of the PRICED procedure are not compromised or reversed.

HARM

Heat: Application of heat increases blood flow causing further bleeding into injury.

Alcohol: Also increases blood flow and perhaps can mask pain.

Running (dancing): Discontinuation of activity following injury is important for preventing further damage.

Massage: Contraindicated at the acute injury stage, especially at the actual site of the injury, because it increases blood flow to the area and induces pain through pressure.

By observing recommended injury procedures at the point that an injury occurs, or by using strategies to minimise symptoms, dancers can protect themselves in both the short and long term.

It is important to note that qualified therapists may prescribe heat or massage, and especially mobility, as part of a recovery programme. However, the dancer or dance leader should follow the above guidelines in the immediate management of injury to guarantee that any action on their part does not further contribute to the injury. Smoking is a detrimental habit for dancers, and should especially be avoided when recovering from an injury, particularly in the first day or two, because nicotine constricts the small blood vessels that assist in rebuilding damaged tissues, so reducing the local metabolism (Simmel, 2014).

RETURNING SAFELY TO DANCE POST INJURY

If the dancer returns too soon after an initial injury, called the **primary injury**, other muscles and joints may compensate and result in additional injury, a secondary injury. The localised primary injury can produce biomechanical changes to a dancer's body. The dancer may redistribute workload through a conscious or unconscious tendency to avoid work in the affected area to protect it. This creates vulnerability at other sites through what is known as the kinetic chain, a link or functional relationship between body parts in which one part affects the movement of another.

Consequently, the strain that is imposed by favouring or relying on alternative muscles or joints, or both, has an additional effect. All secondary injuries are therefore intrinsic because they are a result of the body's inability to function properly. Failing to treat or fully resolve a primary injury may be likely to lead to a secondary injury. For example, ankle sprain is very common in dance, with reported injury rates as high as 31 percent across all forms of dance (Russell, 2010). It usually occurs as a result of awkward landings from jumps or lack of co-ordination, or perhaps overbalancing when turning or falling off high heels. If ankle sprain is not treated effectively, it is likely that compensatory movement patterns may come into play, for example, affecting the knee and hip joints of the same leg or various structures in the opposite side of the body. Hip adductor, knee flexor and knee extensor weakness have been linked to ankle instability (Russell, 2010), so it is not simply a matter of fixing the isolated part but approaching rehabilitation in a holistic way, taking into account the combination of factors that have influenced the occurrence of the injury and those that will affect its healing. This is true for all injuries. To allow the complete healing of the primary injury, dancers must not resume activity too soon—if they attempt functional activities too early, they may reinjure the new tissue, extending overall healing time (Potts & Irrgang, 2001).

The initial stage of injury is the time to limit the effects of the damage, when rest and immobilisation are advocated, but subsequently longer-term management is needed. To avoid the problems caused by the over-restrictive formation and adherence of scar tissue and weakening of connective tissue, advice now includes recommendations for some gentle mobility and weight-bearing activities that help develop strong and mobile scar tissue and increase the range of motion of the injured area (Potts & Irrgang, 2001). The appropriate time to attempt movement of the injured body part should be decided with the guidance of the therapist. Similarly the amount of activity should be gauged with professional advice. Although the absence of pain is often the impetus, it may not mean that the injury has healed, so care should be taken here. The use of medication will obviously have an effect on pain perception.

Returning to full function needs to be progressive and planned. Complete rehabilitation can be divided into four stages: restriction, restoration, reacquisition and refinement (Liederbach, 2000). First, dancers should follow the PRICED procedures and avoid further risk. Movement should be limited, with support such as taping where appropriate. Second, range of motion can be restored, basic movement carefully performed and attention given to maintain overall conditioning. Third, more specific activities can be attempted, underpinned by complementary techniques and increased fitness. Finally, dancers can be unrestricted in their work, securely performing more complicated skills and increased loads with confidence. At this stage, steps should also be taken to educate and inform the dancer as to how to avoid re-injury and maintain the regained function, including recognising the significance of fitness and conditioning, maintaining good nutrition and lifestyle habits as well as investigating the potential of psychological tools and skills to support rehabilitation (Clippinger, 2016; Liederbach, 2000; Sevey Fitt, 1996).

Depending on the type of injury, the return to some level of dance participation may actually happen within a few days or may follow a longer-term absence. Particularly if the latter is the case, functional supplementary conditioning to maintain strength, flexibility and overall fitness during the rehabilitation process, without compromising the injury, is advised. Techniques such as Pilates are useful for maintaining neuromuscular connections (Comfort & Abraham, 2010; Motta-Valencia, 2006; Potts & Irrgang, 2001). Following injury and illness, it is likely that dancers will experience some negative effects on their balance and proprioceptive abilities, placing them at increased risk of further injury. Training to regain proprioception (the body's ability to sense the relative positioning and co-ordination of body parts) could be included in rehabilitation exercises (Liederbach, 2000; Potts & Irrgang, 2001). Increased attention to warming up and cooling down the previously injured area is also very important. Classwork itself is not enough to increase the dancer's capacity in strength, power and endurance, so the training principles of periodization, specificity and overload can be incorporated into the rehabilitation programme, obviously bearing in mind the reduced capacity of injured muscles or joints.

> *Following an injury, dancers should return to activity gradually and modify their activity accordingly, rather than trying to get back to their previous level immediately. If the injury is longer term, they must maintain or regain general fitness before attempting intensive dance movements.*

Chapters 3, 4 and 8 provide more detail on all the aspects of safe practice that can be productively applied in injury recovery.

Injury management and rehabilitation requires regimented organisation to safely return to practice. This should not be overlooked or taken for granted. Although rehabilitation should be guided by a qualified therapist, there must be co-operation from dancers themselves and a partnership with their dance leaders. Communication is key so that the responsibility for increased protection and minimisation of further risk can be shared. Realistic and manageable expectations, rehabilitation goals and training plans must be devised in conjunction with treatment and clearly communicated in order for dancers to achieve a safe return to activity.

Education about the causes and effects of injury, as outlined within this chapter, is essential, especially for young dancers. An increased awareness of injury risk can help dancers better understand the range of physiological and psychological factors involved and provide them with the knowledge to be able to modify their practice. Recommendations for professional dancers can be heeded productively in all contexts and situations (Liederbach, 2000): 'Rehabilitation begins immediately after injury and ends when the dancer returns to full activity, without limitations imposed by the injury, with full confidence in the stylistic demands of the movement, stage sets, costumes and partners and an understanding of how the injury happened and how future injuries can be avoided' (p. 59).

Using the common example of an ankle sprain from earlier, table 9.2 illustrates the practical implementation of these rehabilitation principles.

The psychological effects of injury must not be underestimated. The mental consequences must be considered in combination with the physical aspects when dancers are trying to regain their abilities and, in some cases, relearn their skills. Researchers report that dancers with first-time

Table 9.2 Example Plan for Recovery From Ankle Injury

Stage of ankle injury	Type and objectives of activity	Examples and specifics
Initial/immediate	• PRICED/HARM procedures: Prevent further injury	• Crutches supplied if injury is severe • Dancer removed from working environment • Rest with ankle elevated. Apply ice for 10 minutes, every 60 minutes, for up to 72 hours. Apply compression with an elastic bandage. • Avoid heat and massage. • Avoid alcohol.
Second stage: Beginning of recovery	• Injury plan from therapist following diagnosis • Dancer, teacher and therapist create goals for recovery • Basic motion of the ankle joint to avoid unproductive scar tissue formation	• Taping for support • Gentle, pain-free foot/ankle circles, flexion and extension • Maintain overall fitness, no weight-bearing activities, swimming if possible, resistance work for the rest of the body. Use supportive techniques such as Pilates. • Use imagery and mental practice to participate in alternative ways. • Avoid smoking and alcohol.
Third stage: Progression of recovery	• Proprioceptive exercises progressing gradually • Concentrate on maintaining alignment and stability and improving technique. • Apply training principles of overload, specificity and periodization. • Modify stressful movements that could aggravate recovering injury.	• Standing on one leg (flat foot) with support (for example, a chair/barre), without support, with eyes closed, moving between flat and rising positions with eyes open, on uneven surfaces (for example, balance cushions, wobble boards). • Focus on alignment and correct technique as you begin to return to class, adapting activities. • Increase fitness levels with supplementary activities. • Work with weights or bands to increase resistance. • Increase dynamic technical exercises. • Avoid repetitive jumps.
Fourth stage: Completion of recovery	• Greater complexity and specificity of dance movements • Physical and mental skills back to pre-injury levels • Ensure full physical fitness: attention to strength, endurance, flexibility, stamina, balance and co-ordination • Implementation of good nutrition habits • Education on cause and effects of ankle injury and injury in general	• Return to full class participation with increased awareness and concentration. • Maintain fitness levels through supplementary activities without excessive workload. • Eat an appropriate balance of carbohydrate, protein and fat to support energy demands and avoid fatigue. • Pay attention to hydration levels to maintain concentration and avoid fatigue.

serious injuries experience shock, frustration, depression, anxiety, fear and anger in the first few weeks post injury, and can become demoralised and suffer from sleep problems and fatigue (Krasnow et al., 1999; Potts & Irrgang, 2001). However, dancers' initial negative reactions to injury may become more positive as the injury heals; optimism and happiness are associated with perceived gains in rehabilitation (Krasnow et al., 1999).

While some of these negative consequences might be expected to amplify with continuous reoccurrence of either the primary or secondary injuries, there is evidence to support that it may become easier for some dancers to cope with injuries the second and third time due to a greater capacity to accept injury and decreased anxiety over subsequent injury (Krasnow et al., 1999). Motivation, self-confidence, anxiety and concentration all have a significant effect on injury rehabilitation (Taylor & Taylor, 1995). Dancers need to believe in the effectiveness of their rehabilitation programmes as well as understand them fully, and they must maintain a high level of motivation during the discomfort and anxiety induced by an injury experience. Dance leaders can play their part in helping injured dancers set appropriate physical and psychological goals that can enhance their concentration, for example, by continuing to provide verbal support and feedback, assisting them in modifying their activities and encouraging the use of imagery or mental practice in place of actual activity during this time (Mainwaring et al., 2001). (See chapter 8.) Physiological and biomechanical goals to deal with improving alignment, strength, stamina or flexibility and psychological goals based on maintaining self-confidence and motivation will focus dancers on their rehabilitation process. Whether the rehabilitation period is short or long term, the goals are the same.

Allowing the dancer to work with protective clothing (for example, to maintain body warmth) or equipment (such as knee pads or shock-absorbing footwear) will give practical support. Keeping injured dancers as much as possible in their practice environment is advised, so teachers and directors could provide them with related tasks to stay involved, for example, in making practice or rehearsal notes, contributing to teaching, giving feedback to their peers or helping with other production aspects. It is important that teachers avoid pressuring dancers and that dancers do not impose pressure on themselves to return too quickly, even if their injury would result in replacement with understudies, reduction in

TRUST

Treatment: Essential for promoting speedy recovery (by following the recommendations in the text and consulting a therapist)

Reassurance: To give dancers confidence that they will be able to recover

Understanding: Of the injury, the consequences and the recovery process

Support: From teachers, choreographers, directors, fellow dancers, family and friends

Training: Finding positive ways to continue participation with increased injury awareness and constructive rehabilitative activity to ensure a safe return to full practice

rehearsal time or lack of preparation for assessment. Injured dancers need support from their leaders so that they feel they can take sufficient time to recuperate.

Another mnemonic, TRUST, highlights the psychological aspects of injury to help dancers in their recovery: treatment, reassurance, understanding, support, and training.

Dancers returning from injury are often discouraged by comparisons with their own pre-injury level of skill and the increased skills development of their peers or colleagues during the time they have been away. If this factor is recognised, expectations can be mediated so that neither dancer nor leader pushes too much too soon, and assurance can be given that things will return to normal.

INJURY DOCUMENTATION

A focus on risk limitation has given rise to the necessity for both recording and **documentation of injuries**. Organisations usually have procedures in place for documenting and preserving records should evidence be required or an audit of safe practice undertaken. Accident books should be provided, and managers should ensure that all dance leaders become familiar with how to comply with accident and injury reporting. An example of an accident report form can be found in appendix D. This documentation is an efficient way of tracking injuries and their reoc-

Dance Injury Procedure

■ ■ ■

The dance leader, Jane, is conducting a modern dance session for students (over 18*) at a vocational dance school. The students are practising inverted balances and transfer of weight using one hand. Because they cannot see each other due to the blocked line of sight, two students collide. One student, Daniel, is pushed while weight bearing on one hand that is supporting the whole body in the air.

Jane stops the session immediately. She directs the remaining students to clear space around Daniel, whom she assesses straight away. He is pale and clearly in pain and distress, and is holding his arm and shoulder close to his body. The shoulder appears to be out of place. She suspects a shoulder dislocation.

One of the other students is sent to contact a first-aider. Jane does not attempt to touch Daniel but directs him not to move his arm. The first-aider arrives and Jane requests that an ambulance be called. Daniel, along with a friend, is then taken to the emergency room. Jane ensures that the companion of the injured student is also over 18 years old,* and has a contact phone number to call to provide an update on Daniel's condition.

Jane gives instructions to the other students regarding cooling themselves down before seeking out the accident/injury report book. A report on the incident is completed. Jane provides Daniel's full name and his level of ability, her own name and that of the first-aider plus a witness, the studio in which the accident happened, the date and time of the incident, the mechanism and a description of the injury (in this case, the technique class, as well as a description of the inverted movement and the clash of dancers). The observed symptoms are also recorded. The report indicates that PRICED procedures were not administered on site in this case and that the emergency services attended.

Later, Jane follows up by making contact with Daniel's companion to check the outcome and the diagnosis. She makes a note of this, along with the recommendations from the medical professionals, returning to the original accident report to update it. Daniel's condition is communicated to the relevant tutors (and his parents as he requests*). A co-ordinated rehabilitation programme is planned with Daniel, his therapists, Jane and his other teachers.

* Note that if Daniel had been under 18, his parents would need to be contacted and a responsible adult, rather than another student, would accompany him to the hospital.

currence if necessary, but it can also provide dance leaders with information for reflection on the safety of their practice. The need to interact with colleagues and parents or dancers is vital. If incidents are shared, the outcome can be managed successfully and steps put in place to reduce the risk of them occurring again. Chapter 1 deals with the legal requirements for injury and accident reporting, but the following case study illustrates how a competent dance leader practically manages an injury in the studio.

SUMMARY

To reduce injury occurrence, steps should be taken to identify and minimise potential risk factors. Dance leaders in all teaching and leading situations should carry out a health and injury status check of their participants at the beginning of each session. In addition, the leader could prepare some advance information on the activities to be encountered during the session, advising against full participation or identifying aspects that may involve modification for specific groups where necessary, for example, types of disclaimers for sufferers of heart conditions or warnings for pregnant dancers. A risk assessment is advisable, especially if the dance activity is set in a not-for-purpose environment (see example risk assessment in appendix C).

Dance leaders cannot be expected to have in-depth medical knowledge, and should not attempt to diagnose any injury, but an awareness of the common injuries in their own genre will help them to take the appropriate action when necessary and inform the rehabilitation of both short- and longer-term injury. A working understanding of the types of injury, basic symptoms and effects will ensure that the leader can direct the dancer to get the most relevant help and treatment. It is important to cultivate a culture in which injury and rest are not seen as indicators of weakness. Dance leaders must avoid overtly or inadvertently apply- ing psychological pressure to the injured dancer, even when an absent dancer could cause major difficulties. Injury documentation can protect both the dancer who is injured in a session and the dili- gent leader in whose session the injury occurred.

KEY POINTS

Dancers, dance leaders and managers should do the following:

- Carry out a health and injury status check before leading a dance session.
- Follow recommendations for an effective warm-up and cool-down.
- Work within individual capabilities and limitations to minimise injury.
- Be able to recognise potential physical, psychological and environmental intrinsic and extrinsic risk factors in their activity and understand how to minimise the potential effects.
- Appreciate the warning signs and symptoms of injury and act on them as soon as possible.
- Know how to apply the PRICED, HARM and TRUST guidelines.
- Be aware of lifestyle factors such as nutrition, sleep and the effects of smoking and stimulants on injury occurrence and recovery.
- Maintain overall good functional fitness to protect the body from injury.
- Set realistic and achievable work and training schedules to avoid overwork and fatigue.
- Allow time for preparation for and adaptation to new or unusual movement activities.
- Document injuries and accidents.
- Understand how to continue safely with dance activity following injury.

chapter 10

Adaptations for Specific Populations

After reading this chapter you should be able to do the following:

- Target and apply safe dance practice principles to individuals or participant groups to allow full involvement while accounting for their unique characteristics.
- Select activities that consider any inherent health conditions, disabilities, developmental stages or changes to the dancing body in order to promote inclusive practice.
- Deal knowledgeably with any specific issues and requirements so that dancers feel supported and any ill effects can be avoided.

≡ *Key Terms*

abdominal separation	FAST (face, arms, speech, time)	perinatal period
adolescence		physical disability
allergic asthma	fracture	relaxin
Alzheimer's disease	hearing impairment	rheumatoid arthritis
bone health	hyperglycaemia	stroke
bronchoconstriction	hypoglycaemia	trimesters
bronchodilation	insulin	total hip replacement
dementia	ketones	type 1 diabetes
diabetes mellitus	learning difficulties	type 2 diabetes
dyslexia	middle childhood	vascular dementia
dyspraxia	non-allergic asthma	visual impairment
early childhood	osteoarthritis	
exercise-induced asthma (EIA)	Parkinson's disease (PD)	

In the previous chapters of this book, the individual components of safe dance practice have been explored. The importance of practical application of this knowledge has already been highlighted, but the single most important factor affecting successful application is an understanding of the people participating. Paramount to the realisation of safe dance practice principles are: Differentiation between learners, adaptation due to the level of ability and physical needs, and the overall considerations regarding individual experience, characteristics, and physiological and psychological development. These factors, influenced by the precise aims and purpose of the session and the amount of contact over time, should be merged together to produce a unique and targeted experience for each group, accommodating the individual as far as possible.

This chapter will look at a range of populations that require additional, and frequently more specialised, knowledge in order to tailor dance activities to meet specific needs. When bodies have unique considerations, either through age-related factors, disability or certain health conditions, dance leaders must have a more detailed appreciation of their role and their responsibilities in each case. Physiological and psychological understanding is the foundation for this, overlaid with practical knowledge that can be applied to dance activity in a variety of contexts.

Dancers with specific health conditions must seek professional medical opinion to support them in dancing safely. The use of the health questionnaire (see appendix A) will be beneficial, and dance leaders might also consider how risk assessment (see chapter 1 and appendix C) contributes to the support of these specific populations.

CHILDREN AND YOUNG PEOPLE IN DANCE

Working with young dancers can bring many joys as they develop their skills and passion, but this population is also undergoing rapid physical and biological developments that are often accompanied by psychological and emotional upheaval, as well as potential injury risk. This group of dancers also requires particular consideration of safe practice principles because appropriate dance experiences in childhood and **adolescence** can affect dance participation, and even general well-being, in later years. Unsuitable movement choices or inappropriate expectations, such as pushing young people to excessively high intensities, coupled with inadequate body conditioning and particular aspects of training undertaken too soon, such as pointe work, can have a major effect on developing bodies in both the short and longer term. It is therefore important to bear in mind that young dancers are not miniature adults, and their physical and psychological make-up is different to that of an adult. The expectations of what these young dancers can and should produce needs to be tempered by a knowledge and understanding of the specific developments that are occurring during their journey towards adulthood. In addition, this population will be the future generation of dance leaders; therefore safe and effective practice in their formative years will have implications for the dance participants of the future.

Growth Considerations

Three broad stages of child development exist (Tomonari, 2011): **early childhood** (birth to approximately 8 years old), **middle childhood** (approximately 8 to 12 years old) and adolescence (approximately 12 to 18 years old). Physical growth is generally quite rapid at the beginning of early childhood, but slows down between 5 and 8 years of age. In middle childhood, physical development occurs steadily, and it is not as rapid as it can be in early childhood and in adolescence in particular. The adolescent years represent the most accelerated period of growth and development, which is accompanied by the hormonal changes of puberty. This can be quite a turbulent physical and emotional time for the soon-to-be adult dancer.

The adolescent growth phase, more than the earlier growth phases, notably differs for boys and girls. On average, girls commence their adolescent growth phase between the ages of 11 and 13, whereas boys begin between ages 13 and 15 (Stacey, 1999), but boys experience a more rapid physical change. This growth phase can last for 18 to 24 months (Daniels & IADMS, 2000). During this time girls significantly increase their percentage of body fat (Noughton, Farpour-Lambert, Carlson, Bradney, & Van Praagh, 2000), which is essential for healthy menstrual cycles, but can have implications for perceptions of body image, resulting in decreased body satisfaction. Conversely, boys will see a substantial gain in lean muscle mass (Noughton et al., 2000), which can increase body satisfaction. Early maturing adolescents often result in a shorter, heavier stature than their later-maturing peers, which again can have implications for perceptions of body image and associations with the ideal dancing body (Hamilton, 1999), causing some to dropout of dance participation during this growth phase.

Throughout childhood and adolescence, bones are growing in length and width as a result of increased calcium deposits at three sites: the growth plate (see figure 10.1), the joint surface and the point of attachment of major musculotendinous units (Shah, 2009). The growth plate, a particularly sensitive area for injury potential, will be present longer in later maturing dancers. Skeletal growth begins in the extremities (hands and feet, followed by the limbs), and then the trunk (spine, pelvis and shoulder girdle). This growth pattern can affect the centre of balance, limb control and core stability, resulting in decreased co-ordination and increased clumsiness. The bones also grow at a faster rate than the soft tissues attached to them, meaning that periods of growth are accompanied by tightness in the muscle and tendon fibres, which can result in flexibility and strength restrictions. During times of rapid physical growth, motor skill development can appear to be stalled. However, the opposite is also true;

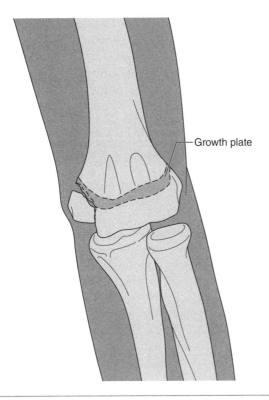
Growth plate

Figure 10.1 An illustration of a growth plate which is present in long bones until the skeleton reaches physical maturity.

motor skills become more refined in the periods of reduced physical growth (Ford et al., 2002). Therefore dancers who were once progressing positively with their skills and technique may find that their physical capabilities plateau or even temporarily decline at different stages. The dance leader should be sympathetic to the changing physical appearance and physical abilities as well as associated psychological feelings that occur as growth progresses, and support the dancer by following the guidelines outlined in this section.

Despite general categorisations of growth, chronological age is not a sufficient indicator of biological age (Matthews et al., 2006). Although this section will address general growth aspects in relation to the young dancer, given the particular issues associated with the adolescent growth spurt, there is a larger focus on the adolescent.

Impact of Growth on Alignment

Since the bones are growing faster than the soft tissues (muscles, tendons and ligaments) and bone growth is occurring asymmetrically, temporary misalignments can be common. For example, presence of a mild scoliosis and accompanying leg length discrepancy can be seen, with a tendency for a left lateral spinal deviation in infants, but a right lateral spinal deviation in older children and adolescents (Stacey, 1999). A kyphotic posture (exaggerated curve in the thoracic spine) can also be prevalent in dancers experiencing a rapid change in height (van der Eerden, Karperien, & Wit, 2003). The changing ratios of spine to leg length can also result in difficulty maintaining neutral alignment of the pelvis and torso (Daniels & IADMS, 2000). Other common misalignments that can develop or can be exacerbated during growth include increased internal rotation of the femur bone (femoral anteversion), swayback or hyper-

---

Growth and Injury

Growth brings about changes that affect performance potential, but also represent injury risk, especially contributing to occurrence of chronic injuries (Poggini, Losasso, & Iannone, 1999). Unsuitable movement choices or inappropriate expectations can have a major effect on the developing bones and muscles, in both the short and longer term. Injury-prone areas in young dancers include the following:

- Knees, specifically the tendon of the kneecap (the patellar tendon)
- Foot and ankle, specifically the Achilles tendon and the big toe joint (especially if experiencing pointe work)

- Hips, specifically issues such as 'snapping hip'
- Lower back, most commonly mechanical pain caused by temporary trunk muscle imbalances, which occur during growth spurts
- Lower leg, specifically shin pain

Research suggests that as the young dancer progresses through to adolescence, the risk of injury is increased (Redding, Nordin-Bates, & Walker, 2011; Steinberg et al., 2013; Roberts, Nelson, & McKenzie, 2013).

extended knees, external rotation of the shin bone (tibial torsion), exaggerated curve in the lower spine (hyperlordosis), and raised arches (cavus foot; Poggini et al., 1999). These alignment variations are discussed further in chapter 2. Repetitive movements, lack of rest and frequent lateral bias in movement material can perpetuate these alignment issues, and could result in permanent problems once the skeleton has fully matured. As with any alignment deviation, the dance leader should work to minimise potential negative effects and challenge dancers to work safely and effectively, taking account of any anatomical restrictions and promoting balanced muscle activation (refer to chapter 2), whether these issues are genetic or as a result of asymmetrical growth.

Young children can also appear hypermobile because they have more bones in their skeleton than the fully matured adult. However, as growth progresses the extent of hypermobility in any one dancer might decrease or disappear altogether. During the more rapid growth phases, such as adolescence, care needs to be taken to maintain flexibility by continuing to safely engage in controlled stretches. However, dance leaders should mediate against excessive stretching, which can

Young dancers should be introduced to the benefits of warming up and cooling down early in their training, which can also include social interaction and play.

cause additional strain to the musculotendinous unit and the ligaments. These areas are already under tension from the rapidly growing bones to which they are attached.

Warm-Up and Cool-Down Specifics

Needless to say the generic principles of warming up and cooling down addressed in chapter 3 are as applicable to the young dancer as to any other dancer. Leaders must instil education and application of appropriate warm-up and cool-down procedures in this young dancing population so as to create a lifelong habit of safe practice. Therefore dance teachers should initially take responsibility to lead young dancers through an appropriate warm-up and cool-down, explaining the what, why and how. Such functional aspects of their training can appear boring to young dancers, so the dance leader should be mindful to ensure that these vital elements of the dance session are interesting and inspiring, as well as functional. Adding elements of play and imagery for very young dancers can be beneficial, such as 'Let's imagine we are sunflowers stretching up towards the sun' for a full body stretch or 'Imagine a ball is wriggling around inside you' for mobility. In time young dancers can begin to take responsibility for their own class warm-up and cool-down.

Given the nature of growth patterns and the identified areas of injury risk, particular care and attention should be paid to warming up knees and the lower back. The joint mobility section should ease these known risk areas into action. In addition, contraindicated stretches and movements, as identified in chapters 4 and 6 respectively, should be reduced or avoided altogether where possible; for example, care should be taken not to hyperextend the neck by letting the head flop back on the spine. In the case of the knee joint, gentle weight and non-weight-bearing activities should be included, but deep knee bends or grand pliés should not be included in the warm-up. Similarly cooling down should attend to these at risk joints and their surrounding muscles, focusing on movements that counteract patterns of muscle activation used during the session. Particular attention should be paid to safe stretching (see chapters 3 and 4), especially of the quadriceps muscle group, ensuring the stretch is conducted with control, appropriate limb alignment (ankles, knees, hips in the same plane) and inclusion of the breath to aid relaxation in the stretch. Remember that the muscles can be quite tight during growth; therefore dance leaders should promote slow, steady, controlled and relaxed stretching at all times, with an emphasis on maintaining the current levels of flexibility rather than an overemphasis on improvement of flexibility. In order to address issues of reduced proprioception and co-ordination associated with growth, the warm-up should also include elements such as body rubbing, or lying, sitting or standing with eyes closed and gently moving the limbs with an awareness of their connection to the centre of the body.

Activities, Progression and Conditioning

Children are less efficient at temperature regulation than adults, and can more easily overheat. They should wear layers that can be added and removed as necessary, as well as expose their skin to allow any perspiration to evaporate, which promotes a cooling effect. Dance leaders should create opportunities for hydration, especially throughout longer sessions, and monitor the intensity levels of the dance session.

Recommendations for appropriate activities and progression within the session for young dancers include focusing on intermittent actions (exercises that vary in intensity) with frequent rest periods, which should be favoured over long-duration activities or excessive repetitions of high-intensity actions (Stacey, 1999). New technical aspects should be introduced gradually, ensuring that appropriate co-ordination and dynamic alignment are attained before progressing to the next technical challenge (Poggini et al.,

Quality over quantity is essential when working with a growing body. The aim is to promote control and provide a safe maintenance of physiological capabilities in preparation for pursuing more targeted training post growth spurt. Instead of increasing intensity, the focus should be on reinforcing effective technique, promoting safe dynamic alignment and posture, and improving artistry and expression, thereby minimising unnecessary stress on already overwhelmed bodily systems.

1999). Dancers are likely to have difficulty remaining focused and concentrated during periods of rapid growth, affecting the amount of information that they can take in – too much to think about at any one time may lead to lack of focus and potentially contribute to injury. Rather than repetitively targeting discrete actions, teachers should focus on full-body movements to maximise motor learning and development (Ford et al., 2012). Material should allow for individual stages of growth, and lateral bias (right- or left-sided preferences) should be minimised. Exercises that promote proprioception (see chapter 4) will also be advantageous within the session.

Appropriate strength, power and flexibility work can be incorporated as young dancers progress in their training, but the degree to which these are included in the dance session should be based on the stage of growth and development. For example, older dancers (post adolescent growth spurt) could be challenged more in relation to jumping and upper body weight-bearing actions than younger dancers (Walker, Nordin-Bates, & Redding, 2011). While recommendations on strength training activities with young bodies are varied, all advice on targeting discrete strength elements promotes caution and advises against maximal strength work and using strength-based actions that could induce pain, especially in and around the knee and spine. A dancer's own body weight, a resistance band or another similarly-proportioned dancer (such as in preparation for dance lifts) can provide sufficient resistance for maintaining and cautiously developing the strength of the growing body. The focus of attention should be on improving overall motor co-ordination for the specific actions that require strength, rather than pushing the boundaries of maximal force production. Given the changing ratio between torso and limb length, it is worth focusing on trunk and pelvis stability training during this rapid growth phase. If this stability work is conducted appropriately, it can minimise the likelihood of experiencing mechanical lower back pain, which is caused by temporary imbalances in the trunk muscles as the skeleton grows (Poggini et al., 1999). For safe execution, adhere to generic guidelines and principles of training, as outlined in chapter 4.

As young dancers progress in their dance activity, levels of commitment and expectation tend to increase, along with frequency of classes or competition events. However, any increase in intensity or duration of hours of dancing

Actions to Avoid or Minimise During Adolescent Growth

The following actions should be minimised within the dance session, if not removed completely, for those experiencing growth spurts (Daniels & IADMS, 2000):

- Movements that involve direct impacts, such as large jumps and sudden drops to the floor, especially drops, rolls or slides that land directly on the knee
- Balancing on one leg on pointe without the support of the barre
- Unfamiliar lifts that demand extreme strength or range of motion
- Any movements that place unnecessary or excessive strain on the knees, such as deep lunges, deep knee bends and grand pliés, as well as jumps that turn in the air and risk landing on the knee before the in-air rotation has been completed

should be undertaken gradually in order to avoid increased injury risk (Di Fiori, 2010). Recommendations state that a minimum of one rest day each week will provide essential recovery time, promoting both physical and emotional adaptations to the new demands of training. An annual extended break from training, performance or competition, in any one year is recommended for young dancers.

Where classes include a mixed-age group, awareness of individual stages of physical development should be considered ahead of technical or artistic capabilities for appropriate progression. This is especially important when considering the right time for commencing pointe work in ballet, for example, or if considering fast-tracking young people by moving them up to a more advanced or older group based on their artistic ability. Ignoring the dancer's physical stage of development in these instances might have negative implications for both the artistic development and physiological well-being of the young person (Walker et al., 2011). Dance leaders should feel confident to delay such decisions during growth spurts and to resist any pressure from parents.

Examples of Varying Age-Group Needs in Planning and Execution of Classes for Young People
■ ■ ■

Suzanne teaches a range of young dancers in a community centre. She has completed first aid training with a relevant paediatric element, and has undergone a safeguarding check in order to be able to work with young children. She has also completed professional development training on child protection issues. Suzanne completes relevant risk assessments and environment checks, including inspecting all props, prior to her classes each week. She also has to maintain effective communication with the parents, guardians or carers of all her dancers, and ensures that relevant contact details are with her at all times so that she can contact a parent in the event of injury or hospitalisation. Given the disparate ages she teaches, each session requires different planning, delivery and attention to safe practice application.

For her Teenie Tots group (up to the age of 3 years old), Suzanne has to account for the safe participation of parents and guardians as well as the young dancers. The sessions are short (40 to

45 minutes) and focus on guided improvisation, movement patterning and movement to music. The delivery incorporates imagery, play and props. Each activity is reasonably brief so as to continually engage the very active minds and bodies of these young participants, and their parents. The emphasis is on enjoyment. Suzanne has a teaching assistant for this group so that an additional pair of eyes is present.

Parents or guardians are not present in class for the Beanie Bop group (ages 4 to 6), but they must drop off and collect their children before and after class. These sessions are 60 minutes long. They still incorporate improvisation, creativity, the use of imagery and some props, but basic technical elements are now being introduced in a fun manner. Suzanne makes sure that she starts the session gently with familiar full-body movements that gradually increase in effort and intensity and that she allows time for a wind-down, both physically and mentally, towards the end of the session.

(continued)

Varying Age-Group Needs   *(continued)*

The Ignition group (ages 7 to 10) is not dissimilar to the Beanie Bop group, but classes are 75 minutes long, and a larger section of the class is dedicated to finding basic posture and alignment required of the style, as well as attending more to skill acquisition and technical enhancement. Suzanne keeps a lookout for any alignment deviations that might be apparent and ensures that she provides appropriate movement challenges to promote balanced muscle activation and alignment patterning. With this group, Suzanne also encourages increased opportunity for vocal exchange within the class and learning experience, for example providing limited options to the group to choose from such as whether to repeat an exercise or not, or choosing between one way of finishing an exercise over another.

Suzanne's Trailblazers group (ages 11 to 14) is the most challenging. Every person in this group is developing at a different rate. Mood, behaviour and confidence levels fluctuate on a weekly basis, and changes in physical capabilities also occur. Classes are 90 minutes long. Within this time Suzanne ensures she pays particular attention to a thorough warm-up and cool-down and tries to educate the group on the importance of these elements, encouraging the dancers to begin to take responsibility for their individual needs. The main body of the class focuses on technical skill development and progression. Suzanne has to provide alternative movement options for some class exercises because one dancer is showing symptoms of Osgood-Schlatter disease (an inflammation at the site of attachment of the patellar tendon at the knee), and needs to avoid deep knee bends, lunges and direct impacts to the front of his knee. Two others are complaining of aches in their legs, likely a result of growing bones pulling on muscle and tendon attachments, so these dancers need to be careful with actions requiring excessive leg flexibility. This group is also notorious for slumping into one hip and relaxing the abdominal muscles, letting the pelvis tip forwards, in between exercises, so Suzanne has to remind the dancers to maintain appropriate posture in between exercises as well as during exercises.

Finally, with Suzanne's oldest group, Frontier (ages 15 to nearly 18), she expects more in terms of taking individual responsibility for their personal warm-up and cool-down and managing any adaptations to class material as necessary. Appropriate posture and alignment are expected to be maintained throughout the class. Some of the participants in this group are hoping to go on to full-time dance study or training, so Suzanne is helping to prepare them for audition situations by providing a solid technical and physical fitness grounding and also frequently providing new dance material, which she encourages the young dancers to perform with confidence, even when they make mistakes. Suzanne provides handouts and leaflets from recognised dance organisations with additional information such as nutrition and hydration for dance, injury management, and supplementary fitness activities. By sourcing these up-to-date leaflets for her students, Suzanne also remains abreast of recent recommendations and works to ensure that she is applying these recommendations to her own practice as well.

Nutrition for Young Dancers

All the changes that are occurring during phases of growth demand additional energy and therefore additional nourishment. The average person will gain up to 48 percent of their skeletal mass during adolescence (Hamilton, 1999). While impact activities such as dance can contribute to increased **bone health**, this benefit will be lost if there is a nutrient deficit (Robson, 2002; Burckhardt, Wynn, Krieg, Bagutti, & Faouzi, 2011), and any bone mineral density lost during this crucial stage of growth is thought to be irreversible (Robson, 2002). The double-edged sword is that the bodily changes occurring during puberty result in heightened body awareness and, especially for girls, increased body dissatisfaction. Therefore adolescent dancers are at risk of reducing their nutrient intake at the very time that an increased nutrient intake is required. Boys often wish to increase muscle mass and gain a strong physique, while girls frequently wish to remain lean, which can lead to restricted nutrient intakes (Hamilton, 1999). The nutritional guidelines provided in chapter 7 are essential for the young dancer to follow. In addition, due to the aforementioned inefficiency of internal temperature regulation in young dancers, effective hydration is required. Despite many young people's preference for sugary, carbonated drinks, water should be the recommended drink for the dance session.

Nutritional education for growing dancers should reinforce the important role of balanced intake of carbohydrate, fat and protein for the needs of their growing bodies. Consuming protein from a variety of sources is vital, given the role of protein in building and repairing the body. This will be especially important for young vegetarian and vegan dancers. Often adolescents misinterpret consuming dietary fats as getting fat. This association should be clarified, and education on the importance of essential fatty nutrients for healthy growth of the brain and nervous system, balanced hormone production (including growth and sex hormones) and healthy joint function should prevail. Adolescent dancers should also be advised on the negative effects of alcohol consumption in relation to energy production and the oxygen-carrying capacity of the blood.

> Restricted and inappropriately balanced nutrient consumption can negatively affect physical growth, especially bone growth, the effects of which can be irreversible. Energy deficits can also result, which are associated with increased risk of bone-related injuries and injuries caused by fatigue. Education is the key to fostering good nutrition habits.

Dance teachers should never take it upon themselves to weigh their dancers, although vocational schools may be affiliated with a healthcare expert who might refer to body mass index guidelines in order to monitor the health of their dancers (further information on BMI is available in chapter 7). In addition, teachers should avoid making flippant comments or using inappropriate language in relation to body size, shape or weight, such as making comparisons between the dancer's pregrowth body and current body or comparing one dancer's body with another. Dance leaders who have concerns for their participants' nutrient intake should follow the advice in chapter 7.

Psychological Considerations

During middle childhood and on into adolescence, dance participation often becomes more serious. Frequently dance leaders and parents place additional expectations on these young dancers. Academic examinations, transitions between levels of education, auditions for vocational dance training schools, involvement in other activities and consciousness over changing physiques are all compounding factors that can increase psycho-

logical pressures in an already intense period in the young person's physical development. These stressors could result in behavioural and mood changes, decreases in self-esteem, interruption of sleep patterns, or negatively affect nutritional intake, all of which will make dancers more vulnerable to injury.

The dance leader needs to be sensitive to the outcomes of the increased pressures. Adhering to recommendations regarding creating a positive psychological environment, as outlined in chapter 8, is particularly important when teaching growing dancers. Positive reinforcement of individual efforts are paramount, along with reassurance that any decline in physical or technical aspects of their dancing due to their growth phase will be temporary. Additionally, acknowledgement that dancers might need more individual support during this time, without overtly isolating any participants from the wider group, is also necessary. Both the dancer and dance leader will require increased patience during this 12- to 24-month period of change.

Regardless of dance setting, dance leaders should aim to provide a supportive and nurturing dance environment throughout childhood and adolescence, which prioritises positive learning environments as discussed in chapter 8. This is also an opportune time to include education about the dancer's body and mind, highlighting that every body is unique and encouraging maturing dancers to begin to take responsibility for their personal needs.

Footwear and Pointe Work

The age at which dancers should start pointe work is a common question in ballet training. Less common, but just as pertinent, is the question of young dancers wearing heeled shoes, such as in ballroom, Latin, Irish, tap and flamenco. Given that the latter is less frequently asked, there is consequently less research on the effect of heeled footwear on young dancers. However, it could be reasonably assumed that the effect of a heeled shoe on lower back pain, foot problems and alignment is similar for the young dancer as it is for the adult (see Chapter 2), except that the young dancer's musculoskeletal system is still developing, and therefore is likely to be more susceptible to alignment deviations and muscular imbalances. If this is the case, these imbalances may be sustained into adulthood, especially if suitable preparatory and counter activities are not conducted.

The limited research on heeled footwear in young dancers does not provide conclusive support for any specific negative effect, but it does recommend viewing each dancer as an individual, since compensatory effects can be diverse (Wilmerding, Gurney, & Torres, 2003; Fong Yan, Hiller, Smith, & Vanwanseele, 2011). Specifically, focusing on achieving trunk stability to support pelvis and spine alignment, which can be affected by the inclination of the heeled shoe, is advised, along with increasing proprioceptive awareness. Foot and ankle strengthening and stretching should also be pursued (see the recommendations in the sidebar later in this chapter).

More research has been conducted on the effects of pointe shoe use in dance than for any other footwear. Of particular concern is the impact of biomechanical stress on the growth plates in the feet of young and growing dancers, especially the growth plates in the big toe (Shah, 2009). Based on dance and exercise research, as well as practitioner wisdom, dance medicine and science specialists have produced guidelines on the multiple signs of readiness for pursuing pointe work. Despite this, it appears that age remains one of the most common deciding factors on when to start pointe work, with an average age of 11.2 years being reported (Meck, Hess, Helldobler, & Roh, 2004; Richardson, Liederbach, & Sandow, 2010). However, this is not a sufficient determinant of pointe readiness, especially since this age coincides with the beginnings of the adolescent growth spurt. Chronological age is not a suitable representation of physical maturation, rather physical maturity along with other factors must be considered for the prolonged health and well-being of these young dancing bodies.

> By using an arbitrary age to signify suitability for starting pointe work, dance teachers risk creating lasting damage on a growing musculoskeletal system.

Literature states the following considerations for deciding when to start pointe work (Weiss, Rist, & Grossman, 2009; Shah, 2009):

- Do not start before the fourth year of training, assuming that dancers are taking part in dance class twice per week and adhering to the additional following points. This is a minimum recommendation.

- Ensure correct technical execution of basic preparatory actions such as plié and relevé.

- Observe for any muscular imbalances, postural instabilities or alignment issues.

- Hypermobility in the foot and ankle will require work on strength, stability and proprioception on the whole kinetic chain of the lower limb, before commencing pointe work.

- Current and past injury history of the lower limb, pelvis and trunk should also be considered as an indicator of potential weakness. Therefore time spent on increasing strength and proprioception will be necessary.

- Pointe work should begin with no more than 15 minutes of exercises at the end of the regular class and before the cool-down section begins.

- Recreational dancers not involved in regular training with the intention of pursuing preprofessional or professional ballet pathways should especially be discouraged from starting pointe work, unless the preceding criteria are fulfilled.

In order to assess whether an individual dancer has sufficient strength and stability of the ankle, along with lower limb, pelvis, spine and trunk alignment, dance teachers can conduct functional and dance-specific tests (Shah, 2009; Richardson et al., 2010).

These guidelines listed in the sidebar are also relevant to other dance forms that utilise similar stylistic requirements, such as the pivot position in Irish dance. Should the dancer have inadequate alignment, strength, stability or proprioception in the tests, then these same actions can be used as training mechanisms in order to enhance any musculoskeletal deficits. If young dancers are considered capable of pointe work, they should be encouraged to progress from soft ballet shoe to demi-pointe to pointe shoe (Pearson & Whitaker, 2012). The duration of time spent in the pointe shoe should be monitored (Steinberg et al., 2013), and as noted in chapter 2 the pointe shoes should not be worn all through the class. In addition preparatory and compensatory actions must be pursued at all times, according to individual needs. If dance teachers are feeling pressure from parents, they should refer to these guidelines to reinforce their decision to delay the

Assessments for Gauging Pointe Readiness

- Have dancers perform a relevé on each leg, with the gesture leg in passé. Ideally they will be able to complete this without support from the barre, and with maximum balance control and suitable alignment. Presence of excess lumbar curve, sickling or winging of the standing foot or misalignment of the foot, ankle, knee, hip kinetic chain denotes unsuitability for progressing to pointe work. A suitably strong and well-trained dancer will be capable of holding this balance for 30 seconds with eyes closed.

- Have dancers perform a grand plié in various positions (e.g., first, second, fifth). Ensure that the trunk can remain stable; the alignment of the foot, ankle, knee and hip is appropriate; and the weight is equally distributed between the metatarsal heads (ball of the foot).

- Have dancers perform a pirouette on relevé with the gesture leg in passé (referred to as the topple test). This should be possible with controlled balance, including recovering effectively from the turn to complete a controlled landing.

- Have dancers perform a specific dynamic balance called the airplane test by standing in parallel on one leg, hinging at the hip and placing the body and other leg horizontal to the floor, with the arms outstretched perpendicular to the body. From this position, the dancer should perform five controlled pliés while allowing the arms to simultaneously reach to the floor on the downward phase and return to being outstretched in the upward phase of the plié. A minimum of four of the plies should maintain alignment of the lower limb (ankles, knees and hips in the same plane) as well as maintaining neutral alignment of the pelvis and spine. Look for pelvic tilting, excessive knee sway, and rolling in or out of the foot, all of which will indicate that the dancer is not yet strong enough in the lower limb for pointe work. Although not mentioned within the literature, this test could also be carried out with the supporting leg in a turned out position, as long as ankle, knee and hip alignment remains in place. This test should be completed on both legs.

- Have dancers perform a repetitive single-leg hop (16 consecutive hops), referred to as the sauté test. Dancers should have a fully extended (straight) knee and pointed foot while in the air, and use their plié and work through the foot on landing. The aim is to maintain neutral pelvic position, a stable trunk, neutral lower limb alignment and proper toe-heel landing for all 16 hops, but at least 8 out of 16 hops must be properly executed. This test should be completed on both legs.

(Shah, 2009; Richardson et al., 2010)

young dancer and explain that this decision is for the long-term physical health and well-being of the child.

Child, pre-adolescent and adolescent dancers are experiencing many changes in physical and emotional maturation. This is not a linear progression, and despite generic age-related identified periods of change, every young person should be viewed as an individual, and his or her personal journey towards adulthood should be considered. One size will not fit all, and young people are not adults in miniature.

From a physical perspective, dance leaders should understand the inter-relationship between the maturing musculoskeletal system and the developing nervous system, as well as the fluctuating effects these can have on aspects of dance training such as flexibility, strength, co-ordination and balance. From a psychological perspective leaders should also acknowledge the effects of bodily and technical fluctuations on elements such as self-esteem. Ensuring healthy and balanced nutrition intake will be key for the growing dancing body, and dance leaders should be aware of the potential to restrict or engage in unhealthy nutrition practices during adolescence in particular. Encouraging excessive participation in training, performance or competition during this sensitive time can lead to early burnout and occurrence of overuse injuries that could persist to adulthood or lead students to stop dancing altogether.

OLDER DANCERS

Participation in dance as a community activity for older participants is becoming more popular and accessible. Brands such as Zumba have created the Zumba Gold programme, and recognition of the health benefits for elderly people taking part in chair-based exercise is on the rise. However it is difficult to define who we are talking about when we use the term *elderly* because people age at varying rates. Compare two 70-year-old adults, for example: One may live independently, and be physically very active, while the other may need care and assistance in completing everyday tasks. Many recreational settings have fitness classes for the 'over 50s' or even 'over 40s', many of whom could be just as fit and healthy as younger people. Ideally classes are designed to suit people's abilities. The age range of participants may vary, for example, in some classes 40- and 70-year-olds may dance together. On the other hand if for health reasons dance leaders feel that their sessions are more suited to a particular age or ability level, they should specify this.

We know that dance participation can help older adults in improving overall physical function, health and well-being (Keogh, Kilding, Pidgeon, Ashley, & Gillis, 2007) and that exercise in the elderly helps to prevent falls and loss of bone density (Minne, 2005). More specific research into a 10-week dance programme found that traditional dance can be an effective activity for improving both static and dynamic balance control in elderly adults (Sofianidis, Hatzitaki, Douka, & Grouios, 2009). Another study found that tango dance participation is effective in increasing strength and speed of walking, and could support balancing ability (McKinley et al., 2008). Research focusing on Scottish Country dance found that elderly people who danced had similar measurements in body composition, functional ability and balance as their younger counterparts, but elderly people who did not dance had poorer results (Dewhurst, Nelson, Dougall, & Bampouras, 2014).

Interestingly, even with no dance experience at all, research suggests that just one beginner dance class will be beneficial for balance for the elderly participant (Guzman-Garcia, Johannsen, & Wing, 2011). Aerobic dance is said to have a positive effect on health and well-being of older people. One specific study found that aerobic dance resulted in improvements in peak oxygen uptake, lower extremity muscle strength and psychological vigour (Engels, Drouin, Zhu, & Kazmierski, 1998). With a growing awareness of the benefits of dance for older people and with an increase in participation, safe practice in this area needs to be addressed so that dance leaders can be confident in their delivery and provide a safe, effective and enjoyable experience for all those taking part.

Preparation and Environmental Factors

A suitably sized, clear dance space is required. Disability access and facilities must be easily available. Chairs should be provided for any dancer who chooses to participate while seated or for participants to sit and rest when necessary. However, other unused obstacles within the space should be removed. As the body ages, the skin is more prone to bruising and skin damage; therefore knocks can be painful, and can cause injury. The floor should be smooth, not slippery, and footwear should provide some grip to help decrease likelihood of trips or falls but not so much grip that it could cause twisting of the knee or ankle. The dance leader should be able to advise participants on suitable footwear for their dance activity. Setting the right temperature is key; older participants may feel the cold more due to reduced circulation. Where possible the temperature should be adjusted accordingly and layers of clothing could be advised. Participants should always perform a gradual and effective warm-up.

Addressing sound and noise levels is also important because hearing loss has been recognised as one of the most frequently encountered problems in the elderly worldwide (Arenson et al., 2009). However, what one participant may find a comfortable volume, another may find too loud or too quiet, so the practitioner must ask the group and acquire feedback on volume levels. Dance leaders must also care for themselves. They should not have to shout or strain their voices. In some environments a head microphone may be suitable.

Lighting and positioning of participants should be addressed to provide them with the best possible viewpoint of the instructor. It has been estimated that 'over 10% of individuals ages 55-84 years, and over 20% of individuals aged 85 and older, suffer from visual impairment' (Arenson et al., 2009, p. 45). All individual needs should be addressed prior to the dance class through medical forms and discussion. Participants should complete a health questionnaire or a PAR-Q (physical activity readiness questionnaire) before their first dance class and should amend these if any of their circumstances change over time. Dance leaders should have access to these forms in all

As the body ages, the risk of succumbing to health conditions increases. If dance leaders are at all concerned about the dancer's readiness to participate, or a change in the health status of regular attendees, approval from their healthcare provider should be requested.

classes in case of emergency. They should also ask at the start of any of their dance sessions whether participants have any injuries or illnesses that leaders do not know about. For an example of a health questionnaire, please see appendix A.

Creating a warm, friendly and welcoming environment is key. All participants will have their own reasons for coming to class, which may be to socialise with friends, to learn new skills or to improve health. For some, this can be quite daunting, so leaders should try to minimise any feelings of anxiety. This is explained later in this chapter, and more information on creating a positive learning environment is discussed in chapter 8.

Alignment and Musculoskeletal Issues

With age the body will naturally experience a reduction in muscular strength, stamina and flexibility, as well as joint mobility. Tendons become less elastic, shortening their length, which also compromises flexibility. Reduced circulation can cause swelling, particularly in the lower legs, making flexibility and range of motion in the ankles more limited. Although this may make the lower limbs more prone to injury, any exercise that encourages safe movement for the feet, ankles and knees is recommended to help maintain joint range and improve circulation (Amans, 2013).

Osteoarthritis (a degenerative joint disease also known as wear and tear in the joints), **rheumatoid arthritis** (an autoimmune disease that can result in the person experiencing pain, decreased movement, instability of the joints, muscle weakness, reduced stamina, swelling and heat in the joints and tiredness; Amans, 2013) and **osteoporosis** (a condition of decreased bone mineral density) are common joint and bone issues in the aging body. Gentle weight-bearing exercise can delay the onset of these conditions and improve symptoms by keeping the muscles surrounding the joints strong, providing increased joint support and also helping to maintain range of motion. On

any given day the symptoms of these conditions will change in severity; therefore the dance leader needs to be prepared to adapt as necessary. Some days the dancers' participation may be extremely limited, so dancers could be involved in the session in another way, for example, choosing music for a section of the class if not working on a set repertoire, observing and providing feedback, sitting rather than standing or taking a less active role within the choreography. Although weight-bearing exercise is recommended to prevent further deterioration and to regain strength, it is not the dance leader's job to provide these supplementary exercises for older people. These should be prescribed from their healthcare provider or physiotherapist. The job of dance leaders is to provide alternatives for the participant if something feels painful or not right and to encourage rest periods within the dance class.

Fractures are common in older people, due to the bones becoming weaker, as with osteoporosis, and falls becoming more regular. The older and more frail adults become, the less able they are to protect themselves when they fall. If a fracture has occurred, this will usually require surgery and a timely recovery phase. In some cases dance participants may have had a **total hip replacement**, usually because of a fracture at the neck of the femur or because the joint is severely affected due to osteoarthritis. As with any injury, participants must receive permission from their health advisor or medical practitioner before returning to or beginning dance classes. They will need to undergo an active programme of rehabilitation first, and again they must follow a gradual approach when they return to physical activity. The dance leader should ask participants to communicate the advice received from their health or medical specialist to ensure safe practice. Dance leaders must not be afraid to ask questions. Teachers are not doctors, and should not be expected to be experts, but the more information they can obtain about the physical capability of their participants, the more effectively they can tailor activities to suit particular needs.

Over time, as joint mobility and muscular strength reduces a decrease in range of movement and strength in the fingers can make it more difficult for elderly dancers to use specific props. This should not be discouraged, since using resources such as scarves, light dance canes and soft balls helps participants maintain strength and mobility for longer.

Safety Tips for Dancers in the Early Stages Following a Hip Replacement

- Have seats that enable participants to sit in an upright position, with the knees level or lower than the hips, and the feet resting flat on the floor.

- Do not let the affected leg cross the midline of the body, that is, do not have dancers sit cross-legged or do activities that take the foot across the body (for example, a step-together-step will be just as effective as a grapevine step).

- Dancers should not stand and rotate the affected leg inwards. For example, when needing to change direction while walking, participants can turn by taking small steps to walk round, rather than twisting on the feet. This will also help to prevent any twisting in the knee joint.

- Participants should not bend all the way over from the waist.

- Before including affected participants in dance activities, take advice from the appropriate health professional and ask them to get permission from their medical practitioner.

- Make sure that the participant completes an updated medical/PAR-Q form and that they agree to take part in the dance activity at their own risk.

- Provide rest periods and alternative movement options.

(adapted from Amans, 2013, p. 103-104)

Health Considerations

'Almost everyone over 60 will have some kind of physical complaint to a greater or lesser degree—creaky joints at best, or as severe as recovering from major operations, [and] problems with eyesight or hearing also become more common' (Pethybridge, 2010, p. 24). Dance leaders are not expected to diagnose or treat any condition, but they must be aware of any health conditions among participants in case an emergency occurs so that they can fully inform the medical assistants dealing with the situation. They should also be aware that when suffering from various health conditions, dance participants often benefit from being offered a lower intensity adaptation to choreography to suit their individual needs and level of ability on that particular day. Older people can have a higher pain threshold, which is a concern because they may feel that some pain in a movement session is the norm or that they do not need to disclose this information because they can deal with it (Amans, 2013).

Dance leaders should stress that participants should not feel pain within the movement activity. If they do, they should cease movement or ask for an adaptation.

Dance for people with **Parkinson's disease (PD)** and **dementia** is becoming a more popular activity. PD is a progressive neurological condition. The main symptoms of PD are that movements become slower, and the person will usually experience tremors and rigidity of movement. Other issues may include tiredness, pain, poor co-ordination, shaking, depression and constipation, any of which can have a negative effect on everyday life. As the condition develops, so do the symptoms, but in no particular order. Symptoms vary from one person to another. Regular exercise is particularly important for people with Parkinson's because it can help physically in maintaining abilities, strengthening muscles, and increasing balance and mobility, and psychologically in reducing feelings of stress, anxiety and depression (Hackney, Kantorovich, Levin, & Earhart, 2007).

To help with stability, participants can use a chair, ballet barre, or the wall when performing balancing exercises. Steps may become smaller and travelling phrases may take longer to achieve. Because co-ordination is affected, it may take participants longer to accurately perform choreography, so patience is key. To create a more relaxed experience, dance leaders could allow participants to improvise and make their own decisions on where to place their limbs throughout the movement.

Participants may be experiencing some memory loss, and so might struggle with remembering material. Also, because symptoms can rapidly change, dance leaders need to accept that some days, participants will be able to do more or less than the previous week, making adaptability even more important. Because participants with PD may feel tiredness regularly, dance leaders should offer them frequent opportunities for rest periods. Due to the increased risk of falls in this population, support workers or caregivers could be invited to join the sessions, since they will probably have a greater understanding of their patient's capabilities.

Dementia is an umbrella term that describes a set of conditions resulting in symptoms such as memory loss and difficulties with thinking, problem solving and language. There are many types of dementia, the most common two being **Alzheimer's disease** and **vascular dementia**. Alzheimer's is a progressive disease, which means that over time more parts of the brain become damaged. Sufferers may become confused, forgetful or withdrawn due to a loss of confidence or communication problems, experience mood swings, feel scared or frustrated by their memory loss, and have difficulty completing everyday tasks (Alzheimer's Society, 2012). Vascular dementia is caused by problems in the blood supply to the brain. It usually begins suddenly, following a **stroke,** for example. Symptoms can be very similar to those of Alzheimer's, but in particular include problems with thinking speed, concentration and communication, and depression and anxiety. Other symptoms of stroke include physical weakness or paralysis, memory problems, seizures, and periods of severe confusion (Alzheimer's Society, 2012). Further symptoms could include visual mistakes and misperceptions, changes in behaviour, difficulties with walking and unsteadiness, hallucinations, problems with continence, and psychological symptoms such as obsessive behaviour. Impaired cognitive functioning will affect a person's ability to carry out everyday activities, which can be upsetting and frustrating. Dance leaders must be aware that participants with dementia may struggle to remember not just the dance itself, but why they are attending the dance sessions. Patience and a gentle approach to these sensitive issues will help in creating a safe and supportive environment. Communication with carers can help the dance leader stay up to date with the participant's current health status, and health questionnaires (see appendix A) must be completed to inform the dance leader of a participant's health status and emergency and medical information.

The dance leader must not ignore any signs of physical change that the participant makes because these could be early signs of stroke. The acronym **FAST** (face, arms, speech, time) should be remembered, and could be displayed within the dance leader's file or as a poster within the dance environment.

Participants who have suffered a stroke need to be monitored carefully during a dance session, and it is imperative that the dance leader has all their relevant medical information. Stroke to one side of the brain affects the movement ability of the opposite side of the body, for example, if the right side of the brain was affected, the left side of the body may experience physical difficulties. This will affect balance and stability, which must be taken into account within the dance class.

A number of other health conditions exist that could affect the brain, heart, lungs or circulation, which are way beyond the scope of this book. Of great importance however is that dance leaders are aware of these conditions. They should practise good communication with participants and obtain up-to-date, accurately completed health questionnaires. If at all concerned, dancers should seek advice from their medical practitioner. If an emergency were to occur the dance leader should know what to do and immediately call emergency services.

FAST: Early Signs of Stroke

Face: Can the person smile, or has the face fallen on one side?

Arms: Can the person raise both arms above the head and hold them there?

Speech: Can the person speak clearly and understand what is being said? Is their speech slurred?

Time: If the participant demonstrates any of the above symptoms, it is then time to call emergency assistance. The quicker the person arrives at a hospital for treatment, the more likely they are to make a better recovery.

(Stroke Association, 2014)

Warm-Up and Cool-Down Specifics

The components that make a warm-up and cool-down (see chapter 3) are no different for older people than for any other group. However, activities may vary slightly, and the importance of a gradual progression from rest to activity, and activity to rest, is heightened. The intensity of the warm-up will need to take longer to build, emphasising a steadier pace to prepare the joints, raise temperature and focus on posture and stability, whether travelling, standing or sitting. Equally the cool-down must have the same gradual focus. The heart of an older person is less able to accommodate increases in workload, and therefore is less efficient at pumping blood and oxygen around the body for increased activity, resulting in the older body taking longer to recover from exercise. Older people may feel the cold more easily so several layers of clothing could be advised, particularly at the start and end of the session. The older body will have decreased elasticity within the lungs and in the strength of the respiratory muscles, which will affect breathing, decreasing the amount of air that can be inhaled and exhaled per breath (Amans, 2013). Remember that for an elderly participant, walking around may be more challenging than running is for a younger person. During the warm-up, movements should remain smooth to begin with and should start small, gradually increasing range of motion through gentle and controlled dynamic stretches. Reminders should be given about correct posture and safe technique, using both spoken and visual instruction to aid understanding. It is important that the warm-up is used for preparation and not for a work-out. It is equally important that the cool-down is used for recovery, and does not come to a halt suddenly. Extra time should be allowed for gentle stretches in the cool-down. Relaxation exercises can also be used at the end or beginning of the session as a tool for focusing the mind away from other stresses (see chapter 8 for information on relaxation). Following the cool-down dance leaders should ask the participants how they feel to ensure that no-one feels unwell as they leave the session.

Activities and Progression

When planning a session with elderly participants there is much to bear in mind about the content and pace of the session. As the body ages, nerve impulses take longer to travel to and from the brain, making reaction time slower. This needs to be taken into consideration when leading any dance activity and judging the pace of a class. Older dancers may need longer to recall previous choreography and to process and respond to information, and will need to work at a calmer pace than in earlier years due to their reduction in stamina. Reduction in circulation may affect the brain and the capacity to learn or memorise new things. Again dance leaders must be patient

Dance activities should be set at an appropriate level for the needs of the group with consideration of the specific context, for example an adult community dance class.

within the dance session. Regular water breaks will need to be included and choreography needs to be chosen carefully. Many participants might attend the dance class for social interaction, and therefore partner dancing can be welcomed. For shy participants, however, this can be quite daunting, so the dance leader should think carefully about who pairs with whom in this situation.

As mentioned earlier, steps that cross the centre line of the body, the grapevine step, for example, need to be avoided for dancers who have had hip replacements. The grapevine could be replaced with a step-together-step movement instead. This will also be more suitable for those who struggle with balance during motion. Although dance leaders should want to help improve or maintain balance, they should choose steps wisely because 'poor balance and a weak or unstable gait can contribute to an increased risk of falls in older people' (Connolly & Redding, 2010, p. 15). In more advanced dance classes for older adults, some people may still struggle with getting down and up from the floor. If this is the case, the dance leader should avoid incorporating floor material or offer an alternative motion. Floor work should only be used when working with more technically advanced participants who are able to do this comfortably, and if it is appropriate to the session and the dance style. If turns are included, a non-turning alternative should be offered to avoid risk of trips, falls, dizziness or nausea. When performing balances or stretches, some participants may be safer doing these exercises holding on to a wall for support.

Considerations and Adaptations for Older Dancers

Margaret is aged 77, and takes part in two dance classes per week, one being a jazz and musical theatre class, the other being Zumba Gold. Before starting either class, she completed health questionnaires so that the dance leader was aware of her health issues. Margaret has angina (a heart condition where blood supply to the heart is restricted, causing chest pain) as well as osteoarthritis. Margaret says that she struggles to walk far without a stick, but she loves to dance. Occasionally Margaret will sit and have a rest. She feels comfortable to do this because of the friendly and supportive environment of the dance sessions. She will use these opportunities to drink water also. When performing travelling phrases Margaret will perform a walk and a lift of the knee rather than a run and a hop. Margaret does not turn in class but performs the same choreography facing forwards. She will also perform a step-together-step movement rather than a grapevine. If anything else needs adapting Margaret is happy to ask the dance teacher, who is experienced enough to provide safe alternatives. The classes have become a social occasion, and Margaret has made some very close friends whom she now sees every week. Both Margaret and the session leader have noticed improvements in her confidence, posture, balance, stability and gait.

Colin is aged 78 and attends dance classes with his wife Pat who is 76. Pat has always danced, from doing ballet at a young age, to then dancing socially for enjoyment, and in more recent years she has joined line dancing, sequence dancing, aerobics and Movement for All classes where the dance style changes regularly from contemporary dance to musical theatre. For the past 7 years Colin has joined Pat in a number of these classes, partly for enjoyment, but also to participate in a fun activity that they can do together. Colin enjoys the lively nature of the classes. He sometimes struggles with a bad chest and cough, but finds that this does not have a negative effect on his participation, and he believes that the dance classes are good for his memory skills. Pat has arthritis in her back and neck, and she found that the aerobics classes became too fast for her and often caused her back pain. However, she does not experience difficulties in the other dance classes. She sometimes struggles with balance, so chooses to hold on to a chair and keep both feet on the ground when possible. Pat also has a fixed ankle with a pin to hold her fused bones in place. This restricts some range of motion, but it has not affected her participation. Her circular ankle movements are simply smaller on that one side. Both Colin and Pat enjoy the social aspect of the dance classes and both benefit from the exercise.

When working with a less able group, a seated class in residential care, for example, the warm-up itself may be enough exercise for some participants, so the leader should accept and praise this amount of participation. Ideally there would be a chance to meet the care staff before the classes begin in order to determine the abilities of the group. Using props here can be useful; if participants know that they are going to exercise, they may feel less motivated because they feel the work will be tiring. However, if the emphasis is on moving and enjoying the music, the experience can be more pleasurable, and achievements can be gained with less anxiety. Musical accompaniment should also take consideration. The dance leader should strive for the session to be a positive experience; therefore simply choosing music from the era in which the participants grew up may not always be wise because this may remind some of loved ones who have passed, which could result in either happy memories or cause upset. Observation is key. The session leader needs to watch and respond to the level of participation within the group, and adapt content when necessary.

Nutrition for Older Dancers

Good nutrition and hydration are of great importance, particularly for the elderly. Therefore times of classes should be considered carefully. Dancers need to have enough fuel for the activity, but must not dance or exercise on a full stomach. Refuelling after the dance activity should also be encouraged to regain energy. Water breaks are a must, since many older people may not recognise when they are thirsty, and some may put off drinking water to avoid as many visits to the toilet. Reminding older participants to drink is paramount for healthy hydration and safe practice overall. The advice that the dance leader can give other than this is quite limited due to health concerns at this age. For example, it may seem a good idea to advise eating plenty of fruit; however, some participants may have been told by their GP to avoid too much fruit due to its high levels of natural sugars. Advising a healthy diet full of variety with plenty of fluids for hydration is sufficient, and further advice should come from the participant's medical practitioner. For more detailed information on nutrition see chapter 7.

Psychological Considerations

Getting older is not just about the physiological changes that happen to the body. Older people also experience psychological changes. Tasks may take longer to achieve, and what was once easy is now more of an effort to complete, which can be a frustrating realisation. Each day can vary emotionally, and there can be regular changes in energy levels, mood, concentration and motivation. Older people will most probably start to lose friends and loved ones and so will have to deal with bereavement, possible loneliness and in some cases isolation. Many will experience depression. On the other hand some may hold a positive attitude towards ageing, and enjoy retirement, keeping active and trying new hobbies.

Research states that dance can have psychological benefits and can help participants combat loneliness (Connolly & Redding, 2010), which could be why it is becoming a more popular form of exercise. Some participants will be quite confident, and might come along with a friend. Others may find attending that first session daunting, and may experience nerves and anxiety. Dance leaders must ensure that they provide a friendly and welcoming environment to help in easing any worries that participants may experience. Dancers must understand that there is no pressure of right or wrong and that it is okay to participate at their own level of ability, particularly in the recreational setting. Praise should be delivered in a non-patronising way to ensure that participants are aware of their achievements. This will help the dancers feel

---

Communication and Instruction Tips for Older Dancers

- Eliminate all distracting background noise.
- Face the person to whom you are speaking.
- Talk slowly and clearly.
- Provide concise and simple directions.
- Physically demonstrate desired position or exercise.
- Use effective kinaesthetic cues.
- Provide more time for them to internalise and process the instructions.
- Continually monitor participant's feedback.

(Alter, 2004)

good about themselves and encourage them to want to come to the class again the following week. Dance leaders should spend time being interested in their participants by talking to them about their reasons for attending and about the information on their health questionnaires. This can also make the dancer feel valued and safer about their participation. Chapter 8 offers generic guidelines for creating positive psychological settings in dance.

DANCERS WITH DISABILITIES

Dance for people with disabilities is becoming more popular, either in inclusive or integrated formats (where disabled and non-disabled people work together in the same session), or within group activities designed solely for people with **learning difficulties** or **physical disabilities**. The range of disabilities is vast, and to define and explain each one is beyond the scope of this book. Broadly speaking physical disabilities can be categorised as either *static* (remain the same over time), such as the loss of a limb or permanent paralysis of a body part, or *progressive* (worsen over time), such as motor neurone disease or muscular dystrophy. Learning difficulties, encompassing cognitive disabilities, relate to mental processes and include examples such as autism or Down's syndrome. Other specific learning difficulties such as **dyslexia** and **dyspraxia** are discussed later in this chapter.

Inclusive dance is also growing internationally in Australia, parts of Europe, America and Canada (Zitomer, 2013). Candoco Dance Company (UK), Dancing Wheels (USA) and Restless Dance Theatre (Australia) are examples of successful integrated companies for disabled and non-disabled dancers. Other companies solely for people with learning difficulties are being developed as the benefits of dance are becoming further understood. For example, Magpie Dance and Anjali Dance Company are two UK-based dance companies that produce performance works and offer dance classes specifically for adults or young people with cognitive disabilities. There is no wrong approach—it simply depends on how that dance company wants to work and whom their sessions are designed for. In sports, athletes are often grouped in classification of disability. This is not the case in dance; therefore the dance leader is often faced with the challenge to meet the needs of a wide range of abilities at the same time, which requires both knowledge and experience. If the company offer classes that

> *Every person is individual, and all participants have their own needs, capabilities and limitations that must be acknowledged and fully considered for safe and healthy dance practice.*

are marketed as being suitable for everyone, then dance leaders need to be prepared to work in a fully inclusive environment.

Dance can play an integral role in developing physical and emotional capabilities of people with disabilities. It can have a positive effect on mobility of the body and in the development of strength, co-ordination, flexibility and cardiorespiratory fitness. It also stimulates the mind–body connection, improving spatial awareness and social skills (Inal, 2014). Research regarding working safely with disabled dancers is currently limited. One study titled 'Changing Perceptions' highlights that young people with disabilities in the UK are striving towards a career in dance (Aujla & Redding, 2013). Therefore more dance-science research needs to take place with this growing dance population.

Preparation and Environmental Factors

As with any dance class, the environment needs to be suitable for the activity; therefore a clear dance space is needed with disability access, and it should be big enough for each dancer to safely move around the space without collision. Chairs must be available for the dancer who chooses to take part in class while being seated, or for when the dancers choose to sit down during rest periods. As explained in chapter 1, it is important that sound and lighting meet necessary requirements. Many dancers with **visual impairments** will be able to locate the dance leader more easily if the leader wears clothing that contrasts to the surroundings (Benjamin, 2002). Dance leaders should also think about where they place themselves in the room while speaking and demonstrating, which is especially important for dancers who lip-read. Sign language interpreters, will also need to see and hear the dance leader clearly. In all buildings, fire alarms must be fitted, but for those with **hearing impairments**, a visual cue should be identified in case of this emergency. Many fire alarms may also be fitted with a flashing light, which would be more suitable. Hearing-impaired students will benefit from a room with good acoustics. Bad acoustics can be a distraction, and also cause difficulty for blind and visually impaired participants, who are relying on verbal instruction (Benjamin, 2002).

Up-to-date health questionnaires (see appendix A) are essential in order for the dance leader to gain information about the dancers' health situation and ability, along with increasing knowledge about the dancers' individual limitations. Dance leaders should discuss the questionnaire with each dancer before participation; this will help them in the planning and delivery of their sessions, and should an accident, upset or emergency occur, they will also have the knowledge and information to successfully manage the situation and contact the relevant people.

Depending on the age or ability of each participant, it may be appropriate to speak to the dancer's parent, guardian or support worker to gain more knowledge about the participant's disability. Every person is unique, and it is of great importance for the dance leader to understand each dancer's strengths and challenges. If participants do have support, then their support worker should be invited to join in with the dance activities. If dancers are severely visually impaired or blind, they should have their support person with them in order to help them safely travel in the space. If this participant feels safer staying in one space or using a chair then this should be an option.

The dance leader should start the session with ground rules that are aimed at health and safety as well as respect for each other. These could range from making sure the dancers are in suitable kit (for example, loose clothing caught in wheelchairs can cause serious harm) to making sure that participants do not use unnecessary force when working in contact with another dancer. Making sure that permission is granted before leading other dancers around the space, particularly if they are visually impaired or working in a wheelchair will also be important. The floor needs to remain clean and dry. Just as clean suitable footwear or bare feet are expected for all dancers, wheelchair users should make sure that wheels are clean and dry. The session leader could have access to cleaning materials such as dry rags or cloths to assist in cleaning the wheels if need be. Some dancers may be fortunate enough to have a separate wheelchair that they use solely for dancing. Carpeted flooring needs to be avoided because it can restrict the manoeuvrability of wheelchairs and can cause friction burns to the skin. Ideally the space will have a smooth sprung floor, as described in chapter 1.

Passageways must be kept clear; this should be common practice in all dance studios, but is even more important when wheelchair users or visually impaired dancers are using the space. As with any equipment, wheelchairs need to be checked for safety. If dancing regularly, the dancer's wheelchair is likely to undergo more stress than that of the less active user. Tyres must be well pumped and brakes kept in good working order. Chairs sometimes have sharp edges or unnecessary fittings that could be removed or taped to prevent causing injury (Benjamin, 2002). If dance leaders or choreographers are not wheelchair users, they should practice in a wheelchair in order to gain experience in how the chair works, moves, tilts and travels, therefore gaining knowledge of what is safe and what is not.

Alignment and Musculoskeletal Issues

Specific alignment and musculoskeletal issues will vary depending on the disability, therefore so will the dancer's needs, abilities and limitations. For example, dancers with spinal cord injuries that have caused paralysis of the lower extremities and trunk muscles will mainly use their arms, upper trunk, shoulders, neck and head for dancing, and they may need extra support for the lower back and pelvis to prevent instability during motion (Inal, 2014). Knowledge of safe alignment will be beneficial for the dancer and dance leader when working with any body type. When in a wheelchair, leaders can assess alignment by having dancers place both feet flat on the footplates or on the floor and looking for symmetry from one side of the body to the other; when symmetry is possible, usually the body can perform equally on each side (Batavia, 2010). However, dancers often prefer to use their right or left side more than the other, which can cause or perpetuate existing muscular imbalance.

Dancers who do have limited movement in certain body parts are more at risk of overworking other muscle groups, and therefore need to take regular rest and recovery periods to avoid overuse injuries. It is advised that people with joint diseases should avoid gymnastic-like movements that involve weight bearing to upper extremities and the cervical spine (Inal, 2014). It is not for the dance leader to try to fix or alter the person's anatomical make-up; rather leaders should work in a safe way with the specific alignment (chapter 2) and movement limitations.

Warm-Up and Cool-Down Specifics

As stressed earlier in this book, the principles of warm-up and cool-down are the same for all dancers, but certain factors do need to be taken into account for those with disabilities. For example, some dancers with spinal injuries are not able to feel body temperature changes, so they probably won't know when they are warm. Some disabled participants may get tired very quickly, and therefore would need a more gradual, steady-paced warm-up, whereas other participants, particularly with attention deficit hyperactive disorder (ADHD), might benefit from more frequent variations of activity to remain focused. In contrast, some dancers may need a longer time to focus on one activity. The most important element is for dance leaders to remember why they do a warm-up and cool-down—to safely prepare the body, physically and mentally, for the following activities and then to bring the body back to a resting state in the safest possible way (see chapter 3 for more on warming up and cooling down).

Activities and Progression

Dance activities and choreography should always be planned with the capabilities of the dancers in mind, and leaders should be able to adapt or change them as necessary. To aid understanding and encourage creativity, it may be useful to introduce and experiment with visual (pictures) or tactile (fabric, balls, feathers, props) stimulants for dancers with learning difficulties. As always the dance leader must make sure beforehand that all teaching aids are fit for purpose and safe to use. The use of touch and contact work can be valuable but there should always be a safe and gradual progression. Trust and physical skills need to be developed before performing contact work that involves lifting and supporting other dancers. When working with blind or visually impaired dancers, their consent must be given before touching or leading them through the space. Verbally addressing the use of touch beforehand will be appreciated, and will make dancers aware that they are about to be touched or moved.

When creating work or rehearsing material with physically disabled dancers, just because one

Dancers and dance leaders should be prepared to work inclusively in both practice and performance settings.

body part is not able to be involved (for example, a wheelchair user with a lower-limb disability), this does not mean that another body part should be overused to compensate, which would cause too much repetition in a more limited group of muscles. There needs to be gradual progression from the start of the session, through the warm-up and into the following exercises with regular rest periods at suitable intervals. (See chapter 6 for more information on progression of activities.)

Although the dance leader can gain knowledge of the needs of each dancer, participants must be encouraged to take responsibility for their own body and to let the leader or group know of any movements that they think could potentially lead to injury, be it through a temporary injury the dancer is carrying or due to a physical or sensory impairment (Benjamin, 2002). It must be highlighted that dancers should follow any advice given by their medical practitioner and communicate any changes to their health or well-being to their dance leader.

Supplementary Fitness and Personal Practice

Adults, adolescents and children, with disabilities or without, benefit from regular and varied physical exercise, such as cross-training (Lockette & Keys, 1994). Cardiorespiratory fitness, strength and flexibility should all be included for overall health and mobility, as well as for improving dance performance. Exercise to improve these important areas of health and fitness should be adaptable for the disabled participant, still following the principles explained in chapter 4. Most gymnasiums and leisure centres have disability access, and some will have instructors who can help in providing exercise programmes to meet the dancer's goals. Although, if dancers are training for improved performance and technique, this should be made clear to the gym instructor because if overworked (and experiencing DOMS), dancers will not work at their best on subsequent day, and may be at an increased risk of injury. Following the guidelines

> Constructive feedback from the dance leader within the dance session, and discussion between leader and participant, will support in setting realistic goals on what can be achieved when practising outside of scheduled studio time.

in chapter 4 dancers must choose their supplementary fitness wisely to suit their goals and capabilities. If unsure they should ask a specialist fitness trainer or medical practitioner for advice.

If dancers wanted to continue to rehearse at home or outside of their usual dance sessions they would still need to follow the general rules of safe practice, remembering to include an effective warm-up and finish with an effective cool-down, as well as including appropriate rest periods so as not to overwork certain body parts. One strategy could be for dancers to take notes during the actual dance sessions and read through these notes in their own time, recapping the work achieved so far. With the permission from the dance leader and all other members of the group, the dance sessions could be filmed so that dancers could watch the choreography privately, which would help in memorising material and evaluating their performance for improved practice. The dancer could also use mental rehearsal (as explained in chapter 8). All of these methods are useful tools for any dancer of any ability.

Psychological Considerations

All participants have their own reason for wanting to dance; maybe, for technical training, for performance opportunities, as a fitness or social activity, or to use dance as movement therapy. For any of these reasons a positive psychological effect is likely, but an inappropriate learning environment or work ethic could also lead to psychological stress. Dance leaders should ask themselves the following:

- Have I created a warm and friendly environment?
- Do the dancers feel safe here?
- Have I provided enough physical support?
- Can I communicate effectively with each dancer? How do I do this?
- Are the dance activities appropriate for the group so that they feel a sense of challenge as well as achievement?

Addressing these questions will help the dance leader in creating a positive dance experience for their participants in an optimal environment (also see chapters 1, 8 and 11).

A key area for further consideration is communication. Some learners may work with sign language or lip-reading, others will learn by listening, and others may use visual or tactile stimulus. Dance

> *Dance leaders should communicate with the dancers to find out what works well and not so well when learning or creating material, rehearsing, sharing ideas and performing, and they should not be afraid to ask about each person's disabilities.*

leaders need to use a combination of stimuli that work well for the dancers involved. Language and tone of voice are key in effective communication. Dance leaders must speak clearly and be aware of volume levels, particularly if trying to deliver when music is also being used. They should think about the ways they describe instructions, for example, not asking a dancer to 'walk through the space', which would be inconsiderate of anyone who cannot do this. Instead they could say 'let's travel' or 'let's move through the space.' Other examples could be to state 'reach high' rather than 'hands up in the air', or 'long limbs' rather than 'stretch your arms or legs', which would give dancers a choice more suitable to their particular capabilities. Pace of movement retention and motor ability is likely to also differ. What will be fast for one dancer may be slow for another, so racing through the movement may not be appropriate. Dance leaders must not be afraid to ask participants about their disabilities and to create an atmosphere where the dancers are honest with each other. For example a dancer might say 'I have brittle bones and cannot take much weight on my legs', or 'I can't do weight-bearing exercises with my upper body.' Having heard this, the leader and the fellow dancers within the group can work with this information and create dance in a truthful and open environment.

PREGNANT DANCERS

Continuing or even beginning to exercise during pregnancy is recognised to be positive for the well-being of both mother and baby, with the consensus being that it appears to provide more benefits than risk (Hammer, Perkins, & Parr, 2000; Nascimento, Surita, & Cecatti, 2012; Pivarnik et al., 2006; Sanders, 2008; Smith & Campbell, 2013; Wang & Apgar, 1998). Of course, how much and what type of exercise are paramount. All exercise is not the same, and many forms of physical activity have not received a great deal of research attention in relation to pregnancy (Pivarnik et al., 2006). The main issue is the lack of specificity

in the generalised descriptions of exercise and physical activity. For example, guidelines do not always provide detail on what counts as vigorous or strenuous; therefore it is not clear if there might be an upper limit for what is considered safe for women who engage in high-performance exercise (Smith & Campbell, 2013; Szymanski & Satin, 2012). Most sources recommend moderate exercise for health benefits, but individual interpretations of what this means, or feels like, can vary. It will also depend on previous fitness levels.

Because dance covers such a broad spectrum of activities, definitive recommendations have been slow to emerge; those that do offer advice wisely play it safe and provide good general outlines (Sanders, 2008). This is understandable in that the physical demands of each genre or context can vary considerably, from upright and gestural vocabularies to more extreme, energetic, athletic rolling on the floor or jumping types of movement.

It could be supposed that common sense would guide a pregnant dancer and that listening to her body could help her to determine when to ease off activity. It has been reported that many women often independently modify their activities based on observable symptoms, discomfort and perceived risk (Sanders, 2008). However, given that dancers are notoriously motivated and are used to working through discomfort, and could have financial concerns about their jobs, this may not always be the case. Because, as previously mentioned, a level of exercise is now advised during pregnancy, some recreational exercisers might begin to attend dance classes that they feel can combine a degree of supplementary fitness and an enjoyable experience. In either case, both the dancer and her leader need to be able to make informed decisions on how much and what kind of activity they can safely undertake. The guidelines provided here will take into account the general recommendations that promote health and well-being for exercising pregnant women, but will also indicate where further questioning and precautions might be necessary for the dancer.

The general advice is that it is safe to continue to exercise at both a recreational and professional level only if there are no medically indicated complications—if there are any doubts on this score, a more conservative approach is warranted (ACOG, 2002; RCOG, 2006; Wang & Apgar, 1998). In the first instance, it is advisable for all dancers, regardless of their ability level, to check with their medical care provider that their degree of participation and style of dance are not likely to have any individual adverse effects, and update this assessment as their pregnancy progresses. They should then present the dance leader with this evaluation. A preparticipation health questionnaire is also strongly advised, for example, the PARmed-X for pregnancy, which includes specific antenatal information (DiFiore, 1998; Hammer et al., 2000; Pivarnik et al., 2006). Women at either end of the spectrum for activity level need the most detailed evaluation: those who are just starting to participate, having previously not done so, or those who want to sustain a high level of professional demand for as long as possible (Hammer et al., 2000). Researchers stress that even women who have higher fitness levels should periodically seek individual medical evaluations of their physical condition in pregnancy with respect to the continuation of their usual activities, so that these can be adjusted if necessary (Nascimento et al., 2012; Powers & Howley, 2012; RCOG, 2006).

Some definitive contraindications exist for exercise during pregnancy that can be readily applied to dance sessions. As well as pre-existing medical conditions that could be stressed by pregnancy, other complications that can affect the ability to move safely can develop in some women, regardless of their previous level of fitness (Artal & O'Toole, 2003).

Contraindications to exercise in pregnancy include the following:

- Severe anemia
- Being extremely underweight
- Pregnancy-induced hypertension (high blood pressure)
- Unmanaged type 1 diabetes
- Unevaluated cardiac arrhythmia
- Persistent second or third trimester bleeding or incompetent cervix

(ACOG, 2002; Artal & O'Toole, 2003)

Caution regarding exercise is advised in early pregnancy (during the first **trimester**), but this is mainly due to residual concerns because of the lack of definitive research and the worry over possible litigation (Hammer et al., 2000). Physical exercise in the second trimester (weeks 13 to 28) is seen to have positive benefits for both mother and baby in regular exercisers and those new to physical activity (Wang & Apgar, 1998). The third trimester (weeks 29 to 40) often sees a natural reduction in activity by individual women, but research also recommends avoiding overly vigorous weight-bearing activity at this time, suggesting relaxation practices instead (Karr, n.d.; Selby, 2002; Sports Medicine Australia, 2009; Wang & Apgar, 1998). A summary of the recommendations for any dancer during each stage can be seen in table 10.1.

The dance leader should continue to observe and monitor the individual dancer carefully as her

Table 10.1 General Recommendations for Physical Activity During Stages of Pregnancy

Stage of pregnancy	Reported physical activity guidelines
First trimester	• Approach new physical activity with caution if you have not been previously active. • Do not increase intensity or frequency of usual activity. • Avoid overly strenuous activity.
Second trimester	• If you have not been previously active, new physical activity is generally considered acceptable. • Moderate exercise is recommended to help prevent excessive weight gain for mother and foetus. • In later stages of this trimester some modifications may be necessary. • Transition to more non-weight-bearing activities.
Third trimester	• There will be a natural self-imposed reduction in activity due to physical changes and discomfort. • Reduce intensity and avoid overly vigorous activity. • Gentle non-weight-bearing activities can be sustained.

ACOG 2002; Hammer et al. 2000; Karr, n.d.; Selby 2002; Sports Medicine Australia 2009; Wang and Apgar 1998

pregnancy progresses so that the dance activity can be tailored when necessary. However, a degree of responsibility must be taken by the dancer herself to assess her own responses to the activity and take the decision to stop moving if she feels unwell, uncomfortable or fatigued (ACPWH, 2010). It is especially important that the dancer does not ignore pain signals.

Signs to stop dancing include the following:

- Headache, dizziness, faintness or shortness of breath
- Chest pain
- Muscle weakness, calf pain or swelling
- Excessive fatigue
- Abdominal pain, particularly in back or pubic area
- Pelvic girdle pain
- Fluid leaking or vaginal bleeding
- Uterine contractions

(Artal & O'Toole, 2003; RCOG, 2006; Sanders, 2008)

Preparation and Environmental Factors

The main issue regarding environmental conditions for pregnant dancers is temperature. Warm-up and exercise will raise body temperature, which is generally positive for exercise, but women should avoid exercise at an intensity or duration that causes the body temperature to rise above 39 degrees Celsius (102 degrees Fahrenheit) to avoid detrimental effects for the baby (Hammer et al., 2000). Appropriate ventilation or air conditioning is advised to prevent overheating, as is avoiding exercise when the weather is very hot and humid (over 27 degrees Celsius or 80 degrees Fahrenheit). Exercising in the early morning or evening can improve the dancer's heat dissipation in these conditions (Kaar, n.d.; Hammer et al., 2000; Wang & Apgar, 1998). Advisable clothing for the pregnant dancer is a layer of light, cool items, with fully supportive footwear where appropriate. The additional weight of the growing breasts can add strain on the neck and upper back, resulting in round shoulders, so a supportive, well-fitting sports bra is needed. If abdominal or pelvic discomfort is experienced in the later stages, a maternity abdominal support belt or simply a wide elastic bandage can provide some relief, although this should be for

general day-to-day activities. Remember that discomfort and pain when dancing should be a sign to stop.

Alignment, Musculoskeletal Issues and Injury Risk

Even if the dancer generally has good posture, pregnancy can be a time when it deteriorates (Selby, 2002). Pregnancy obviously results in a natural, gradual weight gain. As the uterus grows, increased biomechanical stress is placed on the lumbar spine because of the increased anterior tilt of the pelvis, the resulting increase in lumbar lordosis and the alteration of the spinal curves, which affects the biomechanical loading on the body, changes the centre of gravity and affects balance (see figure 10.2; ACPWH, 2010; Alter, 2004; DiFiore, 1998). Once this happens there is also the likelihood of consequential kyphosis (accentuated by the additional weight of the breasts) and forward head.

Studies have shown that 50 to 90 percent of pregnant women experience some kind of back pain, which is attributed to the increased stress on the spine and the altered hormonal influences (Pivarnik et al., 2006). The biomechanical changes will prevent the dancer from effectively managing vertical impact forces (Wang & Apgar, 1998), and the body may be more vulnerable to sprains and strains due to the reduced stability of the joints. The main factor to consider is the effect of the pregnancy hormone on the body's connective tissue. The action of the hormone **relaxin** allows the pelvis to adapt to the developing baby's size and to prepare for birth by increasing the size and pliability of ligaments, tendons and cartilage. It is produced as early as the second week of pregnancy, but remains present in the body until after the birth (DiFiore, 1998). As discussed in chapter 2, the function of ligaments is stabilisation. The joints most at risk of the reduced stability are the symphysis pubis at the front of the pelvis and the sacroiliac joint at the back of the pelvis (ACPWH, 2010; DiFiore, 1998). Injuries of the hip and lower extremities may also be hormone-related, for example, damage to the labrum of the hip and the meniscus of the knee (Pivarnik et al., 2006). While the pregnant dancer may experience an enjoyable sensation of looseness and flexibility she did not previously have, it is important that she does not exploit the effects of relaxin and push her body

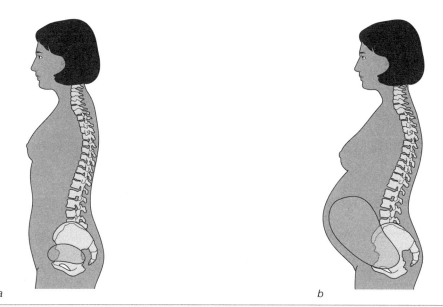

Figure 10.2 Changes to spinal curves in pregnancy.

in new ranges of motion. Because of the lack of protective stability, if the joints are severely overextended during pregnancy, any damage could be permanent (DiFiore, 1998).

The stability of the spine is also compromised by the reduced contribution of the abdominal muscles and the muscles of the pelvic floor. Relaxin has an effect on the abdominal muscles by allowing them to stretch as the abdomen gets bigger. **Abdominal separation**, or diastasis, of the two lengths of the rectus abdominis, which are normally joined at the midline of connective tissue (the linea alba), occurs in approximately 67 percent of women (Pivarnik et al., 2006). The rectus abdominis can increase in length by up to 20 centimetres (7.5 inches), with the gap between the two bands ranging from 2 to 20 centimetres (0.8 to 7.5 inches; DiFiore, 1998). In movements that curl up through the spine (sit-ups and crunches, or simply sitting up from a supine position), often a bulge or dome in the abdominal wall can be seen due to the underlying

tissue being pushed up through the separated bands of muscles. This clearly should be avoided, because it additionally weakens the abdominals, reducing core support even further and jeopardising full recovery of the muscles after birth (McCoid, Harris, & Rafiefar, 2013). The pelvic floor muscles are also weakened in pregnancy due the combined weight of the uterus, amniotic fluid and the baby.

Hand pain (from carpal tunnel syndrome) is the second most frequent injury issue in pregnancy, especially in third trimester, with pain worsening with repetitive wrist flexion and extension (Pivarnik et al., 2006). Dancers who use their hands, wrists and fingers extensively, for example, flamenco dancers or classical Indian dancers may find that this type of pain is intensified in their dance practice. Following injury prevention procedures (rest, ice and strapping or splinting) can be beneficial in reducing some of the pain (Sanders, 2008). See chapter 9 for further information.

Because the changes to the body in pregnancy can amplify the risks of many familiar movements that could normally be managed by the dancer, some types of vocabulary will need to be reassessed. Certainly, the level of intensity, amount of repetition and range of motion will need to be lowered in comparison to prepregnancy states to reduce the risk of injury. The dancer needs to bear in mind that all these physiological factors will result in altered mechanics throughout her body and that she will not be able to carry on as before. Care and attention to modify her regular

Dancers are frequently used to pushing their bodies. The effect of hormones on flexibility should not be ignored. Pregnant dancers should take care not to exploit a greater feeling of looseness and increased range of motion. Instead, rest and relaxation should become the focus in the later stages of pregnancy.

Joint and Muscle Health in Pregnancy

Pregnant dancers must consider the following:

- The stability of all joints, but especially those of the pelvis, is reduced during pregnancy. Range of motion should be comparatively conservative and the increases in flexibility managed carefully.

- Active elongation of the spine to maintain neutral is helpful to avoid stress on the spinal curves.

- Simple pelvic floor exercises to maintain strength and tone will assist in stabilising the spine and will also help to combat urinary incontinence.

- Abdominal muscles will not be able to work in their usual way in assisting active flexion of the spine (curling or rolling up, or even getting up from sitting or lying down), so alternative actions need to be found, for example, rolling onto the side and getting on all fours on the way up from the floor. Sit-ups and stability exercises such as planks should not be attempted.

activities will be wise, ideally in consultation with her healthcare provider.

Activities and Progression

Warm-up and cool-down are even more important in pregnancy so that the body can gently prepare for and recover from exercise (Hammer et al., 2000). The usual guidelines apply (see chapter 3), but pregnant dancers should take care to not to heat the body too much when raising the body temperature. Dynamic movement should be slow and controlled. It is safe to stretch within the usual recommendations, emphasising relaxation during cool-down. It is reported that the pectorals, hamstrings, hip adductors and hip flexors may have a tendency to become tight, so these muscle groups can be addressed with careful static stretching after the dance session. In partner-assisted stretches that are common in antenatal classes, care should be taken not to push the joints into extreme ranges of motion (Hammer et al., 2000). Remember that pregnancy is not the time to work

for increased flexibility, but maintaining flexibility is important for postnatal health and fitness for the dancer.

Pregnant dancers should take care with some specific actions, or avoid them completely, particularly in the last trimester. These include low squats, crossover steps, jumping, repetitive twisting, rapid changes of direction or body position, for example, lying to standing, and any bouncing or ballistic type of movement (ACPWH, 2010; Sports Medicine Australia, 2009; Wang & Apgar, 1998). Contraindicated dance-specific movements are low or wide knee bends, high kicks and deep lunges, and class exercises should emphasise symmetry through the body rather than performance of one-sided sequences (McCoid et al., 2013; Sanders, 2008). Pregnant dancers should completely avoid complicated balances or any dance movements that could present a risk of falling, abdominal trauma or significant joint stress (Rahl, 2010; Sports Medicine Australia, 2009; Wang & Apgar, 1998).

Some difference in opinion exists regarding lying on the back to exercise or rest. Many sources have stated that exercises in the supine position are inadvisable from around 16 weeks because of a danger of the compression of the blood supply to and from the uterus (ACPWH, 2010; Rahl, 2010; Selby, 2002; Wang & Apgar, 1998). Others have suggested that this might be the case when resting but not when actually exercising (Sanders, 2008). Three to seven minutes of exercise in this position have been reported in inducing symptoms such as shortness of breath, dizziness, nausea and tachycardia (Alter, 2004). Given this difference in guidelines, it may be prudent to avoid staying in this position for any length of time.

In terms of fitness, the pregnant dancer may experience feelings of shortness of breath at relatively low exertion because of increased blood volume, a rise in respiratory rate and the pressure of the enlarged uterus on the diaphragm (ACPWH, 2010; Artal & O'Toole, 2003). Consequently, a decrease in performance capacity is normal, especially later in pregnancy (Wang & Apgar, 1998). Because the heightened heart rate makes monitoring exercise intensity difficult, a rate of perceived exertion (RPE) measure, for example the Borg scale, can guide the dancer: Exercising at a 'somewhat hard (13)' level is a recommended maximum (Nascimento et al., 2012; Sanders, 2008; Sports Medicine Australia, 2009).

Towards the third trimester, swimming and cycling are good supplementary activities. Both

In the final stages of pregnancy, dancers should begin to reduce their activity levels towards gentle exercise that does not tax the body, then in the few weeks before the birth, take time for rest and relaxation.

Pilates and yoga classes are frequently adapted for pregnant women, but dancers should be reminded to work within their prepregnancy range of motion and avoid extended stretching (also refer to the earlier advice regarding exercise in the supine position). In particular, they should avoid movements that overload the back muscles (Alter, 2004). It is best for the dancer to seek out a qualified instructor with experience teaching pregnant women if she wants to participate in these types of classes. Relaxation and breathing techniques are very valuable in the later stages of pregnancy.

Nutrition for Pregnant Dancers

Both exercise and pregnancy require additional energy; therefore the pregnant dancer needs to consume enough calories to supply the needs of both. Guidelines suggest that an extra 150 kilocalories per day are required in pregnancy during the first trimester and, in the second and third, an extra 300 kilocalories per day (Artal & O'Toole, 2003; Kenney, Wilmore, & Costill, 2012; Wang &

Apgar, 1998). The energy demands of any activity then need to be estimated in addition to this. To avoid fatigue, consuming some carbohydrate (such as fresh or dried fruit or a sports drink) before (more than 1 hour in advance), during and immediately following the dance session (for example, a sandwich or cereal bar) will be beneficial (Hammer et al., 2000).

Pregnant dancers participating in research studies highlight that they have concerns about weight gain (Sanders, 2008). Recreational dancers may participate in antenatal exercise classes precisely to try to minimise excessive weight gain in pregnancy. Therefore providing information on how to balance diet and exercise for the most positive outcome is the responsibility of dance leaders, although, once again, the advice of the individual dancer's healthcare provider should be paramount.

Hydration is very important in pregnancy. Even if the dancer does not feel thirsty, she should take on water or liquid frequently before, during and after exercise. The dancer may be more reluctant to do this because it may feel uncomfortable due to the extra pressure on the bladder, and it will increase the frequency and necessity of bathroom breaks. Also, because of the increased weakness of the pelvic floor, she may not be as much in control of a full bladder. Nevertheless, she is advised to rehydrate regularly, especially during early pregnancy when blood volume is low, and during endurance exercise lasting longer than 30 minutes, when a carbohydrate drink is useful (Hammer et al., 2000). In hot and humid conditions, loss of fluid as sweat may compromise the ability to dissipate heat during prolonged exercise (Artal & O'Toole, 2003). Because overheating is cautioned in pregnancy, hydration is more critical in this type of environment.

Psychological Considerations

It has been reported that most women experience negative moods at some point during the **perinatal period** and that stress, anxiety and fatigue are common (Pivarnik et al., 2006). However, moderate exercise can alleviate some of the symptoms by increasing energy levels, encouraging a greater sense of control and boosting self-esteem, body image and confidence; exercising with others can also provide peer support (ACPWH, 2010; Gaston & Prapavessis, 2013; Hammer et al., 2000). It is supposed that these benefits are very valuable for dancers—as a population, they can suffer from low

Key Points for Pregnant Dancers

- Obtain medical advice before beginning dance activity.
- Warm up gently but efficiently.
- Avoid overheating and try not to exercise in very warm and humid environments.
- Do not aim to improve fitness and flexibility.
- Avoid stretching beyond prepregnancy normal range of motion.
- Eat well without restricting calories, but not just before exercise.
- Drink plenty of water to avoid dehydration.

- Add more rest periods within the dance activity.
- Listen to the body. Do not work to overload and stop if feeling fatigued.
- Do not ignore pain.
- Understand the physical signs to stop dancing.
- In the last trimester of pregnancy, reduce weight-bearing activities.
- Return to dancing gradually.

(ACPWH, 2010; Kenney et al., 2012; Sanders, 2008)

self-esteem and issues with body image (Sanders, 2008). Continuing to dance is important for the psychological well-being of the dancing mother because it helps her to maintain her identity as a dancer while she makes the transition into motherhood. In the early months after the birth, the lack of personal time and opportunities to return to and focus on dancing also presents psychological challenges.

Returning to Dance Post Pregnancy

It will take time for the dancer's body to return to its prepregnancy state. Even if outwardly the body appears to have resumed its former shape and condition, the effects of pregnancy hormones can remain in the body for some time. Realignment to regain neutral posture is a priority. This may be more difficult when sitting in asymmetrical or slumped breast-feeding positions for prolonged periods of time, and carrying the baby may cause further imbalance. Similarly, learning how to perform new physical tasks such as strapping in car seats, changing and bathing the baby can be demanding on the body in different ways (DiFiore, 1998).

Depending on the type of delivery and any subsequent complications, the dancer must always seek medical advice as to when it is safe to attempt activity, for example, when the two sides of the rectus abdominis have begun to come together again (the so-called rec test, when the amount of space in the separation is less than two fingers or under 2 centimetres or 1 inch wide). While small pelvic tilts are

encouraged from very early after the birth, to avoid the doming effect mentioned earlier, more ambitious curl-ups and especially oblique work should not be attempted until the rectus abdominis returns to normal position and function (DiFiore, 1998). It is important that any discharge (this is normal for several weeks after the birth) has stopped, since this indicates when the uterus has closed; there is a risk of complications when exercising if this is not the case (McCoid et al., 2013). Tears and scars must be healed properly.

Just like returning from injury, developing dance fitness again must be gradual. Stretched and weakened muscles must be reconditioned, bearing in mind that joint stability will still be an issue. The muscles can take up to 6 weeks to repair, so while stretching to maintain muscle length is recommended, any additional flexibility training is not advised until 16 to 20 weeks after the birth and longer if breast-feeding (DiFiore, 1998; Sports Medicine Australia, 2009). There may also be some discomfort from scarring while stretching, for example, following a caesarean section.

For the dance leader, requesting further medical information from the returning dancer is essential. The result of the dancer's postnatal medical check (usually around 6 weeks post birth) and details of any lingering joint problems are relevant in helping them to plan their dance activities safely.

DANCERS WITH ASTHMA

Asthma is a chronic respiratory condition in which the bronchial tubes can become narrowed and inflamed (**bronchoconstriction**), making it difficult to breathe efficiently. The incidence and severity of asthma is increasing in the general population, although the reasons for this are as yet not fully known (Koutedakis & Sharp, 1999). Asthma affects both adults and children, and is the most common chronic disease in childhood, reportedly affecting up to 25 percent of children in Western urban environments (Welsh, Roberts, & Kemp, 2004). Although it is more common in children, with half of sufferers developing it before the age of 10, symptoms can decrease over time, with more than 50 percent of children with mild asthma growing out of it by the time they are 21 (American Running & Fitness Association, 2013; Koutedakis & Sharp, 1999).

Being asthmatic does not prevent athletes and dancers from competing or performing, even at the highest levels, since mild to moderate asthma does not necessarily affect physical performance (Koutedakis & Sharp, 1999). However, active people need to use strategies in order to minimise any possible negative effects. Firstly, asthmatic dancers should seek specific advice from the medical personnel who help them to manage their asthma before they begin or significantly change the type or intensity of their training or dance activities. For leaders to help dancers manage asthma effectively, they must understand what it is and how it affects dance exercise. Several different types and triggers exist, including **allergic asthma**, **non-allergic asthma** and a very common form, **exercise-induced asthma (EIA)**, otherwise known as sports asthma.

Preparation and Environmental Factors

Allergic asthma is affected by exposure to specific allergens that may be different for individuals. The most common outdoor allergen is pollen and the most common indoor ones are mould, dust mites in carpets or upholstery and animals with fur or feathers (shedding microscopic skin cells). Strong odours or fumes from products such as pesticides, paint, perfumes and cleaning chemicals will also affect some people. Non-allergic asthma can be triggered by respiratory tract infections, environmental irritants such as air pollution and temperature changes (American Running & Fitness Association, 2013; The Asthma Center, 2013).

People with asthma are more sensitive to cold, dry air and sudden changes in temperature and humidity. During strenuous activity, it is usual to breathe through the mouth, which means that cold air directly enters the airways without first having been warmed by the passages of the nose (American Running & Fitness Association, 2013). Good indoor air quality in the working environment (not too dry) is important (The Asthma Center, 2013). As a matter of course, smoking should be permitted only in outside designated areas. While it may be entirely apparent that asthmatic dancers should not smoke, it is worth reinforcing because of a reported high incidence of smoking in the dance population (Koutedakis & Sharp, 1999).

The implications for dance practice is that the environment should ideally be as free as possible from indoor allergens and that precautions are taken where necessary if dancing outside, such as using protective masks when rehearsing. Wearing a scarf or mask can protect the dancer from pollen in the warmer months and can help to trap moisture in colder weather (Powers & Howley, 2012). If a venue is shared with other activities, leaders should ensure that it is clean and chemical free before the dance session. For competition and performances when dancers are sharing dressing rooms, it is good practice to ask all dancers to refrain from spraying aerosols (deodorants or hair spray) in the general backstage or preparation area. Instead leaders can designate a single dressing room for the use of sprays. This will help asthmatic dancers to avoid coming into contact with any potential irritants.

Activities and Progression

Exercise-induced asthma (EIA) has a higher incidence among active individuals (Koutedakis & Sharp, 1999). This type of asthma is triggered by aerobic exercise, and symptoms can include the following:

- Chest tightness or pain
- Cough, shortness of breath or wheezing
- Underperformance or poor performance
- Fatigue and prolonged recovery time
- Gastrointestinal discomfort

(Garry, 2013)

EIA may exist by itself or co-exist with other forms (American Running & Fitness Association, 2013). The bronchoconstriction associated with EIA is brought on more by strenuous, long-duration exercise rather than short-term exercise at moderate intensities. Symptoms can be experienced within 20 minutes after the onset of exercise, but usually either occur between 5 and 15 minutes post exercise or up to 6 hours afterwards (Powers & Howley, 2012). Lung vibrations and cold, dry air are the two main triggers of EIA. Impactive dance activities could fall into this category, although good, shock-absorbing shoes and suitable floor construction and surfaces can minimise the risks (Koutedakis & Sharp, 1999). The increased ventilation during exercise and resulting greater loss of heat and water through respiration leads to bronchial constriction, the effects of which can be compounded by repeated daily physical activity during training (Carlsen, 2011).

To help prevent asthma attacks during exercise, a thorough warm-up is recommended, which has a marked positive effect on breathing (Garry, 2013; Powers & Howley, 2012). Because moderate activity can induce **bronchodilation** (widening and opening of the airways), which can last for 1 to 4 hours, dancers can exploit this effect by using moderate intensity activity when warming up (Koutedakis & Sharp, 1999). Rest breaks within the session are helpful. If the dancer uses anti-asthma medication or an inhaler to dilate the airways, these can be used about 15 minutes before the session to reduce symptoms of EIA and help prevent an attack (American Running & Fitness Association, 2013; Garry, 2013; Powers & Howley, 2012). However, dancers themselves have reported that inhaling corticosteroids can sometimes make them feel anxious and shaky before they go on stage because these drugs speed up the metabolism and make the heart race (Wozny, 2010). To combat this, it is suggested that dancers use inhalers approximately 30 minutes before the performance.

In terms of supplementary activities for asthmatic dancers, swimming is a very good choice (if they are not allergic to chlorine) because the air above the water contains more moisture (Powers & Howley, 2012). Practices that emphasise breathing techniques, meditation and relaxation—for example, gentle types of yoga—are also recommended (Koutedakis & Sharp, 1999; Wozny, 2010).

Nutrition for Asthmatic Dancers

Much of the advice concerning diet for asthmatics is similar to that for all dancers, that is, to eat a wide range of fruit and vegetables to boost the immune system and to help prevent any respiratory problems associated with colds and flu. However, some foods have been found to protect against asthma and improve lung function; in particular, vitamins C and E are believed to help reduce the severity of the inflammatory response in the lungs of asthmatic people (Asthma UK, n.d.-b). Increasing antioxidants, which include beta-carotene and selenium, taking fish oil and reducing salt intake have also been identified as beneficial in managing EIA (Powers & Howley, 2012).

Dealing With an Asthma Attack

Dance leaders should always know what to do if a dancer in their session has an asthma attack. This is especially important when working with children. A preparticipation health questionnaire (see appendix A) will flag up any asthmatic dancers, and leaders can then collect further detail on relevant procedures should an attack occur.

Dancers should carry their inhalers at all times, and the dance leader should know where to locate the inhalers and which one to used in an emergency (the reliever colour or type of medication). If dancers are showing signs of distress, they should stop dancing and sit down in a comfortable position, take slow, steady breaths and use a reliever inhaler as directed for their type of asthma. If possible, asthmatic dancers should administer their own medication, with assistance provided if necessary.

Dance leaders should take further action if symptoms do not subside and if they observe any of the following effects in the asthmatic dancer:

- The reliever inhaler is not helping the dancer to recover.
- The symptoms are getting worse (coughing, breathlessness, wheezing).
- The dancer is too breathless to speak.
- The breathing rate increases, and the dancer either cannot get a breath in properly or is breathing very slowly.
- The dancer is showing signs of anxiety or panic.
- The dancer complains of chest pain.
- The dancer has a pale face or blue lips or fingers.
- The dancer is hunching over.
- The dancer (if a child) complains of a tummy ache.

(Asthma UK, n.d.-a; MedlinePlus, 2014)

Asthma does not prevent dancers participating fully in dance exercise. Limiting allergens and triggers in the dance environment, monitoring symptoms and ensuring medication or inhalers are used supportively all help the dancer to work safely. Dance leaders should be able to recognise the symptoms of an asthma attack and act accordingly.

If any of these can be registered, the emergency services should be called, or the dancer taken to Accident and Emergency/Emergency Room. Parents of dancers under 18 years old should be contacted. Even if an asthma attack does not result in a hospital visit, affected dancers should seek an appointment with their own healthcare provider for a medical check following any significant episode.

DANCERS WITH DIABETES

Diabetes mellitus is a metabolic disease in which the body is not able to produce adequate **insulin** (**type 1 diabetes**), or it cannot respond properly to the insulin that is produced (**type 2 diabetes**) or both. Insulin regulates the blood sugar, which in diabetics is too high (**hyperglycaemia**). Type 1 can develop at any age, but it usually quickly appears before the age of 40, and it is the most common type of diabetes found in childhood, whereas type 2 can develop slowly over a long period of time, and is associated with upper body obesity and physical inactivity (Diabetes UK, n.d.; Powers & Howley, 2012). Type 1 affects about 10 to 15 percent of all diabetics, who need to manage their blood sugar levels with insulin injections. Type 2 is more common, and can be managed with diet and exercise, although many people also need medication to stimulate insulin release or improve insulin sensitivity (Meade, 2014).

Exercise increases insulin sensitivity. To meet the energy demands of physical activity, skeletal muscle uses its own stores of glycogen and glucose released from the liver at a greatly increased rate (American Diabetes Association, 2004; Meade, 2014). The management of blood sugar levels in exercise is complicated. First, there must be sufficient insulin so that the muscles can use the glucose; otherwise the amount between that released by the liver and that taken up by the muscles becomes imbalanced, resulting in high blood sugar (hyperglycaemia). If there is too much insulin before exercise, the rate at which glucose is used by the muscles is accelerated while that released from the liver is decelerated, resulting in low blood sugar (**hypoglycaemia**; Powers & Howley, 2012). Therefore diabetics who exercise must be in control of their blood sugar levels before they begin any activity. Diabetic dancers are likely to understand how to manage their blood sugar effectively because they will have had substantial medical attention since their diagnosis, but both dancers and their leaders must understand how this complicated balance plays out in practice, since the consequences can be serious. Regular consultation with their medical advisor should be a fundamental part of diabetic dancers' regime, especially as they grow, develop and age, but also if they alter their activity patterns substantially.

Preparation for Diabetic Dancers

Advance preparation is essential for diabetic dancers of all ages. They should consult with their healthcare specialist before beginning any new form of exercise or dancing and explain what the new activity will entail so that they can gauge the likely intensity and suitability. Dancers must let their leader know that they are diabetic and communicate relevant information that will be necessary in the event of a hypoglycaemic episode, such as where they keep their kit and emergency supplies or snacks (a preparticipation health questionnaire would already have flagged up the condition). In addition, the dancer should always carry medical information and ID or wear a bracelet, necklace or shoe tag that identifies them as a diabetic (NDIC, 2014; Diabetes.co.uk, n.d.). During dance activities, these should not be worn on the body (see chapter 1 for alternatives), but instead could be temporarily and prominently attached to the dancer's kit bag, which should remain nearby. It is also wise for diabetic dancers to avoid exercising alone. Instead, good precautions include working with a friend who knows about their diabetes, carrying a mobile phone and letting someone know their intended whereabouts (Meade, 2014). It is extremely beneficial for the dance leader (or a first-aider who is regularly on hand) to have some basic training in how to recognise and deal with hypoglycaemia appropriately (Lumb & Gallen, 2009).

Diabetic dancers will be used to measuring and monitoring their blood glucose concentration, and will do so before they begin the activity to check that it is under control and ready for exercise. They will know how much insulin they need to administer and whether to eat specific foods to create the necessary balance (see the section Nutrition for Diabetic Dancers). The level of **ketones** (chemicals that indicate whether the blood glucose level is too high and the insulin level is too low) in the blood or urine will tell them whether they are able to begin exercising or must delay starting to work. If the dancer performs strenuous exercise when ketones are present, the blood glucose level may go even higher (NDIC, 2014).

The appropriate dose of insulin can be calculated and then either administered by injection or delivered by an insulin pump worn by the dancer. Both have implications for the dancer's proposed activity. The site of the injection can vary, but it is best to avoid areas of the body that will be worked during the dance activity or at least avoid exercising a muscle that underlies the injection site of short-acting insulin for about 1 hour where possible, since the elevated blood flow results in an increased rate of insulin uptake (Kenney, Wilmore, & Costill, 2012; Meade, 2014; Powers & Howley, 2012). If they need to be worn when dancing, insulin pumps can be taped or held on the body within tighter clothing, although this can be impractical at times in styles that require close contact and athletic manoeuvres when there is a danger of the pump dislodging or the dancer falling onto it (American Diabetes Association, 2013). If the pump is disconnected, the dancer must understand how this affects the insulin dosage (called a *bolus*) and monitor their glucose levels carefully. A teenage dancer with type 1 diabetes describes how she manages an insulin pump in her training:

'I calculate how much insulin I need, which is put into my body by an insulin pump. There's a tube inserted into my skin at my hip that allows the insulin to enter my bloodstream. I change the insertion location every two or three days and take it off when I shower or dance. I don't need to wear it when I'm dancing because exercise helps to balance out glucose levels. If I had insulin constantly going into my body during dance, my blood sugar would drop too low. The pump is also bulky, so it would get in the way' (Schmid, 2012).

The time of day may have an effect on the diabetic dancer's response to exercise. The risk of hypoglycaemia during exercise is reduced if insulin levels are low and liver and muscle glycogen stores are sufficiently high. Providing that the dancer has consumed a good meal the previous

night and taken regular meals during the day, the most appropriate times to exercise may be before breakfast (and morning insulin) or late afternoon (before evening insulin), while late-evening exercise should ideally be avoided (Meade, 2014; Kenney et al., 2012).

Because weight-bearing exercise places additional stress on the feet, good shock-absorbing footwear and appropriate preventive foot care are important. It is common for people with diabetes to have impaired circulation and experience some loss of sensation in the feet (Kenney et al., 2012). Individuals should monitor blisters and any other potential damage to their feet both before and after physical activity (American Diabetes Association, 2004).

In very hot or cold environments, care should be taken to avoid large fluctuations in blood glucose levels (American Diabetes Association, 2004; Meade, 2014). Exercise in extreme weather conditions should be avoided (Diabetes.co.uk, n.d.). Dancers who tour internationally need to carry a copy of their prescription so that they can travel easily through security with insulin, needles and syringes. Travel across time zones can affect blood glucose levels, so meals and medication doses may need to be adjusted (Bye, 2014).

Activities and Progression

To add to the challenges in managing diabetes and activity, different exercise intensities can affect the blood sugar levels in different ways, and the individual dancer's response can vary. Knowing the intensity of the activity to be performed can greatly assist the dancer in creating strategies to manage their diabetes. Moderate-intensity activity is linked to hypoglycaemia and high-intensity exercise to hyperglycaemia (Lumb & Gallen, 2009). Unplanned or intermittent exercise increases the risk of hypoglycaemia, especially if insulin has been taken beforehand (Meade, 2014). Table 10.2 gives an indication of how blood sugar levels fluctuate when exercising at different intensities.

Nutrition for Diabetic Dancers

An understanding of how nutrition and hydration affect safe dance practice is important for all dancers (see chapter 7 for more information) but clearly, managing their nutrition will be especially vital for diabetic dancers. To prevent hypoglycaemia during and after exercise, carbohydrate needs to be consumed (Powers & Howley, 2012).

Table 10.2 Effect of Exercise Intensity on Blood Glucose Levels

Maximum heart rate (%)	Type of activity	Effect on blood sugar
Less than 60%	Low intensity	Little effect on blood glucose
60–70%	Aerobic activity	Falls after 20–30 minutes
70–85%	Mixed or intermittent activity	Marked fall
More than 85%	Anaerobic	Rises

Gallen 2004

The ideal components of the diabetic diet (sugar-free foods or those with a low glycaemic index) are not suitable during exercise, but should remain an important part of the diet on rest days (Gallen, 2004). Ideally active diabetics should consume a carbohydrate-rich snack, meal or drink 1 to 3 hours before exercise. This should contain approximately 15 to 30 grams (0.5 to 1.0 ounces) of carbohydrate per 30 minutes of anticipated moderate-intensity activity, although the requirements will be higher if intensity increases (Meade, 2014; Kenney et al., 2012).

Ingestion of glucose during exercise can be useful, and dance leaders should both allow and encourage diabetic dancers to eat during sessions if they need to. Foods and drinks that do not cause gastrointestinal disturbances are the best options at this point. Glucose tablets and bananas are rapidly assimilated forms of carbohydrate, and cereal bars are useful during longer periods of exercise (Lumb & Gallen, 2009). Sports drinks typically contain about 6 grams (0.2 ounces) of glucose per 100 millilitres (3.5 fluid ounces) and include salts (potassium and sodium) – these are useful for replacing fluids when blood glucose is not falling rapidly whereas higher concentration drinks (15 grams of glucose per 100 millilitres) are better for raising glucose levels quickly (Gallen, 2004). Dancers can make their own sports drinks to a concentration that suits their individual needs using simple and readily available ingredients (table salt and sugar), or can use powdered sports drinks and vary the ratio of glucose to water content (Gallen, 2004).

During recovery from exercise, glucose uptake continues to replace muscle glycogen stores, and insulin sensitivity remains elevated for several hours (Meade, 2014). As for all dancers, carbohy-

drate, protein and fluid replacement are important. Approximately 1.5 grams (0.05 ounces) of carbohydrate per kilogram (35 ounces) of body weight, usually taken with insulin soon after exercise in a drink or snack form, can to help restore muscle and liver glycogen (Meade, 2014; Gallen, 2004).

Table 10.3 provides some examples of what the diabetic dancer might eat and drink before, during and after exercise, and also gives suggestions for emergency foods or drinks when a hypoglycaemic attack occurs.

Proper hydration is also essential because dehydration can adversely affect blood glucose levels. Adequate hydration before and during physical activity is recommended: 500 millilitres (17 fluid ounces) of fluid 2 hours before activity and a frequent intake during activity that also compensates for fluid losses in sweat (with special attention to maintaining hydration in hot environments; American Diabetes Association, 2004).

Injury Risk for Diabetic Dancers

Hypoglycaemia leads to fatigue, loss of co-ordination and mental focus and reductions in strength (American Diabetes Association, 2004). Because these are all risk factors for injury (see chapter 9), dancers should be aware of the onset of hypoglycaemic symptoms, and take action to

Good preparation for dance activity is essential for diabetic dancers. Assessing the blood sugar level and knowing when and how much carbohydrate to consume before they begin dancing helps them to get the best out of their sessions and work safely.

Table 10.3 Food and Drink Suggestions for Dancers With Diabetes

When to eat	What to eat	How much to eat
Before exercise	• Banana: 1 • Bread: 1 slice or 1/2 roll • Cooked pasta: 1/2 cup • Cooked rice: 1/3 cup • Juice or milk: 1 glass • Sports drink with 6% carbohydrate: 250 ml (8.5 fluid oz)	Approximately 15 g (0.5 oz) of carbohydrate per 30 min of moderate exercise *
During exercise	• Bananas: 2 • Cereal bar:1 • Sports drink (6%): 500 ml (16 fluid oz)	Approximately 30 g (1 oz) of carbohydrate per 30 min of moderate exercise
After exercise	• Postexercise recovery meal (carbohydrate and protein) as soon as possible • Avoid alcohol because its effects are similar to those of hypoglycaemia (masking symptoms). It also impairs muscle and liver glycogen replacement.	Approximately 1.5 g (0.05 oz) per kg (35 oz) of body weight
Emergency intake during/following a hypoglycaemic episode	• Glucose tablets: 3 or 4 • Glucose gel (15 g of carbohydrate equivalent) • Fruit juice or soft drink (not diet): 110 ml or 1/2 cup • Milk: 220 ml or 1 cup • Hard sweets (candy): 5 or 6 pieces • Sugar or honey: 1 tbsp	

Meade 2014; NDIC 2014

*If blood glucose is low before exercise, extra carbohydrate is recommended, but if blood glucose is adequate and ketones are negative, extra carbohydrate may not be necessary if exercise is of short duration (Meade, 2014).

address their blood glucose levels during exercise if necessary. The symptoms include weakness, confusion, irritability and fatigue, increased sweating and headaches, and can happen while exercising, immediately afterwards or up to a day later (NDIC, 2014).

Some sources report that active diabetic people are more prone to developing overuse injuries with a slower onset that can limit movement around joints (Colberg, 2013). Additionally, some long-standing diabetics can be prone to nerve compression syndromes at the elbow and wrist, which may be aggravated by repetitive activities, although flexibility with resistance exercises can help to maintain a full range of motion (Colberg, 2013).

Ultimately, it is the dancers' own responsibility to manage their diabetes when exercising, but dance leaders must be aware of any dancers who have this condition, and have to be ready to practically deal with a hypoglycaemic episode that could occur during their sessions. Specific populations also have different considerations: Children may be prone to greater variability in blood sugar levels because their activities are often play-based, with a wide spectrum of energy demands, while hormonal changes in adolescents can make it difficult to control blood glucose levels (American Diabetes Association, 2004). Older individuals with diabetes should be encouraged to be physically active. In normal aging, there is a gradual degeneration of muscles, ligaments, bones and joints,

Practical Guidelines for Diabetic Dancers

- Regular glucose monitoring is essential for safe exercise, especially if exercising for more than 1 hour.

- Consume enough carbohydrate before and during exercise to meet the energy demands of the dance activity.

- Always have a carbohydrate snack or drink to hand that can be quickly absorbed.

- Avoid exercise when blood sugar is high and ketones are present.

- Always carry identification and medical information.

- Wherever possible, do not exercise alone.

- Consult a diabetes specialist for advice on exercise.

(Meade, 2014; NDIC, 2014)

which could be exacerbated both by disuse and diabetes (American Diabetes Association, 2004). However, there is no reason why diabetic dancers should not be able to fully participate in dance activities if they prepare and monitor themselves properly and if their dance leaders are aware of how to assist them in managing the demands.

Forward planning is extremely helpful. If diabetic dancers understand the level of intensity of the session in advance, they can take appropriate action to gauge their medication and food intake. Although this is sometimes not practical or possible, the dance leader might indicate what dancers can expect to be doing in the subsequent session.

Consultation with a healthcare professional prior to starting dance activity and good communication between dancer and dance leader are helpful in managing diabetes. Knowledge and understanding of how diabetes affects the body during exercise and awareness of the procedures for dealing with potential problems are essential for the dancers themselves and are highly recommended for the dance leader.

Administering insulin or medication is beyond the role of the dance leader, but at the very least, leaders should know where to access the dancer's kit and emergency supplies to assist in managing a hypoglycaemic situation. If leaders regularly work with a diabetic dancer, they could carry a supply of suitable carbohydrate-based snacks or drinks in their own first aid kit, especially when travelling to events or performances outside the normal context and environment.

DANCERS WITH DYSLEXIA OR DYSPRAXIA

Dyslexia is a specific learning difficulty that affects the way the brain functions. It can alter how, and at what speed, people process information. Dyspraxia (sometimes referred to as development co-ordination disorder) is also a result of disorganised connections in the brain, which then translate to difficulties with co-ordination and becomes apparent through reduced language or movement skills (Daunt, 2012; Listen and Learn Centre, n.d.). Although other medical conditions (such as cerebral palsy, hemiplegia or muscular dystrophy) can also result in similar disruption to motor co-ordination, the causes are different (Wilkinson et al., 2008).

Both of these learning difficulties have great significance for dancers who are expected to process and translate information from brain to body relatively quickly. Dancers do not always know if they have one or both of these conditions, and even if they do, they are not always keen to disclose a diagnosis or reveal that they have any problems in doing what is expected of them. Often, they do not want to feel singled out for special attention or to have their issues highlighted to the whole group. However, it is becoming much more common that dyslexic and dyspraxic dancers are seeking help in order to be able to cope with learning to dance. To support these dancers, dance leaders could increase their awareness of the symptoms and effects, since these can be misinterpreted as lack of ability. Dyslexic dancers are not slow, and they do not lack intelligence. Similarly dyspraxic dancers are not physically weak or inept.

Certain features can be commonly experienced and observed between the two difficulties, although some are more common in those dancers affected by dyspraxia. By no means does every dyslexic or dyspraxic dancer exhibit all of these features or to the same degree. In line with the inherent message in this book, every participant is individual, and strategies that may be helpful for one person may not be so for another. However, any of the following may be expected:

- Issues with movement memory, such as difficulty picking up and retaining movement patterns and adapting them to different situations
- Confusion with mirroring movement and translating sequences from left to right
- Difficulties with overall co-ordination, such as changing direction, or an apparent lack of spatial awareness
- Problems with alignment, posture, balance and proprioception
- Increased muscle fatigue
- Lack of awareness of rhythm and a reduced sense of time and speed
- Over- or undersensitivity to touch or dislike of tight or overly loose clothing
- Tendency to become stressed, depressed and anxious; prone to low self-esteem
- Sometimes problems with working as part of a team
- Issues with processing written notes, handouts and feedback or reading text

(Daunt, 2012; Dyspraxia Foundation, 2014; Wilkinson et al., 2008)

If dance leaders are aware of these factors, they can introduce some simple strategies into the session that are likely to benefit the whole group as well as make things easier for the dyslexic or dyspraxic dancer.

Dance leaders can try the following during sessions:

- Change facing and orientation in the room or studio when teaching physical information: Work facing the dancers or away from them, or stand next to the individual dancer, facing the same way.
- Move the dancers around the room so that they each take turns being at the front (check with dancers first to be sure that they are comfortable doing this).
- Break the movement material down into smaller chunks and reinforce the essentials frequently.

- Emphasise the dynamics and quality of the material, using imagery to help to focus the intention.
- Repeat exercises and sequences a little more frequently, allowing dancers more time to work on things so that they can refine the material more slowly.
- Be sensitive. Try to stay patient and positive, and do not admonish dancers for a perceived lack of ability.

(Wilkinson et al., 2008)

SUMMARY

Within any dance session, dancers will have various needs, abilities and limitations. It would be impossible for dance leaders to comprehensively understand every scenario, but they must be flexible enough to make their session suit the participants involved. This should include providing a safe environment, communicating effectively with participants and choosing activities wisely to provide the best experience for their dancers. Dance leaders need to be fully aware of injuries, illnesses, the health status of dancers and any psychological implications so that they can plan the sessions and adapt them successfully to provide an experience that is safe, productive and enjoyable. Their advice to the dancers must be knowledgeable and appropriate. Particularly for the population groups covered within this chapter, more detailed guidance regarding health, injury and readiness to participate must come from a specialist practitioner; it should not be expected of the dance leader. If participants do have a condition that affects their physical or psychological health or their ability to learn in the practical dance context, the dancer and dance leader are prompted to investigate the condition so that they are fully aware of any adaptations needed and of what to do if an emergency occurs. The more understanding that dance leaders can gain into working with specific populations through research, conversations with the dancers themselves and continued professional development opportunities, the better they will deliver sessions appropriate to the needs of their dancers and develop into more experienced, safe and well-informed dance professionals.

KEY POINTS

- Dancers and dance leaders should be aware of any contraindications to dance exercise with regard to specific physical conditions, health issues or stages of development.

- Awareness of personal and professional limitations is essential in knowing when to refer participants to a health practitioner for specific care and advice.

- Dancers should always follow the advice given to them by their medical or health practitioner and should inform the dance leader of this information.

- If regularly leading sessions targeted for specific participant groups or a group that includes a dancer with unique health issues, dance leaders must become familiar with any potential complications and must have procedures in place to deal with any adverse scenarios.

- Dance leaders should undertake regular continuing professional development or education to develop their knowledge and understanding with regard to the needs of their specific participants.

- Familiarity with the environmental factors that exacerbate negative effects for individuals or specific populations, as well as the ability to recognise signs of physical distress, is highly recommended.

chapter 11

Evaluating and Appreciating
Safe Dance Practice

After reading this chapter you should be able to do the following:

- Recognise and understand the importance of evaluation.
- Identify what should be evaluated, why it needs to be done and when to do it.
- Record your evaluation for future reference.

Evaluation is an integral part of good practice, and most dance teacher training courses will encourage dance leaders to examine the effectiveness of their own strategies in delivering dance material. Evaluation means to assess the value of something. It is by successful evaluation that dance leaders can reflect on their practice in order to improve. The difficulty arises in knowing exactly what to evaluate, when to evaluate and how to do it. Often evaluation is rightly used to reflect on the learning experience of the participants, yet it is just as important for dance leaders to evaluate their knowledge and application of safe practice, as well as that of their dancers, to support healthy progression for all involved. Evaluation should not be associated with injury occurrence alone, such as reflecting on whether or not the injury could have been avoided. Instead it should be a frequent process undertaken in order to prevent ill-being of self and others. A good teacher is usually a safe teacher, but analysis of the physiological, psychological and environmental components of practice, outlined in the several previous chapters, leads to enhanced dance wellness along with successful learning experiences. Dance leaders should therefore be ready and able to appraise their application of safe practice along with their pedagogical delivery.

REASONS TO EVALUATE REGULARLY

With so many interrelated components of safe practice, it is difficult to incorporate every aspect all of the time. Thorough and frequent evaluation can support a review of safe practice principles and the extent to which each of these are being effectively applied to dance sessions. While it is sometimes seen as superfluous or perhaps over-cautious, evaluation should be a normal part of the working process, and should be conducted regularly. Dance leaders should critically reflect on and honestly appraise aspects of their practice that naturally follow safe practice principles, as well as identify areas that are in conflict with these principles and then seek out strategies for improving them. Evaluating dance sessions in this way will help dance leaders perform quality assurance for their own practice. It will result in an improved experience and working environment for dancers, a decreased risk of injury and an increased likelihood of enhanced performance potential. Evaluation also highlights the importance and value of careful planning. Having different options and potential modifications at the ready, as well as being in control of their own material, will increase dance leaders' ability to offer instant adaptations as necessary. Busking through a session (an unprepared, on-the-spot decision on the arrangement of activities) is unlikely to be conducive to safe practice unless leaders are extremely experienced and are confident with their ability to delve into their repertoire of delivery as the need arises without negatively affecting their participants.

WHAT AND WHEN TO EVALUATE

Evaluation should take place frequently, since ongoing monitoring ensures that safe practice remains current and responsive to changing needs of dance leaders and participants alike. It can be seen as a preparation for activity (what is done before the session) and a subsequent appraisal of the session itself. Before the session, the evalu-

Attention to safe practice and awareness of risk factors supports choreographic creativity, effective rehearsal and optimum performance. Dance leaders can get the best from their sessions and their dancers by planning appropriately and regularly evaluating their methods and strategies.

ation should focus on the status of the environment to ascertain whether it is supportive of the planned session, for example, the floor surface, the temperature and ventilation, access to first aid and ice, the dance leader's professional preparation (holding relevant insurance, completion of risk assessments) as well as whether appropriate clothing and footwear guidelines are upheld. Following the dance session, the degree to which these factors were managed can be assessed. For example, was the environment left in an appropriate state? Were any pre-identified risk factors managed properly? Did the leader follow up with any individual participants on the status of their health, injury and recovery? Observations such as these should be addressed immediately in readiness for the subsequent session.

Evaluation is also a reflective activity in which dance leaders will ideally take time to look back on their session and take note of, and remedy where possible, any shortfalls. Individual dance leaders are encouraged to examine and assess their own understanding and application of safe practice principles with relation to the content of their sessions, following an individual session or as a periodic self-monitoring activity to maintain awareness of safe practice as contexts and job roles change. By acknowledging areas that require improved application or greater depth of knowledge and understanding, leaders can consistently enhance their application of safe practice and get the best from their sessions. For example, following the session, the leader might note whether any important elements were missing: Were necessary strengthening exercises omitted? Did the session promote lateral bias by performing certain exercises on only one side due to time constraints? Further strategic and systematic evaluation can take place at more dispersed intervals, for example, to consider updates on content in response to the development of the group and its changing needs. Depending on the amount of dance delivery and contact time, monthly, termly, or seasonally should suffice.

HOW TO EVALUATE

The most effective method is to film the dance session from time to time or to invite a colleague with safe dance knowledge to observe and provide feedback. By using these strategies dance leaders can regularly review their application of safe practice and set targets for improving relevant aspects for future sessions, as well as identify where gaps in knowledge and application may occur.

Evaluation can also be a two-way process. In many educational environments it is common practice for students to formally evaluate the effectiveness of the teaching provided in order for the institution to evidence good practice or perhaps to flag up areas that can be addressed to enhance the student experience. This appraisal usually centres on delivery and resource provision, and it is frequently done through online surveys or other monitoring procedures. Independent dance leaders could also consider asking their participants for feedback, formally or informally. Leaders could give out an end-of-course or end-of-year questionnaire, asking pertinent questions that might help them see their safe dance practice objectively, for example, 'Do you feel that the material in the class was delivered at an appropriate level to provide a challenge without contributing to risk or injury?' or 'Were you given enough personal information and feedback to help you work correctly?' With adult participants, these viewpoints can give leaders a good overview of the strengths of their sessions and can also pinpoint areas that they could modify if necessary. For children and young people, an informal chat at the end of the year to round up their experience might provide information on whether they felt comfortable with their learning environment and enjoyed their activities. Although in the main parents are not usually present during sessions, their viewpoint can also be requested. For example, they might be asked if their child experiences undue fatigue or has any pain following the dance activity, especially if this regularly presents in a specific joint or muscle group. However, it also must be stressed that the leader should not be swayed by parents who wish their child to progress further and more quickly if this is not appropriate. Ultimately, dance leaders will have the expertise to make sound judgments, and two-way feedback will simply serve to refine their safe practice.

As a monitoring tool, a safe dance practice checklist is a quick and easy reminder to help dance leaders focus on the factors that they could consider. The sample checklist in figure 11.1 provides guidelines on what needs to be addressed with regard to the dance environment before and after the dance session. In addition, details of how to conduct a risk assessment can be found both in chapter 1 and appendix C. Some of the questions to be addressed in advance may only need to be asked once, for example, when assessing and beginning to work in a new space, while others will need ongoing appraisal. With more experience and familiarity with a particular environment and context, some of the checklist elements can become more intuitive than formal. However, it is recommended that dance leaders regularly conduct a check on all aspects of safe practice to ensure consistency of provision. If the answer to any of the questions is no, then the dance leader can instigate a mediating plan of action that supports future safe practice.

In addition to the practical checklist, the personal practice evaluation form (figure 11.2) suggests aspects of safe practice that relate to personal delivery, for example, commenting on content and strategies that integrate safe practice principles. This can be productively used in conjunction with a formal lesson or teaching plan if necessary. Using a version or template of the safe dance practice checklist and the personal evaluation form to keep on file can provide evidence of ongoing commitment to safe practice, thereby ensuring peace of mind for dance leaders and their participants, as well as evidencing to parents, guardians and employers that the dance activity is delivered considerately and safely.

Apart from the dance leader's evaluation, dance managers responsible for training, education and the organisation of dance activities should also ask the following questions in order to support general safe dance practice and assist their employees in observing recommendations:

- Do the studio spaces and facilities meet the latest safe practice recommendations? If not, why not? How soon can this be rectified? What mediating factors can be put into place in the meantime, and whose responsibility is it to ensure these are followed?

- Are my staff members up to date with relevant policies that support safe dance practice, both in terms of national regulations and our individual policies and guidelines?

- If my staff members are teaching a specific population group, such as young people, elderly dancers and participants with learning or physical disabilities, do they know the specific and unique safe practice requirements and potential risks associated with that group of participants?
- Are there any further continuing professional development or continuing professional education (CPD/CPE) opportunities that my staff could complete in order to make sure that they are fully aware of how to deliver safe and effective dance sessions?
- Are first aid kits provided and are ice or cool packs accessible?
- Are enough members of staff trained in first aid?

FIGURE 11.1
SAFE DANCE PRACTICE CHECKLIST

Safe practice factors to check before conducting a dance session:

- ☐ Is the environment appropriate for the dance activity (e.g., size, flooring, temperature and ventilation)?
- ☐ Is the space or environment clear of any hazards?
- ☐ Has a risk assessment been completed if necessary?
- ☐ Is there access to drinking water?
- ☐ Is there a first aid box readily available?
- ☐ Is there access to ice or cool packs?
- ☐ Are all props and equipment safe for use?
- ☐ Am I aware of relevant policies related to my place of delivery (for example, safeguarding policy or accident and injury policy)?
- ☐ Am I appropriately insured?
- ☐ Do I know what to do if an injury occurs?
- ☐ Have I identified any dancers that may need modifications during the session?

Safe practice factors to consider following the dance session:

- ☐ Did I conduct a health and injury check that allowed me to identify specific dancers, then adapt material for these participants if necessary?
- ☐ Were all dancers dressed appropriately and all personal effects removed?
- ☐ Did I wear appropriate clothing and footwear for safe practice?
- ☐ Were potential risk factors, identified before the session, effectively managed?
- ☐ If any injury occurred during the session, was I able to follow recommended procedures confidently?
- ☐ Have I documented any injuries in accordance with specific requirements?
- ☐ Did I check with the dancers who needed modifications to gauge any subsequent effects?
- ☐ Did I leave the space in an appropriate and safe state in preparation for the next user?

FIGURE 11.2
PERSONAL PRACTICE EVALUATION FORM

Name:	Date:	Session:
Factors to evaluate	**Comments**	**Response and action**
Warm-up and cool down • Do I understand how to prepare my dancers and help them to recover from my sessions through my awareness of physiological recommendations? • Were the dancers warm enough and effectively prepared for this session? • Did I leave enough time for an effective cool-down, including activities that brought the body gradually towards a resting state? • Did I address my own warm-up and cool-down?		
Alignment • Am I able to communicate the genre-specific alignment and techniques effectively to ensure safe and effective learning and practice? • Could I confidently address the specific alignment issues of the dancers in the group to ensure efficient execution? • Do I know how to deal with alignment anomalies and how to avoid setting unrealistic expectations?		
Sequencing and progression • Did I plan my session, considering physiological progression, with enough variations to allow for adaptations as necessary? • Did the session progress at the most suitable pace and speed for the group's ability and skill level, ensuring the body was effectively and logically prepared for each exercise or activity? • Do I understand the most appropriate way to include different types of stretching in my session to reduce injury risk?		
Rest and recovery • Did I include suitable opportunities for rest periods within the session and between sessions if applicable? • Am I able to provide appropriate advice regarding preparation for and recovery from the session, for example, by suggesting additional warm-up and cool-down activities, rest, and nutrition strategies to support my activity? • Do I understand how to construct sessions that are healthy and safe in their demands and the effects these have over time?		
Nutrition and hydration • Am I able to advise on nutrition and hydration before and after the session? • Did I include and direct sufficient fluid replacement breaks, depending on the level of activity and the specific environmental factors affecting temperature?		

Factors to evaluate	Comments	Response and action
Injury • Did I understand the effects of injury or illness on dancers in my session? • Was I able to offer strategies for helping dancers participate in the session safely or give appropriate advice on non-participation? • Did I understand and communicate the potential risk factors for injury within my genre-specific practice and take steps to minimise any negative effects through adaptation or by considering the necessity of repetition?		
Psychological factors • Was the learning environment supportive for the group through appropriate use of instructional techniques, language and tone? • Was my feedback delivered in appropriate manner, acknowledging the efforts of the dancer and taking account of safeguarding issues and equal opportunities? • Did my delivery strategies create a dominantly task-involving learning environment that encouraged all participants?		
Individual differences • Were the selected activities and adaptations age- and ability-appropriate? • Did I offer a range of adaptations for those who needed them, for example, dancers with specific health conditions or those recovering from injury? • Did I observe and respond to the individual needs of my learners enough?		
Observation and feedback • Was I able to observe my participants effectively and make sound judgements on their technical ability based on my physiological knowledge? • Did I explain style-specific requirements properly in terms of safety as well as aesthetics and by using clear demonstration and language? • Did I effectively communicate the need for safe execution to my participants?		

Benefits of Evaluation

∎ ∎ ∎

Eve is a popular and respected dance teacher working in an institution that trains young pre-professional dancers. She is very experienced, with a successful performing career behind her. Eve has been teaching for many years but previously has had no reason to re-evaluate her methods because they seem to be successful, and she is usually satisfied with how her dancers develop. Aisha is starting work at the same institution. She also enjoyed a short performing career and then began to study for a formal teaching qualification. Her course involved learning how to reflect on and evaluate different delivery strategies. This is Aisha's first job as a teacher. As part of her induction to the new role, Eve is asked to mentor her.

This process involves peer review, with Eve sitting in on Aisha's sessions and vice versa. Aisha is impressed with Eve's anatomical knowledge and ability to give specific feedback, as well as her capacity to respond to student's stylistic questions clearly and directly. Her teaching style is encouraging and positive, and the students are motivated and enthusiastic. The students say that they are especially tired that day following a late rehearsal the previous evening, so Eve tells them she will reduce the repetitions of their exercises so as not to increase their fatigue. One dancer is not able to jump in class, and Aisha notes that Eve gives this dancer some specific lower-leg strengthening exercises to practise at the side while the other dancers are working on their jump technique.

Aisha shows Eve her lesson plan and a safe practice checklist prior to her session. Eve observes that Aisha conducts a general health and injury check for all the students at the beginning of the class. Unfortunately, one student injures himself by landing badly from a jump. After managing the injury with advice on PRICED*, at the end of the session Aisha also seeks out the accident/injury book to document the incident. Because she is nervous, Aisha later tells Eve that she became distracted by trying to making an impression on the students, and feels that she did not leave enough time to practise her final sequence equally on both sides or for an effective cooldown. She reflects that she will need to address this in her subsequent session.

Through these exchanges, Eve realises that she rarely questions her own practice in this way. She finds out more about the value of safe practice, and is introduced to aspects of delivery that she simply had not encountered or considered before. Aisha realises the value of knowing her dancers and the importance of gaining expertise and understanding in order to be able to adapt the teaching material on the spot, deviating from preconceived plans if necessary. The two teachers learn from each other, and each resolves to refresh and develop their strategies by increasing their genre-specific knowledge and continuing thoughtful preparation and evaluation.

* Information on the PRICED procedure for injury management can be found in chapter 9.

CONTINUING PROFESSIONAL DEVELOPMENT AND EDUCATION

Updating their knowledge regularly through personal research, further education and sharing practice is a positive step for dance leaders. Continuing professional development and education (CPD/CPE) helps them to maintain their currency, stay ahead of variations in choreographic fashions and, most importantly, prepare and protect their dancers so that they can play a part in developing the art form with capable and healthy bodies.

Dancers and dance leaders can now examine and discuss their safe practice in many ways, with online communities dedicated to specific genres, as well as blogs and forums to share experiences and queries. As mentioned throughout the book, unfortunately this advice is not always reliable or fully informed, but nevertheless it is positive that members of the dance community are asking pertinent questions and looking for definitive answers. The notion of safe practice is thankfully more established, and as the profession continues to tighten up regulation for dance leader accreditation and qualifications, those who can demonstrate their awareness of the relevant principles can gain added recognition and status. Many dance teacher associations have introduced safe practice education, and are both recommending and requiring their members to develop their understanding in this area. Readers should check with their regional and national branches on the types of activities offered.

Worldwide, dance organisations are promoting health and well-being for the dancer and providing lectures, workshops and events that focus on physiology, psychology and injury prevention. Several international organisations are actively promoting and supporting safe and healthy dance practice knowledge. Safe in Dance International (SiDI) offers endorsement of safe dance practice CPD/CPE through the Healthy Dance Practice Certificate and the Healthy Dancer Certificate. The International Association for Dance Medicine and Science (IADMS) provides free resource papers and teachers' bulletins to support the development of many topics associated with safe practice. Similarly, Ausdance, Dance UK and the Healthier Dancer Programme, Dance/USA, Tanzmedizin Deutschland (tamed) and the National Centre for the Performing Arts (NCPA) all distribute information and initiate ways to develop healthy dance education. These are only a small number of examples. For a more comprehensive list of relevant organisations, see appendix F.

SUMMARY

Regular evaluation is essential in order to help dance leaders spot gaps in professional knowledge and apply new information to ongoing practice. It is also valuable for highlighting areas of accomplishment as well areas that warrant improvement, helping dance leaders identify aspects of their practice that require updated or increased knowledge or expertise, as well as to consolidate their strengths. It can be used to select and target professional qualifications or relevant courses, encourage and direct independent reading and research or simply to set and reset goals to support planning and implementation. Evaluation is a professional expectation, but in the case of safe dance practice, it represents a significant contribution to the maintenance of the health and well-being of dancers.

Looking back on the various chapters, *Safe Dance Practice* has aimed to address the wide-ranging principles of safe practice by drawing on developments within dance medicine and science research. The information contained in each chapter is comprehensive, but the take-home messages can be clearly distilled: It is the successful application of the research that will provide the means for making it pertinent and realistic.

The authors are all deeply committed to spreading the message that safe practice should be an integral part of dancing, and hope that all dancers and dance leaders can familiarise themselves with the concepts presented in this book. The aim is to stimulate dancers and dance leaders to see safe practice as much more than health and safety, but rather as a framework for the well-being of all those who participate, one that can significantly improve the quality, performance and potential of the dance experience.

KEY POINTS

- Evaluation is key to reflection on and improvement of the application of safe dance practice.
- All dance leaders should frequently evaluate their individual dance sessions and the effects of these sessions over time.
- Regular documentation of the evaluation process can evidence commitment to safe dance practice.
- Continuing professional development/education (CPD/CPE) can encourage dance leaders to keep up to date with safe dance research, which will be of benefit to their own practice and to their participants.

Health Questionnaire

Name: _____   Class in which taking part: _____

DOB: _____

Questions	Information
How much and what type of exercise do you do currently?	
Do you have any disabilities, learning difficulties or special needs?	
Do you have any illnesses, conditions, or injuries that may affect you during dance exercise (e.g. muscle or joint problems, asthma, diabetes or permanent/long term medical issues such as arthritis, high blood pressure) or have you had a recent pregnancy?	
If yes, have you consulted your medical practitioner for advice on participation?	
Do you need to take any medication before, during or after exercise?	
Do you have any relevant allergies?	

I declare that the information I have given above is correct to the best of my knowledge. I understand that I am taking part in dance activity at my own risk.

Date: _____

Signature: _____

Please provide a phone number for next of kin to be used in an emergency.

Contact phone number: _____

Equal Opportunities Statement

- It is my policy to treat all participants equally and fairly regardless of their age, race or ethnicity, culture, religion or beliefs, socio-economic status, gender, sexual orientation, physical ability or disability, or learning ability.

- I will appreciate the diversity of each individual and ensure that all involved in my dance sessions are able to participate to their full potential and without disadvantage.

- I am committed to creating a safe and inclusive working environment that is free from any discrimination and in which all participants feel respected and valued.

- I will ensure that no participant experiences any harassment or bullying during the dance session of which I am in charge.

- I will take positive action to counteract and report any discrimination or harassment that occurs during my session.

- I will regularly review my practice to ensure that the above aims are consistently met.

Signed: _____

Date: _____

From E. Quin, S. Rafferty and C. Tomlinson, 2015, *Safe dance practice*. (Champaign, IL: Human Kinetics).

Risk Assessment Form

ACTIVITY	LOCATION	RISK ASSESSED BY (name)		DATE

IDENTIFY RISK Type of hazard	PEOPLE Who is at risk and why	LIKELIHOOD Low (L), medium (M), or high (H) risk	CONTROL Measures already in place	ACTION Further measures necessary	ACTION Responsibility (name)	DATE Action completed

REVIEW OF RISK Type of hazard	LIKELIHOOD Low (L), medium (M), or high (H) risk	RESULTS OF ACTION AND CONTROL MEASURES	REVIEWER (name)	DATE

Accident Report Form

ACCIDENT REPORT   Details of injured dancer:

Name _____   Date of Birth _____

Contact telephone number _____

Date and time of accident or injury _____

Location in which injury occurred _____

Nature of injury (where on body) _____

Specific activity during which injury occurred _____

_____

Identifiable risk factors in injury onset _____

_____

Person in charge of session _____

Name of witness to injury _____

Name of first-aider, if attending _____

Treatment on site or injury protocols administered _____

_____

Action taken (e.g., emergency services called, dancer sent home) _____

_____

Next of kin contacted _____

Any further details _____

FOLLOW-UP

Diagnosis by health professional _____

Recommendations _____

Date: _____   Name: _____

Signature: _____

From E. Quin, S. Rafferty and C. Tomlinson, 2015, *Safe dance practice*. (Champaign, IL: Human Kinetics).

Nutrition Intake Record

Name: _____ Date: _____ Date of birth: _____

Day	Breakfast	Snacks	Lunch	Snacks	Dinner	Snacks	Fluids	Workload log*
Monday								
Tuesday								
Wednesday								
Thursday								
Friday								
Saturday								
Sunday								
Notes (targets for improvements):								

From E. Quin, S. Rafferty and C. Tomlinson, 2015, *Safe dance practice*. (Champaign, IL: Human Kinetics).

*Number of dance/training sessions, total activity, workload intensity: low/medium/high.

Sources for Additional Information

Actsafe www.actsafe.ca

Artists' Health Alliance http://artistshealth.com

Arts Medicine Aotearoa New Zealand www.converge.org.nz/amanz

Arts Medicine France www.medecine-des-arts.com

Association Danse Médecine Recherche (ADMR) www.admrdanse.com

Association of Dance Professionals of Catalonia (APdC) www.dansacat.org

Ausdance www.ausdance.org.au

Australian Society for Performing Arts Healthcare (ASPAH) www.aspah.org.au

British Association for Performing Arts Medicine (BAPAM) www.bapam.org.uk

Dance Health Finland (DHF) www.dhf.fi

Dance UK www.danceuk.org

Dance USA www.danceusa.org

Dutch Dancer's Health Care Foundation (Stichting Gezondheidszorg voor Dansers, SGD) www.dansgezond.nl

Foundation for Community Dance www.communitydance.org.uk

Foundations for Excellence www.foundations-for-excellence.org

Harkness Centre for Dance Injuries www.med.nyu.edu/hjd/harkness

Institute for Dance Medicine (Fit for Dance) www.fitfordance.de

International Association for Dance Medicine & Science (IADMS) www.iadms.org

Italian Interdisciplinary Center for Performing Arts Medicine (CEIMArs) www.ceimars.it

National Institute of Dance Medicine and Science (NIDMS) www.nidms.co.uk

National Centre Performing Arts (NCPA) http://ncpa.eu

The Rudolph Nureyev Foundation Medical Website www.nureyev-medical.org

Safe in Dance International (SiDI) http://safeindance.com

Tanzmedizin Deutschland e. V (tamed) [website in German] www.tamed.de

Total Health Care for Artists Japan www.artists-care.com

abdominal separation—The normal separation of the two bands of the rectus abdominis muscle into right and left halves during pregnancy so that the abdomen can accommodate the growing baby. Also known as diastasis recti.

accident and injury report—A documented record of an unplanned incident that involves injury to an individual. Often a legal requirement, it provides details of the potential causes and therefore helps to identify possible risks of the incident reoccurring.

active rest—When people remain active at a less strenuous level than their normal training intensity.

adolescence—A transitional period of growth and development occurring in young people as they progress to adulthood, occurring between the ages of 12 and 18 years.

aerobic—Activity of low to moderate intensity that requires the use of oxygen.

agonist—A muscle that, when it contracts, is directly involved in causing specific movements.

allergic asthma—Common type of respiratory condition that causes breathing difficulties, initiated as a reaction to airborne allergens.

Alzheimer's disease—A brain disease that is the most common cause of dementia.

amenorrhoea—Absence of menstrual periods.

anaerobic—Activity of high intensity that is short lasting without the use of oxygen.

antagonist—A muscle that works in a functional partnership with the agonist muscle, relaxing to oppose the agonist's contraction in order to control the joint movement.

autonomic nervous system—A division of the nervous system that is responsible for the involuntary inner functioning of the human body (digestion, regulation of pulse and breathing rates).

autonomy—Having a sense of choice, ownership or control over one's actions; being able to contribute to one's dance experiences.

balance—Ability to sustain a position or movement with stability and control.

ballistic stretch—Stretching with a bouncing momentum.

basic psychological needs—An encompassing term for the three psychological needs considered essential for human well-being: autonomy, competency and relatedness or belonging.

belonging (relatedness)—Having a sense of connection to the group and the activity of dancing.

body mass index (BMI)—Measurement of body fat percentage using sex, height and weight.

bone health—Overall health and strength within the bones.

bony landmarks—Prominent and observable skeletal reference points on the body, used to make judgments on its alignment.

bronchoconstriction—The tightening and narrowing of the muscles of the airways in the lungs that occurs during an asthma attack, affecting the ability to breathe effectively.

bronchodilation—The process by which the tubes in the lungs are expanded, increasing airflow.

burnout—A result of overtraining causing the dancer to discontinue dance activity.

calorie—Molecule of energy provided by food.

carbohydrate—Organic compound found in foods that provides energy for the working muscles and general bodily functions.

cardiorespiratory fitness—Ability to use the circulatory and respiratory systems during physical activity.

cardiovascular stimulation—An increase of the pulse by stimulating the heart rate through gentle, full-body movement.

centre of mass—A point in the body where its combined mass is concentrated and around which the body is balanced.

child protection—Procedures to prevent minors (usually under 18 years of age) against harm, exploitation and possible abuse.

codes of conduct—Rules or professional guidelines that outline recommended values or principles that refer to ethics, responsibilities and behaviour.

competency—Having a sense of being capable; able to partake in and progress within dance activity.

complete rest—When physical activity is ceased for a period of time.

concentric contraction—The resulting action in a muscle when its fibres shorten to affect joint movement.

constructive rest—Rest during relaxation or meditation where imagery is used to assist the release of stress or tension.

core stability—The muscular control required to maintain stability of the spine and trunk.

cues—Shorthand directions that contain information relevant to the technique, quality and performance of dance movement.

delayed-onset muscle soreness (DOMS)—Pain and stiffness in the muscles appearing 24 to 48 hours following activity, usually as a result of unaccustomed or particularly intense activity which has overemphasised the use of eccentric muscle contractions

dementia—A condition that occurs when the brain is damaged by diseases that can result in memory loss, confusion and difficulties with problem-solving and language.

diabetes mellitus—A group of diseases affecting the body's ability to produce or regulate insulin when breaking down food, resulting in abnormally high blood sugar levels.

discrimination—Prejudicial, unfair or less favourable treatment of one group or category of people with specific characteristics.

distributed practice—Work periods are spaced out to provide regular rest periods within and in between physical training sessions.

documentation of injury—The process of recording the details of an injury occurrence in the workplace in order to accurately communicate the potential causes and actual effects to safeguard future health and comply with legal requirements.

duty of care—A legal or moral obligation towards an individual or group of people that upholds standards to ensure their health, safety and well-being.

dynamic stretching—A mode of stretching that takes the limb through its full range of motion utilising gravity and momentum to support a gradual increase in range of motion.

dyslexia—A specific learning disability, most commonly associated with problems in processing linguistic information.

dyspraxia—A motor learning disability that impairs the organisation of movement skills, resulting in decreased perceptual abilities and co-ordination.

early childhood—A developmental period determined by age and encompassing children between the ages of 0 and 8 years.

eccentric contraction—Also referred to paradoxically as a 'lengthening contraction', this is the controlled elongation of a muscle to produce tension against resistance.

ego-involving—A term referring to a less-than-ideal psychological environment in which dancers are frequently and publicly compared with others, talent or ability is preferred over effort and mistakes are considered unacceptable.

equal opportunities—A policy or legislation to ensure that people of any race, religion, sexual orienta-tion, disability or age are not subjected to biased treatment.

exercise-induced asthma—A condition in which inflammation and narrowing of the airways is triggered by the increased breathing rate during physical exertion.

extrinsic risk factors—External, situational characteristics that can increase the likelihood of injury occurring.

FAST (face, arm, speech, time)—An acronym to assess early signs of stroke, in which case emergency help may be needed.

fast glycolytic system—Also known as anaerobic system used for high-intensity activity.

fast stretching—A mode of stretching similar to brief static stretching that holds a stretch for just 5 or 6 seconds. Often used as a quick recovery stretch.

fat—A nutrient found in foods providing a high calorie source for the body.

fatigue—Exhaustion of the mind or body.

first aid—Immediate assistance or care given to a person suffering from a sudden illness or injury.

FITTE (frequency, intensity, time, type and enjoyment)—Five principles used for physical training and development.

forces—Loads that interact with the body (pushing or pulling) and exert an influence on it to cause physical change.

fracture—The breaking or cracking of a bone.

goal setting—A systematic process that identifies clear targets, as well as methods for accomplishing these targets.

HARM—An acronym relating the actions to avoid in the initial management of an acute injury (heat, alcohol, running, massage).

health and safety—Measures put in place to control risks and prevent harm.

hearing impairment—A partial or total inability to hear.

hydration—The absorption of water, essential for life and athletic performance.

hyperglycaemia—A condition, associated with diabetes, in which excessive amounts of sugar are found in the blood.

hypermobility—Some or all of the body's joints are able to move in excess of normal range of motion.

hypoglycaemia—A condition, associated with regulation of diabetes, in which abnormally low levels of sugar are present in the blood.

ill-being—General negative state of being that emphasises both physical and psychological ill-health.

imagery (as a psychological skill)—A systematic use of mental imaging as a means to psychologically prepare for dance activity (e.g., audition, competition, performance), to practise movement material or to promote or reinforce positive feelings associated with a dance situation.

individuality—Training designed to suit the needs of the individual.

instructional feedback—Provision of feedback that is constructive rather than judgemental and that provides guidance on what and how to improve.

insulin—A hormone, made by the body in the pancreas, that regulates the metabolism and utilisation of sugar.

insurance—A form of risk management in which an individual or business can pay a premium to protect themselves from liability or to be compensated for adverse situations.

intrinsic risk factors—Injuries that can occur from personal actions that are under an individual's control.

isometric contraction—A static activation of the muscle that produces no change to the muscle length or angle at the joint.

joint mobilisation—A section of a general warm-up that focuses on the mobilisation of the joints through their available range of motion, promoting the shock-absorbing qualities of synovial fluid.

ketones—Substances that are made in the body when it breaks down fat for energy; in diabetics, their presence indicates prolonged high blood sugar or insulin deficiency.

kinesiology—The scientific analysis of human movement.

kinetic chain—A combination of joints and body segments (bones, muscles and nerves) arranged in a successive sequence.

kyphosis—Displacement of the thoracic spine in which the upper back rounds forward more than usual.

lateral bias—Involves motor actions that either dominate or focus on one particular side of the body, resulting in asymmetry.

learning difficulties—A group of neurological disabilities that affect the way that information is typically learned and processed.

liability—An obligation or legal responsibility towards a person or situation.

line of gravity—An imaginary line that runs vertically downwards through the body from the head via the centre of gravity to the base of support (contact with the ground). It determines the distribution of body weight to create stability and balance.

lordosis—Increased curvature of the spine in which the lower back curves inward or arches more than usual.

macronutrient—Fundamental energy sources broken down into carbohydrate, fat and protein.

massed practice—Work periods that provide little or no rest in between.

middle childhood—A developmental period determined by age and encompassing children between the ages of 8 and 12 years.

micronutrient—Small nutrients needed for bodily function, broken down into vitamins and minerals.

minerals—Essential micronutrients found in foods which are needed for good health

motor learning—The process of learning and improving new movement actions through practice and experience.

movement descriptors—Anatomical terms of reference to describe the range of movement of joints and their position in space.

muscle flexibility and joint mobility (MFJM)—The combination of stretchiness of the muscle fibres with the available range of motion permitted by the joint capsule.

muscle imbalance—Difference or deficits in the strength and length of muscles as a result of inefficient use, faulty posture, strain or injury.

muscle lengthening—A section of a general warm-up that focuses on lengthening the muscle fibres through controlled and brief static or dynamic stretches.

muscle power—Ability to apply explosive force with muscle strength.

muscle strength—Maximum force of a muscle or muscle group.

muscle synergy—How muscles work together, adopting roles that complement each other in order to create stability and promote refined and efficient movement.

muscular endurance—The muscle's ability to work for a continued period of time.

neutraliser muscle—The role a muscle can take to cancel out excessive movement initiated by the contraction of other primary muscles.

neutral pelvis—The position of the pelvis in its most anatomically efficient placement, maintaining the integrity of the natural spinal curves.

non-allergic asthma—Respiratory condition in which increased sensitivity to environmental irritants causes breathing difficulties.

nutrition—The nutrients (food) that we eat and the science of how the body uses these nutrients.

osteoarthritis—A condition where the surface of the joints becomes damaged.

osteoporosis—A condition causing the bones to become brittle, weak and fragile.

overload—A positive physiological adaptation through an increase in training load.

overtraining—When the body experiences a decrease in performance ability and high levels of fatigue for no apparent medical reason, often as a result of an increase in training load and a decrease in effective recovery.

overuse injury—Damage to a body part that occurs as a result of repetitive and cumulative trauma. Symptoms may remain present over time or reoccur. Alternative term: chronic injury.

Parkinson's disease—A condition in which part of the brain becomes progressively damaged.

pedagogy—The science, art and practice of teaching and learning.

perinatal period—Relates to the time encompassing pregnancy, childbirth and postnatal periods, from approximately the 20th week of pregnancy to 4 weeks after the birth.

periodization—Systematic planning of a training schedule or year that incorporates decreases in training intensity following periods of increased intensity.

physical disability—A disability that involves a total or partial loss of bodily functions or a body part, resulting in a limitation in one's mobility or dexterity.

planes of movement—Imaginary axes that three-dimensionally trisect the body, used to describe the relationship of the body to space and provide reference terms for orientation.

plumb line—A vertical straight line used as a marker for assessing ideal alignment and posture, as well as the degree of deviation from the ideal.

posture—The relationship between the skeleton and the muscles, as well as different body parts, that determines how the body maintains its functional alignment.

PRICED—An acronym relating the actions recommended for the initial management of an acute injury (prevention/protection, rest, ice, compression, elevation, diagnosis).

primary injury—Damage occurring to the body as a direct result of the initial cause.

proprioception—A dancer's kinaesthetic awareness of his or her body in space.

proprioceptive neuromuscular facilitation (PNF)—A type of stretch that involves an isometric activation (maximum contraction, with no movement) of the muscle fibres, against a resistance, followed by a passive repositioning of the limb.

protein—A nutrient found in food made up of amino acids.

psychological environment—The social and emotional environment that is created by the people present, largely influenced by the leader of the group.

psychological skills—Systematic strategies that can support a positive healthy attitude such as goal setting, self-talk, imagery and relaxation.

pulse raiser—A section of a general warm-up that gradually increases the heart rate through full-body movements.

pulse reducer—A section of a cool-down that gradually decreases the heart rate through full-body movements.

range of motion (ROM)—The movement available at a specific joint, when accounting for muscle flexibility and joint mobility (MFJM).

rehabilitation—The process to facilitate recovery from injury through co-ordinated medical treatment and training plans to bring the body back to its normal pre-injury condition.

relaxation (as a psychological skill)—A strategic approach to balancing activity and training with systematic rest in order to support well-being.

relaxin—A hormone released in pregnancy by the placenta to increase pliancy in the tissues that will facilitate the birth process.

repetition—In dance terms, the reiteration of particular movements in order to improve their execution.

rheumatoid arthritis—An autoimmune disease that causes inflammation of the joints.

risk assessment—An examination of potential hazards to determine the potential for accidents to arise and to formulate strategies to minimise the possible threat to safety.

recovery—A process of healing physiologically or psychologically.

rest—To cease or decrease activity to allow the mind or body to recover.

reversibility—When physical training gains are lost or diminished due to not being maintained.

safeguarding—The protection of children, young people and vulnerable adults from neglect or abuse and the provision of appropriate care to ensure their well-being.

scoliosis—A condition affecting the spine that results in abnormal lateral curvatures.

secondary injury—Damage occurring to the body as a consequence of the related effects of a primary injury.

self-talk—The internal voice of one's thoughts and feelings, which can have negative or positive implications.

skill acquisition—The process of learning and developing a new ability through instruction and practice.

somatic nervous system—A division of the nervous system that transmits messages to and from the musculoskeletal system and the central nervous system. It is responsible for voluntary movement.

somatic practice—Gentle activity focusing on reducing unnecessary or inefficient muscular effort while refining proprioceptive awareness.

specificity—Exercises designed to be specific to meet a dancer's training aims.

sprung floor—A floor system constructed to provide increased shock absorption and reduce stress on the body to minimise injury and improve performance in physical activity.

stabiliser muscle—The role a muscle can take to immobilize and control a body part, preventing or limiting unnecessary joint action when another body part is moving.

stability—The ability to resist displacement, maintaining control and balance in static and dynamic alignment.

static stretching—Assuming a stretch position and holding it for a period of time.

stretch-shortening cycle—The cycle of brief eccentric or lengthening contraction prior to a concentric or shortening muscular contraction, such as in the plié prior to a jump.

stroke—A medical condition that occurs when part of the blood supply to the brain is cut off.

synovial fluid—A viscous fluid that lubricates and provides shock absorption for the synovial joints.

synovial joint—The most common and most mobile type of joint in the body, bound by a capsule that contains a viscous and lubricating (synovial) fluid.

tapering—A reduction in training in order for the body's energy reserves to be fully replenished immediately before performance or competition.

task-involving—A term referring to a positive psychological environment, which includes attributes such as acknowledgment of individual effort, promotion of self-referenced progression and an understanding that mistakes are part of the learning process.

total hip replacement—Surgery is performed to replace the head of the femur and resurface the hip socket in the pelvis.

touch—Physical contact between two or more individuals that enables the transfer of sensory information, correction or feedback in order to improve learning and skills. Also necessary for sharing body weight in dance choreography.

transfer of learning—Occurs when skills learned in one situation or context are successfully applied in another.

traumatic injury—Damage to the body as a result of force or impact due to external causes. Alternative term: acute injury.

trimesters—The three stages of pregnancy, dividing the 40 weeks of gestation, each of which involves specific developments of the growing foetus and maternal changes and symptoms.

turnout—The position of the legs, used in many dance forms that involves outward (external) rotation of the legs, initiated from the hip joint.

type 1 diabetes—A lifelong disease, usually diagnosed in children or young adults and requiring constant management, in which the body's own immune system destroys insulin-producing cells, causing blood sugar levels to rise higher than normal.

type 2 diabetes—A disease, often manifesting first in adults or with increasing age, in which the body cells do not react to insulin effectively (insulin resistance). Requires management of blood sugar levels.

vascular dementia—A common form of dementia caused by reduced blood flow to the brain.

visual impairment—A loss of sight that cannot be fully corrected using glasses or contact lenses.

vitamins—Essential micronutrients found in foods (and supplementation) which are either fat or water soluble

well-being—General positive state of being that encompasses both physical and psychological health.

References

Introduction

Aujla, I. (2012). *Commitment, adherence and dropout among young talented dancers: A multidisciplinary mixed methods investigation* (Unpublished doctoral thesis). City University, London, England. Retrieved from http://openaccess.city.ac.uk/1948/1/Aujla%2C_Imogen.pdf

Burns, S., & Harrison, S. (2009). *Dance mapping: A window on dance, 2004-2008*. London, England: Arts Council England.

Laws, H. (2005). *Fit to dance 2*. London, England: Dance UK.

Mainwaring, L., Krasnow, D., & Kerr, G. (2001). And the dance goes on: Psychological impact of injury. *Journal of Dance Medicine and Science, 5*(4), 105-115.

Mosston, M., & Ashworth, S. (2002). *Teaching physical education* (5th ed.). San Francisco, CA: B. Cummings.

National Dance Education Organisation. (2014). Statistics: General US education and dance education. Retrieved from http://www.ndeo.org/content.aspx?page_id=22&club_id=893257&module_id=55774

Russell, J.A. (2013). Preventing dance injuries: Current perspectives. *Open Access Journal of Sports Medicine, 2013*(4), 199-210. Retrieved from http://www.dovepress.com/getfile.php?fileID=17662

Shah, S., Weiss, D.S., & Burchette, R.J. (2012). Injuries in professional modern dancers: Incidence, risk factors, and management. *Journal of Dance Medicine and Science, 16*(1), 17-25.

Warburton, E.C. (2008). Beyond steps: The need for pedagogical knowledge in dance. *Journal of Dance Education, 8*(1), 7-12.

Chapter 1

American College of Sports Medicine (ACSM). (2000). ACSM's guidelines for exercise testing and prescription (6th ed.). Philadelphia, PA: Lippincott Williams & Wilkins.

Ausaid. (2013). Child protection policy. Retrieved from http://aid.dfat.gov.au/aidissues/childprotection/Documents/ausaid-child-protection-policy.pdf

Ausdance. (2012). Safe dance floors: Fact sheet 7. Retrieved from http://ausdance.org.au/articles/details/safe-dance-floors

Ausport. (2014). Images of children. Retrieved from http://www.ausport.gov.au/supporting/clubs/resource_library/managing_risks/child_protection/guidelines_use_children_images/images_of_children

Bramley, I. (2002). *Dance teaching essentials*. London, England: Dance UK.

British Association of Advisors & Lecturers in Physical Education (BAALPE). (2004). *Safe practice in physical education and school sport*. Leeds, England: Coachwise Solutions.

Carlon, B. (2011). First aid kit 101. Retrieved from http://www.dance-teacher.com/2011/05/first-aid-101/

Council for Dance Education and Training (CDET). (n.d.). Children and vulnerable adult protection policy guidelines. Retrieved from http://www.cdet.org.uk/images/RA_SUpporting_Documentation/Children_and_Vulnerable_Adult_Protection_Policy_Guidelines.doc

Coussins, C. (2009). Lacing highland dance shoes. Retrieved from http://www.dance.net/topic/8154542/1/Highland/Lacing-Highland-Dance-Shoes-A-note-from-Craig-Coussins-Hullachan.html

Dance UK. (2011). Industry standards for dancers' health, well being and performance. Retrieved from http://www.danceuk.org/healthier-dancer-programme/industry-standards/

Equity. (2011). Guide to health and safety. Retrieved from http://www.equity.org.uk/documents/equity-guide-to-health-and-safety/

Evans, R.W, Evans, R.I., & and Carvajal, S. (1998). Survey of injuries among West End performers. *Occupational & Environmental Medicine, 55*, 585-559.

Exercise, Movement and Dance Partnership. (n.d.). Child protection policies and procedures. Retrieved from http://www.keepfit.org.uk/about-us/ethics-welfare/childprotectionpolicy.pdf

Foley, M. (1998). Dance floors: Dance UK information sheet 6. London, England: Dance UK.

Fong Yan, A., Hiller, C., Smith, R., & Vanwanseele, B. (2011). Effect of footwear on dancers: A systematic review. *Journal of Dance Medicine and Science, 15* (2), 86-92.

Foundation for Community Dance. (2013). Introduction to risk assessment for community dance practitioners. Retrieved from http://www.communitydance.org.uk/public/31286/Introduction%20to%20risk%20assessment.pdf

Foundation for Community Dance. (2014). Definitions, values and codes of conduct. Retrieved from http://www.communitydance.org.uk/member-services/professional-code-of-conduct/the-document.html

Harlequin. (2013). Harlequin's range of ballet barres. Retrieved from http://uk.harlequinfloors.com/uploads/1/downloads/Harlequin_ballet_barres_and_brackets_leaflet_-_UK_-_LR.pdf

Health and Safety Executive. (2011). Five steps to risk assessment. Retrieved from http://www.equity.org.uk/documents/hse-five-steps-to-risk-assessment/

Hernandez, B.L., & Strickland, G. (2005). School health and safety: Standards for dance education and dance in physical education. *Joperd 76*(4), 20-25.

Hopper, L., Allen, N., Wyon, M., Alderson, J.A., Elliott, B.C., & Ackland, T.R. (2014). Dance floor mechanical properties and dancer injuries in a touring ballet company. *Journal of Science and Medicine in Sport, 17*(1), 29-33.

Howard, P. (2009, January 26). How modern law makes us powerless. Retrieved from http://online.wsj.com/news/articles/SB123293018734014067?mg=reno64-wsj&url=http%3A%2F%2Fonline.wsj.com%2Farticle%2FSB123293018734014067.html

Huwyler, J.S. (1999). *The dancer's body: A medical perspective on dance training.* McLean,VA: International Medical Publishing

Kenney, L.W., Wilmore, J.H., & Costill, D.L. (2012). *Physiology of sport and exercise* (5th ed.). Champaign, IL: Human Kinetics

Laws, K. (2008). *Physics and the art of dance: Understanding movement* (2nd ed.). Oxford, England: Oxford University Press.

Love Our Children USA. (2014). Retrieved from www.loveourchildrenusa.org/

Motta-Valencia, K. (2006). Dance related injury. *Physical Medicine and Rehabilitation Clinics of North America, 17*(3), 697-723.

National Dance Teachers Association (NDTA). (n.d.). Advice and information—Dance teachers insurance. Retrieved from http://www.ndta.org.uk/advice-information/dance-teachers-insurance/

National Network for Child Employment and Entertainment (NNCEE). (2014). Chaperone responsibilities. Retrieved from http://www.nncee.org.uk/legislation-employment-a-entertainment/chaperones/detailed-chaperones

National Society for the Prevention of Cruelty to Children (NSPCC). (2013). Using photographs of children for publication. Retrieved from http://www.nspcc.org.uk/search/?query=using+photographs+of+children+for+publication

Pappas, E., & Hagins, M. (2008). The effect of "raked" stages on standing postures on dancers. *Journal of Dance Medicine and Science, 12*(2), 54-58.

Pearson S.J. & Whitaker, A. (2012). Footwear in Classical Ballet A Study of Pressure Distribution and Related Foot Injury in the Adolescent Dancer. *Journal of Dance Medicine & Science. 16*(2): 51-56.

Royal Academy of Dance. (n.d.). Policy and procedures on safeguarding children and vulnerable adults. Retrieved from www.rad.org.uk/documents/about-docs/safeguarding-policy-nov13.pdf

Shell, C.G. (Ed.). (1984). *The dancer as athlete: The 1984 Olympic Scientific Congress proceedings, volume 8.* Champaign, IL: Human Kinetics.

Sport England. (2008). Fitness and exercise spaces. Retrieved from http://www.sportengland.org/media/32375/Fitness-and-exercise-spaces.pdf

Stein, C.J., Kinney, S.A., McCrystal, T., Carew, E.A., Bottino, N.M., Meehan, W.P., & Micheli, L.J. (2014). Dance-related concussion: A case series. *Journal of Dance Medicine and Science, 18*(2), 53-61.

Theatre Safety Committee. (2007). Guidelines for the use of rakes in theatre productions. Retrieved from http://www.equity.org.uk/documents/theatre-safety-committee-rakes-in-theatrical-productions/

UNICEF. (n.d.). The Convention on the rights of the child: Guiding principles. Retrieved from http://www.unicef.org/crc/files/Guiding_Principles.pdf

Wanke, E., Mill, H., Wanke, A., Davenport, J., Koch, F., & Gronenberg, D.A. (2012). Dance floors as injury risk. *Medical Problems of Performing Artists, 27*(3), 137-142.

Whitlam, P. (2012). Safe practice in physical education and sport (8th ed.). The Association for Physical Education (afPE), Leeds: Coachwise Ltd

Youth Dance England. (2013). Dance spaces. Retrieved from http://www.yde.org.uk/main.cfm?type=DS

Chapter 2

Alderson, J., Hopper, L., Elliott, B., & Ackland, T. (2009). Risk factors for lower back injury in male dancers performing ballet lifts. *Journal of Dance Medicine and Science, 13*(3), 83-89.

Batson, G., and International Association of Dance Medicine and Science (IADMS). (2008). Proprioception. IADMS resource paper: Retrieved from http://c.ymcdn.com/sites/www.iadms.org/resource/resmgr/resource_papers/proprioception.pdf

Berardi, G. (2005). *Finding balance; Fitness, training and health for a lifetime in dance* (2nd ed.). New York, NY: Routledge.

Champion, L.M., & Chatfield, S.J. (2008). Measurement of turnout in dance research: A critical review.

Journal of Dance Medicine and Science, 12(4), 121-135.

Clippinger, K. (2016). *Dance anatomy and kinesiology.* Champaign, IL: Human Kinetics.

Conti, S.F., & Wong, Y.S. (2001). Foot and ankle injuries in the dancer. *Journal of Dance Medicine and Science, 5*(2), 43-50.

Deckert, J., Barry, S., & Welsh, T.M. (2007). Analysis of pelvic alignment in university ballet majors. *Journal of Dance Medicine and Science, 11*(4), 110-117.

Deckert, J. (2009). Improving pelvic alignment. *IADMS Bulletin for Teachers, Volume 1, Number 1*

De Oliveira Pezzan, P.A., João, S.M., Ribeiro, A.P., & Manfio, E.F. (2011). Postural assessment of lumbar lordosis and pelvic alignment angles in adolescent users and nonusers of high-heeled shoes. *Journal of Manipulative and Physiological Therapeutics, 34*(9), 614-621.

Franklin, E. (2004). Conditioning for dance. Champaign, IL: Human Kinetics

Gamboian, N., Chatfield, S.J., Woollacott, M.H., Barr, S., & Klug, G.A. (1999). Effect of dance technique training and somatic training on pelvic tilt and lumbar lordosis alignment during quiet stance and dynamic dance movement. *Journal of Dance Medicine and Science, 3*(1), 5-14.

Grieg, V. (1994). *Inside ballet technique.* Hightstown, NJ: Princeton.

Grossman, G. (2003). Measuring dancer's active and passive turnout. *Journal of Dance Medicine and Science, 7*(2), 49-55.

Haas, J.G. (2010). *Dance anatomy.* Champaign, IL: Human Kinetics.

Hamill, J., & Knutzen, K.M. (2009). *Biomechanical basis of human movement* (3rd ed.). Philadelphia, PA: Lippincott, Williams and Wilkins.

Heyward, V.H., and Gibson, A. (2014). *Advanced fitness assessment and exercise prescription* (7th ed.). Champaign, IL: Human Kinetics.

Holt, K.M., Welsh, T.M., & Speights, J.A. (2011). Within-subject analysis of the effects of remote cueing on pelvic alignment in dancers. *Journal of Dance Medicine and Science, 15*(1), 15-22.

Hong, W.H., Lee, Y.H., Lin, Y.H., Tang, S.F., & Chen, H.C. (2013). Effect of shoe heel height and total-contact insert on muscle loading and foot stability while walking. *Foot & Ankle International, 34*(2), 273-281.

Howse, J., & McCormack, M. (2009). *Anatomy, dance technique and injury prevention* (4th ed.). London, England: A & C Black.

Huwyler, J.S. (1999). *The dancer's body: A medical perspective on dance training.* McLean, VA: International Medical Publishing.

Ives, J.C. (2014). *Motor behavior: Connecting mind and body for optimal performance.* Philadelphia, PA: Lippincott, Williams & Wilkins.

Kassing, G., & Jay, D.M. (2003). *Dance teaching methods and curriculum design.* Champaign, IL: Human Kinetics.

Kay, L. (2008). Heel appeal. Retrieved from http://www.dancemagazine.com/issues/December-2008/Heel-Appeal

Kendall, F., McCreary, E., & Provance, P. (1983). *Muscles: Testing and function* (4th ed.). Philadelphia, PA: Lippincott, Williams & Wilkins.

Kenney, L.W., Wilmore, J.H., & Costill, D.L. (2012). *Physiology of sport and exercise* (5th ed.). Champaign, IL: Human Kinetics

Kline, J.B., Krauss, J.R., Maher, S.F., & Xianggui, Q. (2013). Core strength using a combination of home exercises and a dynamic sling system for the management of low back pain in pre-professional ballet dancers: A case series. *Journal of Dance Medicine and Science, 17*(1), 24-33.

Koutedakis, Y., & Sharp, N.C.C. (1999). *The fit and healthy dancer.* Chichester, England: John Wiley & Sons.

Krasnow, D., Monasterio, R., & Chatfield, S.J. (2001). Emerging concepts of posture and alignment. *Medical Problems of Performing Artists, 16*(1), 8-16.

Lamberty, R. (2011). Dancing posture. Retrieved from http://www.rounddancing.net/dance/articles/guest/lamberty/dancingposture.html

Lee, C., Jeong, E., & Freivalds, A. (2001). Biomechanical effect of wearing high heeled shoes. *International Journal of Industrial Ergonomics, 28,* 321-326.

Leiderbach, M. (2010). Perspectives on dance science rehabilitation: Understanding whole body mechanics and four key principles of motor control as a basis for healthy movement. *Journal of Dance Medicine and Science, 14*(3), 114-124.

Lewton- Brain, P. (2009). Dynamic alignment, performance enhancement and the demi-plié. *The IADMS Bulletin for Teachers, 1*(2), 8-10.

Luttgens, K., & Hamilton, N. (1997). *Kinesiology.* Boston, MA: McGraw Hill.

McCabe, T.R., Hopkins, J.T., Vehrs, P., & O'Draper, D.O. (2013). Contributions of muscle fatigue to a neuromuscular neck injury in female ballroom dancers. *Medical Problems of Performing Artists, 28*(2), 84-90.

McCormack, M. (2010). Teaching the hypermobile dancer. *The IADMS Bulletin for Teachers, 2* (1), 5-8.

McMeekin, J., Tully, E., Nattrass, C., & Stillman, B. (2002). The effect of spinal and pelvic posture and mobility on back pain in young dancers and non-dancers. *Journal of Dance Medicine and Science, 6*(3), 79-86.

Mika, A., Oleksy, L., Mika, P., Marchewka, A., & Clark, B.C. (2012). The effect of walking in high- and low-heeled shoes on erector spinae activity and pelvis kinematics during gait. *American Journal of Physical Medicine and Rehabilitation, 91*(5), 425-434.

Opila, K.A., Wagner, S.S., Schiowitz, S., & Chen, J. (1988). Postural alignment in barefoot and high-heeled stance. *Spine (Phila Pa 1976), 13*(5), 542-547.

Pedersen, E., & Wilmerding, E. (1998). Injury profiles of student and professional student flamenco dancers. *Journal of Dance Medicine and Science, 2*, 108-114.

Philips, C. (2005). Stability in dance training. *Journal of Dance Medicine and Science, 9*(1), 24-28.

Potts, J.C., & Irrgang, J.J. (2001). Principles of rehabilitation of lower extremity injuries in dancers. *Journal of Dance Medicine and Science, 5*(2), 51-61.

Safety & Health in Arts Production & Entertainment (SHAPE). (2002). Preventing musculoskeletal injury (MSI) for musicians and dancers: A resource guide. Retrieved from http://www.musicianshealth.co.uk/injuriesmusiciansdancers.pdf

Sevey Fitt, S. (1996). *Dance kinesiology* (2nd ed.). New York, NY: Schirmer.

Simmel, L. (2014). *Dance medicine in practice: Anatomy, injury prevention, training.* London, England: Routledge.

Smith, J. (2005). *Structural bodywork.* Edinburgh, Scotland: Elsevier, Churchill Livingstone

Smith, J. (2009). Moving beyond the neutral spine: Stabilizing the dancer with lumbar extension dysfunction. *Journal of Dance Medicine and Science, 13*(3), 73-82.

Solomon, R., Solomon, J., & Minton, S. (2005). *Preventing dance injuries* (2nd ed.). Champaign, IL: Human Kinetics.

Staugaard-Jones, J. (2011). *The anatomy of exercise and movement for the study of dance, Pilates, sports and yoga.* Chichester, England: Lotus Publishing.

Sweigard, L. (2013). Human movement potential: Its ideokinetic facilitation. Oregon, USA: Allegro Editions.

Watkins, A., & Clarkson, P.M. (1990). *Dancing longer, dancing stronger: A dancer's guide to improving technique and preventing injury.* Princeton, NJ: Dance Horizons.

Welsh, T.M., Rodriguez, M., Beare, L.W., Barton, B., & Judge, T. (2008). Assessing turnout in university dancers. *Journal of Dance Medicine and Science, 12*(4), 136-141.

Welsh, T. (2009). *Conditioning for dancers.* Gainsville, FL: University Press of Florida.

Whiting, W.C., & Rugg, S. (2006). *Dynatomy: Dynamic human anatomy.* Champaign, IL: Human Kinetics.

Wilmerding, V., Gurney, B., & Torres, V. (2003). The effect of positive heel inclination on posture in young children training in flamenco dance. *Journal of Dance Medicine and Science, 7*(3), 85-90.

Chapter 3

Alter, M.J. (2004). *Science of flexibility* (3rd ed.). Champaign, IL: Human Kinetics.

American College of Sports Medicine (ACSM). (2014). *ACSM's guidelines for exercise testing and prescription* (9th ed.). Philadelphia, PA: Lippincott, Williams & Wilkins.

Borg, G. (1982). Psychophysical bases of perceived exertion. *Medicine and Science in Sports and Exercise, 14*(5), 377-381.

Cheung, K., Hume, P.A., & Maxwell, L. (2003). Delayed onset muscle soreness treatment strategies and performance factors. *Sports Medicine, 33*(2), 145-164.

Critchfield, B. (2011). *Stretching for dancers.* International Association of Dance Medicine and Science (IADMS) resource paper. Retrieved from www.iadms.org

Harris, J., & Elbourne, J. (2002). *Warming up and cooling down: Practical ideas for ensuring a fun and beneficial exercise experience* (2nd ed.). Champaign, IL: Human Kinetics.

Herbert, R.D., & Gabriel, M. (2002). Effects of stretching before and after exercising on muscle soreness and risk of injury: Systematic review. *British Medical Journal, 325*, 1-5.

Herbert, R.D., de Noronha, M., & Kamper, S.J. (2011). Stretching to prevent or reduce muscle soreness after exercise (review). *Cochrane Database of Systematic Reviews, 2011*(7), CD004577.

Hindle, K.B., Whitcomb, T.J., Briggs, W.O., & Hong, J. (2012). Proprioceptive neuromuscular facilitation (PNF): Its mechanisms and effects on range of motion and muscular function. *Journal of Human Kinetics: Section II- Exercise Physiology & Sports Medicine, 31*, 105-113. doi: 10.2478/v10078-012-0011-y

Kallerud, H., & Gleeson, N. (2013). Effects of stretching on performances involving stretch-shortening cycles. *Sports Medicine, 43*, 733-750. doi: 10.1007/s40279-013-0053-x

Koutedakis, Y., Pacy, P.J., Carson, R.J., & Dick, F. (1997). Health and fitness in professional dancers. *Medical Problems of Performing Artists, 12*(1), 23-27.

Laws, H. (2005). *Fit to Dance 2*. London, England: Dance UK

Laws, H., Marsh, C., & Wyon, M. (2006). *Warming up and cooling down*. Dance UK information sheet. London, England: Dance UK.

Malliou, P., Rokka, S., Beneka, A., Mavridis, G., & Godolias, G. (2007). Reducing risk of injury due to warm up and cool down in dance aerobic instructors. *Journal of Back and Musculoskeletal Rehabilitation, 20*, 29-35.

McArdle, W.D., Katch, F.I., & Katch, V.L. (2014). *Exercise physiology: Energy, nutrition and human performance* (8th ed.). Philadelphia, PA: Lippincott Williams & Wilkins.

Morrin, N., & Redding, E. (2013). Acute effects of warm-up stretch protocols on balance, vertical jump height, and range of motion in dancers. *Journal of Dance Medicine and Science, 17*(1), 34-40.

Murphy, J.R., Di Santo, M.C., Alkanani, T., & Behm, D.G. (2010). Aerobic activity before and following short-duration static stretching improves range of motion and performance vs. a traditional warm-up. *Applied Physiology Nutrition and Metabolism, 35*, 679-690.

Olsen, O., Sjøhaug, M., van Beekvelt, M., & Mork, P.J. (2012). The effect of warm-up and cool-down exercise on delayed onset muscle soreness in the quadriceps muscle: A randomized controlled trial. *Journal of Human Kinetics. Section II- Exercise Physiology & Sports Medicine, 35*, 59-68. doi: 10.2478/v10078-012-0079-4

Rey, E., Lago-Peñas, C., Casáis, L., & Lago-Ballesteros, J. (2012). The effect of immediate post-training active and passive recovery interventions on anaerobic performance and lower limb flexibility in professional soccer players. *Journal of Human Kinetics, 31*, 121-129. doi: 10.2478/v10078-012-0013-9 121

Samson, M., Button, D.C., Chaouachi, A., & Behm, D.G. (2012). Effects of dynamic and static stretching within general and activity specific warm-up protocols. *Journal of Sports Science and Medicine, 11*, 279-285.

Subasi, S.S., Gelecek, N., & Aksakoglu, G. (2008). Effects of different warm-up periods on knee proprioception and balance in healthy young individuals. *Journal of Sport Rehabilitation, 17*, 186-205.

Taylor, J., & Taylor, C. (1995). *Psychology of dance*. Champaign, IL: Human Kinetics.

Tsolakis, C., & Bogdanis, G.C. (2012). Acute effects of two different warm-up protocols on flexibility and lower limb explosive performance in male and female high level athletes. *Journal of Sports Science and Medicine, 11*, 669-675.

Volianitis, S., Koutedakis, Y., & Carson, R.J. (2001). Warm-up: A brief review. *Journal of Dance Medicine and Science, 5*(3), 75-81.

Wyon, M. (2010b). Stretching for dance. *The IADMS Bulletin for Teachers, 2*(1), 1-12.

Young, W.B., & Behm, D.G. (2003). Effects of running, static stretching and practice jumps on explosive force production and jumping performance. *Journal of Sports Medicine and Physical Fitness, 43*, 21-27.

Chapter 4

Alter, M.J. (2004). *Science of flexibility*. Champaign, IL: Human Kinetics.

Ambegaonkar, J.P., Caswell, S., Winchester, J.B., Caswell, A.A., & Andre, M.J. (2012). Upper-body muscular endurance in female university-level modern dancer: A pilot study. *Journal of Dance Medicine and Science, 16*(1), 3-7.

Angioi, M. Metsios, G,S. Twitchett, E. Koutedakis, Y & Wyon, M. (2009). Association between selected physical fitness parameters and aesthetic competence in contemporary dancers. *Journal of Dance Medicine and Science, 13 (4), 115-123.*

Batson, G., & the International Association of Dance Medicine and Science (IADMS). (2008). Proprioception. Retrieved from www.iadms.org/associations/2991/files/info/proprioception.pdf

Berardi, G. (2005). *Finding balance: Fitness, training and health for a lifetime in dance* (2nd ed.). London, England: Routledge.

Borg, G. (1982). Psychophysical bases of perceived exertion. *Medicine and Science in Sports and Exercise, 14*(5): 377-81.

Bronner, S., & Ojofeitimi, S. (2010). Injuries in hip hop dancers: Breakers, Poppers, Lockers, and New Schoolers. *International Association for Dance Medicine & Science 20th Annual Meeting Abstracts*, 14-15.

Brown, A.C., Wells, T.J., Schade, M.L., Smith, D.L., & Fehling, P.C. (2007). Effects of plyometric training versus traditional weight training on strength, power, and aesthetic jumping ability in female collegiate dancers. *Journal of Dance Medicine and Science, 11*(2), 38-44.

Clippinger, K. (2016). *Dance anatomy and kinesiology*. Champaign, IL: Human Kinetics.

Clippinger-Robertson, K. (1990). Flexibility in dance. *Kinesiology and Medicine for Dance, 12*(2), 1-13.

Critchfield, B., & the International Association of Dance Medicine and Science (IADMS). (2011). Stretching for dancers. Retrieved from http://c.ymcdn.com/sites/www.iadms.org/resource/resmgr/resource_papers/stretching.pdf

Deighan, M. A. (2005). Flexibility in dance. *Journal of Dance Medicine and Science, 9*(1), 13-17.

Dunn, J. (2014). Stretching healthy: A primer for dancers. Retrieved from www.4dancers.org/2014/02/stretching-healthy-a-primer-for-dancers/

Franklin, E. (2012). *Conditioning for dance.* Champaign, IL: Human Kinetics.

Grossman, G., & Wilmerding, M.V. (2000). The effect of conditioning on the height of dancer's extension in à la seconde. *Journal of Dance Medicine and Science, 4*(4), 117-121.

Haas, J.G. (2010). *Dance anatomy.* Champaign, IL: Human Kinetics.

Hamilton, L. (2009). *The dancer's way.* New York, NY: St. Martin's Griffin.

Harley, Y.X.R. Gibson, A St C. Harley, E. Lambert, M, I. Vaughan, C & Noakes, T,D. (2002) Quadriceps strength and jumping efficiency in dancers. *Journal of Dance Medicine and Science. 6*(3), 87-94.

Hindle, K.B., Whitcomb, T.J., Briggs, W.O., & Hong, J. (2012). Proprioceptive neuromuscular facilitation (PNF): Its mechanisms and effects on range of motion and muscular function. *Journal of Human Kinetics: Section II—Exercise Physiology & Sports Medicine, 31,* 105-113. doi: 10.2478/v10078-012-0011-y

Hewitt, T,E. Stroup, A,L. Nance T.A & Noyes F,R. (1996). Plyometric training in female athletes. Decreased impact forces and increased hamstring torques. *America Journal of Sports Medicine. 24 960 765-773.*

Heyward, V.H., and Gibson, A. (2014). *Advanced fitness assessment and exercise prescription* (7th ed.). Champaign, IL: Human Kinetics.

Howse, J., & McCormick, M. (2009). *Anatomy dance technique and injury prevention* (4th ed.). London, England: A & C Black.

Irvine, S., Redding, E., Rafferty, S., & the International Association of Dance Medicine and Science (IADMS). (2011). Dance fitness. Retrieved from www.iadms.org/associations/2991/files/info/dance_fitness.pdf

Kassing, G., & Jay, D.M. (2003). *Dance teaching methods and curriculum design.* Champaign, IL: Human Kinetics.

Kenney, W.L., Wilmore, J.H., & Costill, D.L. (2012). *Physiology of sport and exercise* (5th ed.). Champaign, IL: Human Kinetics.

Kirkendall, D.T., & Calabrese, L.H. (1983). Physiological aspects of dance. *Clinics in Sports Medicine, 2*(3), 525-536.

Kline, J.B., Krauss, J.R., Maher, S.F., & Qu, X. (2013). Core strength training using a combination of home exercises and a dynamic sling system for the management of low back pain in pre-professional ballet dancers. *Journal of Dance Medicine and Science, 17*(1), 24-33.

Koutedakis, Y. (2005). Fitness for Dance. *Journal of Dance Medicine and Science, 9*(1), 5-6.

Koutedakis, Y., & Sharp, N.C.C. (1999). *The fit and healthy dancer.* London, England: Wiley.

Koutedakis, Y., Stavropoulos-Kalinoglou, A., & Metsios, G. (2005). The significance of muscular strength in dance. *Journal of Dance Medicine and Science, 9*(1), 29-34.

Kozai, A. (2012). Supplementary muscular fitness training for dancers. *Journal of Dance Medicine and Science, 4*(1), 15-17.

Krasnow, D. (1997). C-I training: The merger of conditioning and imagery as an alternative training methodology for dance. *Medical Problems of Performing Artists, 12*(1), 3-8.

Krasnow, D., & Deveau, J. (2011). *Conditioning with imagery for dancers.* Toronto, ON: Thompson.

Malkogeorgos, A., Zaggelidou, E., Zaggelidis, G., & Christos, G. (2013). Physiological elements required by dancers. *Sport Science Review, 22*(5/6), 343-368.

McAtee, R.E., & Charland, J. (2013). *Facilitated stretching* (4th ed.). Champaign, IL: Human Kinetics.

Murgia, C. (2013). Overuse, fatigue and injury: Neurological, psychological, physiological and clinical aspects. *Journal of Dance Medicine and Science, 17*(2), 51-52.

Phillips, C. (2005). Stability in dance training. *Journal of Dance Medicine and Science, 9*(1), 24-28.

Rafferty, S. (2010). Considerations for integrating fitness into dance training. *Journal of Dance Medicine and Science, 14*(2), 45-49.

Redding, E., & Wyon, M. (2003). Strengths and weaknesses of current methods for evaluating the aerobic power of dancers. *Journal of Dance Medicine and Science, 7*(1), 10-16.

Rodrigues-Krause, J., Santos Cunha, G., Lima Alberton, C., Follmer, B., Krause, M., & Reischak-Oliveira, A. (2014). Oxygen consumption and heart rate responses to isolated ballet exercise sets. *Journal of Dance Medicine and Science, 18*(3), 99-105.

Twitchett, E., Brodrick, A., Neville, A.M., Koutedakis, Y., Angioni, M., & Wyon, M. (2010). Does physical fitness affect injury occurrence and time loss due to injury in elite vocational ballet students? *Journal of Dance Medicine and Science, 14*(1), 26-31.

Twitchett, E., Nevill, A., Angioi, M., Koutedakis, Y., & Wyon. M. (2011). Development, validity, and reliability of a ballet specific aerobic fitness test. *Journal of Dance Medicine and Science, 15*(3), 123-127.

Wyon, M. (2005). Cardiorespiratory training for dancers. *Journal of Dance Medicine and Science, 9*(1), 7-12.

Wyon, M. (2010b). Stretching for dance. *IADMS Bulletin for Dance Teachers, 2*(1), 9-12.

Chapter 5

Amans, D. (2013). *Age and dancing: Older people and community dance practice.* London, England: Palgrave Macmillan.

Batson, G. (2009). The somatic practice of intentional rest in dance education—Preliminary steps towards a method of study. *Journal of Dance and Somatic Practices, 1*(2), 177-197.

Batson, G., & Schwartz, R.E. (2007). Revisiting the value of somatic education in dance training through an inquiry into practice schedules. *Journal of Dance Education, 7*(2), 47-56.

Bompa, T.O. (2009). *Periodization: Theory and methodology of training* (5th ed.). Champaign, IL: Human Kinetics.

Brinson, P., & Dick, F. (1996). *Fit to Dance?* London, England: Calouste Gulbenkain Foundation.

Budgett, R. (1990). Overtraining syndrome. *British Journal of Sports Medicine, 24*(4), 231-236.

Budgett, R. (1998). Fatigue and underperformance in athletes: The overtraining syndrome. *British Journal of Sports Medicine, 32,* 101-110.

Clarkson, P.M., & Skrinar, M. (Eds.). (1988). *Science of dance training.* Champaign, IL: Human Kinetics.

Franklin, E. (2013). *Dance imagery for technique and performance* (2nd ed.). Champaign, IL: Human Kinetics.

Kenney, W.L., Wilmore, J.H., & Costill, D.L. (2012). *Physiology of sport and exercise* (5th ed.). Champaign, IL: Human Kinetics.

Kent, M. (1996). *The Oxford dictionary of sports science and medicine.* New York, NY: Oxford University Press.

Kentta, G., Hassmen, P., & Raglin, J. (2001). Training practices and overtraining syndrome in Swedish age-group athletes. *International Journal of Sports Medicine, 22*(6), 460-465.

Koutedakis, Y. (2000). Burnout in dance: A physiological point of view. *Journal of Dance Medicine and Science, 4*(4), 122-127.

Koutedakis, Y., Budgett, R., & Faulmann, L. (1990). Rest and underperforming elite competitors. *The British Journal of Sports Medicine, 24*(4), 248-252.

Koutedakis, Y., Myszkewycz, L., Soulas, D., Papapostolou, I., & Sharp, N.N.C. (1999). The effects of rest and subsequent training on selected physiological parameters in professional female classical dancers. *International Journal of Sports Medicine, 20,* 379-383.

Kreider, R.B., Fry, A.C., & O'Toole, M.L. (Eds.). (1998). *Training and overtraining in sport.* Champaign, IL: Human Kinetics.

Laws, H. (2005). *Fit to Dance 2.* London, England: Dance UK.

Liederbach, M., Schanfein, L., & Kremenic, I.J. (2013). What is known about the effect of fatigue on injury occurrence among dancers? *Journal of Dance Medicine and Science, 17*(3), 101-108.

Manchester, R.A. (2012). The role of rest. *Medical Problems of Performing Artists,* 121-122.

Murgia, C. (2010). Overuse, fatigue and injury: Neurological, psychological, and clinical aspects. *Journal of Dance Medicine and Science, 17*(2), 51-52.

Murgia, C. (2013). Overuse, tissue fatigue and injuries. *Journal of Dance Medicine and Science, 17*(3), 92-100.

The National Sleep Foundation. (n.d.). How much sleep do we really need? Retrieved from http://www.sleepfoundation.org/article/how-sleep-works/how-much-sleep-do-we-really-need

Schmidt, R.A., & Lee, T. (2011). *Motor control and learning: A behavioural emphasis* (5th ed.). Champaign, IL: Human Kinetics.

Twitchett, E., Angioi, M., Koutedakis, Y., & Wyon, M. (2010). The demands of a working day among female professional ballet dancers. *Journal of Dance Medicine and Science, 14*(4), 127-132.

Williams, J. (2006). *Applied sport psychology: Personal growth to peak performance.* New York, NY: McGraw-Hill.

Wyon, M. (2010a). Preparing to perform: Periodization in dance. *Journal of Dance Medicine and Science, 14*(2), 67-72.

Chapter 6

Alter, M.J. (2004). *Science of flexibility* (3rd ed.). Champaign, IL: Human Kinetics.

Barnes, M.A., Krasnow, D., Tupling, S.J., & Thomas, M. (2000). Knee rotation in classical dancers during the grand plié. *Medical Problems of Performing Artists, 15*(4), 140-147.

Batson, G. (2009). The somatic practice of intentional rest in dance education—Preliminary steps towards a method of study. *Journal of Dance and Somatic Practices, 1*(2), 177-197.

Batson, G., & Schwarz, R.E. (2007). Revisiting the value of somatic education in dance training through an inquiry into practice schedules. *Journal of Dance Education, 7* (2), 47-56.

Berardi, G. (2005). *Finding balance: Fitness, training and health for a lifetime in dance* (2nd ed.). London, England: Routledge.

Bompa, T.O., & Haff, C.G. (2009). Periodization: Theory and methodology of training (5th ed.). Champaign, IL: Human Kinetics.

Clarkson, P.M., & Skrinar, M. (Eds.). (1988). *Science of dance training.* Champaign, IL: Human Kinetics.

Clippinger, K. (2016). *Dance anatomy and kinesiology.* Champaign, IL: Human Kinetics

Critchfield, B., & the International Association for Dance Medicine and Science (IADMS). (2012). Stretching for dancers. Retrieved from http://c.ymcdn.com/sites/www.iadms.org/resource/resmgr/resource_papers/stretching.pdf

Daniels, K. (2009). Teaching to the whole dancer: Synthesising pedagogy, anatomy and psychology. *IADMS Bulletin for Teachers, 1*(1), 8-10.

Dunn, J. (2014). Stretching healthy: A primer for dancers. Retrieved from www.4dancers.org/2014/02/stretching-healthy-a-primer-for-dancers/

Erkert, J. (2003). *Harnessing the wind: The art of teaching modern dance.* Champaign, IL: Human Kinetics.

Fitt, S. (1996). *Dance kinesiology* (2nd ed.). New York, NY: Schirmer.

Franklin, E. (2012). *Dynamic alignment through imagery* (2nd ed.). Champaign, IL: Human Kinetics.

Franklin, E. (2004). *Conditioning for dance.* Champaign, IL: Human Kinetics.

Gibbons, E. (2007). *Teaching dance: The spectrum of styles.* Bloomington, IN: AuthorHouse.

Gibbs, J., Appleton, J., & Appleton, R. (2007). Dyspraxia or developmental coordination disorder? Unravelling the enigma. *Archives of Disease in Childhood, 92*(6), 534-539.

Gray, J. (1989). *Dance instruction: Science applied to the art of movement.* Champaign, IL: Human Kinetics.

Grove, J., Main, L., & Sharp, L. (2013). Stressors, recovery processes and manifestations of training distress in dance. *Journal of Dance Medicine and Science, 17*(2), 70-78.

Haas, J. (2010). The importance of visualization. Retrieved from www.humankinetics.com/excerpts/excerpts/dance-imagery

Heyward, V.H., and Gibson, A. (2014). *Advanced fitness assessment and exercise prescription* (7th ed.). Champaign, IL: Human Kinetics.

Ives, J.C. (2014). *Motor behavior: Connecting mind and body for optimal performance.* Philadelphia, PA: Lippincott, Williams & Wilkins.

Kassing, G., & Jay, D.M. (2003). *Dance teaching methods and curriculum design.* Champaign, IL: Human Kinetics.

Kenney, L.W., Wilmore, J.H., & Costill, D.L. (2012). *Physiology of sport and exercise* (5th ed.). Champaign, IL: Human Kinetics.

Kimmerle, M., & Côté-Laurence, P. (2003). *Teaching dance skills: A motor learning and development approach.* Andover, NJ: J Michael Ryan.

Koutedakis, Y., & Sharp, N.C.C. (1999). *The fit and healthy dancer.* Chichester, England: John Wiley & Sons.

Krasnow, D.H., & Chatfield, S.J. (1996). Dance science and the dance technique class. *a* 162-172.

Krasnow, D., & Deveau, J. (2011). *Conditioning with imagery for dancers.* Toronto, ON: Thompson.

Lafortune, S. (2008). A classification of lifts in dance: Terminology and biomechanical principles. *Journal of Dance Education, 8*(1), 13-22.

Laws, H. (2005). *Fit to Dance 2.* London, England: Dance UK.

Mainwaring, L.M., & Krasnow, D. (2010). Teaching the dance class: Strategies to enhance skill acquisition, mastery and positive self-image. *Journal of Dance Education, 10*(1), 15-21.

Rafferty, S., & Wyon, M. (2006). Leadership behavior in dance: Application of the leadership scale for sports to dance technique teaching. *Journal of Dance Medicine and Science, 10*(1-2), 6-13.

Redding, E., & Wyon, M. (2003). Strengths and weaknesses of current methods for evaluating the aerobic power of dancers. *Journal of Dance Medicine and Science, 7*(1), 10-16.

Schmidt, R.A., & Lee, T. (2011). *Motor control and learning: A behavioral emphasis* (5th ed.). Champaign, IL: Human Kinetics.

Simmel, L. (2014). *Dance medicine in practice: Anatomy, injury prevention, training.* London, England: Routledge.

Welsh, T. (2009). *Conditioning for dancers.* Gainesville, FL: University Press of Florida.

White, J. (1996). *Teaching classical ballet.* Gainesville, FL: University Press of Florida.

Whiting, W.C., & Rugg, S. (2006). *Dynatomy: Dynamic human anatomy.* Champaign, IL: Human Kinetics.

Wilmerding, M.V., Krasnow, D., & the International Association for Dance Medicine and Science (IADMS). (2009). Motor learning and teaching dance. Retrieved from http://c.ymcdn.com/sites/www.iadms.org/resource/resmgr/resource_papers/motor_learning.pdf

Wyon, M. (2010 a). Preparing to perform: Periodization in dance. *Journal of Dance Medicine and Science, 14*(2), 67-72.

Wyon, M. (2010b). Stretching for dance. *IADMS Bulletin for Teachers, 2*(1), 9-12.

Wyon, M., & Koutedakis, Y. (2013). Muscular fatigue: Considerations for dance. *Journal of Dance Medicine and Science, 17*(2), 63-69.

Wyon, M., & Redding, E. (2005). Physiological monitoring of cardiorespiratory adaptations during rehearsal and performance of contemporary dance.

Journal of Strength and Conditioning Research, 19(3), 611-614.

Chapter 7

American College of Sports Medicine (ACSM). (2011). The female athlete triad. Retrieved from http://www.acsm.org/access-public-information/articles/2011/10/04/the-female-athlete-triad

Bean, A. (2009). *A complete guide to sports nutrition* (6th ed.). London, England: A & C Black.

Benson, J., Gillien, D.M., Bourdet, K., & Loosli, A.R. (1985). Inadequate nutrition and chronic calorie restriction in adolescent ballerinas. *The Physician and Sports Medicine, 13*(10), 79-90.

Brinson, P., & Dick, F. (2001). *Fit to dance?* London, England: Calouste Gulbenkian Foundation.

Burckhardt, P., Wynn, E., Krieg, M.A., Bagutti, C., & Faouzi, M. (2011). The effects of nutrition, puberty and dancing on bone density in adolescent ballet dancers. *Journal of Dance Medicine and Science, 15*(2), 51-60.

Challis, J. (2014). *Nutrition for dancers. Dance UK information sheet 12.* London, England: Dance UK.

Chartrand, D., & Chatfield, S. (2005). A critical review of the prevalence of secondary amenorrhea in ballet dancers. *Journal of Dance Medicine and Science, 9*(3&4), 74-80.

Clarkson, P.M. (1998). An overview of nutrition for female dancers. *Journal of Dance Medicine and Science, 2*(1), 32-39.

Clarkson, P., & the International Association for Dance Medicine and Science (IADMS). (2003). Nutrition fact sheet: Fueling the dancer. Retrieved from http://c.ymcdn.com/sites/www.iadms.org/resource/resmgr/imported/info/dance_nutrition.pdf

Dare, A., & O'Donavon, M. (2009). *A practical guide to child nutrition* (3rd ed.). Cheltenham, England: Nelson Thornes.

De Souza, M.J., Nattiv, A., Joy, E., Misra, M., Williams, N.I., Mallinson, R.J., . . . &

Doyal-Lucas, A.F., & Davy, B.M. (2011). Development and evaluation of an educational intervention program for pre-professional adolescent ballet dancers: Nutrition for optimal performance. *Journal of Dance Medicine and Science, 15*(2), 65-75.

Dyke, S. (2001). *Your body, your risk.* London, England: Dance UK.

Frieson, K.J., Rozeneck, R., Clippinger, K., Gunter, K., Russo, A.C., & Sklar, S.E. (2011). *Journal of Dance Medicine and Science, 15*(1), 31-36.

Frusztajer, N.T., Dhuper, S., Warren, M.P., Brooks-Gunn, J., & Fox, R.P. (1990). Nutrition and the incidence of stress fractures in ballet dancers.

The American Journal of Clinical Nutrition, 51(5), 779-783.

Hamilton, L.H. (2008). *The dancer's way.* New York, NY: St. Martin's Griffin.

Harvard School of Public Health (HSPH). (2015). Healthy Beverage Guidelines. Retrieved from http://www.hsph.harvard.edu/nutritionsource/healthy-drinks-full-story 2015/01/04

International Osteoporosis Foundation. (2014). Calcium. Retrieved from www.iofbonehealth.org/calcium

Kadel, N.J., Donaldson-Fletcher, E.A., Gerberg, L.F., & Micheli, L.J. (2005). Anthropometric measurements of young ballet dancers: Examining body composition, puberty, flexibility, and joint range of motion in comparison with non-dancer controls. *Journal of Dance Medicine and Science 9*(3&4), 84-90.

Koutedakis, Y. (1996). The male and female professional dance: Aspects related to injuries, fitness and nutrition. *Dance Research, 14,* 76-93.

Koutedakis, Y., & Sharp, N.C.C. (1999). *The fit and healthy dancer.* London, England: John Wiley & Sons.

Laws, H. (2005). *Fit to Dance 2.* London, England: Dance UK.

Lopez-Varela, S., Montero, A., Chandra, R.K., & Marcos, A. (1999). Effect of the diet on the nutritional status of ballerinas: Immunologic markers [article in Spanish]. *Nutrición Hospitalaria Sep-Oct 14*(5), 184-190.

Mastin, Z. (2009). *Nutrition for the dancer.* Binsted, England: Dance Books.

Mastin, Z. (2014) *Fluid for dancers. Dance UK information sheet 15.* London, England: Dance UK.

Micheli, L.J., Cassella, M., Faigenbaum, A.D., Southwick, H., & Ho, V. (2005). Preseason to postseason changes in body composition of professional ballet dancers. *Journal of Dance Medicine and Science, 9*(2), 56-59.

Mihajlovic, B., & Mijatov, S. (2003). Body composition analysis in ballet dancers. *Med Pregl, 56*(11-12), 579-583.

Nazarewicz, R., & Babicz-Zielinska, E. (2000). Selected indices of nutritional status and food habits among young ballet dancers [Article in Polish]. *Rocz Pantsw Zakl Hig, 51*(4), 393-401.

Ribeiro, L.G., & Veiga, G.V. (2010). Risk behaviours for eating disorders in Brazilian dancers. *International Journal Sports Medicine, 31*(4), 283-288.

Rinzler, C.A. (2011). *Nutrition for dummies* (5th ed.). Hoboken, NJ: Wiley.

Robson, B., Chertoff, A., & the International Association for Dance Medicine and Science (IADMS). (2010). Bone health and female dancers: Physical and nutritional guidelines. Retrieved from http://c.ymcdn.com/sites/www.iadms.org/resource/resmgr/resource_papers/bone_health_female_dancers.pdf

Sayce, V. (2012). *How to have healthy bones. Dance UK Fact Sheet 11.* London, England: Dance UK.

Shah, S. (2010). *Vitamin D deficiency: A cause for concern.* The 20th Annual Meeting of the International Association for Dance Medicine and Science Abstracts.

The Society for Adolescent Health and Medicine. (2013). Recommended vitamin D intake and management of low vitamin D status in adolescents: A position statement of the society for adolescent health and medicine. *Journal of Adolescent Health, 52,* 801-803. Retrieved from www.adolescenthealth.org/SAHM_Main/media/Advocacy/Positions/Jun-13-SAHM_VitaminD_Position_Final.pdf

Spampinato, A. (2011). *Dehydration and performance: Possible implications for a dancer's hydration status.* The 21st Annual Meeting of the International Association for Dance Medicine and Science Abstracts.

Stensland, S.H., & Sobal, J. (1992). Dietary practices of ballet, jazz, and modern dancers. *Journal of the American Dietetic Association, 92*(3), 319-324.

Torres-McGehee, T.M., Green, J.M., Leaver-Dunn, D., Leeper, J.D., Bishop, P.A., & Wilmerding, M.V., McKinnon, M.M., & Mermier, C. (2005). Body composition in dancers: A review. *Journal of Dance Medicine and Science, 9*(1), 18-23.

Wyon, M.A., Hutchings, K.M., Wells, A., & Neville, A.M. (2013). Body mass index, nutritional knowledge, and eating behaviours in elite student and professional ballet dancers. *Clinical Journal of Sports Medicine, 24*(5), 390-396.

Yang, L.C., Lan, Y., Hu, J., Yang, Y.H., Zhang, Q., & Piao, J.H. (2010). Relatively high bone mineral density in Chinese adolescent dancers despite lower energy intake and menstrual disorder. *Biomedical and Environmental Sciences, 23*(2), 130-136.

Yannakoulia, M., Keramopoulos, A., & Matalas, A.L. (2004). Bone mineral density in young active females: The case of dancers. *International Journal of Sports Nutrition and Exercise Metabolism, 14*(3), 285-297.

Chapter 8

Carr, S., & Wyon, M. (2003). The impact of motivational climate on dance students' achievement goals, trait anxiety, and perfectionism. *Journal of Dance Medicine and Science, 7*(4), 105-114.

Deci, E.L., & Ryan, R.M. (2000). The 'what' and 'why' of goal pursuits: Human needs and the self-determination of behavior. *Psychological Inquiry, 11,* 227-268.

Dickstein, R., & Deutsch, J.E. (2007). Motor imagery in physical therapist practice. *Physical Therapy, 87*(7), 942-953.

Hamilton, L. (1999). A psychological profile of the adolescent dancer. *Journal of Dance Medicine and Science, 3*(2), 48-50.

Hamilton, R.A., Scott, D., & MacDougall, M.P. (2007). Assessing the effectiveness of self-talk interventions on endurance performance. *Journal of Applied Sport Psychology, 19,* 226-239.

Hanrahan, S.J. (1996). Dancers' perceptions of psychological skills. *Revista de Psicología del Deporte,* 19-27.

Holmes, P.S., & Collins, D.J. (2001). The PETTLEP approach to motor imagery: A functional equivalence model for sport psychologists. *Journal of Applied Sport Psychology, 13,* 60-83.

Klockarea, E., Gustafsson, H., & Nordin-Bates, S.M. (2011). An interpretative phenomenological analysis of how professional dance teachers implement psychological skills training in practice. *Research in Dance Education, 12*(3), 277-293.

Krasnow, D., Mainwaring, L., & Kerr, G. (1999). Injury, stress, and perfectionism in young dancers and gymnasts. *Journal of Dance Medicine & Science, 3,* 51-58.

Laws, H. (2005). *Fit to Dance 2.* London, England: Dance UK.

Lench, H., Levine, L., & Roe, E. (2010). Trait anxiety and achievement goals as predictors of self-reported health in dancers. *Journal of Dance Medicine and Science, 14*(4), 163-170.

Miulli, M., & Nordin-Bates, S.M. (2011). Motivational climates: What they are, and why they matter. *The IADMS Bulletin for Teachers, 3*(2), 5-8.

Morgan, K., & Kingston, K. (2010). Promoting a mastery motivational climate in a higher education sports class. *Journal of Hospitality, Leisure, Sport and Tourism Education, 9*(1), 73-84.

Nordin, S.M., & Cumming, J. (2006a). The development of imagery in dance part I: Qualitative findings from a mixed sample of dancers. *Journal of Dance Medicine and Science, 10*(1&2), 21-27.

Nordin, S.M., & Cumming, J. (2006b). The development of imagery in dance part II: Quantitative findings from a mixed sample of dancers. *Journal of Dance Medicine and Science, 10*(1&2), 28-34.

Nordin, S.M., & McGill, A. (2009). Standing on the shoulders of a young giant: How dance teachers can benefit from learning about positive psychology. *The IADMS Bulletin for Teachers, 1*(1), 4-6.

Norfield, J., & Nordin-Bates, S.M. (2012). How community dance leads to positive outcomes: A self-determination theory perspective. *Journal of Applied Arts and Health, 2*(3), 257-272.

Pan, Y. (2014). Teachers' efficacy and students' satisfaction. *Journal of Teaching in Physical Education, 33,* 68-92.

Patterson, E.L., Smith, R.E., Everett, J.J., & Ptacek, J.T. (1998). Psychosocial factors as predictors of ballet injuries: Interactive effects of life stress and social support. *Journal of Sport Behavior, 21,* 101-112.

Quested, E., & Duda, J. (2009). Perceptions of the motivational climate, need satisfaction, and indices of well- and ill-being among hip hop dancers. *Journal of Dance Medicine and Science, 13*(1), 10-19.

Rafferty, S., & Wyon, M. (2006). Leadership behavior in dance: Application of the Leadership Scale for Sports to dance technique teaching. *Journal of Dance Medicine and Science, 10*(1&2), 6-13.

Redding, E., Nordin-Bates, S., & Walker, I. (2011). Passion, pathways and potential in dance: An interdisciplinary, longitudinal study into dance talent development. Trinity Laban research report. Retrieved from http://www.trinitylaban.ac.uk/media/573037/laban_report_single_pages.pdf

Sweigard, L. (2013). Human movement potential: Its ideokinetic facilitation. Oregon, USA: Allegro Editions.

Taylor, J., & Taylor, C. (1995). *Psychology for dancers.* Champaign, IL: Human Kinetics.

Tod, D., Hardy, J., & Oliver, E. (2011). Effects of self-talk: A systematic review. *Journal of Sport & Exercise Psychology, 33,* 666-687.

Tremayne, P., & Ballinger, D.A. (2008). Performance enhancement for ballroom dancers: Psychological perspectives. *The Sport Psychologist, 22,* 90-108.

Walker, I., & Nordin-Bates, S. (2010). Performance anxiety experiences of professional ballet dancers: The importance of control. *Journal of Dance Medicine & Science, 14*(4), 133-145.

Walker, I.J., Nordin-Bates, S.M., & Redding, E. (2011). Characteristics of talented dancers and age group differences: Findings from the UK Centres for Advanced Training. *High Ability Studies, 22*(1), 43-60.

Weinberg, R. (2010). Making goals effective: A primer for coaches *Journal of Sport Psychology in Action, 1,* 57-65.

Chapter 9

Anbarasi, V., Rajan, D., & Adalarasu, K. (2012). Analysis of lower extremity muscle flexibility among Indian classical Bharathnatyam dancers. World Academy of Science, Engineering and Technology, International Science Index 66, 6(6), 161-166.

Beijani, F.J., Halpern, N., Pio, A., Dominguez, R., Voloshin, A., & Frankel, V.H. (1988). Musculoskeletal demands on flamenco dancers: A clinical and biomechanical study. *Foot & Ankle 8*(5), 254-263.

Blake, H. (2010). Young mother paralysed in pole-dancing accident. Retrieved from www.telegraph.co.uk/culture/theatre/dance/8005408/Young-mother-paralysed-in-pole-dancing-accident.html

Bronner, S., Ojofeitimi, S., & Mayers, L. (2006). Comprehensive surveillance of dance injuries: A proposal for uniform reporting guidelines. *Journal of Dance Medicine and Science, 10*(3-4), 69-80.

Brown, A.C., Wells, T.J., Schade, M.L., Smith, D.L., & Fehling P.C. (2007). Effects of plyometric training versus traditional weight training on strength, power and aesthetic jumping ability in female collegiate dancers. *Journal of Dance Medicine and Science, 11*(2), 38-44.

Caldwell, C. (2001). *Dance and dance injuries.* Chichester, England: Corpus.

Campoy, F.A.S., De Oliveira Coelho, L.R., Nascimento Bastos, F., Netto Júnior, J., Marques Vanderlei, L.C., Monteiro, H.L., . . . & Pastre, C.M. (2011). Investigation of risk factors and characteristics of dance injuries. *Clinical Journal of Sport Medicine, 21*(6), 493-498.

Clippinger, K. (2016). *Dance anatomy and kinesiology.* Champaign, IL: Human Kinetics.

Comfort, P., & Abraham, E. (2010). *Sports rehabilitation and injury prevention.* Chichester, England: Wiley & Sons.

Conti, S.F., & Wong, Y.S. (2001). Foot and ankle injuries in the dancer. *Journal of Dance Medicine and Science, 5*(2), 43-50.

Crookshanks, D. (1999). *Safe dance, report 3.* Braddon, ACT: Ausdance, Australian Dance Council.

Harkness Center for Dance Injuries. (n.d.). Injury frequencies. Retrieved from http://hjd.med.nyu.edu/harkness/sites/default/files/harkness/injury-rates_within_different_dance_disciplines.pdf

Henderson, J., & MacIntyre, D. (2006). A descriptive survey of injury patterns in Canadian premier Highland dancers. *Physiotherapy Canada, 58*(1), 61-73.

Howse, J., & Mc Cormack, M. (2009). *Anatomy, dance technique and injury prevention* (4th ed.). London, England: A&C Black.

Inouye, J., Nichols, A., Maskarinec, G., & Tseng, C. (2013). A survey of musculoskeletal injuries associated with Zumba. *Hawaii Journal of Medicine and Public Health, 72*(12), 433-436.

Jacobs, C.L., Hincapié, C.A., & Cassidy, J.D. (2012). Musculoskeletal pain and injuries in dancers; A systematic review update. *Journal of Dance Medicine and Science, 16*(2), 74- 84.

Kauther, M.D., Wedemeyer, C., Wegner, A., Kauther, K.M., & von Knoch, M. (2009). Breakdance injuries and overuse syndromes in amateurs and professionals. *The American Journal of Sports Medicine, 37*(4), 797-802.

Kenney, L.W., Wilmore, J.H., & Costill, D.L. (2012). *Physiology of sport and exercise* (5th ed.). Champaign, IL: Human Kinetics

Koutedakis, Y. (2005). Fitness for dance. *Journal of Dance Medicine and Science, 9*(1), 5-6.

Koutedakis, Y., Cross, V., & Sharp, N.C.C. (1996). Strength training in male ballet dancers. *Impulse, 4,* 210-219.

Koutedakis, Y., & Jamurtas, A. (2004). The dancer as performing athlete: Physiological considerations. *Sports Medicine, 34*(10), 651-661.

Koutedakis, Y., & Sharp, N.C.C. (1999). *The fit and healthy dancer.* Chichester, England: Wiley.

Koutedakis, Y., Stavropoulos-Kalinoglou, A., & Metsios G. (2005). The significance of muscular strength in dance. *Journal of Dance Medicine and Science, 9*(1), 29-34.

Krasnow, D.H., & Chatfield, S.J. (1996). Dance science and the technique class. *Impulse, 4,* 162-172.

Krasnow, D., Mainwaring, L., & Kerr, G. (1999). Injury, stress and perfectionism in young dancers and gymnasts. *Journal of Dance Medicine and Science, 3*(2), 51-58.

Kuisis, S.M., Camacho, T., Krüger, E., & Camacho, A.L. (2012). Self-reported incidence of injuries among ballroom dancers. *African Journal for Physical, Health Education, Recreation and Dance,* S107-S119.

Lai, R.J., Krasnow, D., & Martin, T. (2008). Communication between medical practitioners and dancers. *Journal of Dance Medicine and Science, 12*(2), 47-53.

Laws, H. (2005). *Fit to dance 2.* London, England: Dance UK.

Liederbach, M. (2000). General considerations for guiding dance injury rehabilitation. *Journal of Dance Medicine and Science, 4*(2), 54-65.

Luke, A., Kinney, S.A., D'Hemecourt, P.A., Baum, J., Owen, M., & Micheli, L.J. (2002). Determinants of injury in young dancers. *Journal of Dance Medicine and Science, 17*(3), 105-112.

Luke, A., & Micheli, L.J. (2000). Management of injuries in the young dancer. *Journal of Dance Medicine and Science, 4*(1), 6-15.

Mainwaring, L., Krasnow, D., & Kerr, G. (2001). And the dance goes on: Psychological impact of injury. *Journal of Dance Medicine and Science, 5*(4), 105-115.

Martin, S.A., Pence, B.D., & Woods, J.A. (2009). Exercise and respiratory tract viral infections. *Exercise and Sport Sciences Reviews, 37*(4), 157-164.

Mayers, L., Judelson, D., & Bronner, S. (2003). The prevalence of injury among tap dancers. *Journal of Dance Medicine and Science, 7*(4), 121-125.

Motta-Valencia, K. (2006). Dance related injury. *Physical Medicine and Rehabilitation Clinics of North America, 17*(3), 697-723.

Noon, M., Hoch, A.Z., McNamara, L., & Schimke, J. (2010). Injury patterns in female Irish dancers. *Physical Medicine & Rehabilitation, 2*(11), 1030-1034.

Ojofeitimi, S., Bronner, S., & Woo, H. (2012). Injury incidence in hip hop dance. *Scandinavian Journal of Medicine and Science in Sports, 22*(3), 347-355.

Pedersen, E., & Wilmerding, E. (1998). Injury profiles of student and professional student flamenco dancers. *Journal of Dance Medicine and Science, 2,* 108-114.

Peterson, L., & Renström, P. (2005). *Sports injuries: Their prevention and treatment* (3rd ed.). London, England: Taylor & Francis.

Poggini, L., Losasso, S., & Iannone, S. (1999). Injuries during the dancer's growth spurt: Etiology, prevention and treatment. *Journal of Dance Medicine and Science, 3* (2), 73-79.

Potts, J.C., & Irrgang, J.J. (2001). Principles of rehabilitation of lower extremity injuries in dancers. *Journal of Dance Medicine and Science, 5*(2), 51-61.

Roberts, K.J., Nelson, N.G., & McKenzie, L. (2013). Dance-related injuries in children and adolescents treated in US emergency departments in 1991-2007. *Journal of Physical Activity & Health, 10*(2), 143-150.

Russell, J.A. (2010). Acute ankle sprain in dancers. *Journal of Dance Medicine and Science, 14*(3), 89-96.

Russell, J.A. (2013). Preventing dance injuries: Current perspectives. *Open Access Journal of Sports Medicine, 4,* 199-210.

Safety and Health in Arts Production and Entertainment (SHAPE). (2002). Preventing musculoskeletal injury (MSI) for musicians and dancers: A resource guide. Retrieved from www.musicianshealth.co.uk/injuriesmusiciansdancers.pdf

Sevey Fitt, S. (1996). *Dance kinesiology* (2nd ed.). New York, NY: Schirmer.

Shah, S., Weiss, D.S., & Burchette, R.J. (2012). Injuries in professional modern dancers: Incidence, risk factors, and management. *Journal of Dance Medicine and Science, 16*(1), 17-25.

Shira. (n.d.). Avoiding injury from belly dance. Retrieved from www.shira.net/advice/health/avoid-injury.htm

Simmel, L. (2014). *Dance medicine in practice: Anatomy, injury prevention, training.* London, England: Routledge.

Simpson, S. (2006). Dance injury management Retrieved from http://www.danz.org.nz/Downloads/InjuryMgmt.pdf

Stein, C.J., Kinney, S.A., McCrystal, T., Carew, E.A., Bottino, P.A. -C., Meehan, W.P., & Micheli, L.J. (2014). Dance-related concussion: A case series. *Journal of Dance Medicine and Science, 18*(2), 53-61.

Taylor, J., & Taylor, C. (1995). *Psychology of dance.* Champaign, IL: Human Kinetics.

Thomas, H., & Tarr, J. (2009). Dancers' perceptions of pain and injury: Positive and negative effects. *Journal of Dance Medicine and Science, 13*(2), 51-59.

Trégouët, P., & Merland, F. (2013). The effects of different shoes on plantar forces in Irish dance. *Journal of Dance Medicine and Science, 17*(1), 41-46.

Tsien, C., & Trepman, E. (2001). Internal rotation knee injury during ballroom dance: A case report. *Journal of Dance Medicine and Science, 5*(3), 82-86.

Walls, R.J., Brennan, S.A., Hodnett, P., O'Byrne, J.M., Eustace, S.J., & Stephens, M.M. (2010). Overuse ankle injuries in professional Irish dancers. *Journal of Foot and Ankle Surgery, 16*(1), 45-49.

Wyon, M., Redding, E., Abt, G., Head, A., & Sharp, C. (2003). Development, reliability and validity of a multi-stage dance specific aerobic fitness test (DAFT). *Journal of Dance Medicine and Science, 7*(3), 80-84.

Chapter 10

Alter, M.J. (2004). *Science of flexibility.* Champaign, IL: Human Kinetics.

Alzheimer's Society. (2012). What is Alzheimer's disease? Retrieved from www.alzheimers.org.uk/site/scripts/download_info.php?fileID=1755

Amans, D. (2013). *Age and dancing: Older people and community dance practice.* London, England: Palgrave Macmillan.

American College of Obstetricians and Gynecologists (ACOG). (2002). Exercise during pregnancy and the postpartum period. Retrieved from www.acog.org/Resources_And_Publications/Committee_Opinions/Committee_on_Obstetric_Practice/Exercise_During_Pregnancy_and_the_Postpartum_Period

American Diabetes Association. (2004). Physical activity/exercise and diabetes. Retrieved from http://care.diabetesjournals.org/content/27/suppl_1/s58.full

American Diabetes Association. (2013). How do insulin pumps work? Retrieved from www.diabetes.org/living-with-diabetes/treatment-and-care/medication/insulin/how-do-insulin-pumps-work.html

American Running & Fitness Association. (2013). Making sense of asthma. Retrieved from www.thefreelibrary.com/Making+sense+of+asthma.-a0331081789

Arenson, C., Busby-Whitehead, J., Brummel-Smith, K., O'Brien, J.G., Palmer, M.H. & Reichel, W. (2009). *Reichel's care of the elderly.* New York, NY: Cambridge University Press.

Artal, R., & O'Toole, M. (2003). Exercise in pregnancy: Guidelines of the American College of Obstetricians and Gynecologists for exercise during pregnancy and the postpartum period. *British Journal of Sports Medicine, 37,* 6-12.

Association of Chartered Physiotherapists in Women's Health (ACPWH). (2010). *Fit and safe to exercise in the childbearing year.* Retrieved from www.csp.org.uk/documents/fit-safe-exercise-childbearing-year

The Asthma Center Education and Research Fund. (2013). Asthma—Adult and adolescent. Retrieved from www.theasthmacenter.org/index.php/newsletter/asthma_-_adult_and_adolescent/

Asthma UK. (n.d.-a). Asthma attacks. Retrieved from www.asthma.org.uk/advice-asthma-attacks

Asthma UK. (n.d.-b). Diet and food. Retrieved from www.asthma.org.uk/knowledge-bank-diet-and-food

Aujjla, I.J., & Redding, E. (2013). *Barriers to dance training for young people with disabilities.* http://dance4.co.uk/sites/default/files/news/13-03/changing-perceptions-publications-released-2013/barriersv2lo.pdf

Batavia, M. (2010). *The wheelchair evaluation: A clinician's guide* (2nd ed.). London, England: Jones & Bartlett.

Benjamin, A. (2002). *Making an entrance.* Abingdon, England: Routledge.

Burckhardt, P., Wynn, E., Krieg, M.A., Bagutti, C., & Faouzi, M. (2011). The effects of nutrition, puberty and dancing on bone density in adolescent ballet dancers. *Journal of Dance Medicine and Science, 15*(2), 51-60.

Bye, J. (n.d.). Diabetes—How it affects sports and how to combat it. Retrieved from www.pponline.co.uk/encyc/diabetes-how-it-affects-sports-and-how-to-combat-it-33405

Carlsen, K.H. (2011). The breathless adolescent asthmatic athlete. *European Respiratory Journal, 38*(3), 713-720. Retrieved from http://erj.ersjournals.com/content/38/3/713

Colberg, S. (2013). Overuse injuries in diabetes. Retrieved from www.diabetesincontrol.com/articles/64-/15052-overuse-injuries-in-diabetes

Connolly, M.K., and Redding, E. (2010). Dancing towards well-being in the Third Age. Retrieved from www.trinitylaban.ac.uk/media/315435/literature%20review%20impact%20of%20dance%20elderly%20populations%20final%20draft%20with%20logos.pdf

Daniels, K., & the International Association for Dance Medicine & Science (IADMS). (2000). The challenge of the adolescent dancer. Retrieved from http://c.ymcdn.com/sites/www.iadms.org/resource/resmgr/resource_papers/adolescent-dancer.pdf

Daunt, S. (Ed). (2012). *Music, other performing arts and dyslexia*. Bracknell, England: British Dyslexia Association.

Dewhurst, S., Nelson, N., Dougall, P.K., & Bampouras, T.M. (2014). Scottish country dance: Benefits to functional ability in older women. *Journal of Ageing and Physical Activity, 22,* 146-153.

Diabetes.co.uk. (n.d.). Diabetes and exercise. Retrieved from www.diabetes.co.uk/exercise-for-diabetics.html

Diabetes UK. (n.d.). What is diabetes? Retrieved from http://diabetes.org.uk/Guide-to-diabetes/What-is-diabetes/

DiFiore, J. (1998). *The complete guide to postnatal fitness*. London, England: A&C Black.

DiFiori, J.P. (2010). Evaluation of overuse injuries in children and adolescents. *Current Sports Medicine Reports, 9*(6), 372-378.

Dyspraxia Foundation. (2014). About dyspraxia. Retrieved from www.dyspraxiafoundation.org.uk/about-dyspraxia/

Engels, H.J., Drouin, J., Zhu, W., & Kazmierski, J.F. (1998). Effects of low-impact, moderate-intensity exercise training with and without wrist weights on functional capacities and mood states in older adults. *Gerontology, 44*(4), 239-244.

Fong Yan, A., Hiller, C., Smith, R., & Vanwanseele, B. (2011). Effect of footwear on dancers: A systematic review. *Journal of Dance Medicine and Science, 15*(2), 86-92.

Ford, P., Collins, D., Bailey, R., MacNamara, A., Pearce, G., & Toms, M. (2012). Participant development in sport and physical activity: The impact of biological maturation. *European Journal of Sport Science, 12*(6), 515-526.

Gallen, I. (2004). Review: Helping the athlete with Type 1 diabetes. *British Journal of Diabetes and Vascular Disease, 4*(2), 87-92.

Garry, J.P. (2013). Exercise-induced asthma. Retrieved from http://emedicine.medscape.com/article/1938228-overview

Gaston, A., & Prapavessis, H. (2013). Tired, moody and pregnant: Exercise may be the answer. *Psychology and Health, 28*(12), 1353-1369.

Guzman-Garcia, A., Johannsen, L., & Wing, A.M. (2011). Dance exercise for older adults: A pilot study investigating standing balance following a single lesson of Danzon. *American Journal of Dance Therapy, 33,* 148-156.

Hackney, M., Kantorovich, S., Levin, R., & Earhart, G.M. (2007). Effect of functional mobility in Parkinson's disease: A preliminary study. *Journal of Neurologic Physical Therapy, 31*(4), 173-179.

Hamilton, L. (1999). A psychological profile of the adolescent dancer. *Journal of Dance Medicine and Science, 3*(2), 48-50.

Hammer, R.L., Perkins, J., & Parr, R. (2000). Exercise during the childbearing year. *The Journal of Perinatal Education, 9*(1), 1-14.

Inal, S. (2014). Competitive dance for individuals with disabilities. *Palaestra of Sagamore Journals, 28*(1), 32-35.

Kaar, S. (n.d.). Exercise during pregnancy. Retrieved from www.sportsmd.com/SportsMD_Articles/id/315/n/exercise_during_pregnancy.aspx#sthash.YxYUv69s.dpuf

Kenney, L.W., Wilmore, J.H., & Costill, D.L. (2012). *Physiology of sport and exercise* (5th ed.). Champaign, IL: Human Kinetics.

Keogh, J.W.L., Kilding, A., Pidgeon, P., Ashley, L., & Gillis, D. (2007). Physical benefits of dancing for healthy older adults: A review. *Journal of Ageing and Physical Activity, 17,* 479-500.

Koutedakis, Y., & Sharp, N.C.C. (1999). *The fit and healthy dancer*. Chichester, England: John Wiley & Sons.

Listen and Learn Centre. (n.d.). Dyspraxia—A motor planning disorder. Retrieved from http://listenandlearn.com.au/dyspraxia-a-motor-planning-disorder

Lockette, K,F & Keys, A, M. (1994) Conditioning with Physical Disabilities. USA: Human Kinetics

Lumb, A.N., & Gallen, I.W. (2009). Insulin dose adjustment and exercise in Type 1 diabetes: What do we tell the patient? *British Journal of Diabetes and Vascular Health, 9*(6), 273-277.

Matthews, B.L., Bennell, K.L., McKay, H.A., Khan, K.M., Baxter-Jones, A.D.G., Mirwald, R.L., & Wark, J.D. (2006). The influence of dance training on growth and maturation of young females: A mixed longitudinal study. *Annals of Human Biology, 33*(3), 342-356.

McCoid, F., Harris, S., & Rafiefar, R. (2013). *Pregnancy and the dancer. Dance UK information sheet 19*. London, England: Dance UK.

McKinley, P., Jacobson, A., Leroux, A., Bednarczyk, V., Rossignol, M., & Fung, J. (2008). Effect of a community-based Argentine tango dance program on functional balance and confidence in older adults. *Journal of Ageing and Physical Activity, 16,* 435-453.

Meade, A. (2014). The highs and lows of diabetes and exercise. *Sports Dieticians Australia, 29*(1). Retrieved from www.ausport.gov.au/sportscoachmag/nutrition2/the_highs_and_lows_of_diabetes_and_exercise

Meck, C., Hess, R.A., Helldobler, R., & Roh, J. (2004). Pre-pointe evaluation components used by dance schools. *Journal of Dance Medicine and Science, 8*(2), 37-42.

MedlinePlus. (2014). Signs of an asthma attack. Retrieved from www.nlm.nih.gov/medlineplus/ency/patientinstructions/000062.htm

Minne, H.W. (2005). *Invest in your bones: Move it or lose it.* Retrieved from www.bbcbonehealth.org/documents/moveitorloseiten.pdf

Nascimento, S.L., Surita, F.G., & Cecatti, J.G. (2012). Physical exercise during pregnancy: A systematic review. *Current Opinion in Obstetrics and Gynecology, 24*, 2-8.

National Diabetes Clearing House (NDIC). (2014). What I need to know about physical activity and diabetes. Retrieved from http://diabetes.niddk.nih.gov/dm/pubs/physical_ez/

National Health and Medical Research Council (NHMRC). (2006). Calcium. Retrieved from www.nrv.gov.au/nutrients/calcium

Naughton, G., Farpour-Lambert, N.J., Carlson, J., Bradney, M., & Van Praagh, E. (2000). Physiological issues surrounding the performance of adolescent athletes. *Sports Medicine, 30*(5), 309-325.

Pearson, S.J., & Whitaker, A. (2012). Footwear in classical ballet: A study of pressure distribution and related foot injury in the adolescent dancer. *Journal of Dance Medicine & Science, 16*(2), 51-56.

Pethybridge, R. (2010). *Dance and age inclusive practice.* Leicester, England: Foundation for Community Dance.

Pivarnik, M.J., Chambliss, H.O., Clapp, J.F., Dugan, S.A., Hatch, M.C., Lovelady, C.A., . . . & Williams, M.A. (2006). Impact of physical activity during pregnancy and post-partum on chronic disease risk. ACSM Roundtable consensus statement. *Medicine & Science in Sports & Exercise*, 989-1006.

Poggini, L., Losasso, S., & Iannone, S. (1999). Injuries during the dancer's growth spurt etiology, prevention, and treatment. *Journal of Dance Medicine and Science, 3*(2), 73-79.

Powers, S.K., & Howley, E. (2012). *Exercise physiology: Theory and application to fitness and performance.* New York, NY: McGraw-Hill.

Rahl, R. (2010). *Physical activity and health guidelines: Recommendations for various ages, fitness levels, and conditions from 57 authoritative sources.* Champaign, IL: Human Kinetics.

Redding, E., Nordin-Bates, S., & Walker, I. (2011). *Passion, pathways and potential in dance: An interdisciplinary longitudinal study into dance talent development.* Trinity Laban Research Report.

Richardson, M., Liederbach, M., & Sandow, E. (2010). Functional criteria for assessing pointe-readiness. *Journal of Dance Medicine & Science, 14*(3), 82-88.

Roberts, K.J., Nelson, N.G., & McKenzie, L. (2013). Dance-related injuries in children and adolescents treated in US emergency departments in 1991–2007. *Journal of Physical Activity and Health, 10*, 143-150.

Robson, B.E. (2002). Disordered eating in high school dance students some practical considerations. *Journal of Dance Medicine and Science, 6*(1), 7-13.

Royal College of Obstetricians and Gynaecologists (RCOG). (2006). *Exercise in pregnancy: RCOG Statement 4.* Retrieved from www.rcog.org.uk/womens-health/clinical-guidance/exercise-pregnancy

Sanders, S.G. (2008). Dancing through pregnancy: Activity guidelines for professional and recreational dancers. *JDMS, 12*(1), 17-22.

Schmid, G. (2012). *Dancing with diabetes.* Retrieved from www.dancespirit.com/2012/06/dancing-with-diabetes/

Selby, A. (2002). *Pilates for pregnancy.* London, England: Thorsons.

Shah, S. (2009). Determining a young dancer's readiness for dancing on pointe. *Current Sports Medicine Reports, 8*(6), 295-299.

Smith, K.M., & Campbell, C.G. (2013). Physical activity during pregnancy: Impact of applying different physical activity guidelines. Retrieved from: www.hindawi.com/journals/jp/2013/165617/

Sofianidis, G., Hatzitaki, V., Douka, S., & Grouios, G. (2009). Effect of a 10-week traditional dance program on static and dynamic balancer control in elderly adults. *Journal of Ageing and Physical Activity, 17*, 167-180.

Sports Medicine Australia. (2009). *Women in sport: Fact sheet.* Retrieved from http://sma.org.au/wp-content/uploads/2009/10/WIS-ExPreg.pdf

Stacey, J.M. (1999). The physiological development of the adolescent dancer. *Journal of Dance Medicine and Science, 3*(2), 59-65.

Steinberg, N., Siev-Ner, I., Peleg, S., Dar, G., Masharawi, Y., Zeev, A., & Hershkovitz, I. (2013). Injuries in female dancers aged 8 to 16 years. *Journal of Athletic Training, 48*(1), 118-123.

Stroke Association. (2014). Act FAST: Recognise the symptoms of stroke. Retrieved from www.stroke.org.uk/FAST

Szymanski, L.M., & Satin, A.J. (2012). Strenuous exercise during pregnancy: Is there a limit? *American Journal of Obstetrics and Gynecology, 207*(3), 179.e1-6.

Tomonari, R.F.D. (2011). Stages of growth child development—Early childhood (birth to eight years), middle childhood (eight to twelve years). Retrieved from http://education.stateuniversity.com/pages/1826/Child-Development-Stages-Growth.html

Van der Eerden, B.C.J., Karperien, M., & Wit, J.M. (2003). Systemic and local regulation of the growth plate. *Endocrine Reviews, 24*(6), 782-801.

Walker, I.J., Nordin-Bates, S.M., & Redding, E. (2011). Characteristics of talented dancers and age group differences: Findings from the UK Centres for Advanced Training. *High ability Studies, 22*(1), 43-60.

Wang, T.W., & Apgar, B.S. (1998). *Exercise during pregnancy*. Retrieved from www.uni.edu/dolgener/Fitness_Assessment/exercise_and_pregnancy2.pdf

Weiss, D., Rist, R.A., & Grossman, G. (2009). When can I start pointe work? Guidelines for initiating pointe training. *Journal of Dance Medicine and Science, 13*(3), 90-92.

Welsh, L., Roberts, R.G.D., & Kemp, J.G. (2004). Fitness and physical activity in children with asthma. *Sports Medicine, 34*(13), 861-870.

Wilkinson, J., Quin, E., Hitchens, J., Ehrenberg, S., Irvine, S., Redding, E. . . . & Postano, C. (2008). *Phase I of the Trinity Laban TQEF funded project on dyspraxia in music & dance students*. London, England: Trinity Laban Conservatoire of Music and Dance.

Wilmerding, V., Gurney, B., & Torres, V. (2003). The effect of positive heel inclination on posture in young children training in flamenco dance. *Journal of Dance Medicine and Science, 7*(3), 85-90.

Wozny, N. (2010). Deep breaths. *Dance Magazine, 84*(2), 22.

Zitomer, M. (2013). Creating space for every-body in dance education. *Physical and Health Education Journal, 79*(1), 18-21.

Index

A

ABC's 160
abdominal muscles
    pelvic floor and 35
    during pregnancy 222, 223
    sit-up technique 81f, 136
abdominal separation 222, 251
abduction 27, 28f
abuse. *See* safeguarding
accidents
    definition of 251
    form for reporting 248
    insurance 17, 18
    national regulations 19
    reporting 19, 21, 194-195
    tidiness of facilities 8
Achilles tendon problems 4, 51
active rest 95, 251
active-static stretching 64
active stretching 83
adaptations
    alignment issues and 41, 47
    autonomy and 160
    for contraindicated movements 137
    to environment 11, 69, 109
    individuality and 87, 114, 115
    for older dancers 210, 213
    for return from injury 161
    in training 82, 86
adduction 27, 28f
adolescence. *See also* growth
    caloric requirements 151t
    definition of 251
    flexibility training 84
    gender differences 47, 199, 204
    injuries 200
    kyphosis in 46
    motor co-ordination 111
    nutrition 151-152, 204-205
    progression 204, 207
    psychological considerations 205
    typical schedule for 101t
    warm-up 66
aerial dancers
    alignment and 36
    fitness training 90
    injury risk 182
    warm-up 67
aerobic dance classes 68, 78, 208
aerobic fitness 77, 78-79, 251
age-predicted heart rate maximum 58, 78
agonists 33, 251
airplane test 81-82
alcohol consumption 155, 205
alignment. *See also* cues
    anatomical reference points 26-30
    carrying bags 47, 50-51
    common issues 45
    dancer self-perception of 25
    dance styles and 36
    disabled participants 216
    dynamic 32, 36-37
    fatigue and 50, 82
    feedback on 25
    footwear effects on 3, 40, 51-52
    head 45, 46, 48
    ideal (vertical) 32f

    improving 53
    injury and 24-25, 30, 184
    kinetic chain 30-31
    lower body 38-41
    muscle actions 32-34
    pelvis 41-44, 45
    plumb line 31-32
    posture 30
    spine 44-48
    upper body 48-51, 49
    use of imagery 25
allergens 226
allergic asthma 226, 251
Alzheimer's disease 211, 251
amenorrhoea 141, 153, 251
amino acids 142
anaerobic
    definition of 251
    energy system 77, 78
    training 79
ankle joint
    injury recovery plan 193t
    mobilising 59
    sprains 191
antagonists 33, 251
anterior superior iliac spines (ASIS) 41
anteversion 42
anti-gravity muscles 34
anxiety 158, 171, 173
arches. *See* feet
area-elastic floors (sprung floors) 8, 9, 255
arms
    shoulder alignment 48, 49
    styling 49, 50
asthma
    about 225-226
    attacks 227-228
    nutrition and 227
    triggers 226
    types 226
asthmatic dancers
    activity intensity 226-227
    environmental factors 226
    progression 227
    supplementary activities 227
    taking medications 227
    warm-up 227
asymmetry 46, 47, 129
attire 3, 72
auditions 171
Ausdance Safe Dance 180
autonomic nervous system 58, 251
autonomy 160-161, 251

B

back bends 36, 47
background checks 14
back pain 47, 48, 51, 221
balance
    age and 31
    definition of 251
    training 36, 85
balance boards 36
ball-and-socket joints 30
ballet
    barres 6, 85, 123
    fitness training 89-90
    gauging pointe readiness 207

    injuries in 180
    pliés 134
    point shoes 4, 40, 206
    warm-up 67
ballistic movements 127
ballistic stretching 61, 83-84, 251
ballroom dance 162, 180
bare feet 3, 9, 13
basal metabolic rate 141
base of support 31, 32
basic psychological needs 160-164, 251
belonging 161-162, 251
Bharatanatyam dancing
    fitness training 89-90
    injury patterns 180-181
    warm-up 67
biceps curl 81f
biomechanics 24, 44, 184
blisters 182
blood spills 13
blood sugar levels 228, 229, 230t
BMI. *See* body mass index (BMI)
body fat 153, 199
body image 3, 16, 160, 199
body mass index (BMI) 153, 251
body temperature 10, 58, 70
body weight 141, 153
'bone-breaking' 37
bone growth 199, 200f
bone health
    carbonate beverages and 152
    definition of 251
    nutrition and 141, 144, 204
    in older dancers 209
    strength training and 80
bony landmarks 31, 251
Borg scale 58, 79
boundaries 13, 16, 161
bow legs 41f
breakdancers
    alignment 36
    fitness training 89-90
    injury rates for 82, 181
    warm-up and cool-down 67
breathing
    during active-static stretching 64
    difficulties 189, 212, 227
    inefficient 45, 48, 49
    rate 58
    relaxation and 174
    rest periods 116
bronchoconstriction 226, 251
bronchodilation 227, 251
building insurance 17, 18
bunions 39, 52
burnout 97, 251

C

caffeine 146, 147
calcium 144-145, 151, 152
calluses 182
calories
    definition of 251
    recommended intake 141, 151t, 152t
    restricted diets 153, 163, 205, 207
carbohydrates 141-142, 142f, 251
cardiorespiratory fitness 77-79, 251
cardiovascular stimulation 57, 70, 251

About the Authors

Edel Quin, MSc, FHEA, is leader of the master's in dance science programme in the faculty of dance at Trinity Laban Conservatoire of Music and Dance in London, UK. She specializes in the application of dance science theory and research to the teaching and practice of dance across styles, ages and settings. She frequently presents her applied research at national and international conferences and has published numerous papers. A registered course provider with Safe in Dance International (SiDI), Edel is a sought-after speaker on safe dance practice. She also serves on the education committee of the International Association for Dance Medicine & Science (IADMS).

Edel is a trained Irish and contemporary dancer. She has performed in London's West End and toured as a troupe member and lead dancer with *Riverdance* from 1996 to 2001. She has also taught performance enhancement on Trinity Laban's Centre for Advanced Training scheme for gifted and talented young dancers along with directing rehearsals for visiting professional dance artists and choreographers.

Sonia Rafferty, MSc, FHEA, is a senior lecturer at Trinity Laban Conservatoire of Music and Dance in London, UK. She has been a consultant and lead assessor for Trinity College London's certificate in safe and effective dance practice and is now senior associate at Safe in Dance International (SiDI), developing the Healthy Dance Practice and Healthy Dancer certificates. Sonia has published several peer-reviewed articles on dance science and has been a member of the International Association for Dance Medicine & Science education committee.

She is a professional freelance performer, choreographer, artistic director, and company and master class teacher, and she was a drummer and performer in the opening and closing ceremonies of the 2012 London Olympic Games.

Charlotte Tomlinson, MSc, PGCE, is a dance lecturer, community practitioner, and registered course provider for Safe in Dance International (SiDI), for whom she designed and delivered the first healthy dance practice certification course in Europe. She has presented at the International Association for Dance Medicine & Science annual meetings and co-wrote the foundation degree in dance at Leicester College, UK, where she is module leader for community dance practice and anatomy and physiology. She is a member of the International Association for Dance Medicine & Science, Dance UK, Foundation for Community Dance, and FitPro.

Charlotte is artistic director of SideKick Dance, an inclusive dance group for young people with disabilities. She also leads dance classes for older adults and is a listed healthier dancer speaker with Dance UK.

You'll find other outstanding
dance resources at
www.HumanKinetics.com

In the U.S. call 1.800.747.4457
Australia 08 8372 0999
Canada. 1.800.465.7301
Europe . . . . .+44 (0) 113 255 5665
New Zealand 0800 222 062

HUMAN KINETICS
The Information Leader in Physical Activity & Health
P.O. Box 5076 • Champaign, IL 61825-5076